OXFORD CONSTITUTIONAL THEORY

Series Editors:
Martin Loughlin, John P. McCormick, and Neil Walker

Fault Lines of Globalization

OXFORD CONSTITUTIONAL THEORY

Series Editors:
Martin Loughlin, John P. McCormick, and Neil Walker

One consequence of the increase in interest in constitutions and constitutional law in recent years is a growing innovative literature in constitutional theory. The aim of *Oxford Constitutional Theory* is to provide a showcase for the best of these theoretical reflections and a forum for further innovation in the field.

The new series will seek to establish itself as the primary point of reference for scholarly work in the subject by commissioning different types of study. The majority of the works published in the series will be monographs that advance new understandings of the subject. Well-conceived edited collections that bring a variety of perspectives and disciplinary approaches to bear on specific themes in constitutional thought will also be included. Further, in recognition of the fact that there is a great deal of pioneering literature originally written in languages other than English and with regard to non-anglophone constitutional traditions, the series will also seek to publish English translations of leading monographs in constitutional theory.

ALSO AVAILABLE IN THE SERIES

Beyond Constitutionalism
The Pluralist Structure of Postnational Law
Nico Krisch

The Constitutional State
N. W. Barber

Sovereignty's Promise
The State as Fiduciary
Evan Fox-Decent

Constitutional Fragments
Societal Constitutionalism and Globalization
Gunther Teubner

Constitutional Referendums
The Theory and Practice of Republican Deliberation
Stephen Tierney

Constituting Economic and Social Rights
Katharine G. Young

The Global Model of Constitutional Rights
Kai Möller

The Three Branches
A Comparative Model of Separation of Powers
Christoph Möllers

The Cosmopolitan State
H. Patrick Glenn

Fault Lines of Globalization

Legal Order and the Politics of A-Legality

Hans Lindahl

OXFORD
UNIVERSITY PRESS

OXFORD
UNIVERSITY PRESS

Great Clarendon Street, Oxford, OX2 6DP,
United Kingdom

Oxford University Press is a department of the University of Oxford.
It furthers the University's objective of excellence in research, scholarship,
and education by publishing worldwide. Oxford is a registered trade mark of
Oxford University Press in the UK and in certain other countries

First Edition published in 2013

Published in the United States of America by Oxford University Press
198 Madison Avenue, New York, NY 10016, United States of America

British Library Cataloguing in Publication Data
Data available

Library of Congress Control Number: 2013939688

ISBN 978–0–19–960168–4

Voor Annemarie

Acknowledgments

Every book is a collective endeavour. This one is no exception; it has profited immeasurably from the comments, both generous and searching, of many colleagues and friends.

The first draft of Chapters 1–3 was written during a five month research fellowship in 2010 at the Stellenbosch Institute for Advanced Study, in South Africa. I am grateful to its director, Hendrik Geyer, for his gracious hospitality and interest during those wonderfully stimulating months at STIAS. Intense discussions with André van der Walt, Henk Botha, and Philippe van Houte, during my stay in South Africa, were very helpful in mapping out the main lines of the book. I cherish the memories of the times spent together with Paul Cilliers, who unexpectedly passed away after I returned to the Netherlands.

Several audiences have discussed parts of the manuscript with me in the course of drafting and redrafting it, and I refer to them in chronological (and alphabetical) order: members of the research seminar series of the Centre of Criminology at the University of Cape Town, with special thanks to Clifford Shearing; members of the Law Department of the London School of Economics and Political Science, with special thanks to Martin Loughlin, Emmanuel Melissaris, Grégoire Webber, and Michael Wilkinson; members of the Department of Philosophy and of the Law Faculty of the Universidad del Rosario, in Colombia, with special thanks to Beira Aguilar, Adolfo Chaparro, Camila de Gamboa, Wilson Herrera, and Iván Mahecha; the research group of legal theory of the VU University Amsterdam, with special thanks to Luigi Corrias, Lyana Francot, Bart van Klink, Nanda Oudejans, Irena Rosenthal, Wouter Veraart, and Wouter Werner; participants at the Transnational Societal Constitutionalism Conference in Turin, with special thanks to Riccardo Prandini and Gunther Teubner; the research group of international law at Lund University, with special thanks to Matilda Arvidsson, Markus Gunneflo, Gregor Noll, and Aleksandra Popovic; the research group of legal theory at Glasgow University, with special thanks to Emilios Christodoulidis and George Pavlakos; the Grundlegung research seminar of the Faculty of Philosophy at the University of Groningen, with special thanks to Martin van Hees, Frank Hindriks, and Pauline Kleingeld; the Centre for Law and Society at the University of Edinburgh, with special thanks to Cormac Mac Amhlaigh, Christine Bell, Euan MacDonald, Claudio Mechelon, Stephen Tierney, and Neil Walker; the Centre for Political Philosophy at Leiden University, with special thanks to Thomas Fossen and Herman Siemens; a Law and Theory Centre seminar at the University of Westminster, with special thanks to Hendrik Anderson, Victoria Brooks, Julia Chryssostalis, Peter Fitzpatrick, Stuart Motha, Chantal

Mouffe, Andreas Philippopoulous-Mihalopoulos, and Patricia Tuitt; and a seminar with the law and jurisprudence PhD candidates of Finland, with special thanks to Julen Etxabe, Ida Koivisto, Panu Minkkinen, and Kimmo Nuotio.

I appreciate detailed comments to the second draft of the entire manuscript by Bernhard Waldenfels, whose contribution to a phenomenology of strangeness has been an important source of inspiration for this book, and by Jacco Verburgt, whose remarks and suggestions have helped me considerably to tighten up the argument I am making.

It has been a joy to work closely with the participants in the research seminars of legal philosophy at Tilburg University; their encouragement and incisive questioning during the seminars dedicated to the manuscript have greatly improved it. I am grateful to all of them: Daniel Augenstein, Michiel Besters, Morag Goodwin, Sean Gould, Ivana Ivkovic, David Janssens, Quoc Loc Hong, Desire Nizigiyimana, Philip Paiement, Chiara Raucea, Umberto Sconfienza, and Alan Thomas. I am particularly grateful to Bert van Roermund, the former professor of legal philosophy at Tilburg, for his unstinting support during these years; this book bears witness to how much I have learnt from his pioneering contributions to legal philosophy.

This book is dedicated to Annemarie ter Veer, whose support, humour, and patience during the process of writing it mean more to me than what I can put into writing.

This book builds on earlier published material of mine, even though the final result has taken me in directions I could not have envisaged when I began to write it in June 2010. It is appropriate to acknowledge these sources. I am grateful to the copyright holders for the permissions to republish. In particular, Chapter 1 expands on and revises my article, 'Boundaries and the concept of legal order', published in *Jurisprudence: An International Journal of Legal and Political Thought* 2, no. 1 (2011), 73–97. Portions of chapters 2 and 3 draw on my article, 'We and Cyberlaw: Constitutionalism and the Inclusion/Exclusion Difference', published in the *Indiana Journal of Global Legal Studies* 20, no. 2 (forthcoming). Portions of chapters 2 and 7 draw on my article, 'A-Legality: Postnationalism and the Question of Legal Boundaries', published in the *Modern Law Review* 73, no. 1 (2010), 30–56. Part of a section of chapter 2 builds on my article, 'Inside and Outside the EU's "Area of Freedom, Security and Justice": Reflexive Identity and the Unity of Legal Space', published in *Archiv für Rechts- und Sozialphilosophie* 90, no. 4 (2004), 478–497. A section of chapter 3 fleshes out ideas initially outlined in 'Discretion and Public Policy: Timing the Unity and Diversity of Legal Orders', published in Sacha Prechal and Bert van Roermund (eds.), *The Coherence of EU Law: The Search for Unity in Divergent Concepts* (Oxford: Oxford University Press, 2008), 291–313 (by permission of Oxford University Press). A section of chapter 4 builds on my article, 'Constituent Power and Reflexive Identity: Towards an Ontology of Collective Selfhood', published in Martin Loughlin and Neil Walker (eds.), *The Paradox of Constituent Power: Constituent Power and Constitutional Form* (Oxford: Oxford University Press, 2007), 9–24 (by permission of Oxford University Press). Part of a section of chapter 5 draws on my article, 'Dialectic and Revolution: Confronting Kelsen and Gadamer on Legal Interpretation', published in *Cardozo Law Review* 24, no. 2 (2003), 769–798. A section of chapter 5 presents a strongly abridged version of the argument developed in 'Recognition as Domination: Constitutionalism, Reciprocity and the Problem of Singularity', published in Neil Walker, Jo Shaw, and Stephen Tierney (eds.), *Europe's Constitutional Mosaic* (Oxford: Hart, 2011), 205–230. Portions of chapter 6 build on ideas initially presented in my articles, 'Finding a Place for Freedom, Security and Justice: The European Union's Claim to Territorial Unity', published in *European Law Review* 29, no. 4 (2004), 461–484, and 'Acquiring a Community: The Acquis and the Institution of European Legal Order', published in *European Law Journal* 9, no. 4 (2003), 433–450. The final section of chapter 6 draws on ideas presented in 'Breaking Promises to Keep Them: Immigration and the Boundaries of Distributive Justice', published in Hans Lindahl (ed.), *A Right to Inclusion and Exclusion? Normative Fault Lines of the EU's Area of Freedom, Security and Justice* (Oxford: Hart, 2009), 137–159. Finally, a section of chapter 7 draws on my article, 'In Between: Immigration, Distributive Justice, and Political Dialogue', published (in truncated form) in *Contemporary Political Theory* 8, no. 4 (2009), 415–434.

Tilburg, March 2013

Contents

Introduction 1

PART I: LEGAL ORDER

1 Legality, Illegality, A-Legality: A Preliminary Analysis 13
1.1 Reorienting the Problem of the Unity of Legal Orders 13
1.2 Legality 18
1.3 Illegality 26
1.4 A-Legality 30
1.5 Boundaries and Limits 39

2 A Topology of Legal Orders in a Global Setting 44
2.1 The *Nomos* of Nomadism 44
2.2 The Frontiers of Roman Law 49
2.3 Multinationals 56
2.4 *Lex Mercatoria* 58
2.5 The Law of Cyberspace 65
2.6 Overlapping Legal Orders 69
2.7 The Topography of Legal Space Revisited 74

3 The Identity of Legal Collectives 77
3.1 Individuality and Identity 77
3.2 The Collective as a Self and as the Same 81
3.3 Collective Self and Alterity 90
3.4 Implications and Caveats 96
3.5 Exclusive Territoriality Affirmed 101
3.6 An Enlarged First-Person Plural Perspective 106

PART II: LEGAL ORDERING

4 A Genealogy of Legal Ordering 117
4.1 Intentionality and Legal Ordering 118
4.2 Disclosing Something as Something* 122
4.3 We [Ought to] Jointly Disclose Something as Something* in-Order-to-φ 125
4.4 We [Ought to] Jointly Disclose Something as Something* Anew in-Order-to-φ 129
4.5 Ordering and Rationality 133

4.6 Back to the 'First' Constitution 143
4.7 The Paradox of Representation 148
4.8 The A-Legal Origins of (Il)legality 152

5 A-Legality 156
5.1 Estrangement 156
5.2 The Normative Complexity of A-Legality 163
5.3 Fault Lines 174
5.4 Civil Disobedience 182
5.5 Chaos 184

6 Setting Legal Boundaries 187
6.1 The Identification of a Collective as a Thing 187
6.2 The Identification of a Collective as a Self 191
6.3 From Identification to Reidentification 197
6.4 Question and Response 201
6.5 The Hiatus between Question and Response 206
6.6 Collective Transformation 209
6.7 The Emergence of a Novel Legal Collective 215
6.8 Collective De-Identification 218

7 A Politics of A-Legality 222
7.1 Inclusion and Exclusion as a Normative Problem 222
7.2 Reciprocity and a Politics of Boundary-Setting 227
7.3 The Non-Reciprocal Origin of Reciprocity 234
7.4 Human Rights as the Rights of Strangers 239
7.5 Dia-Logos 248

Conclusion 261

Bibliography 269
Index 283

Introduction

Some time back my partner and I were having dinner at a restaurant when a vagrant suddenly came in. All eyes turned on the man when he walked up to the waiter and demanded a dinner. It was clear he would brook no nonsense; it was equally clear that he would not be paying for the dinner. A tense silence settled over the room. The waiter hesitated and, presumably worried about the ruckus that would ensue if he called the police, quickly ushered him to a table close to the kitchen—as it happened the table next to ours. The vagrant was quickly forgotten and his unexpected arrival gave way, once again, to animated conversation. And then something extraordinary happened, even though only a handful of guests noticed it: when the man was brought his dinner, he looked up at the waiter and, with an angelical smile, invited him to sit down and share the meal. The waiter was stunned (and so were we); he fidgeted a bit, awkwardly declined the invitation, and walked back quickly into the kitchen.

However fleetingly, the vagrant's gesture disrupted the flow of an order that had been taken more or less for granted by those who participated in it. The disruption had two faces. For the one, it called attention to the restaurant as part of a concrete order in which boundaries establish that certain persons are to behave in certain ways in certain places and at certain times. For the other, the vagrant's invitation intimated another way of ordering who stands and who sits, who orders and who eats, when one is entitled to enter and leave, and so forth. Notice that realizing the order intimated by the vagrant's behaviour would require a great deal more than simply redefining some legal norms pertaining to restaurants; however discretely, his gesture called into question fundamental features of the *entire* legal order in which restaurants are the kind of place in which one is served a meal if one can pay for it. In short, the vagrant both breached and transgressed extant legal boundaries. Yes, his behaviour was misplaced (rather than emplaced); but it was also *dis*-placed: it took place elsewhere than in the distribution of places made available by the legal order of which that restaurant was a part.

What sense are we to make of this event as concerns the spatial dimension of the legal order it questioned? Can we simply say that the vagrant was 'in' the restaurant? Was he not in a sense both inside and outside a legal order? What does his gesture tell us about how boundaries do their work of including and excluding? Would it suffice to change the boundaries which establish where certain kinds of behaviour ought to take place, such that his invitation could be integrated into the legal order he challenged? Or does his gesture bespeak the possible emergence of a novel legal order that is irreducible to the latter?

These are very local questions, raised by an evanescent event; they are, it seems, far removed from the properly global scale of the developments which have robbed state law of its paradigmatic status for legal theory and the legal doctrine. Nothing could be further from the truth. The vagrant's gesture and the questions to which it gives rise expose what remains largely beyond the pale of reflection in the contemporary debate about law in a global setting; it betokens a neglected field of enquiry which demands sustained and careful attention.

Indeed, the current debate about legal order, which seeks to pin down what has changed when it can no longer be taken for granted that law true and proper falls on either side of the divide between municipal law and international law, assumes that the inside/outside distinction is contingent, a fixture of that historically specific kind of legal order called a 'state'. It has become a truism to assert that contemporary social relations cannot be adequately described and explained as taking place exclusively within—and to some extent between—sovereign states with mutually exclusive territories, populations, and governments. A host of novel legal orders, such as codes of professional self-regulation, *lex mercatoria*, technical standardization, the Internet Corporation for Assigned Names and Numbers (ICANN), and multinationals, can no longer be accommodated in a concept of law that takes the spatially bounded state to be the paradigm of legal order.

These developments have profoundly influenced how contemporary legal theory approaches the concept of law. If the spatial boundaries of states had been largely taken for granted as constituent features of legal order during the acme of the municipal/international law paradigm, the emergence of cross-border legal orders retrospectively exposes those boundaries as a contingent feature of law. Building on this insight, a variety of theories have sought to articulate a general concept of legal order that need not rely on the inside/outside distinction as one of its constituent features, and to think through the normative implications of this epochal transformation for law and politics. In particular, the process by which the state's legal boundaries lose some of their purchase on human behaviour is often celebrated as marking the passage from a monistic understanding of social life to the consolidation of pluralism in law and politics. If the thought patterns that underpinned the state sought to protect the integrity of its legal boundaries, often at the expense of diversity, the advent of non-state legal orders opens up the possibility of a pluralistic politics less mindful of securing legal boundaries and more respectful of differences—or so we are told.

Even though this conceptual and normative reorientation understands itself as introducing a drastic shift away from the paradigm that has dominated Western legal and political theory during the past centuries, one may wonder whether it does not continue to rely on the state-centred thinking about boundaries it claims to leave behind. Indeed, to assert that the inside/outside distinction is not a constituent feature of legal orders is to hold that the borders of the territorial state, or of other comparably bounded communities, exhaust the manner in which legal orders close themselves into an inside vis-à-vis an outside. This assumption has been so overwhelmingly obvious that, to the best of my knowledge, there is not a single contribution to legal or political theory that directly and systematically poses the question whether the kind of closure afforded by the borders of state territories exhausts how legal orders close themselves into an inside in contrast to an outside, let alone whether that kind of closure is the primordial manifestation of the inside/outside divide. More broadly, I know of no legal or political theory that incorporates the question about spatial closure into a systematic and general enquiry into the kinds of boundaries that might be an ingredient to law as a normative order.

Why should we not rest satisfied with this standard picture about legal order in a global setting, regardless of whether one refers to contemporary developments as 'postnationalism', 'transnationalism', 'denationalization', or some such? Why not move directly into a normative appraisal of the threats and opportunities opened up by these developments?

The short answer, as intimated by the vagrant's literally extra-ordinary gesture, is that this diagnosis, however engrained and seemingly obvious, operates with an extremely reductive understanding of the inside/outside distinction and of the ways in which inclusion and exclusion are constitutive features of legal orders. Making sense of law in a global setting requires, or so I will argue, introducing the cardinal three-way distinction between the boundaries, limits, and fault lines of legal orders. The aim of this book is to elucidate and justify the systematic interconnection between these three categories.

Admittedly, the distinction between boundaries, limits, and fault lines is not part of the vocabulary with which legal and political philosophies have been accustomed to conceptualize legal order. These categories are even further removed from the conceptual framework of the legal doctrine. So, although the book will familiarize the reader, step by step, with each of these categories, it may be helpful to introduce them right away by anticipating four theses which lie at the heart of this book: (i) Any legal order we could imagine must have *boundaries*, because law determines who ought to do what, where, and when within the concrete unity of an order. In other words, law regulates—orders—behaviour by setting its subjective, material, spatial, and temporal boundaries. (ii) Whereas boundaries join and separate places, times, subjects, and act-contents within the concrete unity of a legal order, *limits* distinguish a legal order from the domain of what remains legally unordered for it. If boundaries configure a legal order as a realm of practical possibilities available to participant agents, this realm is perforce limited because legal collectives can only configure themselves as concrete legal unities by excluding other possible realms of practical possibilities. (iii) The limits of legal orders become visible in strange behaviour that, irrupting into a legal order from the domain of the unordered, transgresses the spatial, temporal, subjective, and material boundaries that establish whether behaviour is legal or illegal. If the boundaries of legal orders determine what is (il)legal, they manifest themselves as limits when challenged by *a-legality*, that is, by strange behaviour and situations that, evoking another realm of practical possibilities, question the boundaries of (il)legality. (iv) The boundaries of a legal order appear as normative *fault lines* to the extent that a-legal behaviour and situations raise normative claims that surpass the range of practical possibilities which the apposite legal collective could actualize as its own possibilities by reconfiguring the boundaries of who ought to do what, where, and when. A fault line manifests itself in the form of normative claims that are not merely unordered but also unorderable for a given legal collective.

Returning to the questions raised by the vagrant's—the stranger's—gesture, these four theses entail that it is necessary to distinguish between two forms of the inside/outside distinction. The first is the distinction between domestic and foreign legal spaces; the second is the distinction between the space a legal collective deems its own and strange spaces. As the vagrant's gesture shows, these two modes of the inside/outside distinction are irreducible to each other: a strange place need not be foreign; a foreign place need not be strange. Crucially, whereas globalization processes show that the distinction between foreign and domestic spaces is contingent, the distinction between own and strange places is constitutive for legal orders as such, global or otherwise. In this fundamental sense, no legal order is imaginable that does not close itself into an inside vis-à-vis an outside.

The reader may rest assured that this dense set of theses and formulations will be suitably introduced and fleshed out in due course. But their unfamiliarity shows that the three-way distinction between boundaries, limits, and fault lines launches an enquiry into the concept of legal order that differs in decisive ways from the approaches favoured by leading strands of legal and political theory. Borrowing a felicitous formulation from my colleague, Bert van Roermund, I shall sketch out the broad contours of a 'first-person plural' concept of legal order, that is, of a legal order as played out by a 'we' in which a manifold of individuals act jointly. This concept builds on and moves beyond insights derived from analytical theories of collective action and from phenomenology, in particular a phenomenology of the alien or strange. While these two traditions in philosophical thinking about order have developed largely independently of each other, I will attempt to show that a certain—at times uneasy—alliance between the two casts light on law in a global setting in ways that are not available to contemporary conceptual and normative debates about legal order. As concerns the conceptual debate about legal order, this book engages two of its most prominent contemporary exponents, namely *legal positivism* and *systems theory*, which have strongly influenced sociologies oriented to making sense of law in a global setting. Albeit in different ways, or so I will argue, neither strand of thinking succeeds in adequately illuminating the nature of the relation between legal orders and their boundaries, limits, and fault lines. A comparable problem undermines a range of normative theories of legal order. In general, contemporary normative approaches to legal order seek to identify the conditions that could justify legal obligations. Some of these theories are *particularist* in flavour: they hold that legal obligations presuppose and are only binding for a bounded collective. Other theories have a *universalistic* bent: ultimately, they argue, the global setting of law shows that legal obligations are such to the extent that they are binding for—or at least are derived from obligations binding for—everyone and everywhere, rather than only for the members of a bounded collective. I will argue hereinafter that both of these normative approaches to legal order operate with a reductive understanding of how legal boundaries do their work of including and excluding. An adequate understanding of how boundaries include and exclude entails developing an account of the normativity of legal orders alternative to both particularism and universalism, communitarianism and cosmopolitanism.

While the book critically engages this wide range of conceptual and normative theories of legal order, it declines the invitation to do so in their own terms. The concept of law in the first-person plural, as it will be developed hereinafter, seeks to open up and systematically explore a number of conceptual and normative issues that have escaped attention hitherto, rather than defend any of the positions staked out in the current debates about law in a global setting. Because my enquiry is orthogonal to a good deal of these debates, I draw on what is relevant in these discussions for my own purposes, without necessarily taking a stance on them. For this reason, only rarely will I take the trouble of mapping those debates, let alone referring to them at any length.

To give the reader a sense of the direction I will be taking, let me anticipate, however succinctly, the main argumentative line of the book:

Part I of this book holds, more generally, that viewing law as a species of joint action offers an approach to the concept of legal order that is sufficiently capacious to incorporate a very wide range of legal orders while also sufficiently flexible to accommodate their differences. The basic idea, borrowing Margaret Gilbert's adroit formulation, is that there is a fundamental difference between two uses of the indexical 'we', namely, 'we each' and 'we together'. The first is aggregative; the second, integrative. The first speaks to a summation of individuals; the second to a group, to a manifold of individuals who view themselves as a unit by dint of acting jointly. It may remain an open question for the purpose of this book whether this distinction exhausts the range of uses of 'we' with respect to action, and, in particular, whether 'we together' exhausts the domain of 'social facts', as Gilbert puts it. But I will be arguing that joint action by legal collectives provides the template for understanding the concept of legal order and its relation to boundaries, limits, and fault lines. In particular, the structure of joint action under law explains why no legal order can be imagined that does not close itself into a limited unity—not even a global legal order of human rights. And it reveals that while the kind of territoriality proper to states is indeed contingent, legal collectives necessarily lay claim to exclusive territoriality, understood as a collective claim to regulating entry into and circulation within the distribution of ought-places which determine that legal order as a (putative) spatial unity. These findings suggest that a wide range of contemporary legal and political theories, together with many contributions to the sociology of globalization, inadvertently entrench state-centred thinking about legal order when congratulating themselves for having overcome it.

Even though legal orders are perforce limited, boundary-setting can shift these limits, including what had been excluded from legal order, or excluding what had been included therein. Because Part I is primarily concerned with describing the general structure of legal order, it takes for granted that the boundaries of (il)legality and the limit between legal (dis)order and the unordered have already been set. Part II shifts from boundaries and limits as set to the process of setting legal boundaries and limits. In other words, it moves from law as ordered to the process of legal ordering, from *ordo ordinatus* to *ordo ordinans*. So in contrast to the structural approach of Part I, a genetic enquiry is favoured in Part II. The core of this second part is an analysis of the process of boundary-setting that governs the emergence and transformation over time of legal collectives, with particular attention to how the limit between legal (dis)order and the unordered is redrawn in the process of setting legal boundaries. As will transpire, the conditions that govern the genesis of a legal collective also continuously undermine the authoritative claim *that* there is a 'we', the members of whom act jointly, and *what* it is that their joint action is about. The first-person plural perspective always comes second, and never entirely 'arrives': boundary-setting folds pluralization into unification, disintegration into integration, estrangement into what becomes familiar, the second person into the first. Crucially, a theory of legal ordering remains incomplete if it rests content with an account of how resetting the boundaries of (il)legality can shift the limits of legal (dis)order. The boundaries of a legal order not only mark the limit between legal (dis)order and the unordered, but also a *fault line of normativity* to the extent that a-legality raises a normative claim that demands the actualization of practical possibilities that are incompossible with the range of possibilities available to a collective as its own possibilities. The domain of the unordered whence a-legality irrupts into legal order, and to which a collective must respond in one way or another by boundary-setting, encompasses both what is normatively *orderable* and normatively *unorderable* by a legal collective.

The stake of a general account of legal ordering by way of boundary-setting is normative as much as it is conceptual: does the emergence of novel forms of legal order offer hope of moving beyond the logic of inclusion and exclusion that animates the state? Or does that logic continue to hold sway, even though these novel legal orders perhaps transform how it does its work? My answer is unequivocal: in the same way that legal collectives are necessarily limited, so also they cannot order behaviour other than by including and excluding, determining what counts as relevant and important for law, and what does not. Granted, a legal collective can respond to a-legality by resetting the boundaries of (il)legality, thereby obliquely reconfiguring the limit between legal (dis)order and the unordered. But what normative implications follow from this insight? Does it require postulating, in line with universalism, that the *telos* of practical reason, as concerns law, is an all-inclusive legal order, such that boundary-setting should aim for an ever greater inclusiveness? Does it require postulating, in line with particularism, that the *telos* of practical reason, as concerns law, is to articulate a collective identity which is given directly and originally to its members, such that boundary-setting ought to continue including what belongs to the collective's own identity, and excluding what is alien thereto? Or should we be looking for a third interpretation of the normativity of legal ordering?

Regardless of the position one might want to take with respect to this debate, it reveals a further fundamental stake of an enquiry into legal ordering: the problem of practical rationality as it pertains to law. Boundaries, limits, and fault lines certainly deserve our sustained attention because they can shed light on legal order and its disruptions by a-legality. But they are also—and principally—important because *the problem of inclusion and exclusion lies at the heart of modern interpretations of practical rationality*. It is these interpretations of practical rationality which, ultimately, I both want to draw on and qualify when examining how a-legality questions boundaries, and how collectives can respond to a-legality in the process of setting boundaries. Conversely, my claim is that any normative stance on how to deal with the problem of legal inclusion and exclusion presupposes careful scrutiny of how legal boundaries are questioned by a-legality, and how they are posited, in processes of boundary-setting.

Albeit in different ways, both particularism and universalism rely on the principle of reciprocity when explaining the normativity and rationality of boundary-setting. I will defend the thesis that both readings of the principle of reciprocity elude and elide the normative blind spot which is called forth by the non-reciprocal emergence of legal reciprocity, and which, like a birthmark, accompanies a legal collective throughout its career. Indeed, the non-reciprocal origin of legal reciprocity returns from ahead in the form of normative claims which refuse integration into the circle of reciprocity and mutual recognition available to that legal collective, yet which the latter cannot discard as unreasonable other than by falling prey to a *petitio principii*. It is precisely in these situations that the legal boundaries challenged by a-legality manifest themselves as a fault line of normativity, and not merely as a limit that can be shifted by including what ought not to have been excluded, or by excluding what ought not to have been included. Inasmuch as every collective harbours a normative blind spot which it can neither suspend nor entirely justify, the normative question that arises is how a collective ought to deal with this blind spot in the course of setting the boundaries of (il)legality. I will sketch out to this effect the broad contours of a 'politics of a-legality' in which collective self-restraint, in the face of a-legal claims which definitively resist inclusion into the collective's legal order, is incorporated into the ongoing process of boundary-setting.

Globalization, I argue in the conclusion, is no exception to this normative predicament: the emergence of and radical challenges to novel legal orders with a global reach attest to the emergent fault lines of globalization. The assumption that globalization reveals (spatial) closure to be a merely contingent feature of legal orders not only involves a reification of the world into a (very large) thing among other things, but also, and more importantly, a certain 'forgetfulness' about the worldliness of a legal world, namely about its structure as a limited nexus of spatial, temporal, subjective, and personal ought-relations, which, as a home-world, both points to and has cut itself off definitively from the one world. Against the monism of universalism and the simple pluralism (hence the multiplication of monism) of particularism, I argue that the fault lines of globalization attest to the intertwinement of home-worlds and strange worlds, against the background of the one world to which there can be no access if there are to be legal orders.

Addressing this wide range of issues requires a differentiated methodology which integrates conceptual, empirical, normative, ontological, and institutional levels of interrogation and analysis. Let me briefly say something about each of these strata:

- The central *conceptual* problem raised by the dissolution of the doctrinal identity between law and state turns on finding a way to illuminate the internal connection between legal order and boundaries, limits, and fault lines. As anticipated heretofore, I will argue that adumbrating this three-way relation requires developing a general theory of legal order as a first-person plural concept. A legal order is, in a nutshell, a form of joint action in which authorities mediate and uphold who ought to do what, where, and when with a view to realizing the normative point of acting together. By parsing this concept of legal order into its constituent parts, I hope to show why boundaries, limits, and fault lines are ingredients in all and sundry legal orders.
- *Empirically*, the question is whether careful analysis of a sampling of legal orders in a global setting could justify the strong claim that boundaries, limits, and fault lines are part and parcel of all legal orders. I can do no more, within the scope of this book, than scrutinize a range of legal orders which, at first glance, are strong counterexamples to the thesis that all legal orders are limited. With varying degrees of detail, I show that nomadism, Roman law, classical international law, *ius gentium*, multinationals, *lex constructionis*, cyberlaw, overlapping legal orders such as the European Union and its Member States, a global legal regime of human rights, and space law all validate the thesis that a closure in space, time, content, and subjectivity is constitutive for legal order.
- This set of conceptual and empirical problems is intimately linked to a number of *normative* issues. At issue is the practical question confronting every legal collective, namely, what ought our joint action to be about? In other words, what ought to be included in legal (dis)order and excluded therefrom? If, as we shall see, this practical question remains within the circle of reciprocity and the practical possibilities available to a collective as its own possibilities, how, then, to respond to normative claims about practical possibilities which exceed the range of what a given collective can include in its legal order? These are, one and all, questions about practical rationality as it pertains to the process of setting the boundaries of legal orders.
- In turn, the problem of practical rationality bears directly on a fundamental theme of *collective ontology*. Any stance one might want to take on the openness and closure of the boundaries of legal orders is ultimately linked to an interpretation of the finitude proper to a collective self. This is what the distinction between boundaries as limits and as fault lines seeks to clarify. I will argue that boundary-setting in response to a-legality reveals the finite questionability and finite responsiveness of legal collectives. A collective frames the question raised by a-legality in a way that renders it amenable to a response by the collective, that is, a response that, on an authoritative assessment, allows the collective to reidentify itself over time. It is this ontological issue—a strong form of finitude as the mode of existence of a collective self—which is most fundamentally elicited by what I will call a 'politics of a-legality'.

- Finally, the emergence of law in a global setting also brings *institutional* questions to the fore. I will argue that a constitution is a first-person plural concept, hence that constitutions function as the master rule for establishing what counts, for a legal collective, as *our* joint action. If, as has often been argued, constitutions are located at the interface between politics and law because they operate as institutional devices for authoritatively establishing what counts as legal unity in the face of political plurality, then the political problem of setting legal boundaries in response to their questioning by a-legality is as much at the heart of constitutionalism in a global setting as it is of state constitutionalism.

PART I

LEGAL ORDER

Part I seeks to develop a concept of legal order that shows how and why boundaries and limits play a role in making sense of legal order as a specific kind of normative order. This analysis is structural rather than genetic; I will postpone an enquiry into the emergence of legal boundaries and limits (and fault lines) until Part II. The structural account favoured in Part I fleshes out and validates, as anticipated in the Introduction, a first-person plural concept of legal order. By parsing this concept of legal order into its constituent parts, I hope to illuminate why and how legal orders must deploy boundaries and limits if they are to be normative orders. Let me provide a brief overview of the three chapters which compose Part I.

Chapter 1 lays the groundwork for the remainder of Part I, discussing three variations on an entirely mundane joint act whereby a group of friends buy victuals at a food shop with a view to throwing a party. These scenarios have a number of functions. They allow me to describe, in some detail, what it means that legal orders appear as concrete normative orders from the first-person plural perspective of joint action. They lend credence to the claim that it is reductive to view the unity of legal orders as the unity of a manifold of norms. And, crucially, they allow me to introduce the three-way distinction between legality, illegality, and a-legality in a way that illuminates the distinction and relation between the boundaries and limits of legal orders.

Admittedly, the three scenarios take place in the context of a state order. So it is essential to test whether the structure of legal order captured by the description of those three scenarios also holds for non-state law. Such is the task of chapter 2. It validates the findings of chapter 1 by discussing a series of possible counter-examples to the thesis that legal orders must be spatially limited. All the legal orders examined in this chapter display a common topography, which bears out the view that whereas the inside / outside distinction afforded by borders between domestic and foreign spaces is contingent, the inside / outside distinction corresponding to the limit between legal (dis)order and the unordered is a necessary element of legal orders as spatial unities.

Chapter 3 ties together the findings of the first two chapters, further developing a concept of legal order in the first-person plural. To this effect it draws on theories of collective action of analytical provenance and links these to Paul

Ricœur's important contribution to a theory of identity. By grasping why joint action involves collective identity as sameness (*idem*) and as selfhood (*ipse*) it will be possible to explain why legal orders are organized as an interconnected distribution of ought-places, times, subjects and act-contents, that is, as legal orders in which *boundaries* join and separate its elements. Moreover, understanding why joint action involves collective self-inclusion and the exclusion of alterity, i.e. of other than collective self, also explains why legal orders are perforce *limited*, that is, why and how legal (dis)order goes hand in hand with a domain which remains unordered from the first-person perspective of the apposite legal collective. The chapter concludes by exploring some of the implications of these ideas for the current debate about law in a global setting.

1

Legality, Illegality, A-Legality: A Preliminary Analysis

A first and indispensable step towards a systematic account of the internal relation between boundaries, limits, and legal order is to provide a preliminary description and conceptualization of the kinds of boundaries which are constitutive for legal orders as such, regardless of whether what is at stake is, say, state law, international law or any of the host of transnational or even global legal orders which are emerging before our eyes, such as codes of professional self-regulation, *lex mercatoria*, technical standardization, ICANN (the Internet Corporation for Assigned Names and Numbers), and multinationals. Such an exercise generalizes, in that it must identify and characterize the basic and general structure of legal boundaries in a way that does not open it up to the reproach of being state-centred. But this generalizing move must not come at the price of losing concreteness, such that we are left with a concept of legal order incapable of illuminating how legal boundaries contribute to regulating behaviour. The guiding insight I will develop in this chapter is that the general and concrete structure of legal orders becomes visible if one traces the different relations to boundaries deployed by legal, illegal, and a-legal behaviour. If legal and illegal behaviour call attention to the boundaries of a legal order, a-legal behaviour reveals boundaries as the limit of legal (dis)order by intimating strange places, times, subjectivities, and act-contents which interfere with the legal order they transgress.

1.1 REORIENTING THE PROBLEM OF THE UNITY OF LEGAL ORDERS

Hans Kelsen is one of only a handful of legal theorists who has explicitly addressed the problem of legal boundaries within the framework of a general study of the concept of law. What renders him unique for the purpose of my enquiry is that his contribution to legal theory both reveals and conceals how (spatial) boundaries are elements of the concept of law as a normative order. Let us pick out both movements.

Kelsen approaches the problem of boundaries, including but not limited to spatial boundaries, within the framework of what he calls the four spheres or dimensions of validity of legal norms. As, according to Kelsen, legal norms regulate human behaviour, human behaviour can be regulated with regard to four different dimensions: spatial, temporal, material, and subjective. As concerns space and time, Kelsen notes that '[t]he norm must . . . determine in its content both where and when the behaviour takes place—or, in terms of the norm, "ought to take place"'. He adds: 'That a norm is valid will always mean that it is valid in some space or another and for some time or another—in other words, that it refers to events that can only take place somewhere and at some time.'[1] In addition to the spatial and temporal spheres of validity, legal norms involve an objective or material sphere of validity, indicating what kind of human behaviour is to be regulated. In other words, there can be no ordering of the 'where' and the 'when' of behaviour that does not also order the 'what' thereof. Finally, legal norms also deploy a personal sphere of validity, establishing who ought to behave in a certain way. Accordingly, the task of the law is to regulate—order—human behaviour by determining *who* ought to do *what*, *where*, and *when*.

Crucially, and here is where the problem of boundaries comes into the picture, Kelsen distinguishes between 'limited' and 'unlimited' spheres of validity. In this vein, a 'norm may be valid only for a certain space and time... that is, it may govern only those events that occur within a certain space and time' or, to the contrary, 'the norm may be valid... everywhere and always'. In the same way, the personal sphere of validity is unlimited when, for example, the 'norms of a universal morality are addressed to absolutely all human beings', in contrast to, say, legal norms that 'impose obligations on, and grant rights to, certain categories of human beings'.[2] The same holds for the material sphere of validity, which can regulate all or some forms of behaviour. In short, normative orders in general, and legal orders in particular, can in principle be either *limited or unlimited*.

This last point is decisive, because it renders explicit the assumptions that govern contemporary descriptions and analyses of legal orders in a global setting. In effect, by drawing the distinction between limited and unlimited spheres of validity, Kelsen can be read as asserting that there is no necessary relation between (spatial) boundaries and legal orders, nor a fortiori between law-making and setting legal boundaries. This distinction neatly captures the intuitive sense of boundaries that governs much theorizing about global law. At least in principle, or so I construe Kelsen as arguing, it is possible to conceive of a legal order that is not limited in space, time, content, or subjects, that is, which would be valid everywhere, at all times, for all forms of behaviour and for all human beings. In particular, a global legal order, were it ever to be founded, would have a 'territory', defined as its spatial sphere of validity, and it would certainly have spatial boundaries that ordain where forms of behaviour ought to take place, but it would have no 'outside' in the sense of an order contiguous to other legal orders. Moreover, the fact that an unlimited legal order is at least conceivable explains why a theory of legal order can be developed independently of any consideration of legal limits. In fact, the hallmark of a general theory of law would have to be that it *refuses* to integrate limits into the concept of legal order—or so it seems.

[1] Hans Kelsen, *Introduction to the Problems of Legal Theory*, 1st edn. of the *Reine Rechtslehre*, trans. Bonnie Litchewski Paulson and Stanley L. Paulson (Oxford: Clarendon, 2002), 12. See also Hans Kelsen, *Pure Theory of Law*, 2nd edn. of the *Reine Rechtslehre*, trans. Max Knight (Berkeley, CA: University of California Press, 1967), 10 ff.

[2] Kelsen, *Problems of Legal Theory*, 12–13.

Once it has been ascertained that legal orders need not be limited, an investigation of the concept of law as a specific kind of normative *order* turns on making sense of the law as a *unity of legal norms*. In a famous passage of the first edition of the *Pure Theory of Law*, Kelsen notes that:

> The law *qua* order—the legal order—is an order of legal norms. The first questions to answer here have been put by the Pure Theory of law in the following way: what accounts for the unity of a plurality of legal norms, and why does a certain legal norm belong to a certain legal order?[3]

We need not concern ourselves at any length with how Kelsen goes about answering this question. It may suffice to remind the reader that his further analysis of law *qua* order concentrates on clarifying the notion of a basic norm; on explicating a legal order as a *Stufenbau* or hierarchical interconnection of norms; and on elucidating legal acts as acts of norm application and norm creation. What is important for our own enquiry is that Kelsen restricts the problem of legal order as a unity to that of a unity *of norms*.

Kelsen by no means stands alone here. Let us briefly look at Hart. The problem of the unity of legal order receives its initial formulation early on in *The Concept of Law*: 'What are rules and to what extent is law an affair of rules?'[4] The core of Hart's analysis is, of course, the distinction and possible union between primary and secondary rules. Although all legal communities have primary rules of obligation which stipulate what individuals must or must not do, these rules on their own do not give rise to a legal *system* proper. For if a legal community is only governed by primary rules—which is certainly possible and even characteristic for what he calls 'primitive communities'—these rules 'will simply be a set of separate standards, without any identifying or common mark, except of course that they are the rules which a particular group of human beings accepts'.[5] The passage from a 'pre-legal' to a 'legal world' is secured, as Hart sees it, with the emergence of secondary rules, rules which entertain different aspects of primary rules as their object. Most famously, the 'rule of recognition' addresses the problem of uncertainty about which rules belong to a regime of primary rules, indicating the criteria that must be met so that any given rule can be viewed as a rule of the group. The existence of such a rule is constitutive for the systematicity of law, that is, for the possibility of viewing a manifold of legal norms as a *unity*. 'By providing an authoritative mark [the rule of recognition] introduces ... the idea of a legal system: for the rules are now not just a discrete unconnected set but are ... unified'.[6] No less importantly, the rule of recognition is decisive for understanding the validity of legal rules: 'to say that a given rule is valid is to recognize it as passing all the tests provided by the rule of recognition and so as a rule of the system'.[7] All of this has been rehearsed innumerable times in the literature. I repeat it, not to launch yet a new foray into the extraordinarily ramified

[3] Kelsen, *Problems of Legal Theory*, 55 (translation altered: I render '*Rechtsordnung*' throughout this book as 'legal order', rather than as 'legal system').

[4] H.L.A. Hart, *The Concept of Law*, 2nd edn. (Oxford: Clarendon Press, 1994), 13.

[5] Hart, *The Concept of Law*, 92.

[6] Hart, *The Concept of Law*, 95.

[7] Hart, *The Concept of Law*, 103.

and detailed—and increasingly sterile—debate about the rule of recognition, but rather to call attention to the simple but decisive fact that Hart poses the problem of the concept of legal system as a problem of the *unity of a manifold of rules,* i.e. as a problem about rule-affiliation.

Ronald Dworkin has mounted a powerful attack on Hart's concept of legal order, objecting that law's ambit also includes, at a minimum, 'principles' and 'policies'.[8] But including principles and policies in law will not get us any closer to formulating or addressing the problem concerning the relation between boundaries and legal order. While Dworkin's proposal certainly broadens the scope of what counts as law, the *general direction* of the question concerning legal order remains unchanged, namely, identifying the 'standards' that could explain decisions of law as a coherent practice. The unity of the law emerges and is continuously (re)negotiated in a legal practice that seeks to preserve and augment the integrity of the rules, principles, and policies that define the law as a normative order. The same holds a fortiori for Jules Coleman's contribution to legal theory, which seeks amongst others to defend Hart's project against Dworkin's attack by reformulating it in terms of 'inclusive positivism'.[9] Here again, as is also the case with Joseph Raz, the overriding problem that determines a study of law as a normative *order* is to articulate the conditions that allow of identifying a manifold of legal norms as a unity.[10]

But does this range of enquiries exhaust the problem of unity involved in thinking of law as a normative order? Indeed, the question about law as a normative *order* need not be posed only with regard to legal norms (however broadly construed); it can also be posed from the perspective of the behaviour which an order is called on to regulate. If an order, to borrow a Kantian formulation, is the unity of a manifold, then the problem of legal order cannot be only the problem about the unity of a manifold of norms, as Kelsen and many others take for granted. It is also, and no less importantly, a question about *how a legal order manifests itself as a unity with respect to each of the normative dimensions of behaviour regulated by the law*. On this—avowedly unorthodox—reading of Kelsen, law, *qua* normative order, sets up certain kinds of relations between places, between subjects, between times, and between act-contents. It also integrates these four kinds of relations as the dimensions of a *single* order of behaviour, such that certain acts by certain persons are allowed or disallowed at certain times and in certain places. Law is a compound *differentiation and interconnection* of dimensions of behaviour: it differentiates four dimensions of behaviour—subjectivity, content, time, and space—and it differentiates each of these dimensions, splitting them up into an interrelated manifold of places, times, subjects, and rights/obligations. Hence, instead of only asking 'Under what conditions can a manifold of norms manifest themselves as legal unity?', we must redirect our attention to the

[8] Ronald Dworkin, 'Is Law a System of Rules?', repr. in Ronald Dworkin (ed.), *The Philosophy of Law* (Oxford: Oxford University Press, 1977), 38–65.

[9] See Jules Coleman, *The Practice of Principle: In Defence of a Pragmatist Approach to Legal Theory* (Oxford: Oxford University Press, 2001).

[10] See Joseph Raz, *The Authority of Law*, repr. (Oxford: Clarendon Press, 2002), 37–159.

dimensions of behaviour regulated by law: what is the mode of appearance of a legal order as a spatial unity? And as a temporal unity? And as a material unity? And as a subjective unity?[11]

The implication of raising these questions is that law is never only an order of norms that is grafted a posteriori onto the world of fact, such that it thereby transforms the latter's meaning. That no legal norm, nor a fortiori any legal order, is conceivable absent spatial, temporal, material, and subjective dimensions means that law appears, from the *practical* perspective of those whose behaviour it regulates, as a normative unity to the extent that it differentiates and interconnects who ought to do what, where, and when. From this practical perspective, a legal order is not first and foremost the unity of a manifold of norms and only derivatively a spatial, temporal, subjective, and material unity. To the contrary: isolating legal norms as the object of the question about the unity of legal order comes second, as a historically late doctrinal and theoretical achievement.

Nowhere in the Pure Theory of Law is the laying bare of this new area of philosophical exploration and its immediate concealment more manifest than in a passage that appears at the beginning of the second edition of the *Reine Rechtslehre:*

> [W]hen we compare the objects that have been designated by the word 'law' by different peoples at different times, we see that all these objects turn out to be *orders of human behavior*. An 'order' is a system of norms whose unity is constituted by the fact that they all have the same ground of validity; and the ground of validity of a normative order is a basic norm—as we shall see—from which the validity of all norms which belong to the order are derived.[12]

Notice the reduction of the problem of legal order that goes from the first to the second of these two sentences. In the first, it is still possible to raise the question about legal order as the unity of a manifold in a way that begins from what is ordered, namely, behaviour. The question then becomes in what ways the law appears as a unity to those whose behaviour it regulates. Here is where the problem of the spheres of validity as specific modes of legal unity comes into the picture. By contrast, the second sentence immediately closes down this possibility, reducing the problem of legal order to how a manifold of *norms* can be understood as a unity—that is, to the problem of the ground of unity of that manifold of norms. While the subsequent debate about and confrontation with Kelsen

[11] In a recent book Scott Shapiro argues that legal theory should eschew its fixation on law as a unity of norms and approach law as an organizational phenomenon. While we share the conviction that collective action casts new light on the concept of law and on the unity of a legal order, his planning theory does not (and perhaps cannot) raise and deal with the question about legal unity in terms of the internal connection between legal order and its boundaries and limits (and fault lines). In his words, 'The *unity* of a set of legal norms is thus derived from the *sociality* of legal participants. What makes it the case that the laws of a particular system of law are laws of that system is that they are the products of the activity of *one group* sharing a plan and working together in planning for a community'. In the same way, the normative issues raised by boundaries, limits, and fault lines examined in chapter 7 remain well beyond the purview of his planning theory of law. See Scott Shapiro, *Legality* (Cambridge, MA: Harvard University Press, 2010), 208.

[12] Kelsen, *Pure Theory of Law,* 30.

has centred on the viability of the basic norm as conditioning the possibility of viewing a manifold of norms as a unity, many of Kelsen's detractors and allies have already accepted the terms in which he poses the problem about legal order. The forthcoming pages resolutely resist this reductive move; they seek to develop original possibilities opened up by Kelsen's Pure Theory of Law, even if Kelsen himself did not or could not pursue them as a result of some of the premises guiding his thinking about law.

1.2 LEGALITY

I will now outline three scenarios which allow me to describe how the concreteness of legal orders can be illuminated from the perspective of their addressees. There is a danger with this approach, however, against which we must be on guard from the very beginning. And that is to assume that the descriptions exhaust the meaning of the scenarios. If the descriptions of these three scenarios seek to elicit why an act is legal, illegal, or a-legal, so also the descriptions *frame* an act in such a way that it can appear as legal, illegal, or a-legal. We will return to discuss this problem in Part II, when examining what phenomenological and post-structuralist theories refer to as the 'precedence' of questions and the 'retroactivity' of answers. For the moment, these scenarios and their corresponding descriptions and labels are a *heuristic device* that clarifies in what sense legal orders are concrete, and how their concreteness is related to boundaries and to limits.

Consider the following scenario:

> *Scenario 1*: Some thirty friends get together after work at the Galeries Lafayette, in Rennes, on 20 December 2008, to purchase food with a view to throwing a party that evening. In addition to vegetables and basic products they also go for some delicacies, including a top-of-the-line brand of foie gras. They load some twenty-four panniers with the food, queue up at the check-out points, and then leave the *grand magasin* after having paid a not insignificant sum of money for their purchases. The party was memorable.

A doctrinal analysis of the scenario would focus on the apposite legal norms, in particular the norms regulating the contract of sale, indicating the rights and obligations that accrue to the contracting parties. This approach is entirely legitimate as far as it goes; but it says little or nothing about the spatial, temporal, subjective, and material dimensions of the scenario, and how these are interconnected. Accordingly, I will explore the scenario with the following question in mind: how does law manifest itself as a concrete normative order from the perspective of those whose behaviour it regulates?

(i) *Space*. I begin with the trivial assertion that the scenario takes place in the food department of Lafayette—a place to sell and buy food and food-related products. The food department is an *ought*-place, in the sense of a place where certain kinds of behaviour are commanded, authorized, or permitted.[13] Although trivial in a mundane sense, this assertion is of the greatest importance to understanding how law orders space: it differentiates places as ought-places, as places where certain kinds of acts 'ought' to take place. Lafayette is only intelligible as the specific ought-place that it is—a place where one ought to buy and sell food—as part of a broader set of ought-places which includes, say, work-places, street-places, parking-places, and home-places. What is characteristic for a legal order is not only that it splits up space into a manifold of ought-places, but also that it regulates the conditions for entry to and exit from these places: the friends must have entered the food department of Lafayette if they are to purchase food. Some will have entered by crossing the door that separates it from the street; others via the lift, after having driven into the parking lot of the Lafayette. Notice that the relation between these ought-places is normative: at issue is not merely how a potential client *can* enter Lafayette. It would also have been possible, for example, to break one of the windows of the shop and to scramble in after having removed the shards of glass. The same holds for the other legal places to which it is related: one ought to enter the parking lot of Lafayette by the appropriate entrance and by taking a parking ticket before going ahead to park the car, even if one *can* enter by crashing through the barrier. The course of action in which the friends select products and put them into panniers also refers beyond itself, to how one ought to *leave* the food department: when finished with shopping, clients are expected to queue up to pay at the check-out points, rather than try to slip out via the entry or fire doors. As an ought-place, the food department of Lafayette is normatively related in certain ways to other ought-places—*and not in others.* Having paid, the friends go on to walk, drive, or to take a tram, taxi, or bus to the home where the party will take place. And this home is also a legal place in the sense of an ought-place (parties are allowed; (large-scale) cultivation of marijuana in a greenhouse is not) with appropriate ways to enter and leave it.

To summarize: law orders space by differentiating ought-places and interconnecting them normatively, such that, first, one ought to enter and leave certain places in certain ways, and, second, certain forms of behaviour are assigned to certain places. Buying at Lafayette, like all legally ordered behaviour, demands a specific kind of *normative orientation in space*, the kind of dexterity required to move *appropriately* into and out of the shop, which is different to the spatial adeptness of the client who knows 'the quickest' way to enter, or who has his or her 'bearings' in the supermarket and can swiftly locate the products he or she needs,

[13] I borrow here from Kelsen, who encompasses the positive and negative regulation of behaviour under the global term 'ought'. The former comprises commands, in which an individual is obliged to engage in or abstain from a certain act, and authorizations, in which 'an individual is authorized by the normative order to bring about, by a certain act, certain consequences determined by the order' (such as the creation of norms). By contrast, negative or permissive regulations concern situations in which 'behavior is not forbidden by the order without being positively permitted by a norm that limits the sphere of validity of a forbidding norm, and therefore is permitted only in a negative sense' (Kelsen, *Pure Theory of Law*, 15–16).

or who knows which of the check-out points tends to be the least 'congested'. In other words, spatial orientation within a legal order involves exploiting the spatial possibilities that a legal order opens up, and shunning those it forecloses. That a manifold of places are differentiated and interconnected as ought-places entails that the law allows and disallows places for certain kinds of behaviour, as well as ways of circulating between these places. The law orders space (a) by differentiating and interconnecting a manifold of ought-places, such that (b) it makes and limits room for behaviour.

(ii) *Time*. Because law orders behaviour, law differentiates and interconnects time in the form of an arc spanning past, present, and future. I pick up the foie gras and hesitate: it is expensive; can I pay for it if I also want to buy this, that, and the other? I look at how much money I have in my wallet; yes! I flip the can into the pannier. The 'now' of the hesitation points beyond itself, into the future, in the form of what I ought to do in a bit: to pay. This anticipation of what ought to happen opens up the future in the sense of revealing how it might come to pass through my action; but it also closes down the future because the anticipation concerns what I *ought* to do, even though there are other possibilities I *can* actualize: I can pay; leave without buying the products; bide my time and wolf down the foie gras in the toilet room of Lafayette when nobody is watching; and so on. In the same way that my act involves a normative reference to the future, it also involves a normative reference to the past: by selecting the foie gras and putting it into my pannier now, I am 'following up' on what I did by entering the food department, namely, to consider buying products on offer in the shop. Here again, the past is not an indeterminate past but one which both opens up and constrains what I am doing now: I am going about buying food and delicacies... The sequence of acts that make up buying foie gras and other food at the Lafayette, in which past, present, and future appear as normatively linked to each other, is both preceded and followed up by other sequences of acts: I am now paying a two-zone ticket because I stepped on board the tram; I am now paying a two-zone ticket and ought to step out later, when the tram reaches Lafayette. Once again, the law opens up the future as the realm of normative possibilities: I may either travel the two zones, alighting in front of Lafayette, or I may for whatever reason step out earlier, after traversing only one zone. But the law also closes down the future in terms of possibilities available to behaviour now: I ought not to travel beyond the two zones I paid for. And the normative opening up and closing down of future possibilities 'follows up' on what I did in the past: to step on board and pay a two-zone ticket. In all these cases, past, present, and future appear as coordinated modes of *ought*-time.

In short, the law orders time by differentiating and interconnecting behaviour in specific normative articulations of past, present, and future. Conversely, behaviour is temporally ordered, legally speaking, when it occurs at the *proper* time within a certain normative articulation of past, present, and future. In the same way that legally ordered behaviour displays a normative form of spatial orientation, so also it displays a normative form of *temporal* orientation: I know what I ought to do in the sense of the appropriate time at which to do something to pull off a legal act: I ought to step out *now* (the second zone is ending); I ought to pay *now* (the employee at the check-out point has registered all of the products I want to purchase). In any case, the point of differentiating and interconnecting past, present, and future normatively is to enable and disable certain courses of action. The law orders time by (a) differentiating and interconnecting a manifold of ought-times, such that (b) it makes and limits time for behaviour.

(iii) *Content*. As with the spatial and temporal dimensions of the scenario, its legal content also involves differentiation and interconnection. This double operation is already at work within what the legal doctrine tends to view as a single legal act: a 'sale'. In effect, *what* I am now doing—selecting a can of foie gras and putting it into my pannier—is different from what I did earlier, namely to signal that I am considering purchasing products from Lafayette by entering its food department, and different from what I will do in a bit, namely to pay at the check-out point. The differentiation is not artificial, because I can, for example, decide to interrupt my shopping and leave without buying anything. But each of these different acts appears as legally ordered only if it can be interconnected with the others, given the 'point' of the legal act: if I want to purchase goods that are on display, then I ought to select which goods I want to buy and pay for them. The same holds for the example of transportation (signalling I want to travel—stepping on board—paying—stepping out). This normative differentiation and integration within a *single* course of action makes it possible to view the act as legally ordered. Although we need not pursue this point any further here, differentiation and interconnection are obviously far more ramified than this: for instance, what I ought to do, when buying the foie gras from Lafayette, is different from but interconnected to what Lafayette ought to do, as the seller thereof.

In each of these cases, the legal operation of differentiation and interconnection orders the content of behaviour by opening up and foreclosing kinds of behaviour that may take place, where 'foreclosing' means both 'closing down' and 'closing in advance'. In addition to spatial and temporal orientation, also a normative form of *material orientation* is required in our scenario, an orientation concerning what I ought to do, which presupposes but is irreducible to orientation about what I can do. The second aspect of the basic ordering operation of law comes again into view: legal norms facilitate and hinder kinds of behaviour. In the same way that a legal order enables and limits where and when behaviour ought to take place, by (a) differentiating and interconnecting the content of behaviour, a legal order also (b) enables and limits what ought to be done.

(iv) *Subjectivity*. The friends who gather at Lafayette are the *magasin's* prospective clients. But their legal determination as prospective *clients* is unintelligible in the absence of a subjective differentiation and interconnection: Lafayette as the prospective *seller*. Differentiation does not stop here, however: Lafayette is a retail seller, subjectively different to the wholesale sellers from whom it buys products; in turn, the wholesale retailers are different from farmers who manufacture the products, etc. Granted, the interconnection between most of these subjective differentiations remains latent when the friends indulge in their shopping spree at Lafayette. But if the party leads, alas, to collective food poisoning because the foie gras was laced with a dangerous bacterium that slipped into the production process due to sloppy quality control, then the differentiation and interconnection of these legal subjectivities may well be actualized.

Importantly, the differentiation of legal subjectivities is normative because conditions are attached to their exercise and interconnection. As concerns the conditions for their exercise, a person who has no money to shop at the food department may not take on the role of buyer. If the person is penniless, then, under certain conditions, and in certain legal orders, the person may have a right to welfare allowances, such that, if these allowances are sufficient, he or she may accede to the status of a buyer (at Lafayette). Analogously, the status of a buyer is different from but normatively interconnected to the legal subjectivities of, say, an employee, a rentier, or a self-employed dentist. Other forms of differentiation and interconnection would also hold, of course, in this scenario. For example, while minors may be authorized to buy the foie gras at Lafayette, they would not be authorized to purchase alcohol. Or one of the friends may have been barred from shopping at Lafayette altogether because on earlier occasions he has brawled with other clients. Lafayette, for its part, is authorized to sell if it meets certain rules about incorporation, public hygiene and safety, and labour conditions; the farmer, to manufacture the foie gras subject to conditions of craftsmanship and so on.

Hence, the second face of the basic ordering achievement of legal norms comes into view. The normative point of differentiating and interconnecting is, in this case, to establish *who* ought to engage in certain legal behaviour, which requires creating legal subjectivities and restricting to a lesser or a greater extent the actors authorized to assume those subjectivities. Here again, legally ordered behaviour requires a specific form of *subjective orientation:* one knows *who* is authorized to engage in certain forms of behaviour, and one takes on and drops those forms of legal subjectivity in the appropriate circumstances. In the same way that a legal order enables and limits the where, when, and what of behaviour, so also (a) by differentiating and interconnecting legal subjectivities, a legal order (b) enables and limits the who of behaviour.

A legally versed reader will immediately recognize that my description of the material and subjective spheres of validity of the scenario is extremely crude compared to the detail and refinement that the legal doctrine brings to bear on its account of contracts of sale. But my aim is not to emulate the legal doctrine; it is to recover what remains largely implicit and taken for granted in the doctrinal analysis of contracts of sale, and of legally significant behaviour in general: how law manifests itself as a concrete order to those whose behaviour it regulates.

This perspective is particularly clear if we look at the legal ordering of space and time. As to the former, phenomenology has insisted on the fundamental distinction between 'positions' and 'places', between the three-dimensional space of geometry and the space of action of embodied beings. Not only do things, persons, and acts 'have their place', but places belong together as a unity of places—a 'region', as Heidegger would put it.[14] The three-dimensional space of geometry certainly has a role to play in the law (e.g. the architectural blueprint of the building defines where the entries and exits of the food department are to be placed). But the whole point of my description of the differentiation and interconnection between ought-places in the first scenario is to show that we could not even begin to make sense of space as a 'sphere of legal validity' unless we introduce the first-person singular perspective, which involves orientation about how one ought to enter and leave certain places, and what one ought to do in those places. In particular, the legal doctrine and legal theory take this perspective for granted when they refer to persons, products, services, and the like as 'entering' or 'leaving' a territory.

In the same way that it is necessary to distinguish between positions and places, law also depends on the distinction between calendar and subject-relative time. At one level, the law relies on calendar time, as when it determines the date at which a legal norm enters into force or when it is repealed, or when, in our scenario, Lafayette establishes its trading hours and days. But legal time is never only calendar time; the time of the law is first and foremost a subject-relative form of temporality. Whereas calendar time is ordered as the continuum of a before and an after, in which the sequence of events is entirely indifferent, the law orders past, present, and future in terms of the 'appropriate' times to engage in behaviour. We could not even begin to make sense of temporality as a form of legal *validity* if there were no actor for whom past, present, and future ought to unfold in a certain way. The third-person descriptions of legal behaviour of the doctrine and of legal theory tend to underplay or even mask this perspective when referring to the temporal validity of legal norms.[15]

[14] Martin Heidegger, *Being and Time*, repr., trans. John Macquarrie and Edward Robinson (Oxford: Blackwell, 1995), 136. For a parallel distinction between 'site' and 'place', see Edward Casey, *Getting Back Into Place: For a Renewed Understanding of the Place World* (Indianapolis, IN: Indiana University Press, 1993). For a phenomenologically inspired reading of Aristotle's philosophy of place (*topos*), see Rémi Brague, *Aristote et la question du monde* (Paris: Presses Universitaires de France, 1988), 273–322.

[15] In a seminal article Gernet observes that the human mastery of time, in particular of the past and the future as temporal dimensions that collectives can bring under their control, is a late historical acquisition, rather than a constant of the human condition. Indeed, 'an idea such as that of planning is recent'. He adds that '[t]he category of time had to constitute itself in law. "Abstract and quantitative time": this is the framework in which are affirmed, for the purpose of action and regulation, the notion of a past that is valid as such [and] the notion of a future that is secured as such—two faces of the same thought-process that cannot seem "natural" until it has been acquired'. While Gernet is right to warn against the naturalization of a certain interpretation of time, this by no means entails that 'archaic' law is devoid of time or temporal boundaries. In effect, the notion of a ritual, to which such law remains linked, is unthinkable in the absence of the insertion of actions and events into a temporal order organized in terms of their *appropriate* sequence. Although the scenario we are exploring already moves within a relation to time in which legal norms disclose the past and the future as temporal dimensions amenable to collective control, the normative unity of past, present, and future at work in legality is rooted in a more primordial normative ordering of time, according to which it is appropriate to do certain things before, together with, or after other events or situations. Indeed, behaviour is legal in our scenario to

In short, there are proper times and places for the proper legal subjects to engage in the proper kinds of behaviour. That is: the law orders by indicating the spatial, temporal, material, and subjective *boundaries* of behaviour. To begin with, normative relations between ought-places require a bounded form of space: one enters or leaves Lafayette in appropriate ways; one steps in and out of trams in appropriate ways, etc. In this sense, at least, the inside/outside distinction is a constitutive feature of any imaginable legal order, and not merely of state law. Contemporary legal and political theories have been so fixated on proclaiming that law has become de-territorialized that they overlook the simple but tremendously important fact that the distinction between a domestic or national territory and foreign territories is but *one* of the manifold legal manifestations of the inside/outside distinction. Territorial borders are no more than a species of spatial boundaries, all of which distinguish an inside from an outside. Law must also indicate temporal boundaries if it is to order behaviour. It can draw on calendar time, as when Lafayette determines its opening and closing times. But there are also temporal boundaries in the form of 'the right time' to do something, with respect to which behaviour can take place either 'too early' or 'too late'. This is the primordial form of temporal boundaries in the law; it is primordial because it also holds in those cases—and especially in those cases—in which it makes no sense to try and identify an act as 'on time', 'too late', or 'too early' in terms of calendar time. If the law orders behaviour by indicating its spatial and temporal boundaries, so also it orders behaviour by indicating its material boundaries. By indicating what someone ought to do, the law delimits the scope of behaviour: *this* behaviour is commanded, authorized, or permitted. Parallel considerations hold, finally, for the subjective sphere of validity of legal norms: law orders the subjective dimension of behaviour by indicating its boundaries, that is, the conditions for taking on the status of a legal subject who is authorized to engage in certain forms of legally relevant behaviour, and for interconnecting this specific form of legal subjectivity to other forms thereof.

I can now spell out more precisely in what sense legal orders are *concrete* orders. First, a legal order is concrete in that the four spheres of validity belong together: only by an abstractive process can they be discussed separately. Indeed, when unpacking the scenario into its four dimensions, it proved impossible to entirely filter out the other three dimensions in the process of describing each of them separately. For this reason I refer to space, time, subjectivity, and content as *modes* of legal order, that is, as the dimensions that make up a *single* order. Second, a legal order is concrete in that the integration of the four spheres of validity takes place from the perspective of those whose behaviour is regulated by the law. Law appears as a four-dimensional order in which, for example, one finds oneself in Lafayette (place), as a prospective client (subject), in the course of (time) buying a bag of potatoes and other products (content). Only derivatively

the extent that the group of friends engages in an act at the 'right' time, e.g. paying after selecting the food products they want to take away. It is at this most fundamental level that all legal orders, positive or otherwise, set temporal boundaries to behaviour. See Louis Gernet, 'Le temps dans les formes archaïques du droit', *Journal de psychologie normale et pathologique* 53 (1956), 379; 405.

can a legal order be 'objectified', that is, severed from this first-person perspective, with a view to either isolating the 'meaning' of legal norms as the object of doctrinal analysis and 'interpretation', or establishing from a theoretical perspective under what conditions a manifold of norms can be viewed as a legal unity. Third, a legal order is concrete in that it assigns the *appropriate* places and times for the *appropriate* subjects to do the *appropriate* things. Law is concrete because it provides normative markers for what to do, when and where to do it, and by whom it should be done, such that I can orient myself in each of these dimensions, and all of them together.

There is a final point I would like to make about this scenario, which prepares the transition to the second scenario. Indeed, what is characteristic for behaviour as it unfolds in Lafayette is that the two faces of the ordering function of law—the differentiation and interconnection of behaviour, for the one; the opening up and foreclosure of normative possibilities, for the other—remain *unobtrusive* to those who act and those who might have observed what was taking place. No one notices, least of all the party-goers themselves, that for a client to select a can of foie gras and purchase it, space must be differentiated into certain places, which in turn are interconnected in certain ways; that time must be differentiated into appropriate times to do certain things, the appropriateness of which can only be understood in their connection to other appropriate times to do yet other things; that the content of behaviour must be differentiated into specific acts the meaning of which demands their interconnection to other specific acts; that, finally, subjectivities must be differentiated and interconnected. The party-goers simply buy the foie gras, taking no notice of the legal differentiations and interconnections that make their acts possible; if asked, they would simply say 'this is how one goes about getting food if one wants to throw a party'. The hold of law *qua* normative order is at its strongest when it remains unnoticed as an order that opens up and closes down normative possibilities by differentiating and interconnecting four dimensions of behaviour. Yet more pointedly, while the participants understand what it is they ought to do, they do not immediately describe it in specifically legal terms, even if, *ex post*, their behaviour can be shown to be legal and they can interpret it as such. This is important because it suggests that legal orders draw on and *come to stand out* against the background of a more or less anonymous form of normativity, a normativity in which interaction precedes the reflexive operation whereby a manifold of individuals refer to themselves as a 'we' who act together, such that paying at the check-out point is simply what 'one' does. This is not to say, however, that it is a normativity devoid of legality, for law has contributed to shaping these patterns of behaviour. But it does suggest that the qualification of behaviour as legal, in scenarios such as the one we have been probing, already presupposes situations in which behaviour has been *authoritatively qualified* as such, hence in which the legality of behaviour is obtrusive, the outcome of an authoritative decision. In this sense, a pre-reflexive and post-reflexive normativity are interwoven in the scenario under discussion. I will refer to this kind of pre- and post-reflexive interaction as *social* interaction, and to the manifold of individuals who interact in this way as *society*.

The unobtrusiveness of legal behaviour and of legal order in this first scenario impinges directly on how the order's boundaries appear to those whose behaviour it governs. Indeed, boundaries mark the way in which a legal order differentiates and interconnects the elements that make up each of the dimensions of behaviour. And this is another way of saying that boundaries *join* and *separate*. Legality is unobtrusive when it appears as a 'matter of course' that legal boundaries join and separate in the way they do. The doors or lift show me the way into Lafayette and the check-out points indicate the way out; I select the product now because I am going to pay in a bit to be able to move on to organizing the party tonight; I am authorized to draw money with my debit card to buy what I need from Lafayette; I select the products and, when the employee at the check-out point tallies up the products and hands me the bill of sale, I simply take out my debit card and pay the total amount. Legal boundaries separate and join the different aspects of the course of action into a meaningful whole, such that the clients can orient themselves more or less effortlessly at every stage of the course of action with regard to who ought to do what, where, and when. In the first scenario, the unobtrusiveness of legal order is the unobtrusiveness of legal boundaries for those whose behaviour is governed by that order.

1.3 ILLEGALITY

If the first scenario dealt with legality, the second scenario focuses on the problem of illegality. Actually, the problem of illegality had already cropped up indirectly in the analysis of the first scenario. To show that law orders behaviour by opening up and closing down normative possibilities I resorted to the device of presenting behaviour that would breach the law, contrasting it to legal behaviour. But those scattered remarks by no means exhaust how illegality contributes to illuminating the problem of order and legal boundaries. Indeed, illegality involves a specific kind of *interruption* of legal order, one which retrospectively sheds new light on features of law as normative order that would remain in the dark if behaviour only followed its legal course. In particular, illegality sheds light on the role of the first-person *plural* perspective, which functioned as the inchoate but indispensable presupposition of the description of the first scenario. So consider the second scenario:

> Some thirty friends get together after work at the Galeries Lafayette, in Rennes, on 20 December 2008, to purchase food with a view to throwing a party that evening. In addition to vegetables and basic products they also go for some delicacies, including a top-of-the-line brand of foie gras. They load some twenty-four panniers with the food. But they realize they do not have enough money to foot the entire bill. So a member of the group stuffs the cans of foie gras into the inside pockets of his trench coat before they queue up at the check-out points to pay. A security guard has spotted the action and the individual is detained at the doors of the *grand magasin* by two police agents, who charge him with theft. The party was called off *sine die*.

On a standard doctrinal account this scenario is a snapshot of an illegal act: instead of purchasing the foie gras, an individual steals it, or at least attempts to steal it. If criminal charges are brought against the alleged shoplifter, the prosecution would seek to show that the act meets each of the elements of the offence: *actus reus*, consisting in an unauthorized taking, keeping, or using of another's property, and *mens rea*, i.e. dishonesty and/or the intent to permanently deprive the owner or the person with rightful possession of that property or its use. Typically, the indictment would include a perfunctory reference to the place where the offence took place and the apposite calendar date (and time).

While 'correct' as far as it goes, this doctrinal account focuses on legal norms in a way that presupposes, without clarifying, how the scenario sheds light on law as a concrete normative order. From this perspective, a first point to consider is that, although the criminal proceedings would in all probability focus primarily on *mens rea*, hence on the boundaries that define the content of the act, the theft breaches the four kinds of boundaries we have explored in the first scenario. By passing the check-out point without exhibiting and paying for the foie gras, the would-be party-goer also has breached a *spatial* boundary, and therewith also what determines Lafayette's food department as the specific kind of ought-place that it is: a place where one ought to buy (and sell) certain products. By taking the product without paying for it, the would-be party-goer also has breached a *temporal* boundary, namely the appropriate time to do something (exhibit a product and pay for it). By taking the product without paying for it, the would-be party-goer also has breached a *subjective* boundary: because he is a client, rather than, say, a quality control inspector who takes away cans of foie gras to test them, he is only authorized to participate in a contract to buy the foie gras from Lafayette. In short, and returning to the first scenario, in the same way that behaviour is legal insofar as it actualizes four dimensions of legal order, so also illegal behaviour breaches law as a spatial, a temporal, a subjective, and a material order.

But what does it *concretely* mean to say that illegal behaviour 'breaches' legal order? In other words, and more exactly, if law is primordially a concrete order of behaviour, how does legal order manifest itself as concrete in and through illegal behaviour? A first, apparently obvious reaction would be to say that illegality denotes the *absence* of legal order for the case at hand. Actually, the opposite is the case: illegality has a 'positive' significance in that it renders legal order and behaviour *present* in a specific way. I noted at the end of the foregoing section that legal order and behaviour remain unobtrusive as long as behaviour follows its due (legal) course. Phenomenologically speaking—that is to say, in terms of a description that attempts to capture how law manifests itself *qua* concrete normative order to those whose behaviour it regulates—illegal behaviour becomes itself *conspicuous*. Illegality reveals that legal boundaries govern behaviour and also, conversely, that legal boundaries depend on behaviour. The dependence of boundaries on behaviour remains in the background as long as behaviour is legal; only retrospectively, when someone attempts to carry out the products without paying, does it become apparent that, each time that a client pays at the check-out point, he or she is also reiterating, and in this sense resetting, the spatial boundary that joins and separates the food department of Lafayette from what lies beyond it.

Moreover, the conspicuousness of behaviour goes hand in hand with the conspicuousness of legal order *as such*. In particular, illegal behaviour renders conspicuous the two operations that make of law a normative order for each of its spheres of validity: (i) the proper differentiation and interconnection of ought-places, such that one ought to buy food in Lafayette, which requires entering and leaving in the appropriate way; (ii) the proper temporal differentiation and interconnection of a course of action, such that after selecting products one pays for them and then walks out; (iii) the proper differentiation and interconnection of kinds of behaviour, such that one can either select products and pay for them, or desist from buying; (iv) the proper differentiation and interconnection of legal subjects, namely buyer and seller.

All of this becomes obtrusive when behaviour breaches legal norms. Succinctly, the interruption wrought by illegal behaviour has the effect of making legal order manifest *as* legal order. If, in the ordinary course of buying victuals in a food shop, individuals understand what they ought to do as participants in a more or less anonymous and pre-reflexive form of normative order, this normative order becomes differentiated as a *legal* order when the police collar the shoplifter and take him away. And this means that the *boundaries* of legal order become obtrusive: by interrupting the joining and separating functions of boundaries, illegal behaviour renders these two functions visible *as such*. When the would-be party-goer is detained at the doors of Lafayette, the check-out point becomes conspicuous *as* where one ought to pay, that is, as the spatial boundary that separates and joins inside and outside in a certain way: one is authorized to leave the food department if one pays at the check-out point, etc. Moreover, these four boundaries become visible *all together*: the theft retrospectively makes clear that clients (subjectivity) ought to pay (content) at the check-out point (space) before (time) leaving.

Importantly, illegality does not only make legal order and its boundaries visible; to view an act as illegal is to *affirm* their validity, or more exactly, to *re*affirm their binding character for behaviour: clients *ought* to pay at the check-out point before leaving the store. Even though behaviour breaches legal order, its qualification as illegal has a 'positive' normative significance: illegality counts as the privative manifestation of legal order, hence as its reaffirmation, despite—and because of—the interruption of the two ordering operations of the law.

This insight allows us to take two further steps in clarifying the relation between boundaries and legal orders. First, each of the four kinds of boundaries set in legal orders delimits behaviour in terms of the distinction between the *legal and the illegal*. In this vein, behaviour is legal or illegal when someone is 'emplaced' or 'misplaced'; acts in a timely or untimely fashion; acts in the way established in the law—or not; or is the proper subject of a form of behaviour—or not. *To posit the four boundaries of legal orders is to posit the master distinction between legality and illegality—and vice versa*. Second, the *practical* point of setting legal boundaries is to introduce what Charles Taylor calls a 'qualitative distinction' and Bernhard Waldenfels a 'preference in the difference': the reaffirmation of legal boundaries in the face of their breach means that legality is preferred to illegality, and legal order to legal disorder.[16] Also Niklas Luhmann makes this point when, drawing on Gregory Bateson's work, he notes that systems bring about 'a difference that makes a difference'.[17] So, the immediately foregoing thesis can be sharpened as follows: to posit the four boundaries of legal orders is to posit the master *preferential* distinction between legality and illegality. Conversely, to posit the distinction between legality and illegality is to establish that the appropriate way of entering and leaving an ought-place is preferred to inappropriate ways, and so on.

This insight points to yet a fourth way in which legal orders are concrete normative orders. Because the distinction between legality and illegality is a preferential distinction, acts that breach the law are not normally greeted with indifference by those whose behaviour it regulates. Illegal behaviour provokes fear, irritation, anger, and a variety of related emotions. Perhaps the fundamental reason for this is that, to a lesser or greater extent, illegal behaviour effectively undermines our capacity to orient ourselves normatively in the world, thereby exposing our constitutive vulnerability as beings that are not simply 'in' an order but need to take up a relation *to* an order.

'Our' capacity to orient 'ourselves' normatively, I just wrote; the moment has arrived to introduce the first-person *plural* perspective into our conceptual framework of the relation between boundaries and legal order. Indeed, whoever, as an actor, qualifies an act as illegal, does not refer to the latter as 'a' legal order in general, but rather as *our* legal order, as the legal order *we* live by. The qualification of an act as illegal renders *us* thematic as a collective. This follows from the fact that law is a *social* order, such that legal norms regulate relations *between* actors. Kelsen puts it as follows: 'The object of regulation by a legal order is the behavior of one individual in relation to one, several, or all other individuals—the mutual behavior of individuals'.[18] This passage suggests that a distinction can be drawn between 'individual' relations and 'collective' relations. In the former, legal norms regulate the behaviour of an individual vis-à-vis one or several other individuals, such as 'the norm that obliges the debtor to pay the creditor'; in the latter, they regulate behaviour with regard to all members of a collective, for example 'the norm obliging a man to do military service'.[19] But Kelsen himself acknowledges that this distinction is untenable because even norms that regulate individual relations necessarily involve a reference to the collective as a *whole:*

> The legal authority commands a certain human behavior, because the authority, rightly or wrongly, regards such behavior as valuable for the human legal community. In the last analysis, it is this relation to the legal community which is decisive for the legal regulation of the behavior of one individual to another.[20]

[16] See Charles Taylor, *Philosophy and the Human Sciences. Philosophical Papers 2* (Cambridge: Cambridge University Press, 1985), 234. See also Bernhard Waldenfels, *Antwortregister* (Frankfurt: Suhrkamp, 1994), 202–210; and Bernhard Waldenfels, *Vielstimmigkeit der Rede: Studien zur Phänomenologie des Fremden 4* (Frankfurt: Suhrkamp, 1999), 197.

[17] Niklas Luhmann, *Social Systems*, trans. John Bednarz Jr. with Dirk Baecker (Stanford, CA: Stanford University Press, 1995), 74.

[18] Kelsen, *Pure Theory of Law*, 32.

[19] Kelsen, *Pure Theory of Law*, 32.

[20] Kelsen, *Pure Theory of Law*, 32 (translation altered).

What is of interest here is the insight that legal behaviour takes place within a framework of mutual expectations about what the other members of the collective ought to expect of me in a given situation and vice versa, such that mutuality always involves a reference to the apposite collective.[21]

These ideas will be developed more fully in chapter 3, when discussing joint action. For the moment, notice a fifth sense in which legal orders are *concrete* normative orders: they involve a reference to the first-person plural perspective of a 'we'. Whereas this reference remains largely inchoate and taken for granted in the course of legal behaviour as described in section 1.2, illegal behaviour interrupts it, thereby making it explicit as what should not be interrupted. The breach of the spatial boundary separating the food department from what lies outside makes conspicuous the interconnection between the would-be thief and Lafayette, and between the would-be thief and the other clients: the attempted theft involves a rupture of our *mutual* orientation in space. We, as a *whole*, expect of each other that, after entering the food department, those who want to take products away will queue up and pay at the check-out point before leaving, and so on. In turn, the mutuality of expectations is geared to what is taken to be the *point* of behaviour. The term 'point', as I use it here, includes but is not limited to the interests or values served by behaviour. In the same way, the 'point' of behaviour should not be collapsed into a purposive or functional reading thereof. William Twining puts it very well when referring to the point of a social practice or institution: '"Point" is preferable to purpose as it allows for the idea of social practices emerging, developing, becoming entrenched, or changing in response to complex processes of interaction that cannot be accounted for in terms of deliberate purpose, consensus or conscious choice'.[22] Importantly, 'point' refers 'to any motive, value or reason that can be given to explain or justify the practice *from the point of view of the actor*'.[23]

1.4 A-LEGALITY

I now turn to the third of the scenarios described at the outset of this chapter. If the first of the scenarios pictures a situation of legality, and the second of illegality, this third scenario depicts what I will call a-legality. The third scenario marks a decisive rupture with the second: whereas illegality is the privative manifestation of legality, a-legality denotes behaviour that calls into question the distinction

[21] Luhmann deftly refers, in this context, to 'expectations of expectations'. See Niklas Luhmann, *A Sociological Theory of Law*, trans. Elizabeth King-Utz and Martin Albrow (London: Routledge & Kegan Paul, 1985), 28 ff.

[22] William Twining, *General Jurisprudence: Understanding Law from a Global Perspective* (Cambridge: Cambridge University Press, 2009), 111.

[23] Twining, *General Jurisprudence*, 110 (emphasis added). For a powerful criticism of a functionalistic interpretation of meaning and behaviour, see Cornelius Castoriadis, *The Imaginary Institution of Society: Creativity and Autonomy in the Social-Historical World*, trans. Kathleen Blamey (Boston, MA: The MIT Press, 1998), esp. 115 ff.

itself between legality and illegality as drawn by a legal order in a given situation. Here is the scenario:

> Some thirty persons belonging to the *Mouvement des chômeurs et précaires en lutte* (roughly: the 'Movement of the unemployed and vulnerable engaged in struggle') enter the Galeries Lafayette, in Rennes, on 20 December 2008. Their immediate aim is to take food from the shop, without paying for it, and to distribute it among unemployed persons—*autoréduction*, as this kind of action is called in French. More generally, they hope 'to disrupt, for a while, the process of consumption in this Christmas period; to leave with the food that the director of the shop would have kindly offered to us...; to highlight the struggle against the governmental reforms...targeting the poor: the unemployed, the vulnerable, poor workers, pensioners'. They queue up at the eight check-out points of the shop, three in a row. When the first eight panniers are processed and ready to be paid for, the *chômeurs* refuse to pay, all the same remaining in the queues. They explain the motives of their refusal and request that the director of the shop authorize them to depart with the victuals—including the pricy foie gras (not only the rich should be able to enjoy (top-of-the-line) foie gras during Christmas). They avoid any form of violence to ensure that they give no grounds for being taken into custody. Two banners are unrolled and displayed with the caption *chômeurs et précaires en lutte*, and the members of the MCPL engage in a lively discussion with clients about the point of their action. The director initially refuses to negotiate, and the sales operations of the food department of Lafayette grind to a halt, with confused clients milling around, most of them irate about, some sympathetic to, the *autoréduction*, and with ever longer queues of clients shaping up at the check-out points. Some forty minutes later, the director agrees to enter negotiations, upon which the group is finally allowed to leave the premises with ten panniers of victuals, which are promptly distributed to the unemployed standing outside the governmental employment offices at Rennes. If not a party, it was presumably a festive occasion.[24]

Doctrinally speaking, this scenario is interesting because it is unclear which norm is applicable thereto. On the one hand, the *chômeurs* are careful to avoid fulfilling the conditions that could typify their act as theft: there is no *mens rea*, as they request authorization to take Lafayette's property. At the same time, their act is not simply legal either, e.g. a donation by Lafayette. There is a form of duress which they bring to bear on Lafayette by blocking the eight check-out points: an economic loss accrues if the company does not allow the *chômeurs* to leave with the products. The act may well typify the offence of extortion, which Section 312-1 of the French penal code characterizes as 'the fact of obtaining with violence, threats of violence or constraint a signature, a commitment or the renouncement to something, whether the revelation of a secret or the

[24] This account summarizes the *autoréduction* as described in 'Rennes: Autoréduction des chômeurs galeries Lafayette', available at <http://www.ac.eu.org/spip.php?article1947> (accessed on 13 February 2011). More information about the MCPL is available at their home page: <http://www.ac.eu.org> (accessed on 13 February 2013).

delivery of funds, values or any good'.[25] But the *autoréduction* does not fit entirely comfortably under Section 312-1, either. No personal gain accrues to the *chômeurs* by placing Lafayette under duress: their act is called forth by and responds to the duress to which the needy are exposed, a duress to which they *ought not* to be exposed by the legal order, or so the *chômeurs* claim. Their act reveals, or attempts to reveal, an inverted symmetry between Lafayette and the needy. In effect, the law orders behaviour in such a way that the conditions which make it possible to shop in Lafayette are also the conditions that place the needy in a situation of unjust duress; liberating the needy of their situation of duress requires engaging in duress against Lafayette.

These considerations by no means exhaust the significance of the scenario, however. They focus on legal norms in a way that abstracts from the concrete order of which they are part. In particular, what light does the scenario cast on the relation between boundaries and legal order? How does it modify and make more complex the conceptual framework built up over the last two scenarios, according to which law is a concrete normative order?

Notice, to begin with, that the scenario depicts an *interruption* of legal order. The sales operations of the food department literally grind to a halt until the *chômeurs* are authorized to depart with the victuals. From this perspective, there are at least three similarities between the theft and the *autoréduction*. First, both kinds of behaviour become themselves conspicuous in a way that makes legal order conspicuous *as* legal order. In both cases, the two operations of law as a normative order—the differentiation and interconnection of behaviour, and the normative enablement and foreclosure of possible ways of behaving—come into view. Second, both situations render obtrusive all four kinds of boundaries whereby law orders behaviour. In other words, in both cases the two functions of boundaries—to join and to separate—become visible. Third, both the attempted theft and the *autoréduction* interrupt the reference to a collective, such that identity becomes a problem. But each of these similarities is also the locus of a significant difference between illegality and a-legality.

By refusing to pay at the check-out point, indicating that they want to distribute the food amongst the needy, the *chômeurs* call attention to the food department as a specific kind of ought-place and reveal that the shop's spatial boundaries separate it from and join it to certain other ought-places: buying in Lafayette goes together with having a work-place, going to a home-place to throw a party and so on. The point of the action is, however, to call attention to the operation of *normative inclusion and exclusion* that defines the check-out point as a spatial boundary. Inclusion and exclusion should be understood quite literally: the needy are included in the legal order as having a place of their own—the government employment offices, where they are to apply for possible job opportunities—but also excluded from other places, such as shopping at their leisure at Lafayette. This inclusion and exclusion involves marginalization—literally: the

[25] See the article 'Autoréduction, ou extorsion?', posted on 5 January 2009, at <http://www.maitre-eolas.fr/post/2009/01/05/1263-autoreduction-ou-extorsion> (accessed on 22 July 2010). The author, a jurist, is careful, however, to go no further than asserting that the *autoréduction* is 'very probably' extortion.

needy have no place in the differentiation and interconnection of work-places, shopping-places, parking-places, taxi-places, home-places, and cinema-places that the legal order makes possible for those who can pay at the check-out point, and the interconnection of which is viewed as socially valuable and desirable. Crucially, the *chômeurs* hold that the needy *ought not* to be marginalized: the place the legal order assigns to them is not the place they would be assigned by an order in which the distribution of places were a *common* space, or so they claim. So the action *transgresses* the check-out point as a spatial boundary that joins and separates inside and outside. By connecting Lafayette and the governmental employment offices in a way precluded by the legal order, the *chômeurs* evince a possible interconnection of places as ought-places, but one which would transform, to a lesser or greater extent, the *entire* interconnection of places made available by the legal order: work-places, shopping-places, parking-places, home-places, government employment office-places, and so on. Their action seeks, on the one hand, to show that the law has closed down spatial possibilities and, on the other, to open up other spatial possibilities. As a result, the check-out point appears as the spatial boundary that separates the entire distribution of ought-places contested by the *chômeurs* from an outside, understood as a place that cannot be accommodated within the distribution of ought-places made available by the legal order, and also joins it thereto: they cross the check-out point zone on their way to the needy standing in front of the government employment offices.

By refusing to pay, indicating that they want to distribute the food among the needy, the *chômeurs* call attention, secondly, to the temporal boundaries of the legal situation at hand. Indeed, the *autoréduction* reveals how the act of shopping for food at Lafayette sutures past, present, and future into a single temporal arc. Looking into the future, there is a 'right time' to consume the foie gras and other products, which is *after* having paid for them (now). Looking into the past, *now* is the 'right time' to pay *after* having shopped; and it was the 'right time' (then) to shop *after* having engaged in a day's work that provides the financial wherewithal to engage in buying. Past, present, and future appear as normatively different yet interconnected in the temporal sequence 'work—shopping—eating/partying', a temporal sequence (and cycle) that is repeatedly lived through by all those who participate in the 'process of consumption', as their internet page puts it. By refusing to pay, the *chômeurs* seek to throw this ought-temporality out of joint: they claim that now is the 'right time' to take food to the needy, precisely because they *cannot* pay for it; waiting until they find work is 'too late'. Their point is normative: they expose the normative principle that differentiates and interconnects past, present, and future as ought-times, namely the principle of means; and they seek to question it: need, not means, *ought* to determine how a legal order organizes past, present, and future. In other words, they call into question that the principle of means is capable of ensuring the temporal commonality required for the law to assign an *appropriate* time to do something, such that it is possible to distinguish in a legal order between 'the right time', 'too late' and 'too early'. In short, the *chômeurs* expose how in the very process of opening up time by giving it a normative point, the legal order also closes down possible temporal orderings of behaviour—although it ought not to. By taking out products now, without paying for them, to distribute them among the needy, they *transgress* what counts as the right time to do something. Indeed, the 'right time' appears as what separates the temporality of the legal order from another temporal order (now is the right time: after payment), and what joins it thereto (now is the right time: they need it).

The *chômeurs* also seek to interrupt the material boundaries of legal acts. The process of consumption is merely the obverse of a specific process of economic production and distribution, or so they seek to show. By refusing to pay, demanding that they be allowed to give away the food to the needy, the unemployed call attention to the interconnected series of acts and institutions that govern the distribution of food: one must be prepared to buy it from a seller, who owns it, which means that the buyer must have sufficient money to buy it, which, in turn, presupposes other interconnected sets of rights and obligations, such as salaried employment, home ownership, etc. By refusing to pay, the *chômeurs* make explicit that the 'point' of shopping is to *buy;* and that the 'point' of buying is part and parcel of the 'point' of capitalism, in which means, not need, is the key criterion for distribution, both quantitative and qualitative. By selecting foie gras—a top-of-the-line foie gras, to boot—as one of the products to be distributed amongst the needy, the *chômeurs* expose with great precision how the legal order establishes the material boundaries of shopping for food: not only does one select products to buy them, but one (obviously) only selects those products one can pay for: to each according to their means.[26] As with the other forms of boundaries, material boundaries also become conspicuous as joining and separating: not only is buying interconnected to selling, but contracts of sale are different from but interconnected to a wider set of legal institutions such as employment contracts, capital ownership, welfare programmes and the like. Accordingly, the action of the *chômeurs* has a normative purport, as it questions the commonality of the principle of means, that is, its capacity to justify what it is 'appropriate' to do. As a result, their action exposes how the needy are subject to material inclusion and exclusion by the legal order. The needy are included in the legal order as unemployed, hence as obliged to look for a job via the intermediation services of the government unemployment offices; and they are excluded from a range of rights available to the employed. Material marginalization goes hand in hand with spatial and temporal marginalization. By taking the products without paying, their behaviour transgresses a material boundary, which both separates what one ought to do in this scenario from other possible ways of establishing 'appropriate' behaviour, and joins it thereto.

Finally, the subjective boundaries of shopping for food become conspicuous. While the needy may, in principle, buy at Lafayette or anywhere else, sufficient financial wherewithal is a condition for taking on the status of a buyer who must pay immediately after shopping, whether with cash, a debit card, or a credit card. The destitute may not take on the role of buyer, unless they are recipients of

[26] This point proved particularly irksome to a participant in the interventions posted on the internet site of the article, who, in a comment dated 3 January 2009, indignantly exclaimed: 'IT'S SIMPLY THEFT, especially to take foie gras, which is certainly not a vital commodity (*produit de première necessité*)!!! . . .'

a welfare allowance, in which case their purchases ought to be commensurate with their allowance (no foie gras, and certainly not a pricy one). By refusing to pay, and demanding to be allowed to distribute the food amongst the needy, the *chômeurs* thematize the legal subjectivities interconnected as a matter of course in shopping for food: employees, rentiers, self-employed professionals, retailers, farmers, and the like. Once again, inclusion and exclusion become manifest: the needy are included in the legal order in the mode of unemployed, that is, as excluded from participating in a variety of legal subjectivities. It is not surprising, therefore, that the *chômeurs* sought to interpellate the other persons in Lafayette, engaging them in a discussion about the point of their action. By doing so, they address these persons in a way that no longer takes for granted that they are related to each other as clients within a broader network of legal subjectivities. To the contrary, they call into question the commonality of the principles that order their interpersonal relationships as clients, employees, self-employed professionals, unemployed, etc., and, by requesting the solidarity of the clients with the needy, evoke other ways of differentiating and interconnecting legal subjectivities. By refusing the role of a client while doing what a client does—to take away products, the *chômeurs* transgress a subjective boundary, which appears as separating the legal order with its subjectivities from other possible differentiations and interconnections of legal subjectivities, and joining it thereto.[27]

All of this, and more, gets lost if one reduces the scenario to a doctrinal problem of the right legal norm to apply to the situation, or even to the hermeneutical problem of a 'hard case', as Dworkin would put it.[28] The question of the 'right' legal norm to apply to the scenario is inseparable from the problem of 'appropriateness' that irrupts into view with a-legality. Like the interruption of legal order brought about by the attempted theft, so also the four boundaries

[27] There is a further layer of a-legality, which concerns the disruption of the *queue* by the *chômeurs*, yet which I can only briefly discuss here. Pointing to the reflexive structure of collective action involved in queuing, Kevin Gray argues that 'the pattern of structured waiting overseen by the queue is an almost unique kind of self-regulation in which the potentially anomic force of the crowd is converted by tacit agreement into a deferment of individual gratification in the interests of some higher social order or objective'. More pointedly, the queue 'embodies a co-ordinated pattern of relationships, the conduct of individuals within the queue being governed... by a shared set of beliefs relating not least to the importance of distributive justice between queuers'. The queue, I would add, is an elementary manifestation of distributive justice as a spatio-temporal phenomenon: to each his/her own place and time with respect to the object of the queue. What the *chômeurs* effectively do is use the queue in a way that questions the who, what, where, and when of queuing up at the food department of Lafayette. In particular, they show that the counterpart to the inclusiveness of 'distributive justice between queuers' is the exclusion of those who cannot even consider belonging to that queue because they belong in another queue: the queue in front of the employment offices in Rennes. By the same token, they show that waiting to pay up at Lafayette is already a form of power, and not merely of disempowerment, as Gray assumes, namely, the power of those who can literally *afford* to wait to pay. By disrupting the queue they can be viewed as turning on its head 'one of the most iconic political images of the modern British era', namely, 'a photograph, under the striking headline "LABOUR ISN'T WORKING", of a long line of people stretching away into the distance, all supposedly queuing to reach the "Unemployment Office".' See Kevin Gray, 'Property in a Queue', in Gregory S. Alexander and Eduardo M. Peñalver (eds.), *Property and Community* (New York: Oxford University Press, 2009), 165–195. Gray's excellent analysis of queuing, and its appositeness to my description of a-legality, was brought to my attention by André van der Walt.

[28] Ronald Dworkin, *Law's Empire* (Cambridge, MA: Belknap Press, 1986).

of legal order become conspicuous in the *autoréduction:* there are proper times and places for the appropriate persons to engage in the appropriate legal behaviour. But whereas the interruption of illegal behaviour reaffirms the spatial, temporal, material, and subjective boundaries that define behaviour as appropriate or inappropriate, the *autoréduction* calls these boundaries into question; it *challenges* how a certain legal order determines who ought to do what, where, and when. The act does not merely breach the four boundaries that determine behaviour as legal in the given situation; it transgresses the boundaries on the basis of which behaviour is either legal or illegal, creating a situation of *indeterminacy* within the order as it stands. By the same token, legal order becomes obtrusive as legal order, as was earlier the case with illegality. But, in contrast to illegality, it becomes obtrusive in a way that reveals that the possibilities for behaviour opened up by legal differentiation and interconnection go hand-in-hand with the *closing down* of other possibilities, possibilities which claim a normative force of their own. Accordingly, a-legal interruptions *deplete* the normativity a legal order claims for itself. Whereas the qualification of an act as theft implies the (re)affirmation of the legal order and its boundaries—clients ought to pay before leaving with food—the *autoréduction* calls into question the 'ought' that holds together the spatial, temporal, material, and subjective dimensions of what counts as legal and illegal. It depletes the normative hold of places as ought-places, of times as ought-times and so forth.

A strong form of normative disorientation ensues: as noted in the scenario, when the check-out points are blocked and the *chômeurs* unroll their banners, confused clients begin to mill around and ever longer queues shape up. In a more fundamental sense than is the case with the attempted theft of the second scenario, the *autoréduction* creates a situation of normative disorientation: it is not only 'improper'; it (also) challenges the spatial, temporal, subjective, and material criteria that define legal behaviour as *either* proper or improper. Several of the comments posted on the site about the action attest to one strategy of dealing with this situation, namely to qualify the act as illegal, thereby bringing it back into the fold of what is understandable within the framework of the given legal order. 'IT'S SIMPLY THEFT', fulminates the one in capital letters; 'it's pure and simple theft', echoes the other. In both cases, the references to the situation as being 'simple' and 'pure' are as telling as the qualification of theft. Yet other comments deploy other well-tested strategies for dealing with such situations, including jokes—'must look at too many American series!!'—and insults—'gosh, what an imbecility!' (*pff, quelle connerie!*). This strategy is also visible in the web article posted by the jurist, who, with contained anger, argues that the *autoréduction* 'very probably' consists in the offence of extortion. Regardless of the strength of the legal arguments, what is striking is the tone in which they are written, such that anger and irony serve to contain and neutralize the claims raised by the *chômeurs*. Significantly, Helmut Plessner has shown how laughing and crying are ways of reacting to 'boundary situations':

> Unanswerable situations, in which man cannot orient himself, to which he can find no relation, whose condition he cannot discover, which he cannot understand and cannot grasp: with which, therefore, he can do nothing, are... intolerable. He will

> try at any price to change them, to transform them into situations 'answerable' in some way or other, or to escape them.[29]

We will return to more fully discuss the problem of (un)answerability or (un) responsiveness at a later stage of the book. What is important, for the time being, is that, although laughing and crying are extreme cases of losing control, in which 'the relation of man to his body becomes disorganized',[30] the expressive responses to the breakdown of the sales operation of Lafayette's food department are also ways of dealing with what is literally a boundary situation, i.e. to the interruption of the fourfold boundaries that allow of defining behaviour within the situation as legal or illegal. The confusion, jokes, and insults unleashed by the incident attest to normative disorientation, to a situation which many clients cannot understand, and to which they respond in these ways. The *autoréduction* neatly exposes an inverted asymmetry between the needy and the clientele of Lafayette: the vulnerability of the former is mirrored in the vulnerability of clients who can no longer orient themselves spatially, temporally, materially, and subjectively because the distinction itself between legality and illegality, as drawn in a legal order, has been interrupted. For a moment, the clients have become *précaires*, normatively speaking.[31]

I summarize the foregoing analysis as follows: the *autoréduction* resists assimilation to either face of the distinction between legality and illegality; it evokes a situation of a-legality. The 'il' of 'illegality' speaks to a privative form of legal order: legal *dis*order. By contrast, the 'a' of a-legality is not privative, or in any case not only privative: a-legal behaviour (also) intimates *another* legal order. More exactly, the *autoréduction* evokes a *strange* order—a 'xenonomy', not a 'heteronomy'.[32] Not the reaffirmation of boundaries, as drawn by a given legal order for a certain situation, but their questioning is at stake in a-legality. Accordingly, a-legality, like illegality, reveals that legal boundaries govern behaviour and also, conversely, that legal boundaries depend on behaviour. But if the qualification of an act as illegal serves to reaffirm the primacy of boundaries over behaviour, a-legality primarily reveals the capacity of behaviour to draw boundaries otherwise. A-legality makes conspicuous that behaviour *spaces;* that it *times;* that it *materializes;* that it *subjectifies*.

[29] Helmut Plessner, *Laughing and Crying: A Study of the Limits of Human Behavior*, trans. James Spencer Churchill and Marjorie Grene (Evanston, IL: Northwestern University Press, 1970), 141.

[30] Plessner, *Laughing and Crying*, 138.

[31] Elisabeth Ströker points to three distinct aspects of the lived space of human beings, which she calls 'attuned space' (*Stimmungsraum*), the 'space of action' and the 'space of intuition'. Concerning the first of these, she points out that space always has an 'atmosphere' or 'mood' (*Stimmung*), such that, for example, when I go into a café I am pleasantly struck by its coziness but then, a couple of hours later, begin to feel 'hemmed in' with all the noise, and so decide to step out to the street, which is itself fresh and cool, etc. The reactions of the clients in Lafayette intimate the transformation in the atmosphere or mood of the food department effected by the disruption of the queue. A complete phenomenology of legal space that takes its points of departure in the three-way distinction between legality, illegality, and a-legality would have to include a discussion of the atmospheric dimension of lefgal places, which is part of what goes into our existence as embodied beings. See Elisabeth Ströker, *Investigations in Philosophy of Space*, trans. Algis Mickunas (Athens, OH: Ohio University Press, 1987), 19–47.

[32] I am grateful to David Janssens for correcting me on this point.

Why speak of a 'strange' legal order, rather than simply of 'another' legal order? The answer is, briefly, that the interruption of legal order wrought by a-legality disrupts the conditions of *legal intelligibility* of the situation: the act withstands qualification as being simply legal or illegal, and not because it is 'a bit of both', but rather because there is a normative claim that resists *both* terms of the disjunction, as defined by extant law. The same holds for each of the kinds of legal boundaries that configure the situation. There is something in the *autoréduction* that cannot be grasped in any of the four ways in which the legal order organizes the legal/illegal distinction, namely as individuals who are emplaced or misplaced; act in a timely or untimely fashion; act in the way established in the law—or not; and are the proper subject of a form of behaviour—or not. In general, what withstands intelligibility in terms of the categories at our disposition is, strictly speaking, *strange*. By insisting that the *autoréduction* was theft, angry clients seek to *understand* it, to make it familiar by levelling it down a situation that is eminently understandable from a legal point of view because it is legality with a negative sign: illegality. Whereas legality and illegality are the two faces of legal familiarity, a-legality denotes the experience of *estrangement:* what participating actors cannot simply understand as (il)legal, thereby disrupting their capacity to orient themselves spatially, temporally, materially, and subjectively within a given legal order. For this reason, 'interpretation', in the sense of a doctrinal activity oriented to establishing whether a legal norm is applicable to a situation or not, is a derivative activity. The experiences of understanding and misunderstanding, in which our capacity to orient ourselves normatively in the world is put to the test, are prior to the doctrinal hesitation about which norm to apply to a situation, a hesitation that calls forth an interpretative activity leading to an explicit judgement about legality or illegality. Which is why I want to insist, once again, that it is reductive to assume that a legal order, *qua* normative order, is a unity of norms, standards, policies, and some such; instead, this account is a doctrinal and theoretical achievement that abstracts from a legal order's primordial concreteness.

These considerations on ownness and strangeness point to a further aspect of the concreteness of legal orders. I noted earlier that law does not simply introduce the distinction between legality and illegality as a neutral distinction: to distinguish between these terms is also and constitutively to *prefer* one of the two terms: the legal vis-à-vis the illegal. This is, however, what one might call a 'first-level' preferential distinction. There is also a second-level preferential distinction: the own is preferred to the strange, where 'own' includes both the legal and the illegal. For this reason, disgruntled clients qualified the *autoréduction* as simply theft. In other words, legal (dis)order is preferred to what bursts the conditions of legal intelligibility made available by an order because it raises a normative claim that demands realization, yet which refuses qualification as either legal or illegal behaviour. See here, then, yet a sixth reason for which legal orders are concrete: they involve a preferential distinction whereby *(il)legality is preferred to a-legality.*[33]

[33] Schmitt perceptively opposes the move of 'normativism' to '[dissolve] every concrete order and community into a series of valid norms, the "unity" or "systematicity" of which is, in turn, merely normative'. Carl Schmitt, *Über die drei Arten des rechtswissenschaftlichen Denkens*, 2nd edn. (Berlin: Duncker & Humblot, 1993), 15. Remarkably, however, Schmitt says little or nothing about the 'concreteness' of legal orders, either descriptively or conceptually. My aim in the foregoing sections is to offer just such a

1.5 BOUNDARIES AND LIMITS

The foregoing is but a preliminary analysis of the three-way distinction between legality, illegality, and a-legality, so let me lodge four caveats right away before spelling out its implications for the boundaries and limits of legal orders.

The first revisits the remark at the outset of section 1.2 that the descriptions of the three scenarios have a heuristic function. In particular, I have simply taken for granted that the *autoréduction* is an a-legal act, to be able to contrast some of its distinctive features to those of legality and illegality. But was the *chômeurs'* act a-legal? Remember that for many of the clients, the *autoréduction* was a blatantly illegal act. Moreover, need one take for granted that their act is a-legal in the way I have described it? Analogous queries hold, of course, for my descriptions of legality and illegality. Also in these cases my descriptions depict the scenarios in such a way that these seem to demand that they be qualified as 'legal' and 'illegal'. As noted at the outset of section 1.2, we will need to come back to this crucial point in Part II, when discussing the precedence of a-legality and the retroactivity of boundary-setting. In the same vein, it will be necessary at a later stage to deconstruct the sharp distinctions introduced by the three scenarios, which, of course, is not the same as rendering them more blurred or fuzzy.

Second, the sequence of scenarios is not neutral. I begin with a situation of legal order and then consider two variations thereon. This expository strategy leads to viewing the second and third scenarios as (conceptually) dependent on order, as *deviations* thereof. This is particularly the case with the third of the scenarios, which I have dubbed a-legality. By the same token, to the extent that I first discuss legality and illegality, it would seem that I am uncritically favouring *unity* at the expense of the kind of plurality which manifests itself in a-legality. One may wonder, therefore, whether this expository strategy does not end up favouring legal order to the detriment of what disrupts it, and subordinating the familiar to the strange. While there are good reasons for prioritizing legal order at this initial stage of our enquiry, it will be necessary to ask, in Part II, whether and how this prioritization could also be inverted. Can the passage from legality to a-legality be countered by the passage from a-legality to legality, such that (il)legality proves to be dependent on a-legality, and the familiar on the strange?

Third, while I have described an example of a-legality in the third scenario, the introduction of this concept serves a quite narrow purpose at this stage of the argument, namely, to show why all legal orders are necessarily limited. It is by no means exhaustive of the phenomenon. A full analysis of the range and variable intensity of phenomena grouped under this concept will have to wait until Part II.

Fourth and last, further attention must be dedicated to the relation between the more or less anonymous form of normativity deployed in what I called social interaction, and the reflexive acts whereby individuals identify themselves and others as members of a legal collective that is limited in space, time, content, and

description and conceptualization. But this is only half of the story. I will argue at the end of chapter 4 that thinking through the conditions that explain the concreteness of legal orders effectively inverts the main thesis about concrete orders which Schmitt is concerned to defend.

subjectivity. To mark this difference and relation, I will introduce the distinction between legal understanding and legal interpretation at the outset of chapter 4.

Be it as it may, this rough and ready characterization of legality, illegality, and a-legality suffices, as it stands, to cast new light on the question concerning legal order. As noted in the introduction to this book, legal and political theorists, as well as sociologists of globalization, have sought to develop a general concept of law that could release it from the strictures of state-centrism. In particular, it has been assumed that borders are a contingent feature of legal order, as is the inside/outside distinction. The entire thrust of this chapter is to show that this diagnosis and the theoretical framework that underpins it are highly reductive; its advocates inadvertently entrench state-centrism when celebrating that they have overcome it.

Resistance to state-centrism only gets started, or so the foregoing sections suggest, by examining how boundaries actually appear with respect to those whose behaviour they regulate. The three scenarios outlined heretofore attempt to clarify, step by step, the modes of appearance of law as a concrete normative order. The first thesis slowly emerging from this description is that *a legal order appears from the first-person perspective as a normative order organized as a spatial, temporal, subjective, and material unity.* More generally, the foregoing considerations suggest that to speak of an investigation of the relation between boundaries and legal order is imprecise; it is necessary to draw a distinction between *boundaries* and *limits*, and to explore how these are related to each other.

I begin with boundaries. A first desideratum of a general theory of legal order as a concrete normative order is to develop a comprehensive and precise account of legal boundaries. A comprehensive account is required because contemporary political and legal theories tend to concentrate on spatial boundaries. More exactly, they focus almost exclusively on *borders*, that is, on the spatial boundaries which demarcate the territory of a state or other collective. To the extent that citizenship is linked to the territorial state, these theories are also prepared to accommodate subjective boundaries, albeit limited to membership boundaries.[34] But little or no attention is paid to the temporal and material boundaries of legal orders. Nor, for that matter, do I know of any legal or political theory that develops an account of legal order that systematically links together the four kinds of boundaries I have been at pains to identify and illustrate in this chapter. In addition to comprehensiveness, the foregoing considerations aspire to a greater precision in the conceptualization of legal boundaries than is available in contemporary legal and political theory, or in sociologies of globalization. Indeed, what I have sought to show is that legal boundaries, whether spatial, temporal, subjective, or material, both join and separate elements *within a unity*.

The insight that legal boundaries do their job by distinguishing and interconnecting elements within the unity of a legal order allows us to introduce the crucial notion of a *limit*. The crux of the analyses set out earlier in this chapter is the interruption of legal order wrought by a-legal behaviour. Like illegality, a-legal

[34] See, e.g. Balibar's essays, 'What is a Border?' and 'The Borders of Europe', in Étienne Balibar, *Politics and the Other Scene*, trans. Christine Jones, James Swenson, and Chris Turner (London: Verso, 2002), 75–103.

behaviour has the effect of making a legal order conspicuous *as* an order; in both cases the four spheres of validity become visible as aspects of a *single*, interconnected distribution of places, times, contents, and subjectivities. The decisive difference with respect to illegality is, however, that whereas the latter still moves within the orbit of the normative possibilities that a legal order opens up by differentiating and interconnecting, a-legality exposes an order as *foreclosing* normative possibilities. A-legality is the experience of *strange* behaviour, behaviour that demands that an ought-place, ought-time, ought-subjectivity, and ought-act content be actualized that cannot be accommodated within, and is therefore incompatible with, the interconnected distribution of ought-places, times, contents, and subjectivities made available by the extant legal order. This is the experience in which a concrete legal order appears as *limited*. What reveals itself in a-legality is not merely a legal boundary that joins and separates elements within the unity of a legal order, but rather a boundary as the limit of that legal order, such that there is a *discontinuity* between the legal order as a unity and what is beyond the limit. This means that a-legal behaviour manifests itself as *a-civic*, by challenging the distribution of legal subjectivities; as *a-nomic*, by questioning what ought to be done, according to a legal order; as *a-topic*, by contesting the differentiation and distribution of places that make up a legal space; as *a-chronic*, by challenging the 'right time' to engage in legal behaviour. The *autoréduction*, or so I have argued, is a-legal insomuch that it reveals boundaries as marking the limits of a specific legal order, in each of these four senses.

Spatially speaking, the limit of legal order becomes apparent in behaviour that is a-topic, i.e. legally *dis*-placed rather than simply emplaced or misplaced: a-legal behaviour can be assigned an ought-place in the legal order, yet claims an ought-place for itself for which there is no place within the distribution of places made available by a legal order. A-topic behaviour dis-locates law: it intimates a strange place and distribution of places in contrast to the familiar places of the legal order, to the distribution of places that members of a collective call their *own* legal space. This casts new light on the inside/outside distinction. Precisely because they focus exclusively on borders of states, which are part of the more encompassing order of international law, a variety of contemporary legal and political theories take for granted that the inside/outside distinction is equivalent to the distinction between domestic and foreign territories. But the domestic/foreign distinction is *not* the fundamental form of the inside/outside distinction. Law orders space by setting up a distribution of ought-places that are normatively interconnected in certain ways, and not in others; and this means that a legal order emerges through a closure that partitions space into an *inside,* a familiar distribution of places, and an indeterminate *outside*. This outside manifests itself through forms of behaviour that, questioning the claim to commonality raised with respect to the familiar distribution of places, intimate an *ought*-place that has no place within that distribution of places, yet which demands that it be actualized. A-legal behaviour is, in the two fold sense of the term, 'outlandish'. This, as I have sought to show, is the upshot of what happened at the check-out points of Lafayette, when the *chômeurs* refused to pay for the products they wanted to distribute among the needy standing outside the government employment offices of Rennes.

I am well aware that the three scenarios pertain to *state* law, to the law of France, rather than to any of the other legal orders that are emerging or have once again become visible in our 'global' era. There are, however, at least three good reasons for focusing on these scenarios. The first is that a general theory of legal order must be sufficiently capacious to include state law. By beginning with these scenarios, I want to ensure that the theory I am outlining can explain and justify state law as a species of the genus: legal order. The second is that it should be possible, on the basis of these scenarios, to offer an initial justification of why boundaries and limits are constitutive features of *any* legal order (hence *also* of state law). A 'global supplement', so to speak, could have been added to the third scenario, whereby the movement had coordinated its *autoréduction* in Rennes (and elsewhere in France) with sister movements in other countries, such that all the acts took place simultaneously, or at least explicitly referred to each other. In this case the banners unrolled at Lafayette might have read: '*chômeurs et précaires du monde en lutte*...' But no global supplement is necessary to drive home the point I want to make.[35] As legal and political theories have focused so insistently on the borders of the state, proclaiming the slow death of territoriality, the third scenario is valuable because it focuses on a spatial boundary that is *not* a territorial border to show that the distinction between familiar and strange places is the fundamental form of the inside/outside distinction. It is more fundamental than the domestic/foreign distinction because *any* of the spatial boundaries of a state, including but not limited to its territorial boundaries, can be the locus of a-legality. The same would hold for any other legal order. Third, the scenario has the advantage of showing that the two forms of the inside/outside distinction are irreducible to each other: *a strange place need not be foreign;* conversely, *foreign places need not be strange*. If the *autoréduction* reveals that the French legal order harbours strange places within, the structures of legality and illegality described in the first and second scenarios would apply in a wide variety of foreign legal orders, as well. Aldis, Walmarts, Marks & Spencers, Macros, and the like are emplaced in the same world in which the Lafayette at Rennes takes up its place.

This insight casts new light on the problem of de-territorialization. A wide range of contemporary legal and political theories, as well as sociologies of globalization, equate the inside/outside distinction to the distinction between domestic and foreign territories, arguing that this distinction cannot be constitutive for the concept of legal order. Ulrich Beck formulates what for many has become a platitude when asserting that '[t]he association of place with community or society is breaking down'.[36] No doubt these theories are correct in asserting that the inside/outside distinction, when construed as the distinction between domestic and foreign territories, is historically contingent; it is certainly possible to conceive of legal orders that do not require fixed territorial borders like those of the state. For example, a global polity, whatever its political configuration, would have no outside in the form of a foreign territory. But to the extent

[35] But the scenario *can* be viewed as including such a supplement, to the extent that the *chômeurs* contest the capitalist organization of legal space.

[36] Ulrich Beck, *What is Globalization?*, trans. Patrick Camiller (Cambridge: Polity Press, 2000), 74.

that a global polity, if it is to be a legal order, must in some way organize the face of the earth as a distribution of ought-places that is deemed to be common, any of the boundaries that marks off a *single* ought-place from other ought-places in the global polity also appears, when questioned by a-legal behaviour, as marking off the *whole* distribution of ought-places as an inside vis-à-vis a strange outside.

Hence, any and every spatial boundary of a legal order, even the most 'mundane' and apparently insignificant, is also a limit that renders it discontinuous with a strange outside. More exactly, *every spatial boundary of a legal order is a limit*, at least latently. By contrast, the borders of states are not, *qua* borders, limits: what lies beyond is in principle familiar, in the form of, for example, another state. If a state is a distribution of ought-places, so also the state itself can be seen as an ought-place within the broader differentiation and interconnection of ought-places of classical international law. But a border *can* become a limit when a border crossing calls into question the distribution of ought-places in which a state takes up its place. I submit that border crossings by immigrants often have this effect. In such cases, it is not only the borders of the respective state which become conspicuous as spatial limits; to a lesser or greater extent, a-legal border crossings render conspicuous the entire international community of states as a familiar world which is discontinuous with respect to a strange outside. The distinction and correlation between municipal and international law become visible as aspects of a single, bounded space, even though classical international law covers the whole face of the earth, i.e. even though it makes no sense to apply the contrast between foreign and domestic places to it. State borders are one of the (latent) limits of international law. And this is another way of asserting that, although international law covers the whole face of the earth, it is not 'everywhere'. Pending a fuller development of this insight in chapter 2, we can already anticipate that classical international law is *somewhere* in particular; it is no less emplaced and located than the states it differentiates and interconnects, precisely *because* it differentiates and interconnects these legal orders. All forms of legal order are spatially limited, or so I conjecture: in the absence of the distinction between a familiar inside and a strange outside no space can be a legal space. And what I conjecture about spatial boundaries holds for temporal, material, and subjective boundaries, as well: no legal order is conceivable which is not limited in space, time, subjectivity, and content. So the second thesis which has begun to emerge is the following: *a legal order appears from the first-person perspective as a normative order that is limited in space, time, subjectivity, and content*. At a later stage yet a third category will be introduced, in addition to boundaries and limits: fault lines. But this will need to wait till Part II, when considering how a-legality questions a legal order, and thinking through a normative alternative to both universalism and particularism.

To sum up, if one takes borders to be only one specific kind of spatial boundary, rather than its paradigm, and if one acknowledges that spatial boundaries are but one of the four kinds of boundaries that legal orders put in place to regulate behaviour, then one of the tasks confronting a general theory of legal order as a concrete normative order is to systematically articulate the nature of the interrelation between boundaries, limits, and (as we shall see) fault lines.

2

A Topology of Legal Orders in a Global Setting

The first chapter zooms in on a single incident, reading it in three different registers, with a view to unveiling the general structure of legal orders as limited normative orders. This narrow approach had the great advantage of allowing me to introduce the three-way distinction between legality, illegality, and a-legality, and the distinction between boundaries and limits, in a straightforward and uncluttered way. But the strategy also has an important drawback: while I have sought to pitch the analysis of the relation between boundaries and limits at a high level of generality, it would be reckless to assume that the three scenarios I discussed can carry the full weight of a general account of this relation. This shortcoming must now be redressed. It would greatly exceed the scope of this book to engage in a systematic study of the historical permutations of the spatial, temporal, subjective, and material boundaries discussed in chapter 1. So I will concentrate primarily on the spatial boundaries of legal orders, which are widely viewed as the focal point of the transformations leading, first, to the coupling of law and state during the supremacy of the national/international law paradigm, and, subsequently, to the uncoupling thereof in the current, increasingly global setting of law.

As concerns spatial boundaries, chapter 1 outlined and defended the view that there can be no legal order absent a *limited* distribution of ought-places, and that such a distribution requires a first-person plural perspective which introduces a preferential differentiation between inside and outside. The question we must now address is whether this topography of legal order, however abridged, can hold its own when confronted with a range of potential counterexamples. In short, we need to engage in a topology of legal orders—a study of the spatial configurations of a variety of legal orders in a global setting. To this effect I will assess a panoply of legal orders that are irreducible to state law: nomadism, Roman law, classical international law, *ius gentium*, multinationals, *lex mercatoria*, cyberlaw, and the overlap between the EU and its Member States. The final section of the chapter systematizes our findings in seven interlocking propositions that distil a general topography of legal order.

2.1 THE *NOMOS* OF NOMADISM

I launch this enquiry with what is ostensibly the most radical counterexample to the topography outlined in chapter 1: nomadism. For, it might be argued, the preferential differentiation between inside and outside, which I view as central to that topography, remains squarely within the orbit of the concept of legal space presupposed by sedentary communities. The inside/outside distinction, so runs the objection, makes no sense for nomadic communities because the nomadic relation to space does not draw a distinction whereby an inside is preferred to an outside. Insisting on the constitutive character of this distinction would amount to hypostatizing sedentary communities into the single and necessary form of social life, thereby concealing the original possibilities of relating to space held open by nomadism. This hypostasis, to which chapter 1 would have fallen prey, is especially problematic because it blinds us to novel forms of nomadism that could be emerging with globalization. A topology of legal order must begin, accordingly, by addressing this 'threshold' objection, as one might put it.

The etymology of the word 'nomad' harks back to *nomos* and to the root *nem-* in ancient Greek. Drawing on Emmanuel Laroche's study of this root, Gilles Deleuze and Felix Guattari note that '[t]he root "nem" indicates distribution, not allocation [*partage*], even when the two are linked. In the pastoral sense, the distribution of animals is effected in a non-limited space and implies no parcelling out of land'.[1] In this primordial understanding, *nomos* is what lies beyond the town or city, in the form of a plateau, mountain, steppe, or desert. This etymological issue is the prolegomenon to a strong conceptual thesis: nomadism reveals a form of space and social organization—and of law—that is not predicated on closure and exclusion. Deleuze and Guattari contrast the path of the nomad to the road of a sedentary polity, whether it be the Roman *limes* (which we shall shortly discuss) or otherwise:

> [E]ven though the nomadic trajectory may follow trails or customary routes, it does not fulfill the function of the sedentary road, which is to *parcel out a closed space to people*, assigning each person a share and regulating the communication between shares. The nomadic trajectory does the opposite: it *distributes peoples (or animals) in an open space*. One that is indefinite and non-communicating. The *nomos* came to designate the law, but that was because it was originally distribution, a mode of distribution. It is a very special kind of distribution, one without division into shares, in a space without borders or enclosure. The *nomos* is the consistency of a fuzzy whole [*ensemble flou*]...[2]

On this reading, the nomad is exterior to the limited or 'striated' space of sedentary communities, not because the nomad calls into question a particular allocation of legal places, but rather because the nomad relates to space in a way that neither allocates ought-places nor sets boundaries: the nomad inhabits a 'smooth' space. The nomad 'can be called the De-territorialized par excellence' because 'it is the earth that de-territorializes itself, in a way that provides a nomad with a territory. The land ceases to be land, tending to become simply ground (*sol*) or support'.[3] The nomadic *nomos* seems to erase the normative dimension that creases the land into my place and yours; it 'de-creases' the sedentary *nomos*, as one might put it.

[1] Gilles Deleuze and Felix Guattari, *A Thousand Plateaus: Capitalism and Schizophrenia*, trans. Brian Massumi (London: Continuum, 1987), 621.

[2] Deleuze and Guattari, *A Thousand Plateaus*, 420 (translation altered).

[3] Deleuze and Guattari, *A Thousand Plateaus*, 421 (translation altered).

Yet, can there be a collective 'distribution of peoples (or animals)' at all absent a closure of space that localizes a nomadic collective by delimiting it? Can the nomad 'occupy and hold a smooth space',[4] other than by introducing a preferential distinction between inside and outside?

In addressing these questions, a first point to bear in mind is that Deleuze and Guattari systematically refer to 'the nomad', as an individual, and to 'nomadism', as a form of behaviour, in light of their interest in contrasting what they call the 'essence' of the nomadic relation to space to those of the migrant, the transhumant, and the sedentary.[5] But the problem of a nomadic relation to space is a problem confronting nomadic *groups*. As soon as one introduces the first-person plural perspective, the question arises whether 'occupying and holding a smooth space' is possible without a collective distribution of places as *ought*-places of some sort, that is, as places in which certain activities ought or ought not to take place, regardless of the comings and goings of the nomadic group. Deleuze and Guattari refer, in this context, to Toynbee's insight that nomads do not move, an insight which Edward Casey deftly reformulates as follows: '*they move in place*, that is, in a seasonally determined cycle of places within the region they inhabit on the edge of the desert'.[6] Notice that Casey's formulation of the notion of place remains underdetermined: at issue is not only the fact that nomadic groups move from place to place within a region, but that each of these places is itself a specific distribution of ought-places.

George Silberbauer's study of a nomadic people who call themselves the G/wikhwena, and who, at the time of his study, inhabited part of the Kalahari Desert in Botswana, contains a number of indications that this foraging group displays recurrent patterns of spatial organization in the course of its nomadic wanderings. His descriptions show, in particular, that the G/wikhwena relate to places as *ought*-places, even if the normativity that attaches to these places opposes differentiation into the three-way distinction between religion, law, and morality.[7] A newly married couple, for instance, is supposed to set up its household next to the household of the woman's parents and to remain there until their first child is born, at which time the couple is expected to set up their household next to the household of the man's parents.[8] In addition to marital households, a settlement will typically have a collective bachelor shelter,

[4] Deleuze and Guattari, *A Thousand Plateaus*, 452.

[5] Deleuze and Guattari, *A Thousand Plateaus*, 452. The notion of transhumance is important because it correctly captures what many have come to call forms of postnational 'nomadism'.

[6] Casey, *Getting Back into Place*, 306.

[7] This evokes the more general question concerning the specificity of ought-places in what has been called 'mythical space'. In particular, one may ask whether it is possible to oppose mythical and post-mythical normative spaces, or whether all normative spaces, including modern 'functionally' differentiated legal spaces, remain, in essential aspects, mythically structured if they are to function as *normative* spaces. See, amongst others: Georges Gusdorf, *Mythe et métaphysique* (Paris: Flammarion, 1953); and Ernst Cassirer, *Philosophy of Symbolic Forms*, vol. 2, trans. Ralph Mannheim (New Haven, CT: Yale University Press, 1955).

[8] George Silberbauer, *Hunter and Habitat in the Central Kalahari Desert* (Cambridge: Cambridge University Press, 1981), 149. Silberbauer contrasts the name of this nomadic people, which means 'bush people' or 'people of the thorn forests', to G/wi.

which not only houses men who have not yet married, but also accommodates husbands during the period in which their wives go into menarchial seclusion. Although the members of a G/wi group gather together during the summer months, they spread out as individual or extended households during the difficult winter months to maximize their foraging capabilities in light of the harsh climatic conditions. During this period of winter isolation, members of the households are expected not to forage in the areas of the other households.[9] Moreover, and during the periods of joint settlements, the members of a G/wi group are expected to keep out of the shelters of the other households, unless they are permitted to do so. A G/wi settlement, therefore, is organized as a distribution of ought-places, in which each ought-place is different from but interconnected to the other ought-places of the settlement. The distribution of ought-places is not limited, however, to the cincture of the settlement; it also extends to the spatial relation between the settlement and the environing hunting grounds: men are not to sally out into the surroundings to hunt during their wives' menstruation periods.

The relation to space of the G/wi shows that if the concept of nomadic place to which Casey and Deleuze and Guattari refer remains underdetermined, so also Casey's reference to the 'region' in which nomadic places are located. As Silberbauer points out, 'a G/wi group is a community . . . occupying a defined territory and controlling the exploitation of the resources of that territory'. Moreover, G/wi groups delimit their territories with landmarks, or more accurately, with areas surrounding those landmarks. In the same way that a G/wi group organizes settlements within its territory as distributions of ought-places, so also the areas surrounding the landmarks between G/wi groups serve to delimit and distribute ought-places: while it is acceptable that hunters of one G/wi group chase a wounded animal into the territory of a contiguous group, it is unacceptable that they foray into the other group's territory to, say, forage for plants.

The primary bond of the G/wi individual is to his or her group, not to a territory, such that 'the link between the individual and territory is derived from the bond between community and land'. The alleged founder of a group is the 'owner' of a territory 'and is said to be the one from whom visitors and prospective recruits to the group ask permission "to drink water" (i.e., camp with the band and share in the use of their territorial resources) and of whom recruits seek approval to join the band'.[10] In practice, lineage lines give rise to two, three, or even four 'owners' who are deemed to descend from the alleged original founder, and who function as spokespersons for the group as a whole, which decides on the basis of consensus whether a newcomer will be accepted. This open attitude toward membership facilitates considerable intergroup migration, both by

[9] George Silberbauer, 'A Sense of Place', in Ernest S. Burch, Jr. and Linda J. Ellanna (eds.), *Key Issues in Hunter-Gatherer Research* (Oxford: Berg, 1994), 134.

[10] Silberbauer, *Hunter and Habitat in the Central Kalahari Desert*, 99, 141.

individuals and by households. It also allows for the acceptance of non-G/wi into their groups. But

> [a]lthough membership is not closed, it does confer exclusive rights. Permission is never actually withheld and its asking is simply a formality. It is, however, a formality that clearly indicates that the use of territorial resources and residence have to be granted before they are gained. Unwelcome visitors are given permission to remain but are later eased out of the band.[11]

So, G/wi nomadic groups relate to space by setting up a preferential difference between inside and outside from the first-person plural perspective: access to membership, and therewith to the group's territory and its use, is granted to all newcomers, but subject to the possibility of belated exclusion by the collective. That members are preferred to non-members entails that inside is preferred to outside, and vice versa. It is significant, in this respect, that the G/wi word for a stranger met for the first time—*/xajekhwema*—means, literally, 'entering-man'.[12]

These considerations on the G/wi give the nay to Deleuze and Guattari's strong thesis that 'the nomad, nomad space, is localized and not delimited'.[13] There can be no nomadic emplacement in the absence of a spatial closure. A nomadic *nomos* is not, as Deleuze and Guattari hold, an 'open space', but rather a limited space. Even if nomadism implies that persons and animals are distributed in a '*fuzzy* whole' ('*ensemble flou*'), there can be no distribution unless the nomadic *nomos* is a 'fuzzy *whole*', an ensemble—indeed—of ought-places that functions as its background condition. Another way of putting it is that there can be no distribution of persons (and animals) in space that does not involve a normative point providing orientation for spatial distribution, a normative point that, by including certain configurations of ought-places and excluding others, draws a preferential differentiation between inside and outside. Every act of nomadic distribution draws its meaning as a *distributive* act from this preferential differentiation, which it both presupposes and actualizes.[14] In the same vein, the land of a nomadic group does not cease to be land, becoming 'simply ground (*sol*) or support': it is creased by normativity that indicates *where* certain activities ought to take place. While there are certainly significant differences between the territorialities of sedentary and nomadic communities, the nature of these differences is not grasped by the simple opposition between, respectively, 'striated' and 'smooth' spaces. In fact, I wonder whether this distinction, which has captured the imagination of many scholars

[11] Silberbauer, *Hunter and Habitat in the Central Kalahari Desert*, 141. Silberbauer discusses in some detail the social techniques used to 'encourage' unwelcome members of a band to migrate to another band—a soft form of coercion, but coercion nonetheless, by which to enforce the exclusivity, both social and territorial, of the G/wi nomadic bands (*Hunter and Habitat in the Central Kalahari Desert*, 173–174).

[12] Silberbauer, *Hunter and Habitat in the Central Kalahari Desert*, 60–61. I briefly refer to another nomadic example of this preferential differentiation in chapter 3, when discussing the Pintupi of the Australian Western Desert.

[13] Deleuze and Guattari, *A Thousand Plateaus*, 422.

[14] Not only does nomadic distribution, like all distributive acts, require the closure of space, but also a closure of the *who* (in the double sense of by whom and to whom), the *what*, and the *when* of apportioning. This insight calls forth the problem of (distributive) justice as a first-person plural concept, which requires detailed attention in another work.

anxious to move beyond the strictures of state territoriality, makes any sense at all in grasping what it means for a collective to take up a relation to space as a normative space of action. But that is an issue calling for separate discussion.

2.2 THE FRONTIERS OF ROMAN LAW

I would like to take a further step in the examination of possible counterexamples to the general topography of legal order introduced in chapter 1 by delving into what is, on the face of it, the stark contrast between Roman law, on the one hand, and modern national/international law, on the other. In a meticulously documented article that probes the emergence of the 'boundary (*Grenze*) of modernity', Merio Scattola points to a remarkable historical inversion that goes from the Roman treatment of spatial boundaries to that of the national/international law paradigm. In his words, 'the Roman conception [of spatial boundaries] is entirely turned on its head [by modernity]: whereas the boundary in the *Corpus iuris civilis* only enjoys a private law validity, just this private law meaning is now excluded, and only the public [law meaning] is understood as being the original and authentic boundary'.[15] The question that arises is whether the legal topography of chapter 1 is sufficiently general to explain this feature of Roman law. As I will attempt to show, Scattola's analysis of this inversion is particularly apposite because it shows that both situations are governed by the same 'logic': the conditions that explain why Roman law could only elucidate boundaries as a phenomenon of private law are the very same conditions that govern the modern emergence of legal boundaries as a phenomenon of (international) public law between nation-states.

I cannot follow here the details of Scattola's discussion of the rich array of terms and institutions whereby Roman law deals with the problem of spatial boundaries. It suffices to note for our purpose that there are at least two terms in Latin which include a reference to the spatial boundaries of a territory. The first is *finis*, which originally meant the boundaries of a city or an area, and was often equated to the outermost part of a territory circumscribed by a boundary line. The second is *limes*, which originally meant a road that traverses or crosses something, such as a field or forest, and gradually came to mean the road that, in the absence of rivers or other natural boundaries, was built to function as the boundary separating Roman territory from *gentes* and *nationes*. The Romans, accordingly, were well aware that 'peoples possess different regions of the earth's surface; that these [regions] could be divided by means of real or virtual lines; that everything which finds itself within these lines is part of a homogeneous territory; and that such a territory can also be determined by the unitary administration of justice'.[16] And yet, as he immediately adds, neither of these terms has

[15] Merio Scattola, 'Die Grenze der Neuzeit: ihr Begriff in der juristischen und politischen Literatur der Antike und Frühmoderne', in Markus Bauer and Thomas Rahn (eds.), *Die Grenze: Begriff und Inszenierung* (Berlin: Akademie Verlag, 1997), 64–65. Scattola exploits the polysemy of the German word *Grenze*, which includes, in English, 'boundaries' and 'borders'.

[16] Scattola, 'Die Grenze der Neuzeit, 40.

the meaning of a legal border dividing two communities; it was necessary to wait till modernity before legal borders made their appearance. Instead, the non-legal boundaries of the Roman polity delimit the space within which private law can regulate how legal boundaries are drawn, contested and modified. Instances thereof are the *actio finium regundorum*, the 'action for regulating boundaries', used to settle disputes between neighbours concerning the boundaries of their lands,[17] and the distinction between *fines publici* and *fines privati*, whereby the former refers not to the boundaries of the polity but rather to the boundaries of public property, as opposed to the boundaries of private property.

Whence the crucial question: if the Romans had a keen sense of spatial boundaries as delimiting their polity with respect to other polities, why did they not develop a conception of these boundaries as *legal borders*? Scattola's answer to this question is perspicuous, and I quote it in full:

> A boundary arises from the agreement between two owners: the condition thereof is that the property on both sides [of the boundary] is legally protected, hence that both property owners belong to the same legal community. Both owners must therefore recognize the other party, and accept that there is a common law that governs their reciprocal relations and obligations. Roman citizens can draw boundaries between their properties because all of them belong to a single *communio iuris* reflected in the laws of the jurisprudence of the *iuris consulti* and in the law of the *res publica Romana*. Absent such a legal community there can be no common legal understanding, as a result of which common boundaries are unthinkable.[18]

This insight broadly confirms and enriches the account of legal spatiality outlined in chapter 1. I pick out three features that are of particular interest. The first concerns Scattola's observation that legal boundaries are 'common boundaries'. This means that although legal boundaries separate, they also *join* both places—in this case properties—as parts of a single legal space. Yet more forcefully: legal boundaries cannot fulfil their role of separating legal places *unless* they also join them into a whole. Second, legal boundaries can only do their work of separating and joining ought-places if there is a reference to a collective, to a *communio iuris*. However acrimonious and in need of resolution via an *actio finium regundorum*, boundary disputes presuppose and assert the first-person plural perspective of a 'we'. When seeking to disengage from one another by separating their properties, the parties in strife affirm their mutual commitment to each other as members of the polity.

If these two initial points remain largely within the scope of the analysis of chapter 1, my third observation takes this analysis a step further. Although Scattola shows that Roman law conceptualized legal boundaries as a phenomenon of private law, closer consideration requires qualifying his insight. Consider Ulpian's commentary on the distinction between *fines publici* and *fines privati*, to

[17] See Theodor Mommsen and Paul Krueger (eds.), *The Digest of Justinian*, trans. Alan Watson (Philadelphia, PA: University of Pennsylvania Press, 1985), Book 10, 1.

[18] Scattola, 'Die Grenze der Neuzeit', 44. Saskia Sassen makes a similar point in her monograph, *Territory · Authority · Rights: From Medieval to Global Assemblages* (Princeton, NJ: Princeton University Press, 2006), 40.

which Scattola refers when noting that the former remains within the conceptual framework of private law:

> The boundaries of public lands must not be retained by private individuals. Therefore, the Governor of the province shall see that public lands are separated from those belonging to private persons and endeavor to increase the public revenues. If he finds that any public places or buildings are occupied by private persons, he must estimate whether they should be demanded for the benefit of the public, or whether it would be better to lease them for a sufficient rent; and he must always pursue the course which he thinks will be of the greatest advantage to the State.[19]

At one level, Scattola is no doubt right to note that the concept of public lands, places and buildings and their boundaries continues to rely on the private law notion of property. But the more fundamental question is on what basis Roman law could introduce the very distinction between public and private boundaries. For, clearly, both public and private places are part of a *single* distribution of legal places, that is, a space that is deemed to be the *common* space of a collective. In this sense, private and public properties and their boundaries are only conceivable as part and parcel of the public domain. In short, the distinction between *fines publici* and *fines privati* only makes sense because public and private places, in virtue of their mutual implication and differentiation, are locations within a more encompassing spatial unity. Both public and private places presuppose and refer to the totality of places in which they are located, hence to the apposite collective. The distinction between public and private places is public.[20]

Scattola's contribution to our theme goes, however, considerably further. In effect, he shows that the reason for which Roman law could only accommodate legal boundaries in the framework of private law is also the reason that explains why legal boundaries between states *could* emerge in modernity: 'a reliable boundary can only be drawn when peoples and states recognise a common public law. This recognition is, however, the characteristic proper to modern political history, both from a real perspective and that of the history of ideas'.[21] It is for this reason that state and international law are correlative legal orders. Scattola adds: 'both the existence and the effectiveness of state boundaries are conditioned by the existence of a higher legal community between states, such that also different public subjects mutually recognise their boundaries and, when the occasion so demands, can settle their disputes'.[22] Scattola can then construe the expression 'the boundary of modernity' as having a twofold sense: on the one hand, modernity conditions the emergence of legal borders that delimit states;

[19] S.P. Scott (ed. and trans.), *The Digest or Pandects of Justinian*, L, 10, 5, 1, in *The Civil Law* (Cincinnati, OH: The Central Trust Company, 1932), Vol. IX, 245.

[20] Kelsen draws a similar conclusion with respect to the distinction between public and private law: 'To distinguish in principle between a private non-political sphere of the law and a public political sphere is to obscure the fact that the "private" law created in the contract is no less the arena of political power than the public law created in legislation and administration'. See Kelsen, *Problems of Legal Theory*, 95–96.

[21] Scattola, 'Die Grenze der Neuzeit', 45.

[22] Scattola, 'Die Grenze der Neuzeit', 65.

on the other, the emergence of legal borders between states marks the commencement of modernity.

The deeper continuity Scattola reveals between Roman law and the complementary relation in modernity between national and international law is interesting in various ways. More generally, it shows that the scope of the topography sketched out in chapter 1 is consistent with the spatial configuration of both international law and legal orders such as the Roman. As concerns international law, Scattola confirms the insight that it also is a spatial unity in the form of a single distribution of ought-places, in this case of states. If a state manifests itself as a differentiated interconnection of ought-places, so also the international legal order. In the same vein, the spatial unity of international law involves a first-person plural perspective, namely, 'we', the community of states. International law also involves a *determinate* distribution of places: it includes states and state territories, while excluding other possible configurations of legal space and legal communities.

Yet the non-legal boundaries that delimit the Roman polity demand closer scrutiny. Indeed, what more can be said about these boundaries, other than that they circumscribe a territory which is not legally contiguous to another territory? The most direct way of putting it is to assert that these non-legal boundaries are *frontiers*. As such, they mark the confines of a common legal space, confines which are not themselves legal. This is not to say that there is no law on the far side of the frontier; the *Digest*, for example, shows clearly that the Romans were well aware that their enemies had legal orders of their own. The point is, rather, that while there may well be legal collectives beyond the frontier, these are not integrated, together with the Roman polity, into an encompassing legal order recognized as such by all these collectives. This resonates with an insight developed in chapter 1: what lies beyond a limit is an ought-place that has no place in a single distribution of legal places. Regardless of whether it expands or contracts, the frontier of a legal order joins and separates places, but not as ought-places which are part of a legal whole. To cross such a frontier is either to abandon what a collective deems to be the space of law, or to be received into its fold. This side and the far side of the frontier of a legal order are strongly discontinuous because there is no common legal standard which defines them as the kind of legal places that they are. This insight points to a fundamental *asymmetry* between both sides of a frontier: they are not reversible, as are, for instance, relations between property owners who share 'a common law that governs their reciprocal relations and obligations' (Scattola). By the same token, the two sides of the frontier carry different 'existential' valences: the Roman that leaves Roman territory loses his or her status as a Roman citizen, with all the rights and obligations conferred by this legal status, and becomes, quite simply, a human being.

One might want to assume that the notion of a frontier only has a 'historiographical' interest for a theory of legal boundaries, as frontiers would have ceased to play a role in international law. But this would be to miss the radical implication of Scattola's analysis, an implication, however, which he does not draw: by definition, the outermost confines of a legal space *are not themselves legal or illegal*. Roman law has a frontier, not because it is Roman but because it is law. *Frontiers are the spatial limit of a legal order*. This implication has two faces, neither of which he discusses.

The first concerns the boundaries of property. Indeed, if the frontier of a legal order is not a legal boundary, does this not also spill over into the legal boundaries of property, which are contaminated, as it were, with an irreducible aspect of factuality? The traces of this problem are apparent in Scattola's assertion that 'a [legal] boundary arises from the agreement between two owners', hence an agreement which emerges against the background of a situation that is already deemed legal. For the possibility of an agreement between owners about the boundaries that separate their properties already presupposes a prior demarcation of the polity, and of those who are entitled to own property therein: *imperium*. But is this prior demarcation itself ever simply the result of a legal agreement? Scattola inadvertently reveals that the boundaries of *dominium* attest to an intertwinement of legality and factuality that is already effectual in *imperium*, an intertwinement that resonates in the distinction and relation between property and (adverse) possession.

Importantly, it also resonates in the contemporary distinction and relation between property rights and 'informal' settlements of squatters. Brazil's *Movimento dos trabalhadores rurais sem terra* (MST)—Landless Workers Movement—has repeatedly occupied unused land, where, according to its website, 'they have established cooperative farms, constructed houses, schools for children and adults and clinics, promoted indigenous cultures and a healthy and sustainable environment and gender equality'.[23] Land occupation is one of a range of forms of collective action deployed by the MST, which also includes protest marches and the occupation of government agencies and highways, aimed at encouraging the Brazilian government to expropriate and redistribute privately owned land. While landowners have sought to have squatting by the MST declared illegal and to evict squatters from their properties, it is significant that the Landless Workers Movement justifies land occupation with reference to Article 184 of the Brazilian constitution which requires authorities 'to expropriate for the purpose of agrarian reform, rural property that is not performing its social function'.[24] In terms of the considerations of chapter 1, the land occupations by the MST do not only breach the boundaries of properties; they also transgress them, intimating a place that has no place in the distribution of ought-places actualized by the Brazilian legal order, yet which, they claim, ought to.

André van der Walt has shown, in a remarkable study on the process of transformation and land reform in South Africa following the democratic dispensation

[23] <http://www.mstbrazil.org/?q=about> (accessed on 13 February 2013).

[24] See the site 'Constitutional Authority: Legality of Land Occupations', available at: <http://www.mstbrazil.org/?q=constitutionalauthority> (accessed on 13 February 2013). For background information about the MST and its legal and political mobilization to transform property law in Brazil, see Peter P. Houtzager, 'The Movement of the Landless (MST), juridical field, and legal change in Brazil', in Boaventura de Sousa Santos and César A. Rodríguez-Garavito (eds.), *Law and Globalization from Below: Towards a Cosmopolitan Legality* (Cambridge: Cambridge University Press, 2005), 218–240.

of 1994, how squatting, amongst other things, reveals property and property law 'in the margins':

> Property law is not possible without attention, at some level, to property rights and the power they entail... [But we also need] to imagine a perspective on property that includes, in a meaningful way, the interests of those who are not 'normally' considered part of the property elite, without automatically reducing them to the status of weakness and dependency... To think about property in the margins also implies taking note of the strong positions that sometimes feature in the margins, particularly when they are founded on direct rejection of or confrontation with the dominant property regime.[25]

I would add that marginal positions can be strong, rather than merely weak, because the boundaries of property, both spatial and material, arise, paradoxically, in boundary crossings that question them. If we can speak of a 'de-centring' of property law, as Van der Walt puts it, it is because a dominant property regime, and the way in which it draws the legal/illegal distinction, is the sedimentation of a-legal boundary crossings. Eduardo Peñalver and Sonia Katyal have shown, in line with this idea, that 'the apparent stability and order that property law provides owe much to the destabilizing role of the lawbreaker, who occasionally forces shifts of entitlements and law'. Indeed, they further argue, property outlaws expose the paradox of a system of property, which 'is at once stable, perhaps even essentially so, and yet this seemingly ordered system at the same time masks a pervasive, but constructive, instability that is necessary to prevent the entire edifice from becoming outdated'.[26] In this view, the qualification of persons who transgress the spatial boundaries of property law as 'landless' or 'homeless' is not only privative, as the terms suggest: while there is certainly a privative dimension in being landless or homeless, such transgressions intimate other possible configurations of property law.[27] In other words, 'lawbreakers' in such situations are, in the fundamental sense of an outside discussed hitherto, property *out-laws*. This ambiguity at the heart of the term 'outlaw' is the reason for which I have dubbed the transgression of legal boundaries *a*-legal rather than only *il*-legal.

Secondly, a comparable argument concerns international law itself. Scattola could overlook that international law has a frontier because it would seem that international law no longer has 'outermost confines'; after all, it now covers the whole face of the earth. But, as Scattola's account makes clear, (classical) international law regulates relations between *states*. The legal borders of states

[25] André van der Walt, *Property in the Margins* (Oxford: Hart, 2009), 242–243.

[26] Eduardo M. Peñalver and Sonia K. Katyal, 'Property Outlaws', *University of Pennsylvania Law Review* 155 (2007), 1098.

[27] As concerns the 'homeless', Lorna Fox has persuasively argued that, in cases of mortgage arrears and repossessions, Western property law has systematically favoured creditors' claims on the capital asset embodied in property over the home-interest of the occupier. Drawing on philosophical literature on the notions of dwelling, place, and sense of place, she outlines the contours of a 'legally coherent concept of home' that would do justice to its specificity as what I have called an *ought*-place. Her work, as well as that of Van der Walt, exemplifies, on a theoretical level, the reconfiguration of a legal space as a distribution of ought-places intimated by a-legality. Also legal theory can, in this sense, be 'a-legal'. See Lorna Fox, *Conceptualising Home: Theories, Laws and Policies* (Oxford: Hart, 2007), especially 131 ff.

presuppose mutual recognition within the framework of an encompassing community of states. As a result, the logic at work in Roman law remains at work in the tandem state-international law: because 'a boundary is legally recognised when it can point to a higher legal community',[28] the frontier of international law manifests itself in boundary crossings that intimate an ought-place that is not a legal place within the single distribution of legal places made possible by international law. This is no abstract subtlety. Although Scattola has nothing to say about colonization in his article, the emergence of contemporary international law from the *ius publicum europaeum* is by no means innocent. As subordinate indigenous peoples know all too well, the 'mutual recognition' (Scattola) between states which gives rise to international law is not an agreement between the communities that existed prior to their colonization and the colonizing powers; it is between the states that ensued from colonization and the de-colonizing powers. The frontiers of international law manifest themselves, amongst other things, in all those boundary crossings into and from the lands which subordinate indigenous communities claim as their own, yet which obtain no recognition as such in the 'legal community of nations'.[29] We will return to this shortly, when discussing the claim to an own land raised by the U'wa people in what many—but not they—call Colombia.

More generally, a boundary crossing that evokes an ought-place that is not 'a part of a general whole'[30] of legal places attests to a frontier crossing, regardless of whether that distribution of legal places concerns Roman, state or international law. On this reading, intimated towards the end of chapter 1, *any* spatial boundary of whatever legal order can suddenly manifest itself as a frontier—as a spatial limit. The purpose of the *autoréduction* by the *chômeurs* at Galeries Lafayette was to reveal the check-out point of the food department as a frontier, and with it a 'far side' of the law that beckons beyond the check-out points, a beyond which 'generates curiosity, promise, threat, and fear'.[31] If, finally, legal globalization has a frontier, it is not only and not primarily because it unfolds as an expansive process in which the spatial boundaries of a legal order are pushed ever further outward or become ever more inclusive; it is because global legal orders, like all legal orders, have an outside in the strong sense of a strange ought-place, intimated in a-legal crossings of their legal boundaries.

These considerations entail, amongst other things, that 'global law' cannot be construed in such a way that, as *global* law, it involves a first-person plural perspective that stands *above* 'regional', 'national', or 'sub-national' legal orders,

[28] Scattola, 'Die Grenze der Neuzeit', 50.

[29] This point resonates strongly with Jim Tully's criticism of constitutional imperialism to which Vattel, Kant, and their followers, amongst others, made decisive contributions. See James Tully, *Strange Multiplicity: Constitutionalism in an Age of Diversity* (Cambridge: Cambridge University Press, 1995), 79–82. See also the logic of inclusion and exclusion attaching, amongst other things, to the concept of civilization in international law, as portrayed by Martti Koskenniemi, *The Gentle Civilizer of Nations: The Rise and Fall of International Law 1870–1960* (Cambridge: Cambridge University Press, 2002), 127–132.

[30] Scattola, 'Die Grenze der Neuzeit', 66.

[31] Thomas D. Hall, 'Borders, Borderlands, and Frontiers, Global', in Maryanne Klein Horowitz (ed.), *New Dictionary of the History of Ideas* (New York: Charles Scribners and Sons, 1994), vol. 1, 241.

and encompasses all of these. The understanding of the globality of a global perspective as involving a 'higher point of view' amounts to the fallacy of what Merleau-Ponty calls a '*pensée de survol*'. If, as our considerations suggest, global law involves a first-person plural perspective, and with it a necessary closure of legal space into an inside and an outside, then, as we shall see in the forthcoming analyses, any global legal order cannot but encounter other legal orders *from the side*—laterally, as one might put it—and not from above; it is an encounter between differently emplaced first-person plural perspectives. Conversely, it suggests that there could be no first-person plural *perspective* absent the emplacement of a legal order, global or otherwise.

2.3 MULTINATIONALS

These final comments on the frontier of global law need to be tested in a concrete manner. A number of legal theorists have argued that the internal regulations of multinational enterprises are putative legal orders which resist accommodation on either side of the correlation between municipal and international law. In this vein, 'the construction of global de-territorialized legal orders—in other words, multinational enterprises',[32] poses a strong challenge to the exclusive territoriality of the nation-state. Two leading legal theorists have gone so far as to defend the view that transnational economic groups, which are 'non-territorial legal orders', exercise 'delocalized powers'.[33] This process of 'delocalization' is all the more remarkable because the internal regulations of multinational enterprises are not part of public law, whether national or international; multinational enterprises are *private* collectives engaged in self-regulatory activities on a global scale. Bracketing for the moment a discussion of the private character of multinationals, the question that interests me here is the following: what kind of topography defines multinationals as distinct legal orders? In particular, even though multinationals have no territory in the sense of a state, are they *delocalized* orders, such that the inside/outside distinction has ceased to play a role in their configuration as legal orders?

By accepting that multinationals are distinct legal orders, I am also accepting that, although they rely in a variety of ways on the positive law of states, their spatial unity is irreducible to a simple aggregation of patches of state territories. Furthermore, if it is nonsensical to explain the spatial unity of a multinational in terms of state borders, so also it is nonsensical to argue that a multinational's spatial unity gives rise to the distinction between inside and outside in the form of the distinction between 'foreign' and 'domestic' territories. As Robé nicely puts it, 'The existence of these organizations, each with its unity of command, logic and rules (making use of this multiplicity of supports in positive law while existing as one in their functioning), challenges our understanding of law as a phenomenon

[32] Jean-Philippe Robé, 'Multinational Enterprises: The Constitution of a Pluralistic Legal Order', in Gunther Teubner (ed.), *Global Law Without a State* (Aldershot: Dartmouth, 1997), 49.

[33] Michel Kerckove and François Ost, *Le système juridique entre ordre et désordre* (Paris: Presses Universitaires de France, 1988), 203, cited by Robé, 'Multinational Enterprises', 56.

intrinsically based on [territorial] states'.[34] Sassen is more specific about the concrete spatiality of these organizations when noting that the global dispersal of factories and service outlets of integrated corporate systems, in particular multinationals, goes hand in hand with the centralization of their command functions in what she dubs 'global cities'.[35] There is an important difference, however, with respect to other forms of global law, inasmuch as multinationals do not claim to regulate the whole face of the earth; they are more like movable enclaves.

Take Royal Dutch Shell, the oil multinational: it comprises a building or set of buildings that is its world headquarters; a number of other buildings that are the national headquarters scattered throughout the countries in which it is active; yet other buildings which house its research and development programmes; oil extraction rigs; refineries; service stations; and so forth. Notice that these boundaries are not 'fixed': Shell is free to move its headquarters, sell off refineries, acquire concessions to explore and tap expanses of the sea bed, etc., thereby reconfiguring its spatial order as it sees fit. Yet, even despite this important difference with states, Shell is a *single* distribution of places, organized as such in terms of the point guiding the multinational's various activities. In other words, Shell's spatial unity is linked to a first-person plural perspective in terms of the normative point guiding its various activities. Moreover, and in light of that normative point, Shell's internal regulations entitle different sorts of persons to enter certain of these places (e.g. only certain scientists are allowed to enter into its research labs, or only certain IT specialists are allowed to enter its computer facilities), and different kinds of activity are commanded, authorized, or forbidden in different sorts of places (e.g. certain safety procedures are obligatory in the refineries, or certain parking slots are reserved for certain executives). In short, *qua* (more or less movable) spatial unity, Shell consists of a single distribution of *ought*-places.

It is this feature that explains why Shell is spatially limited in terms of the inside/outside distinction. In effect, the occupation of the Brent Spar oil storage and tanker loading buoy by Green Peace activists, and the associated consumer boycott of Shell service stations, can be seen as acts that question the distribution of legal places that define Shell as a spatial unity. In particular, the occupation and boycott call into question the commonality that Shell claims for its space. By occupying the buoy, the activists evoke a way of emplacing Shell's activities in a global distribution of places that is—literally—*outside* of the interests furthered by the way in which Shell's activities distribute and use places. The buoy, when occupied, evokes a *strange* ought-place, an ought-place that has a place in the spatial unity Shell claims for itself, yet also intimates an ought-place outside of that unity of places, and the actualization of which is incompatible with the extant configuration of ought-places deployed by Shell. In this fundamental sense, the contrast between inside and outside, in the sense of the contrast between own and strange places, is no less constitutive of a multinational than it is of any

[34] Robé, 'Multinational Enterprises', 45.

[35] Saskia Sassen, 'Places and Spaces of the Global: An Expanded Analytic Terrain', in David Held and Anthony McGrew (eds.), *Globalization Theory: Approaches and Controversies* (Cambridge: Polity, 2007), 79–105, 84–86.

other legal order.[36] While Shell does not constitute itself as a spatial unity in line with the spatial forms of a state territory, it is not and cannot exercise 'delocalized power', as Van der Kerchove and Ost claim. If Shell is to be a global legal order, then it must emplace itself, closing itself into an inside over and against an outside. To borrow Sassen's turn of phrase, the emergence of multinationals is a specific manifestation of the 'localization of the global'.[37] The ineluctable emplacement of multinationals explains, moreover, why their 'internal regulations' are just that: *internal* regulations. Indeed, by marking off who ought to do what, where, and when, they stake out an inside in the sense of a unity of ought-places in contrast to a strange outside. The activists who occupied the Brent Spar breached a legal boundary and also transgressed it, revealing it as a limit between a unity of ought-places and a strange outside.

Finally, and although I concentrate in this chapter on spatial boundaries, notice that the Brent Spar actions also contest the subjective boundaries that define *who* counts as an interested party to the collective (e.g. the recurrent question concerning shareholders and stakeholders), the *material* boundaries that determine what rights accrue to individuals (e.g. profits for shareholders in light of social costs generated by the firm's activities), and the *temporal* boundaries that define Shell as a collective project (e.g. the tension between the pursuit of profit over time and environmental concerns). In this sense, 'private' self-regulation never has been nor can be insulated from politics. But we will return to explore this issue in chapter 3.

2.4 *LEX MERCATORIA*

The astounding multiplication and consolidation of worldwide commercial practices, transnational professional codes, standardized contracts of economic sectors and branches, international arbitral awards and other related phenomena indicates, or so a leading scholar avers, that '[*l*]*ex mercatoria*, the transnational law of economic transactions, is the most successful example of global law'.[38] Let us unpack the expression 'global law' into its component parts with a view to formulating the question I would like to explore.

[36] See the 'Brent Spar' entry at: <http://en.wikipedia.org/wiki/Brent_Spar_oil_rig> (accessed on 13 February 2013). Evidently, a comparable analysis could be made of action taken against Shell's activities in the Niger Delta.

[37] Saskia Sassen, *A Sociology of Globalization* (New York: W.W. Norton, 2007), 4. Boaventura de Sousa Santos has defended a similar thesis, when characterizing globalization as 'the process by which a given local condition or entity succeeds in extending its reach over the globe and, by doing so, develops the capacity to designate a rival social condition as local'. The question that remains unanswered, both in Sassen and de Sousa Santos, is how legal space is structured such that global legal orders are a form of localization. Moreover, de Sousa Santos seems to view the relation between legal order and localization as contingent, to the extent that he contrasts 'globalized localism' to 'the emergence of issues which, by their nature, are as global as the globe itself and which I would call, drawing loosely from international law, the *common heritage of mankind*'. Boaventura de Sousa Santos, *Toward a New Legal Common Sense*, 2nd edn. (London: Butterworths, 2002), 178, 181.

[38] Gunther Teubner, 'Global Bukowina: Legal Pluralism in the World Society', in *Global Law Without a State*, 3.

Teubner's first point is that *lex mercatoria* is law. This qualification of the new merchant law has been the object of sharp controversy.[39] Against its critics, who deny that *lex mercatoria* is law, Teubner argues that it emerges in relative autonomy from both state law and international public law, in the form of private self-regulation by economic sectors. Although it would be a mistake to view *lex mercatoria* as structurally deficient law because it does not meet the criteria of state law, the new law merchant, like the other forms of global law, is nevertheless a distinct kind of legal order that emerges as a result of the functional differentiation of global society. Importantly, and by contrast to sub-national legal orders of ethnic, religious, or cultural communities, *lex mercatoria* is truly global in reach.

I find Teubner's dismissal of the move to reduce the new law merchant to an underdeveloped form of state law compelling. His claim that the emergence of *lex mercatoria* poses a considerable challenge to state-centred theories of law is no less compelling, to the extent that this novel legal order exposes state territoriality as a merely contingent feature of legal order. But Teubner's claim is stronger: while he grants that the new law merchant, like all law, requires a closure of 'meaning boundaries', it distinguishes itself from state law because, by definition, it no longer relies on spatial closure. In contrast to national or even regional legal orders, which remain localized in space, *lex mercatoria* attests to the delocalization of legal orders.

> The traditional differentiation in line with the political principle of territoriality into relatively autonomous national legal orders is thus overlain by a sectoral differentiation principle: the differentiation of global law into transnational legal regimes, which define the external reach of their jurisdiction along issue-specific rather than territorial lines, and which claim a global validity for themselves.[40]

The reference to 'externality' in this passage points to the crux of the matter: can the new merchant law define the 'external reach' of its content, time, and subjects without also having to close itself spatially as an inside that is preferred to an outside?

Let us consider one of the examples Teubner marshals in favour of his reading of *lex mercatoria*: *lex constructionis*, the transnational law of large construction projects such as airports, harbours, mines, roads, petrochemical plants, and hydroelectric dams. Indeed, *lex constructionis* displays a typical feature of private self-regulation on a global scale: it involves standard contracts drawn up by a handful of sector organizations, including the International Federation of Consulting Engineers (FIDIC), the International European Construction Federation (FIEC), the British Institution of Civil Engineers (ICE), the Engineering Advancement

[39] The literature on *lex mercatoria* is enormous. See, amongst others, Ursula Stein, *Lex Mercatoria: Realität und Theorie* (Frankfurt: Vittorio Klostermann, 1995), 179 ff, for an overview of the theoretical debate. See also Ralf Michaels, 'The True *Lex Mercatoria*: Law Beyond the State', *Indiana Journal of Global Legal Studies* 14, no. 2 (2007), 447–468; Alec Stone Sweet, 'The New *Lex Mercatoria* and Transnational Governance', *Journal of European Public Policy* 13, no. 5 (2006), 627–646.

[40] Andreas Fischer-Lescano and Gunther Teubner, 'Regime-Collisions: The Vain Search for Legal Unity in the Fragmentation of Global Law', *Michigan Journal of International Law* 25, no. 4 (2004), 1009.

Association of Japan (ENAA), the American Institute of Architects (AIA), and the International Bank for Reconstruction and Development (the World Bank). As an important study notes, although these standard contracts are usually tailored to fit each new situation, 'they have a profound effect on the formation of normative expectations in this [global] market'.[41] Furthermore, and this is a second distinguishing feature of *lex mercatoria*, the resolution of disputes about these contracts is almost always assured by international arbitration.

Consider the standard construction contract drawn up by the FIDIC, which has consolidated itself as the dominant construction contract for the sector. Topographically speaking, this contract regulates rights and obligations of the parties germane to the 'Site', which the standard contract defines as 'the places where the Permanent Works are to be executed, including storage and working areas, and to which Plant and Materials are to be delivered, and any other places as may be specified in the Contract as forming part of the Site'. The standard contract also refers to the 'Country', interpreted as 'the country in which the Site (or most of it) is located, where the Permanent Works are to be executed'.[42] In short, the contract defines the site as an *ought*-place, but as a standardized ought-place the normativity of which depends on a contractual model that claims global validity. So, while a given country may have one or more sites under construction, what renders these sites the ought-places that they are is a transnational contract rather than simply the law of the country. In this sense, *lex constructionis* falls beyond the inside/outside distinction proper to the nation-state. But can *lex constructionis* emerge as a novel legal order without a spatial closure?

The struggle of the U'wa indigenous people against oil drilling in their ancestral lands casts light on this question. In effect, the U'wa—the name means 'people who think, people who know how to speak'—have been engaged since the early 1990s and up to the present day in protracted and desperate resistance to attempts, initially by the American oil company Occidental Petroleum (Oxy), subsequently by the Colombian oil company Ecopetrol, to drill and exploit oil resources situated in or contiguous to their lands.[43] This struggle is part of centuries-long resistance of the U'wa to a process of creeping dispossession from their vast ancestral lands, and which saw them confined to a reserve of some 61,115 hectares by 1987. The legal dossier of the struggle includes, amongst other things, successive judgments in 1997 by the Colombian Constitutional Court and Council of State, in which the former ruled in favour, the second against the

[41] Oren Perez, 'Using Private-Public Linkages to Regulate Environmental Conflicts: The Case of International Construction Contracts', *Journal of Law and Society* 29, no. 1 (2002), 84.

[42] 'Conditions of Contract for Construction for Building and Engineering Works Designed by the Employer', 4 and 5: <http://www1.fidic.org/downloads/cons_mdb_gc_jun10_unprotected.pdf> (accessed on 13 September 2010). The Contract for Construction is currently available, upon payment, at: <http://fidic.org/books/construction-contract-1st-ed-1999-red-book> (accessed on 9 May 2013).

[43] For an overview of the U'wa's struggle against Oxy and Ecopetrol, see César A. Rodríguez-Garavito and Luis Carlos Arenas, 'Indigenous Rights, Transnational Activism, and Legal Mobilization: The Struggle of the U'wa People in Colombia', in *Law and Globalization from Below: Towards a Cosmopolitan Legality*. More recent information about the struggle is available on the website of the NGO *Amazon Watch*: <http://amazonwatch.org/> (accessed on 13 February 2013).

U'wa's demand that the drilling activities be terminated. The struggle acquired international notoriety when, confronted with imminent oil drilling in 1995, the U'wa announced that, unless drilling plans were halted, they would commit collective suicide, like one of their groups did in the 16th century, when confronted with the advance of the Spanish Conquistadores.[44]

Strictly speaking, the oil exploration activities of Oxy and Ecopetrol do not fall under the standard construction contract laid down by the FIDIC. But this is immaterial from the point of view of our own questioning: in September 2008 the U'wa announced their opposition to governmental plans to contract the construction of a road linking Colombia and Venezuela, which would traverse part of their ancestral lands.[45] It is in this spirit, therefore, that I would like to examine how the challenge raised by the U'wa against oil drilling casts light on the question concerning the spatial boundaries of *lex constructionis*.

The judgment by the Colombian Constitutional Court provides a first hint concerning the nature of the problem. It is particularly interesting because, of the two judgments noted above, it went furthest in recognizing the legitimacy of the interest of the U'wa in protecting their lands. As a result, the Court struck down the administrative act that granted exploration rights to Oxy, arguing that the act ran foul of Article 330 of the Colombian Constitution of 1991, which requires participation by indigenous peoples in all decisions pertaining to the exploitation of natural resources in their territories. Participation of the indigenous groups is indispensable, held the Court, because:

> The exploitation of natural resources in indigenous territories requires harmonising two conflicting interests: the need to plan the management and use of resources in said territories to guarantee their sustainable development, conservation, replenishment or substitution . . . and [the need] to ensure the protection of the ethnic, cultural, social, and economic integrity of the indigenous communities that occupy said territories.[46]

The Court's judgment is a landmark ruling that was celebrated by many in Colombia and elsewhere. But would the 'harmonization' of interests it defends address the radical challenge raised by the U'wa? Indeed, the harmonization of conflicting interests presupposes the common interest of a single collective. Yet the whole thrust of U'wa contestation is to reject this presupposed commonality. From the very beginning, the U'wa have steadfastly refused to engage in the process of participation and consultation with the Colombian government and with the oil companies in the latter's terms, an engagement which would commit them, as they well understood, to accepting the premise of that process: that while they have a legitimate interest in the outcome of the decision, its

[44] See the article, 'U'wa tribe's suicide pact', posted on: <http://www.vhemt.org/uwa.htm> (accessed on 13 February 2013).

[45] 'Colombia: Resistencia Uwa contra petroleras y megaproyectos, 2009-10-08': <http://www.amazonwatch.org/newsroom/view_news.php?id=1943> (accessed on 13 September 2010).

[46] Constitutional Court of Colombia, *Case SU-039/07*, Derechos Fundamentales de Comunidad Indígena, at: <http://www.corteconstitucional.gov.co/relatoria/1997/SU039-97.htm> (accessed on 13 February 2013), consideración 3.2.

legitimacy has to be assessed in terms of the common good of the Colombian collective and its claim to a shared territory. Theirs is another claim to commonality altogether, as shown by an extraordinary document entitled 'Letter of the U'wa to the white man':

> We were born as children of the earth... That cannot be changed either by Indians or by the white man (*riowa*). More than a thousand times and in a thousand different ways we have said to you that the earth is our mother, that we cannot nor want to sell her, but the white man does not seem to have understood... We ask ourselves: is it the white man's custom to sell his mother?[47]

This is no rhetorical question. The U'wa understand themselves—and the white man—as an integral part of a living whole, in which 'every living being has blood: every tree, every plant, every animal, the earth itself, and this blood of the earth (*ruira*, petroleum) is what gives power to all of us, plants, animals, and men'. But whereas the U'wa seek to live attached to mother earth, the white man has become estranged from her, declaring war on everything except his own internal barrenness. Against the white man's self-betrayal, the U'wa remind him that:

> The universe is of Sira and we the U'wa only administer it; we are merely a yarn of the rounded fabric of the *irokua* (a 'backpack'), whereas the weaver is He. That is why we the U'wa cannot transfer, mistreat or sell the land or its blood, nor its creatures, because these are not the beginning of the fabric.[48]

Accordingly, the referent of 'we' in the document's first sentence, 'We were born as children of the earth...', is not only the U'wa; nor is it only the U'wa and the white man: it is *all* living beings. The U'wa refuse to participate in negotiations concerning a construction contract because the claim to commonality they invoke is inimical to the harmonization of interests of all living beings within a process of collective decision-making about a construction project. Spatially speaking, what the U'wa reject outright is the alleged commonality of negotiations premised on the disclosure of places as construction sites. Is, then, what renders a construction site an ought-place, in terms of *lex constructionis*, also what allows this place to be an ought-place in the ancestral lands of the U'wa?

In the course of their resistance, the U'wa have occupied some of the oil drilling sites, blocked roads leading to these sites, and travelled to New York and Washington, urging US investors, such as JP Morgan, not to purchase shares of Ecopetrol.[49] Now, the journey of an U'wa delegation that travels to Bogotá or to New York is not simply the same journey that government or oil company delegations would undertake when travelling to the lands of the U'wa, albeit

[47] 'Carta de los U'wa al hombre blanco': <http://www.nodo50.org/tortuga/Carta-de-los-U-WA-al-hombre-blanco> (accessed on 13 February 2013). For an anthropological study of the U'wa, see Ann Osborn, *The Four Seasons of the U'wa: A Chibcha Ritual Ecology in the Colombian Andes* (Wantage: Sean Kingston Publishing, 2009).

[48] 'Carta de los U'wa al hombre blanco'.

[49] 'Colombian U'wa indigenous leaders to visit US, urging investors and US Congress to respect human rights', posted on 21 November 2008 at: <http://www.bilaterals.org/spip.php?article13824> (accessed on 13 February 2013).

in the opposite direction. In a very real sense, the U'wa never entirely arrive in the places where their interlocutors are located, nor would their interlocutors entirely arrive in the lands of the U'wa, if they were prepared to undertake such a journey. At one point, the U'wa note in their 'Letter to the white man' that it is not merely their land which is sacred: the *whole* world is sacred, including the places where the offices of Ecopetrol in Bogotá, and of JP Morgan in New York, are located: 'our law is . . . the law of the earth, and the earth is one and only one. . .'. Is not a comparable claim raised by *lex constructionis* as a form of *global* law, such that a construction site in Colombia can only appear as such because it is emplaced in a spatial whole wherein there is also a place for offices of Ecopetrol in Bogotá, of JP Morgan in New York, and for the seat of, say, arbitration proceedings by the International Court of Arbitration if it were necessary to settle a dispute between the contracting parties? The journeys by the U'wa emissaries, on the one hand, and Ecopetrol or JP Morgan officials, on the other, speak to a *double asymmetry*, not to the reciprocity between two correlative ought-places such that although we are here, and you there, we can take up your place, and you ours.

Whence do the U'wa enter the oil drilling sites and these other places? From outside. Their boundary crossings into the drilling sites attest to a *limit* between a familiar unity of ought-places and a strange outside, to an ought-place that has no place in the kinds of ought-places made available by *lex constructionis*, yet which raises a normative claim of its own. The anguished question the U'wa address to the white man—'Who is the savage?'[50]—shows that *lex constructionis*, like all manifestations of *lex mercatoria*, brings about a spatial closure in which an inside is preferred to an outside. Ursula Stein's reference to the '*internal* legal order of private international associations' should be taken literally.[51] Indeed, by breaking down the fences that enclosed the drilling sight, the U'wa breached a legal boundary and also transgressed it, revealing it as a limit between a unity of ought-places and a strange outside.

An afterthought: Teubner is certainly right, on one level, to argue that *lex constructionis*, as all *lex mercatoria*, emerges and develops at a considerable distance from both state law and international public law. On a deeper level, however, and returning to our earlier considerations about frontiers, I wonder whether there is not a more intimate link between international law and *lex constructionis* than what meets the eye from a systems-theoretical perspective. For if the resistance of the U'wa to oil drilling in their lands is part and parcel of a struggle that began with the colonization of their ancestral lands, then the fences that cordon off construction sites are the frontier between this specific site of a global *lex constructionis* and U'wa land, and also one of the myriad frontiers between the ought-places of international law—states—and the ought-places of indigenous laws. To the extent that the FIDIC's standard contract refers to the 'country' or 'countries' in which construction sites are located, the globality of *lex constructionis* has its condition of possibility in the colonization instrumental to the emergence of international law with a planetary reach.

[50] 'Carta de los U'wa al hombre blanco'.

[51] Stein, *Lex Mercatoria*, 46 (emphasis added).

Notice that the recognition by international public law of rights to 'internal' self-determination by indigenous peoples in no way blunts or accommodates the radical questioning of the boundaries of international public law. To the contrary: by refusing to participate in the harmonization of interests required by Article 330 of the Colombian Constitution, the U'wa deny that theirs is a right to indigenous self-determination within—and as part of—the Colombian state. By granting the U'wa a right to self-determination within the Colombian state, international law is, from their point of view, an instrument of domination. A right to 'internal' self-determination is literally internal to international law. In this strong sense, the U'wa enter the construction sites of Ecopetrol from a place that is outside of international law and outside of *lex constructionis*. In the same way that foreign places need not be strange, as shown by construction sites scattered throughout the face of the earth, so also strange places need not be foreign, as shown by the occupation of construction sites by the U'wa.

And for this reason also, returning to a point made earlier, the encounter between *lex constructionis* and the U'wa legal order is not one between a 'global' perspective and a 'local' perspective encompassed by the former: it is a *lateral* encounter. In fact, the challenge raised by the U'wa does not only involve classical international law and *lex constructionis*; it also calls into question Jeremy Waldron's interpretation of *ius gentium*, which he describes as the body of positive law that, surpassing the particularities of different nations, is common to all mankind. More precisely, it is that body of universal principles that '[regulates] relations within states particularly between citizen and government but also sometimes between private individuals'.[52] One of those universal principles is, in his view, the principle of due process. Significantly, the judgment handed down by the Colombian Supreme Court hewed scrupulously to the principle of due process: it struck down the administrative act granting the drilling rights because the interests of the U'wa had not been properly taken into account in the harmonization of interests stipulated by Article 330 of the Colombian Constitution. But this is precisely the problem: because invoking the principle of due process involved taking for granted that the U'wa are members of the Colombian collective, its application required that the Constitutional Court remain deaf to the fundamental nature of their claim: that the U'wa are a distinct group that has been forcibly integrated into the Colombian collective. Precisely because the principle of due process regulates 'relations within states particularly between citizen and government', and more generally between the government and those who are subject to the state, the application of the principle of due process to the U'wa consolidates this forcible integration in the very act of striking down the oil drilling permit, and renders invisible what is excluded from *ius gentium* in the case at hand. *Ius gentium* has an outside. As we shall see in chapter 7, analogous considerations hold for human rights, which Waldron takes to be the hard core of *ius gentium*'s allegedly universal content.

[52] Jeremy Waldron, *'Partly Laws Common to All Mankind': Foreign Law in American Courts* (New Haven, CT: Yale University Press, 2012), 28.

2.5 THE LAW OF CYBERSPACE

The different legal orders we have discussed are permutations of legal space as a concrete space of action, in which boundary crossings are events at once physical and normative. The emergence of the Internet seems to throw this view of law into profound disarray. Because it appears to sever the link between 'legally significant (online) phenomena and physical location', cyberspace would require a novel form of law and legal institutions, one that does not rely on the physical boundaries of real space.[53] Indeed,

> we know that the activities that have traditionally been the subject of regulation must still be engaged in by real people who are, after all, at distinct physical locations. But the interactions of these people now somehow transcend those physical locations. The Net enables forms of interaction in which the shipment of tangible items across geographical boundaries is irrelevant and in which the location of the participants does not matter. Efforts to determine 'where' the events in question occur are decidedly misguided, if not altogether futile.[54]

Does it make sense to continue insisting that, despite the emergence of cyberspace, all legal orders perforce regulate behaviour by determining who ought to do what, when, and *where*? Would not cyberlaw, even if still more or less incipient, mark a decisive threshold in the emancipation of law from space and spatial boundaries, to the extent that information available on the Net is simultaneously available to anybody with an Internet connection, regardless of where that person is located? In the same vein, does not cyberlaw clinch the demise of the spatial distinction between inside and outside as a constitutive feature of legal order?

The objection mounted by Johnson, Post, and others against territorially defined rules for cyberspace is, to begin with, technological in character: 'messages can be transmitted from one physical location to another location without degradation, decay, or substantial delay, and without any physical cues or barriers that might otherwise keep certain geographically remote places and people separate from one another'.[55] In any case, it quickly became apparent that technological developments had given the lie to the apparent recalcitrance of the Internet to legal regulation. Lawrence Lessig has noted that the regulability of behaviour requires knowing 'who did what, where', a formulation that echoes the personal, material, and spatial spheres of validity of legal norms.[56] The architecture of the Net indeed made it initially very difficult to regulate these three aspects of behaviour on the Net. But eleven years after the article by Johnson and Post, architectures of personal identification and authentication, of content control, and of geographical tracing and zoning had been put into place that

[53] David R. Johnson and David Post, 'Law and Borders—The Rise of Law in Cyberspace', *Stanford Law Review* 48 (1995), 1370.

[54] Johnson and Post, 'Law and Borders', 1378.

[55] Johnson and Post, 'Law and Borders', 1370.

[56] Lawrence Lessig, *Code: Version 2.0* (New York: Perseus Books Group, 2006), 38 ff.

allowed state law to re-establish its regulatory purchase on Internet activities.[57] The well-known lawsuit filed in France against Yahoo!, in which the plaintiffs demanded that Yahoo! remove Nazi paraphernalia from its auction site or block access thereto, is a good example of how legal orders set spatial boundaries to Internet activities. Although the corporation argued that the Internet is a global medium, and that it could not block French citizens from Yahoo! sites, the French court not only decided in favour of the plaintiffs but eventually also threatened the company with a fine of 100,000 French francs for each day of delay in complying with its ruling. Soon after, Yahoo! had installed filters that block computers located in France from access to the auction site.[58] In short, the Net has become eminently regulable. Yet more forcefully, Lessig and others argue, the emergence of 'code'—the software and hardware that structure cyberspace—may well make the Net almost perfectly controllable because, although one can disobey the law, which sanctions disobedience *ex post*, 'code' limits behaviour *ex ante* in ways that are very difficult to elude.[59] As a raft of issues ranging from freedom of speech to privacy and intellectual property have made clear, cyberspace has become a new domain in which legal orders, state legal orders in particular, regulate who ought to do what, where, and when, that is, posit personal, material, spatial, and temporal boundaries to activities that use the Internet. The reason for this success lies, ultimately, in what Johnson and Post themselves have to say about cyberlaw: 'the activities that have traditionally been the subject of regulation must still be engaged in by real people who are, after all, at distinct physical locations'.[60]

Johnson, Post, and others also mount an argument about legitimacy against the localization of cyberlaw: 'There is no geographically localized set of constituents with a stronger and more legitimate claim to regulate [the Net] than any other local group. The strongest claim to control comes from the participants themselves, and these could be anywhere'.[61] The argument they invoke is a democratic argument: self-regulation by the community of internet users and service providers should be the criterion of legitimacy of cyberlaw, not regulation by the territorial communities of nation-states.

While cyberlaw raises a number of urgent political issues, my sole question at this moment concerns the problem of spatial boundaries. Imagine that states had not sought to bring cyberspace under control, and that the global community of internet providers and users were able to regulate cyberspace on its own,

[57] 'The architecture of cyberspace will in principle allow for perfect zoning—a way perfectly to exclude those who would cross boundaries'. Lawrence Lessig, 'The Zones of Cyberspace', *Stanford Law Review* 48 (1996), 1409.

[58] 'Ligue contre le racisme et l'antisémitisme et Union des étudiants juifs de France c. Yahoo! Inc. et Société Yahoo! France'. The ruling is available at: <http://www.lapres.net/yahfr.html> (accessed on 13 February 2013).

[59] See Lessig, *Code*, 38 ff. See also Joel R. Reidenberg, 'Lex Informatica: The Formulation of Information Policy Rules through Technology', *Texas Law Review* 76, no. 3 (1998), 553–593; Joel R. Reidenberg, 'Technology and Internet Jurisdiction', *Pennsylvania Law Review* 153 (2005), 1951; Milton Mueller, *Ruling the Root: Internet Governance and the Taming of Cyberspace* (Cambridge, MA: The MIT Press, 2002).

[60] See Johnson and Post, 'Law and Borders', n. 54.

[61] Johnson and Post, 'Law and Borders', 1375.

presumably in an institutional setting quite different to the Internet Corporation for Assigned Names and Numbers (ICANN). Suppose, furthermore, that the inception of cyberlaw was marked by a 'Declaration of Independence for Cyberspace' like that penned by John Perry Barlow: 'Governments of the Industrial World, you weary giants of flesh and steel, I come from Cyberspace, the new home of Mind. On behalf of the future, I ask you of the past to leave us alone. You are not welcome among us. You have no sovereignty where we gather'.[62] In short, imagine the most favourable constellation possible for the (private) self-regulation of the Internet community. The question that arises is whether the cyberlaw that were to emerge from this self-regulatory activity would no longer have an outside, by dint of its global reach.

Let us begin with the final sentence of the passage cited from Barrow's exuberant Declaration, turning it into a question: *where do we gather?* Where do we gather when, bidding farewell to state sovereignty, we enact and follow cyberlaw? The Declaration has a ready answer: we gather in cyberspace, which 'is a world that is both everywhere and nowhere'. And it adds shortly thereafter: 'we are creating a world where *anyone, anywhere* may express his or her beliefs, no matter how singular, without fear of being coerced into silence or conformity' (emphasis added). So, despite the drastic claim that cyberspace is not the world 'where bodies live', what is concretely at stake in the construction of cyberspace is, amongst other things, fostering and protecting its potential to secure free speech for embodied beings who are dispersed across the face of the earth, and who must type or speak somewhere if they are to gain access to the global cyber-community, and who must glance somewhere at a computer screen or listen somewhere to what someone is typing or saying somewhere. Moreover, the 'we' of the cyber-community is, in Barrow's reading, potentially everyone; not, however, as an aggregation of individuals but rather as a *whole*, as a collective that acts jointly, such that it is possible to mock state governments because 'you do not know *our* culture, *our* ethics, or the unwritten codes that already provide *our* society more order than could be obtained by any of your impositions' (emphasis added). In short, and returning to the question, 'where do we gather?', it would seem that 'where' is everywhere, and 'we', everyone. On the face of it, cyberlaw is—or at least can be—a magnificent illustration of what Kelsen had to say about norms, namely that their spatial and personal validity is unlimited when they 'refer to events wherever . . . it is possible for them to occur' and when they are 'addressed to absolutely all human beings'.[63] So, although technological developments have allowed states to capture cyberlaw, setting spatial and temporal boundaries to cyberspace, it remains the case that, given its capacity to refer to everyone, everywhere, given its indifference to place and person, cyberlaw is the exemplar, at least in principle, of an all-inclusive legal order—or so it seems.

This preliminary examination of the question 'where do we gather?' seeks to show that cyberlaw would require a reference to the first-person plural perspective

[62] John Perry Barlow, 'A Declaration of the Independence of Cyberspace', available at: <https://projects.eff.org/~barlow/Declaration-Final.html> (accessed on 13 February 2013).

[63] Kelsen, *Problems of Legal Theory*, 12–13.

of a 'we', on whose behalf legal norms are enacted. It also shows that this reference also implies a reference to a normative point of cyberlaw; in the example, I focused on freedom of speech, which Barrow and many others are anxious to shield from state regulation, as happened in the *Yahoo!* ruling. Johnson and Post, in particular, have stoutly defended what they call a ' "meta-interest" of Net citizens in preserving the global free flow of information', provided that this flow is 'unrelated to vital and localized interests of a territorial government'.[64] This proviso gives away too much, however, on at least two counts: first, the obvious state response would be that *Yahoo!* and similar cases fall within the sphere of public order, and therefore are warranted; second, state assessments of public order would trump the principle of the free flow of information on the Internet, which would thereby become a residual principle, ever vulnerable to further restriction. The only way of preserving this 'meta-interest' would be that Net citizens themselves, through self-regulation, establish which limitations would be authorized to free speech on the Internet. But this would not absolve the Internet community of having to address the problem of what counts as legitimate limitations to the exercise of free speech in cyberspace. Could the normative point of cyberlaw avoid having to include and exclude possible forms of behaviour? In the same vein, would the exercise of free speech in cyberspace cease to be located, even if state interests no longer play a role therein?

Consider the *Jyllands-Posten* Muhammad cartoons controversy in September 2005.[65] This controversy casts doubt, to say the least, on the assumption that agreement could be reached by the global community of Internet users and service providers on access to cartoons of the prophet Muhammad, or even of images of him or, for that matter, of any other prophet. It also calls attention to the question on behalf of whom, where, Barrow speaks when asserting that 'we are creating a world where anyone, anywhere may express his or her beliefs, no matter how singular, without fear of being coerced into silence or conformity'. Now that the *Yahoo!* case has blazed the way, it is tempting to muster technology to the rescue, implementing filters such that persons can be shielded from having to view images of the prophet Muhammad, thereby also allowing those who are less punctilious to view them if they so wish. The Wikipedia entry on the controversy, for example, used to offer helpful instructions on how to modify the user's default browser settings to avoid having to look at images of the prophet Muhammad on the encyclopaedia.[66] But would this solve the problem that the images have been *posted* on the Internet, including the web-pages of the aniconism-friendly Wikipedia? In the case of groups and individuals for whom aniconism is law, the real problem is not to ensure, by the appropriate

[64] Johnson and Post, 'Law and Borders', 1394.

[65] A good overview of the debate and a wealth of background material is available in the apposite Wikipedia entry: <http://en.wikipedia.org/wiki/Jyllands-Posten_Muhammad_cartoons_controversy#cite_note-4> (accessed on 13 February 2013).

[66] 'If you have an account or want to create one, you can change your personal settings so that you don't have to see Muhammad images, without affecting other users. This is done by modifying your CSS (Cascading Style Sheet) page, which is individual to each user. To do this . . .'. See to this effect: <http://en.wikipedia.org/wiki/Template:Muhammad-FAQ-Images> (accessed on 2 September 2010).

technological means, that people need not be confronted with images of the prophet; it is rather that these images are posted on the Net *at all*, the more so because 'information available on the World Wide Web is available simultaneously to anyone with a connection to the global network'.[67] The global reach of cyberspace becomes the global reach of blasphemy and unbearable affront. The assumption that cyberspace allows freedom of speech to 'anyone, anywhere' because it is indifferent to place and person amounts to a *de*-localization, i.e. the denial and erasure of the limited spatial configuration of a religious law, and a novel *localization*, namely, the configuration of a secularized legal space that is spatially limited because images of the prophet can be shown anywhere rather than nowhere.[68]

A play on words? On 1 January 2010 a Somali man 'armed with an axe and a knife in either hand', or so the Danish police claimed, broke down the entrance door of Kurt Westergaard's home in Aarhus and attempted to kill the cartoonist, whose drawing lampooning the prophet in the *Jyllands-Posten* had given rise to the controversy. The Somali allegedly belonged to the al-Shabab militia. *Where* did the man come from when entering Westergaard's home? A BBC news bulletin quotes Sheikh Ali Muhammad Rage, a spokesperson for the group, as saying: 'We appreciate the incident in which a Muslim Somali boy attacked the devil who abused our prophet Mohammed and we call upon all Muslims around the world to target the people like him'.[69] When the Somali man broke down the door with an axe and stepped in, he entered Westergaard's home from one of the places 'around the world' to which the spokesperson refers. This is not simply the same world which Barrow calls 'our world'. It may be asked, furthermore, whether the man's boundary crossing is merely illegal, or whether he was not also entering from a place outside of the world inhabited by Westergaard: a strange place that is not simply 'anywhere', as Barrow puts it, but *else*where—in a strange world. The Somali man breached a legal boundary and also transgressed it, showing it to be a limit that joins and separates a unity of ought-places and a strange outside.

Where, then, do we gather when enacting and following cyberlaw? Somewhere.

2.6 OVERLAPPING LEGAL ORDERS

A final step we must take in assessing the generality of the topography of legal order introduced in chapter 1 is to establish whether it is capable of explaining the notion of 'overlapping' legal orders. This notion plays a crucial role in all contemporary moves to censure the assimilation of law to state law. These censures point out that the claim to exclusive territoriality deployed by nation-states

[67] Johnson and Post, 'Law and Borders', 1375.

[68] This analysis bears, of course, on the alleged universality of human rights law: can it be taken for granted that human rights law has an inside but no outside, as its '*erga omnes*' claim seems to suggest? We will examine this and related issues pertaining to human rights law in chapter 7.

[69] BBC News, 'Somali charged over attack on Danish cartoonist', 2 January 2010, at: <http://news.bbc.co.uk/2/hi/europe/8437652.stm> (accessed on 13 February 2013).

is historically contingent. If there were at least three different and partially competing normative orders—feudalism, church, and empire—in the Middle Ages, our contemporary global setting shows even greater legal pluralism. On the one hand, there is a host of novel legal orders which overlap with state law and with each other. Some of these legal orders are functionally driven, e.g. the World Trade Organization, the Internet Corporation of Assigned Names and Numbers, the Fédération Internationale de Football Association, and the International Organization for Standardization; others are regional, such as the European Union, the South African Development Community, the Association of Southeast Asian Nations and Mercosur. On the other hand, and no less importantly, there are a manifold of overlapping legal orders that have been around a long time, often predating the nation-state, yet which only now are again recognized as putative legal orders irreducible to state law. These include, on Twining's reading, some forms of religious law, such as Islamic, Hindu, and Jewish law; the laws of subordinated peoples, such as the law of indigenous peoples throughout the world and Romani law; and 'illegal legal orders', such as the law of squatter settlements or legal orders set up by insurgent movements in contemporary states.[70]

A typology of overlapping legal order need not concern us here; what is at stake is the phenomenon itself. For, despite its ubiquity in the literature about medieval and global law, it is striking how little attention has been granted to actually making concrete spatial sense of the term 'overlap' as it pertains to legal orders. It remains, by and large, an emblematic metaphor that has eluded theoretical scrutiny. Theories of legal pluralism satisfy themselves with variations on the idea that overlap speaks to the co-existence of legal orders in a 'given spatio-temporal context'.[71] The question that presents itself to our attention is, therefore, what modality of legal space this metaphor seeks to articulate, and whether the topography of legal order deployed in chapter 1 is sufficiently general to explain 'overlap' between legal orders, regardless of their specific spatial configurations.

The key to addressing this question is the *concreteness* of legal space as a normative space of action. By this I mean that the unity of legal space involves two correlative dimensions. The first is normative, and concerns a claim about the normative point with regard to which a manifold of individuals can view themselves as the members of a polity participating in joint action under law. The claim to commonality associated to this normative point is circumscribed. Indeed, the notion of a 'point' captures the idea that commonality arises through a selection that grants legal protection to what is deemed to be relevant and important to a community, or, to use

[70] Twining, *General Jurisprudence*, 70.

[71] Twining, for example, refers to legal pluralism as 'the co-existence of discrete and semi-autonomous legal orders in the same time-space context'; Tamanaha, for his part, refers to legal pluralism as a state that 'exists whenever more than one kind of "law" is recognized through the social practices of a group in a given social arena...'. See Twining, *General Jurisprudence*, ch. 16, 25 (online at: <http://www.cambridge.org/gb/knowledge/isbn/item2427672/?site_locale=en_GB)> (accessed on 18 June 2013) and Brian Tamanaha, *A General Jurisprudence of Law and Society* (Oxford: Oxford University Press, 2001), 194. De Sousa Santos extends this definition to include the 'co-existence' of supra-state, global legal orders with state and infrastate legal orders. See de Sousa Santos, *Toward a New Legal Common Sense*, 92.

historically more recent categories, the common interests and values of a collective, thereby discarding other possible determinations of the normative point as legally irrelevant and unimportant. The second dimension is physical, insofar as the legal order's normative point obtains a spatial insertion by means of boundaries that partition space into a distribution of ought-places. Legal boundaries articulate these two dimensions of legal space: different normative points are spatially articulated in distinct ways of differentiating and interconnecting ought-places. This explains, on the one hand, why boundary-crossings are normative no less than physical events, and, on the other, why boundaries may change, becoming more or less 'porous', even though their physical positioning does not budge an inch. In short, a legal space is never only a geographical surface, never only the material support of one or more legal systems, but rather a concrete articulation of normative and physical dimensions from the first-person plural perspective of a 'we'.

The concreteness of legal space explains, to begin with, why a legal space need not be geographically continuous. Kelsen had already made this point with respect to state law: 'it is essential', he asserts, 'that *one* state also have *one* territory, that the territory of a state form a unity'.[72] But, clearly, it will not do to reduce the unity claimed for the territory of a state or for any other legal order to geographical unity, as some authors have been wont to do. For example, Patrick Twomey has noted that 'the EU is paradoxically not "European" in so far as it encompasses overseas territories. Problematic examples include Spain's Moorish city fortresses of Ceuta and Melilla in North Africa, recently corralled inside "Europe" by newly erected Schengen fences'.[73] This insight then becomes the stepping stone for a criticism of EU legislation that, appealing to the spurious geographical unity of Europe, excludes third-country nationals from rights assigned to citizens of the European Union. Europe is undoubtedly a specious geographical unity; but the point is moot: the spatial unity of law is irreducible to the unity of geographical space (whatever that might mean). By implication, if the spatial unity of law is no more than putative, this is for reasons other than the absence of geographical continuity. As Kelsen trenchantly puts it, 'the unity of a state territory . . . is by no means a natural, geographical unity'.[74] He adds that '[s]ometimes, to one and the same State territory belong parts of space which are not physically contiguous . . . To the territory of a State belong its colonies . . . and also so-called "enclosures" that are completely surrounded by the territory of another State'.[75]

[72] Hans Kelsen, *Allgemeine Staatslehre*, repr. (Vienna: Östereichische Staatsdruckerei, 1993), 138. See also Hans Kelsen, *Das Problem der Souveränität und die Theorie des Völkerrechts. Beitrag zu einer reinen Rechtslehre*, 2nd edn. (Aalen: Scientia Verlag, 1981), 74–75.

[73] Patrick Twomey, 'Constructing a Secure Space: The Area of Freedom, Security and Justice', in David O'Keeffe and Patrick Twomey (eds.), *Legal Issues of the Amsterdam Treaty* (Oxford: Hart, 1999), 352. In a similar vein, Jan Broekman has observed that Europe is not a geographical unity that could serve as the basis for the legal space of the European Union. See Jan M. Broekman, *A Philosophy of European Union Law* (Louvain: Peeters, 1999).

[74] Kelsen, *Allgemeine Staatslehre*, 138. See also Kelsen, *Das Problem der Souveränität und die Theorie des Völkerrechts*, 74–75.

[75] Kelsen, *General Theory of Law and State*, repr. (New Brunswick, NJ: Transaction Publishers, 2007), 208. Kelsen does not succeed, however, in explaining the unity of legal space. See on this issue my paper

Ceuta and Melilla, as parts of the territory of Spain, are cases in point. While it must be possible to move from one ought-place to another if there is to be a legal space, its unity does not depend on geographical continuity but rather on a normative point that allows of linking together a number of ought-places into a single legal space from the first-person plural perspective of a 'we'. The scope of this argument is by no means limited to the state; it holds for *all* legal orders, including a variety of 'overlapping' legal orders that display a considerable measure of geographical discontinuity. For example, Sassen notes that the medieval church was organized as a 'network of ecclesia or bishoprics and in a strong hierarchy headed by Rome'.[76] The aforementioned structure of a legal space allowed this spatial network to function as such even though there might be geographical discontinuities between the ecclesia or bishoprics that made up the church's jurisdiction.

Turning now to 'overlapping' legal orders, the concreteness of legal space reveals that the metaphor gets things right and wrong. What it gets right is that a physical dimension is a constitutive feature of any conceivable legal space, and that any number of legal spaces can share a given physical space. But the metaphor gets at least two things wrong. First, even if distinct legal orders cover exactly the same geographical extension, human behaviour that is relevant to any one of these orders, in terms of the normative point that governs its spatial configuration, might be entirely irrelevant to the other(s). Accordingly, the account of legal order outlined in chapter 1 suggests that, depending on their respective normative points, it is possible that someone or something enters or exits one of these 'overlapping' legal orders *without entering or leaving the other order(s)*. Second, the metaphor is misleading because it suggests a 'layered' structure of legal spaces, such that one is the lowest 'layer' upon which one or more other legal orders are 'superimposed'. Here again, the notion of layered or superimposed legal orders takes for granted that the space of law is a geographical surface, rather than a concrete normative space of action that is at once normative and physical. To insist on the crucial insight, what the metaphor of 'overlap' in law seeks to articulate is that different collectives with different views of what defines them as legal spaces can nonetheless share all or part of a geographical extension. The legal topography unveiled in chapter 1 easily accommodates this situation, no less than the case of 'exclusive' territoriality proper to the nation-state. Indeed, it shows that the mutually exclusive territoriality of states is but an extreme case of a broader spectrum of possibilities covered by the limited spatiality of legal orders, which includes not only the functional and regional legal orders that emerge with the uncoupling of law and state, but also the legal orders of religious communities, subordinate indigenous peoples, and even 'illegal' legal orders, such as Pasagarda, the fictitious name of a squatter community (*favela*) of Rio de Janeiro described by de Sousa Santos.[77]

'Inside and Outside the EU's Area of Freedom, Security and Justice: Reflexive Identity and the Unity of Legal Space', *Archiv für Rechts- und Sozialphilosophie* 90 (2004), 478–497.

[76] Sassen, *Territory · Authority · Rights*, 38.

[77] De Sousa Santos, *Toward a New Legal Common Sense*, 99 ff.

These considerations are borne out by the 'overlapping' legal orders that have emerged in the contemporary global setting. In effect, the crux of the uncoupling of law and state is the differentiation and multiplication of the normative points and first-person plural perspectives governing the configuration of legal orders as concrete spaces of action. Accordingly, the emergence of 'overlapping' legal orders, many of which are functionally driven, is internally linked to the differentiation of their content, that is, to the parsing of their boundaries.

A good example of this is the EU and its Members States. According to Article 1 of the Treaty on European Union (TEU), 'By this Treaty, the High Contracting parties establish among themselves a European Union, hereinafter called "the Union", on which the Member States confer competences to attain objectives they have in common'. Although Article 1 is formulated in the third-person plural perspective, the enactment of the Union takes place from the *first-person* plural perspective. The reason for this is as simple as it is decisive: in the absence of this perspective, the agreement contained in the Treaty would be inconceivable. To agree is to commit *ourselves* to act together. Accordingly, the canonical formulation of Article 1 TEU is the following: 'By this Treaty, *we*, the High Contracting Parties, establish among *ourselves* a European Union . . .'. Moreover, by referring to the 'common objectives' pursued by the Member States, Article 1 anticipates the normative point of the EU, which is spelled out more fully—albeit not exclusively—in Article 3 TEU. I single out part of Section 3 of Article 3 TEU for further consideration:

> 3. The Union shall establish an internal market. It shall work for the sustainable development of Europe based on balanced economic growth and price stability, a highly competitive social market economy, aiming at full employment and social progress, and a high level of protection and improvement of the quality of the environment . . .

Article 3(3) illustrates very well, I think, the correlation between the normative point of joint action under law and the concreteness of legal space. It shows that economic integration is the central—but by no means exclusive—normative point of the EU. Indeed, notions such as 'sustainable development', 'balanced economic growth', and 'social progress' provide normative orientation for economic integration. Moreover, this normative point obtains spatial configuration in the form of an internal market. Regardless of the doctrinal discussion about the distinction between an 'internal' and a 'common' market, the European internal market clearly involves a claim to commonality: to a common market, such that the point of economic integration—what it is *about*—requires calibrating the external borders of the market, and the internal boundaries between the Member States, in such a way that boundary crossings of persons, goods, services, and capital promote 'balanced economic growth', a 'highly competitive social market economy' and the like in the *whole* EU.[78] See here the articulation of normative and physical dimensions in the absence of which the internal market

[78] The opposite also holds, of course: calibrating boundaries involves calibrating the normative point of a legal practice. We will return to this in Part II.

could not be a legal space. Accordingly, participation in and regulation of the internal market involve taking up a first-person plural perspective whence the Member States appear as a differentiated interconnection of ought-places that make up a common—single—legal space.

Each of the Member States retains, however, a first-person plural perspective which is irreducible to the first-person plural perspective made available by the normative point of the EU, not least because the EU is governed by the principle of the specific attribution of competences, as intimated in Article 1 TEU. The legal space of each of the Member States is more than an ought-place within the distribution of places that constitutes the EU as a legal space: the Member States are spatial unities in their own right, which means that they differentiate and interconnect ought-places in light of their own normative points, which they deem to be partially complementary to but distinct from the normative point of the EU. Here again, the EU and its Member States illustrate the basic structure of 'overlapping' legal orders: while two or more legal orders share a given geographical surface, they are different legal spaces because they differentiate and interconnect ought-places from different first-person plural perspectives, and in view of different normative points.

2.7 THE TOPOGRAPHY OF LEGAL SPACE REVISITED

The survey of a variety of legal orders in the course of this chapter sought to test the generality of the topography outlined in chapter 1. Granted, the range of cases explored is relatively small. But it was by no means my aim to offer a comprehensive and exhaustive topology of law in a global setting. Instead, the potential counterexamples were selected because the literature on globalization continuously refers to these and similar cases as confirming that the inside/outside distinction has ceased to be a constitutive feature of legal order. My reconstruction of these cases gives the nay to this widespread view: no legal order is thinkable, or so I argue, absent a spatial closure. More generally, while I have sought to engage in detail with the empirical features of the spatial configuration of these legal orders, the crucial point I am trying to drive home in each case concerns the a priori features of the general topography of legal order. In effect, my argument, as illustrated by each of these cases, is, first, that no sense could be made of legal orders in the absence of a unity of ought-places and, second, that there can be no such unity absent a first-person plural preferential differentiation between inside and outside, where 'outside' has the strong sense of a strange ought-place.

Crucially, the reference to an outside here is not merely 'figurative' or 'metaphorical'. It is tempting to assert that only when we refer, say, to someone stepping in or out of a home, or entering or leaving a state, are we using the inside/outside distinction in its real or literal sense. By contrast, the reference to a strange place as being 'outside' would be simply metaphorical. But we should be very chary of this objection, for it misses altogether the implication of the foregoing analyses: as in all spaces of action, we could not make sense of inside and outside in any given legal order, such that we can speak of someone entering or leaving a courthouse, or entering or leaving a state, unless the more fundamental distinction has already been drawn between what counts as a collective's own space and what lies beyond it, in the form of strange places. Only on the basis of this more fundamental distinction is it at all possible to refer to inside and outside as places that are part of a single (legal) space. To reserve the inside/outside contrast for the latter kind of situation, denying it to the former, is to lose sight of the conditions of possibility under which it is at all possible to understand the distinction between inside and outside as 'literal' or 'real'.

Moreover, I readily grant that I have not discussed the determinability or even 'accuracy' of boundaries, when making the case for the inside/outside distinction. Twining observes that 'while most national legal systems have relatively clear territorial boundaries, this is not the case with many other normative and non-state legal orders'. He is surely right, in some sense. But we cannot be satisfied with a metaphorical description of these other kinds of legal orders as 'more like waves or clouds than hard objects such as rocks or billiard balls'.[79] Nor does it suffice to assert that 'we often have to talk *as if* a legal order is a stable, integrated, discrete unit in much the same way as cartographers represent streams, fields, marshes or cities using discrete symbols, which may suggest that their boundaries are more precise and fixed than they really are'.[80] What would be required is a conceptual framework capable of explaining different ways of determining boundaries and the kinds and levels of 'precision' and 'fixity' they enjoin. I cannot develop such a conceptual framework within the confines of this book. It must suffice here to observe that different kinds of legal practices require different ways of drawing (spatial) boundaries, which have the kind and level of precision required by the normative point of the apposite practice. This is why, for example, even within state law there are sharply demarcated spatial boundaries and other, more or less fuzzy boundary zones and borderlands. Importantly, there is no single scale going from precise to imprecise boundaries that encompasses all legal orders. Twining's remark that states have clear territorial boundaries, whereas other legal orders do not, compares these different legal orders from the perspective of the criteria governing state borders. As such, his approach remains thoroughly state-centred. The point is, instead, that legal practices that are different in kind may call forth altogether different sorts of scales of preciseness and impreciseness of legal boundaries. Although state borders may be precise (or imprecise) according to cartographic criteria, these criteria may be hopelessly unsuitable for determining the spatial boundaries of another kind of legal collective in a sufficiently precise way. A nomadic group, for example, may need to establish what counts as its legal space and the conditions of entry by outsiders according to very different criteria. And what holds for spatial boundaries also holds a fortiori for the 'accuracy' of temporal, subjective, and material boundaries of legal orders.

[79] Twining, *General Jurisprudence*, 20.

[80] Twining, *General Jurisprudence*, 20.

In short, the topography of legal order I have been concerned to outline and test throughout this chapter seeks to clarify, with respect to space, how legal orders actualize what Ernst Cassirer described in passing as the fundamental and most general function of order, namely 'to limit the unlimited, to determine the relatively indeterminate'.[81] More succinctly, the task of order is 'to bound and bind together the boundless' (*das Unbegrenzte zu begrenzen und zu binden*...).[82] This remains, however, an extremely general formulation that does not concretely elucidate how legal orders, as normative orders, set boundaries to behaviour. If chapter 1 provides an initial characterization of how legal orders set spatial, temporal, subjective, and material boundaries to behaviour, this chapter has concentrated on spatial boundaries across a wide range of legal orders, showing how they can reveal themselves as marking the spatial limit of a legal order.

The upshot of our enquiry in this chapter is a general topography of legal order that, for the sake of clarity, can be parsed into the following set of interlocking propositions: (i) Legal orders regulate behaviour by way of a normative point that allows of differentiating and integrating a manifold of ought-places into a spatial unity. (ii) The spatial unity of legal orders involves a closure whereby an inside is preferred to an outside. (iii) The preferential differentiation between inside and outside is linked to a first-person plural perspective: by closing itself as an inside with respect to an outside, a community is deemed to lay claim to a space as its own, and vice versa. (iv) The reference to an 'own' space shows that the inside/outside distinction is ambiguous, as it can mean a domestic space in contrast to foreign spaces, and a familiar space in contrast to a strange space. (v) A strange space is intimated within a legal space by ought-places that have no place in a distribution of places deemed to be a collective's own space, and the realization of which interferes with the collective's spatial unity. (vi) The two modes of the inside/outside distinction are irreducible to each other: a strange place need not be foreign; a foreign place need not be strange. (vii) The spatial boundary between domestic and foreign spaces is contingent; the limit between own and strange places is constitutive of legal orders as spatial orders.

[81] Ernst Cassirer, *Symbol, Technik, Sprache* (Hamburg: Felix Meiner Verlag, 1985), 100.

[82] Cassirer, *Symbol, Technik, Sprache*, 100.

3

The Identity of Legal Collectives

Let us take stock. Chapter 1 suggests that the question whether spatial closure might be a necessary feature of legal orders should be addressed within the more general framework of an examination of the kinds of boundaries at work in the law: why and how are (spatial) boundaries constitutive features of law as a normative order? Building on the insight that legal norms establish who ought to do what, where, and when, it shows that the law, from the first-person perspective of those whose behaviour it regulates, appears as an order—as a unity—to the extent that it is limited in space, time, content, and subjectivity. Focusing on spatial boundaries, chapter 2 tests the generality of the topography of legal order outlined in chapter 1, confronting it with a number of potential counterexamples. Amongst others, it shows why three prime examples of 'global law'—multinationals, *lex mercatoria*, and cyberlaw—are spatially limited. The time is now ripe to gather together the findings of the previous chapters by sketching the contours of a general model of legal order as it pertains to boundaries and limits. The key to this general model, or so I will argue at some length, is collective identity and its contrasting terms. On the one hand, sameness and selfhood, *idem* and *ipse*, show why legal boundaries demand incorporating both poles of identity into a first-person plural concept of legal order. On the other, the contrasting concepts to identity as sameness and selfhood, namely plurality/difference and other than self, explain why each legal boundary is also, albeit latently, a limit of the apposite order. The remainder of the chapter tests and consolidates the findings of this first-person plural model of legal order.

3.1 INDIVIDUALITY AND IDENTITY

I noted at the outset of chapter 1 that the way in which contemporary legal and political theories approach the concept of law tends to block a study of the internal connection between boundaries and legal order. The difficulty, I suggested, arises from the fact that the question about legal order, *qua normative order*, has usually been approached as a question about the unity of a multiplicity of rules, principles, standards, or whatever. Moreover, the debate about the concept of legal order as a unity of norms is also pitched as a debate about the kind of normativity specific to law and, in particular, about the relation between law and morality. To the extent that the central problem of legal and political theory is formulated in this fashion, any systematic development of the question concerning the internal relation between boundaries/limits and legal order is pushed into the background. What shift in the nature of the question about legal order would allow us to examine this internal relation, without forfeiting the question about the normativity specific to law?

I take my cue from William Twining's important contribution to a general jurisprudence. According to Twining, there are three basic questions which guide jurisprudential enquiry:

> First, what counts as one normative order? (the problem of individuation). Second, how should we distinguish the legal and the non-legal in this or similar contexts (the problem of identification of the legal). Third, are there useful ways of categorising the candidates that have been identified for inclusion in this mapping exercise? (the classification of legal traditions, families, systems, and cultures).[1]

The second of these questions attracts the bulk of Twining's attention. Indeed, the concepts of law developed by a wide variety of legal philosophers are beholden, or so he argues, to the particular and highly contingent paradigm of municipal/international law. Not surprisingly, therefore, Twining has sought to generalize the concept of law developed by what he views as largely state-bound contributions to legal theory, paring it down to only those elements which allow of including the entire range of legal orders flourishing in contemporary society, while also excluding other kinds of normative order from that set. Notice, however, that by going down this path Twining reproduces the basic assumption of the theories he censures: the problem of legal order is primarily a problem concerning the criteria that allow of distinguishing between law and other kinds of normative order. While this question is certainly of considerable importance, the attempts to deal with it conceal the problem of the relation between boundaries/limits and legal order. How, then, could this problem be rendered accessible to a theory of law as a normative order? What reorientation is required, such that the problem of legal order can be posed as a problem about boundaries/limits?

Twining himself points the way, when, in the passage cited above, he notes that the question concerning the criteria that distinguish law from other normative orders does not exhaust a theoretical exploration of law in a global setting. Prior to the question about the 'identification of the legal', as he calls it, comes the question about the *individuation of the legal*. '[I]n law there are problems about individuating the *units* to be mapped... What counts as *one* system, order, tradition or other *unit*?'[2] Notice how the problem of unity surfaces discretely but unmistakably in this passage. Closer consideration shows that this is no isolated or coincidental reference to the problem of unity. Indeed, Twining notes with respect to his mapping of legal orders that 'all of the examples are of putative normative or legal *orders*—potential units to be mapped'.[3] And he reiterates this point, asserting that his overview of law in the world 'assumes that these are all sufficiently discrete units to be treated as normative, and possibly legal, orders'.[4] It is this assumption—no doubt legitimate as long as one focuses exclusively on the question concerning the criteria that distinguish law from other normative orders—which demands further investigation.

[1] Twining, *General Jurisprudence*, 73–74.

[2] Twining, *General Jurisprudence*, 67 (emphasis added).

[3] Twining, *General Jurisprudence*, 71.

[4] Twining, *General Jurisprudence*, 72.

Accordingly, I propose to shift attention to individuation as the issue which allows of illuminating the internal connection between boundaries/limits and the unity of legal order. Absent boundaries and limits, it would not be possible to individuate legal orders; absent individuation we could not begin to meaningfully speak of the central descriptive tropes of law in a global setting, such as 'legal pluralism', 'overlapping' legal orders, 'interlegality', 'boundary conflicts' between legal orders and 'scales' or 'levels' of law. In fact, absent individuation it would not even be possible to pick out and speak about any legal order at all. Remarkably, however, the individuation of legal orders, and the role of boundaries/limits in securing their individuality, is largely taken for granted by legal theory and legal sociology, as well as by sociologies of globalization.[5] This state of relative neglect needs to be redressed.

A brief reference to an important essay by Joseph Raz allows me to clarify and illustrate the nature of this shift. 'Laws are part of legal systems; a particular law is a law only if it is part of American law or French law or some other legal system'—so begins his essay, 'The Identity of Legal Systems'.[6] But what do legal theorists mean when they assert that laws form a legal system? In the face of persistent and never entirely satisfactory attempts to answer this question, he sets himself a more modest task: 'to clarify the nature of the problem of the unity of municipal legal systems'.[7] His preliminary and strategic move is to distinguish between the formal and material unity of legal orders. On Raz's reading, 'the material unity of a legal system consists in its distinctive characteristics; it depends on the content of its law and on the manner in which they are applied'. This is the more or less contingent, more or less particular subject matter of the legal doctrine and of legal sociology. By contrast, formal unity, which he also dubs the 'identity' of a legal system, 'is found in the criterion or set of criteria that determines which laws are part of the system and which are not'.[8] It is this latter problem, as he notes, which has attracted the attention of Austin, Hart, and Kelsen, and for good reason: 'a more or less clear concept of the identity of a legal system is presupposed by any investigation into its material unity'.[9] But there is still a preliminary difficulty which needs to be dealt with before the

[5] A good example of this is the concept of legal order advanced by de Sousa Santos in *Toward a New Legal Common Sense*. Whereas the debate about legal pluralism has concentrated hitherto on sub-state legal orders, we have now entered, in de Sousa Santos' opinion, a period of 'postmodern legal plurality', in which supra-state legal orders co-exist with state and sub-state legal orders. But what is a legal order, such that we can speak at all about a situation of legal *plurality*, postmodern or otherwise? 'I conceive law as a body of regularized procedures and normative standards that is considered justiciable—ie, susceptible of being enforced by a judicial authority—in a *given group* and contributes to the creation and prevention of disputes, as well as their settlement through an argumentative discourse coupled with the threat of force'. The problem of individuation appears in this definition, albeit indirectly, in the reference to a 'given group' as the locus of legal order, whether sub-state, state or supra-state in scale. By referring to a group as 'given', de Sousa Santos is by no means assuming that group unity is beyond political contestation, an assumption that would contradict the entire thrust of this incisive book. Instead, what is significant about this definition is that the fundamental problem that merits further consideration, yet which it takes for granted, is the nature and the process of individuation, such that description and analysis can focus on social processes in and between 'given group[s]'. See de Sousa Santos, *Toward a New Legal Common Sense*, 86 (emphasis added).

[6] Raz, *The Authority of Law*, 78.

[7] Raz, *The Authority of Law*, 78.

[8] Raz, *The Authority of Law*, 79.

[9] Raz, *The Authority of Law*, 80.

problem of identity can be properly clarified: the problem of the individuation of laws, i.e. what counts as a complete law.[10] To keep separate the problems of the identity of legal orders and the individuation of laws belonging to a legal order, Raz proposes to reformulate the former as an enquiry into the criteria for a complete description of any legal order, regardless of whether any particular statement describes one complete law within the system or not. On the basis of these distinctions, Raz can go ahead to argue that problems of identity, when properly isolated, demand 'methods of determining the identity of *all* municipal legal systems. Thus conceived, the problem is very different from that facing a legal practitioner looking for an answer in a *particular* legal system to a certain legal problem'.[11] Hence, Raz pitches the problem of identity in a way that is meant to illuminate what he, like Hart and Kelsen, views as the main problem of legal theory, namely, understanding how a manifold of legal norms can be viewed as a unity—as a legal order. I will not further discuss how Raz proceeds to clarify the problem of identity. It may suffice to note that when legal theory distinguishes between formal and material unity, isolating the former as its proper area of enquiry, a theory of legal order that seeks to shed light on legal boundaries is relegated to the status of a derivative, more or less casuistic, enquiry into the material unity of a particular set of legal orders.[12]

Individuation, by contrast, suggests a way of conceptualizing legal order which escapes the simple opposition between what Raz would call a formal approach applicable to 'all' legal systems, and a material approach directed to 'particular' orders, municipal or otherwise. This alternative would have to be an approach that seeks to clarify the general conditions under which *all* legal orders manifest themselves as *particular* orders, that is, as 'discrete units', to borrow Twining's telling expression. At issue is not merely an analysis of particular orders but rather a formal analysis of the particularity of legal orders. The problem, returning to the opening sentence of Raz's essay, is not to articulate the criteria that help us to establish whether 'a particular law . . . is part of American law or French law or some other legal system'. It is to evince the general conditions that allow of individuating a legal order as American or French; as international law; as the World Trade Organization (WTO), the Internet Corporation for Assigned Names and Numbers (ICANN), or the law of the U'wa people. In fact, the term 'particular' does not adequately capture the nature of the problem. At stake is neither the individuation of laws within a legal order nor a description of the 'content, traditions and spirit' of the laws that make up a legal system, as Raz would have it, but rather *the individuation of a legal order as such and as a whole*, whatever its 'level': global, international, regional, transnational, non-state, inter-communal, etc.

Two further comments are appropriate before leaving this section. First, the main thesis to be defended in this chapter is that the problems of the individuality

[10] See Joseph Raz, *The Concept of a Legal System: An Introduction to the Theory of Legal System* (Oxford: Clarendon Press, 1970), 70 ff.

[11] Raz, *Authority of Law*, 81–82.

[12] While giving a new answer to the identity question, Shapiro's theory of legal planning remains within this traditional understanding of it. See Shapiro, *Legality*, 8–10, 225.

and individuation of legal orders should be approached by way of an investigation of, respectively, the identity and identification of legal orders. For reasons that will become clear along the way, I do not follow Twining, Tamanaha, Raz, and others in reserving the terms 'identity' and 'identification' for the criteria which would allow of distinguishing legal order in general from other kinds of normative order. Identity and identification, as I will argue, are primordially about individuation as the collective process of setting legal boundaries. The second comment I would like to make is that although I will be shifting attention to the problem of individuation as a way of illuminating the internal connection between boundaries, limits, and legal order, this entails neither abandoning nor losing sight of the problem of the distinction between legal order and other kinds of normative orders. As we shall shortly see, the concept of law, as a specific kind of normative order, inevitably reappears and must be addressed in the process of thinking through how boundaries/limits are drawn in the process whereby certain kinds of collectives individuate—identify—themselves.

3.2 THE COLLECTIVE AS A SELF AND AS THE SAME

The shift to the problem of individuation was prepared in chapter 1 with the insight that boundaries come into focus from the first-person perspective of those whose behaviour is regulated by law. This insight is decisive because it means that the individuation of legal orders involves a process of *self*-individuation. In turn, the reference to 'self' in self-individuation introduces the problem of identity into our considerations. The aim of this section is, therefore, to clarify the internal connection between collective identity and the boundaries of legal order. Drawing on the two initial scenarios described in chapter 1 I will show how collective identity, in the twofold sense of 'sameness' and 'selfhood', is at issue in the manner in which legal and illegal behaviour relate to boundaries. The limits of legal orders will be discussed in the following section, when introducing the contrasting terms to collective identity.

If we revisit the first two scenarios of chapter 1 the problem of collective identity first appeared when I noted that engaging in legal behaviour from the first-person *singular* perspective of a legal actor, i.e. an actor whose behaviour is legally coordinated with that of others, requires being able to take up the first-person *plural* perspective of a 'we'. I further observed that, insomuch as the mutuality of legally relevant behaviour involves a reference to the first-person plural perspective, legal behaviour actualizes this reference, whereas illegal behaviour interrupts it. I did not pursue the first-person plural perspective any further at that stage of the analysis, holding it in reserve for more detailed development in the present chapter.[13] To get started in a concrete manner, it is helpful to look again at the second of the scenarios—the attempted theft of a number of cans of foie gras from the Galeries Lafayette. Indeed, the attempted theft brings about a double interruption with regard to the first-person plural perspective. On the

[13] I will not attempt to explore the connections between the first-person plural perspective outlined hereinafter and Hart's analyses of the 'internal perspective' in *The Concept of Law*, preferring instead to focus directly on the problem of collective identity as it pertains to the first-person plural perspective.

one hand, the food department ceases to appear as a common place, in the sense of a place with respect to which we all share—are deemed to share—the *same* expectations as to how one ought to enter and leave, what one ought to do in that place, and so forth. On the other, the theft impairs our capacity to view *ourselves* as a group, that is, as a whole or unit the members of which ought to coordinate their action appropriately in the process of buying and selling produce in a food department. The 'same expectations' and 'viewing ourselves as a group'; these expressions suggest that illegality involves a twofold interruption of *identity*: of identity as sameness and as selfhood. Let us dwell on this distinction, for it is of crucial importance to our entire enquiry.[14]

Paul Ricœur has argued that identity can be parsed into two poles that, although related, are irreducible to each other, namely sameness or *idem*-identity, and selfhood or *ipse*-identity. As concerns the former, two cases of 'the same' can be distinguished: numerical and qualitative identity. Numerical identity 'denotes oneness (*unicité*): the contrary is plurality (not one but two or several)'; it involves 'the notion of identification, understood in the sense of the reidentification of the same, which makes cognition recognition: the same thing twice, *n* times'. By contrast, qualitative identity denotes 'extreme resemblance', such that the substitution of two things is possible without semantic loss.[15] The opposite of sameness, in a qualitative sense, is dissemblance, difference, divergence, either in the form of things that are different to each other or in the form of a given individual that becomes different (over time). The numerical and qualitative modes of identity are related in those situations in which the *re*-identification of an individual is at stake, e.g. is this the person (now) who committed the crime (back then)? The temporal dimension points to yet a third component in the concept of identity: 'the *uninterrupted continuity* between the first and the last stage in the development of what we consider to be the same individual', that is, to 'a principle of *permanence in time*' as constitutive of numerical identity.[16] In Ricœur's view, the exemplary manifestation of *idem*-identity, for those beings who are also selves, is *character*: 'By "character" I understand the set of distinctive marks which permit the reidentification of a human individual as being the same'.[17]

The second pole of identity is selfhood or *ipse*-identity. The crucial feature of selfhood is its reflexive character, which Philip Pettit describes as follows: 'That

[14] Some aspects of the following reflections draw inspiration from Bert van Roermund's powerful article, 'First-Person Plural Legislature: Political Reflexivity and Representation', *Philosophical Explorations* 6, no. 3 (2006), 235–252, and to multiple conversations on the topic with him. Van Roermund has further developed insights of this article in his recent book, *Legal Thought and Philosophy: What Legal Scholarship is About* (Cheltenham: Edward Elgar, 2013), and two papers that defend a recognition-based reading of Hans Kelsen's Pure Theory of Law. See Bert van Roermund, 'Kelsen under the Low Skies. Recognition Theory Revisited and Revised', in Robert Walter, Clemens Jabloner, and Klaus Zeleny (eds.), *Hans Kelsen anderswo. Hans Kelsen Abroad* (Vienna: Manz Verlag, 2010), 259–279, and 'Objectifying Legal Norm Claims: Validity and Self-Reference', in John Gardner, Leslie Green, and Luis Duarte de Almeida (eds.), *The Pure Theory of Law Revisited: The Jurisprudence of Hans Kelsen* (Oxford: Oxford University Press, 2013), 11–41.

[15] Paul Ricœur, *Oneself as Another*, trans. Kathleen Blamely (Chicago: Chicago University Press, 1992), 116. See also Peter F. Strawson, *Individuals*, repr. (London: Methuen, 1984), 31 ff.

[16] Ricœur, *Oneself as Another*, 117.

[17] Ricœur, *Oneself as Another*, 119.

an agent is a self means that he can think of himself, or she can think of herself, in the first person as the bearer of certain beliefs and desires and other attitudes and as the author of the actions, and perhaps other effects, to which they give rise'.[18] The reflexivity inscribed in selfhood 'indicate[s] that an attitude or action bears on the agent himself or herself'.[19] Now, as both Ricœur and Pettit acknowledge, self-identity deploys a form of temporal continuity. In the same way that something—a stone, a house, a tree—can be re-identified insomuch that it remains (more or less) the same over time, so also selfhood, as a pole of identity, entails permanence in time, even though irreducible to the form of a substratum or substance.[20] Ricœur and Pettit characterize the temporal continuity of self-identity in similar ways. For Ricœur, the paradigm of self-identity is keeping one's word, such that, regardless of the vicissitudes an agent encounters after promising something, he or she nonetheless makes good on the promise by doing that to which he or she had committed. For Pettit, 'the agent will be the same self as the person they were at an earlier time just so far—and this will be a matter of degree—as they actively own or endorse the claims and attitudes and actions of that earlier agent'.[21] Notice that, in Pettit's formulation, self-identity requires that an agent be the '*same* self' over time. The reason for this is that there could not be permanence over time with 'a purely formal "I", with a thin, commitment-free identity'; thus 'I must give my self a substantive specification; I must assume a substantive *character*'.[22] This returns us to Ricœur's analysis of character as the way in which personal identity manifests itself as *idem*-identity, as sameness, even though Ricœur, like Pettit, is careful to underscore that sameness and selfhood, while conceptually distinct, are never entirely separate.

The foregoing considerations focused on personal identity, on identity in the first-person singular perspective; but they are relevant to collective identity, too. Unfortunately, Ricœur has strikingly little to say about collective identity in *Oneself as Another*. Pettit is considerably more expansive in this respect. In the same way that the words 'person' and 'self' are reserved for agents who can refer to themselves with first-person indexicals such as 'I', 'me', 'my', and 'mine', 'integrated collectives', as Pettit dubs them, have a personal perspective whereby their members can refer to themselves with first-person plural indexicals such as 'we', 'us', 'our', and 'ours'. The contrasting concept for a collective self is 'the other', including 'others' in the form of other collectives: alterity in the form of behaviour which attests to another first-person plural perspective. In the same vein, integrated collectives display self-identity in the form of inter-temporal commitment. 'The words defended in the past... will stand out for those of us in the

[18] Philip Pettit, *A Theory of Freedom: From the Psychology to the Politics of Agency* (Cambridge: Polity, 2001), 79.

[19] Pettit, *A Theory of Freedom*, 80.

[20] Ricœur, *Oneself as Another*, 118.

[21] Pettit, *A Theory of Freedom*, 83. Rawls refers in a similar vein to the 'principle of responsibility to self': 'we are responsible to ourselves as one person over time... One who rejects equally the claims of his future self and the interests of others is not only irresponsible with respect to them but in regard to his own person as well. He does not see himself as one enduring individual'. John Rawls, *A Theory of Justice* (Cambridge, MA: The Belknap Press, 1971), 422–423.

[22] Pettit, *A Theory of Freedom*, 85 (emphasis added).

collectivity as words that "we" as a plural subject maintain'.[23] Pettit's description of collective self-identity in terms of 'maintaining' our word meshes well with Ricœur's characterization of personal self-identity in line with the motto 'I will hold firm' (*je maintiendrai*). Collective self-identity is that pole of identity in which a group agent sticks to its commitments over time, and which is fit to be held to its commitments. To give a collective twist to Ricœur's motto, *nous maintiendrons:* we will hold firm.[24] And although Pettit does not explicitly mention this point, being able to refer to a group as the 'same' collective self over time implies a substantive specification of selfhood—a 'collective character', as one could put it.

So much for collective identity in general. The identity of legal collectives in particular can also be parsed into sameness and selfhood, thus described. Sameness manifests itself, *qua* the 'character' of legal collectives, in the form of mutual normative expectations articulated and actualized in joint action under law. In line with what we have learnt about the spheres of validity of legal norms in chapter 1, these normative expectations are expectations about who ought to do what, where, and when. Accordingly, the 'substantive character' of a legal group—what determines it as a 'we'—is the specific way in which it gives shape to the spatial, temporal, subjective, and material dimensions of behaviour. The character of a legal collective manifests itself to its members—and to others—in how it draws the boundaries that establish the who, what, where, and when of behaviour falling within the scope of its normative point. Returning to the scenarios of chapter 1, the character of the French legal collective is determined, as concerns its spatial dimension, by the manner in which its territory is organized as an interconnected manifold of ought-places (including the food department of Galeries Lafayette in Rennes), as well as the conditions for entering and leaving specific kinds of ought-places therein. Notice that what allows us to re-identify this collective over time is not merely that its territorial borders remain (more or less) the same but rather that its concrete configuration as a spatial unity, in which there are certain kinds of ought-places (and not others) interconnected in certain ways (and not in others), shows a certain permanence over time. The character of legal collectives also holds for each of the other dimensions of legal norms—the subjective, the temporal, and the material—such that, for example, the French collective authorizes the sale of alcohol in a food store (rather than, say, exclusively in a state monopoly store), to part of the population (rather than prohibiting it altogether), and on certain days of the week (rather than seven days a week), and so forth.

A comparable analysis can be made of each of the other legal orders we have discussed in chapter 2. In each of these cases, the 'character' of a legal collective is defined by recognizable patterns of behaviour that respond to concrete mutual

[23] Pettit, *A Theory of Freedom*, 117.

[24] Ricœur, *Oneself as Another*, 124. In a similar line, Arendt notes that the mutual promise between the members of a polity has the power to stabilize time, not because those who promise share 'an identical will which somehow magically inspires them all', but by virtue of 'an agreed purpose for which alone the promises are valid and binding'. Hannah Arendt, *The Human Condition* (Chicago: Chicago University Press, 1985), 245.

normative expectations about who ought to do what, where, and when. This holds first and foremost for the members of a legal collective themselves, who can identify and reidentify their collective as remaining (more or less) the same over time to the extent that, by and large, their expectations are met about how they and their fellow members ought to act.

The notion of a collective character seems particularly apt because it points to an important parallel between individual and collective agents. Ricœur notes, referring to the former, that character appears as 'my manner of existing in accordance with a finite perspective affecting my opening to the world of things, ideas, values, and persons'.[25] Although collective agents are different in important ways to individual agents, their mode of existence is nonetheless also marked by a finite perspective. Notice how the problem of the limit of legal orders introduces the problem of the ontology of collectives, in the form of their *finitude*. It is appropriate to speak of a first-person plural 'perspective' or 'point of view' because the way in which a collective draws the legal boundaries that establish who ought to do what, where, and when determines quite literally its *opening and closure* as a collective. To claim that legal orders are necessarily limited is to claim that legal collectives have a character; to claim that they have a character is to assert that their mode of existence, as responsive agents, is finite. This is one of the lessons to be gleaned from a-legality: by questioning how a concrete legal order draws the legality / illegality distinction, a-legal behaviour reveals that there can be no legal collective without a collective *point of view*. We will develop this insight at greater length in Part II, when discussing the ontology of collective selfhood, in particular finite questionability and finite responsiveness as modes of being of legal collectives.

Now, returning to identity over time, a legal collective remains the same—and this is a matter of degree—not only insofar as the normative expectations about the who, what, where, and when of behaviour remain more or less unchanged over time, but also insomuch that behaviour accords with these normative expectations. In other words, a legal collective remains the same over time to the extent that its members develop and deploy the dispositions that allow them and third parties to say that they are living by its law, i.e. that individuals abide by who ought to do what, where, and when. This situation corresponds to the first of the scenarios outlined in chapter 2, in which individuals orient themselves as a matter of course in Galeries Lafayette as the common place which one enters in certain ways, where one goes about shopping, queues up, and then leaves in certain ways. The coordination of behaviour in the Galeries Lafayette, in the first of the scenarios, is habitual, almost 'second nature' to the participants, such that they do not even think of coordinating their acts by reflecting on what one *ought* to do: paying for the foie gras at the check-out point is simply what one does (blindly) if one wants to lavish it on one's guests. By the same token, as long as behaviour is in accordance with mutual normative expectations, the first-person plural reference to a 'we' deployed in each joint act whereby a client and Lafayette

[25] Ricœur, *Oneself as Another*, 120.

pull off a sales transaction remains more or less implicit; what we stand by—our mutual commitments—remains largely taken for granted. Such situations are the legal manifestation of what Ricœur adroitly calls the 'overlapping (*recouvrement*) of *ipse* by *idem*'.[26]

This last point allows us to introduce ipseity into the picture: how does selfhood play a role in the identity of legal collectives? To clarify this point, it is helpful to begin by focusing on the notion of joint action, which was briefly introduced in chapter 1. To this effect, it is necessary to disambiguate two uses of the pronoun 'we', which Margaret Gilbert refers to as 'we...both' and 'we...together'.[27] To see the difference, consider an example of what Alfred Schütz calls a 'we-experience'. Suppose, he argues, that I am watching a bird in flight and notice out of the corner of my eye that you are, too. I do not know concretely what is going through your mind while you follow the trajectory of the bird's flight; but the 'general correspondence' whereby each of us knows of the other that we are doing the same suffices for a we-experience. 'It is enough for me to know that you are a fellow human being who was watching the same thing that I was. And if you have in a similar way coordinated my experiences with yours, then we can both say that *we* have seen a bird in flight'.[28] In line with Gilbert's distinction, this example illustrates an 'aggregative' sense of the term: 'we...both'. A strong reading of 'we' would arise when, for example, you and I have agreed to look at birds *together*, in the course of which, having spotted a bird flying in the distance, I would point it out to you if I noticed that you had not also spotted it. 'We...together' denotes a strong, integrative sense of 'we': a joint act is irreducible to the summation of acts of individuals, even if there can be no joint act absent agency by the individuals who share in the action—'participatory agency', as she dubs it.[29]

Important practical implications follow from joint agency. Amongst other things, joint action 'entails taking on or accepting a set of responsibilities and rights: it involves accepting a new set of constraints on one's behaviour. (One also accepts certain new entitlements)'.[30] More pointedly, joint action gives rise to 'directed' or 'relational' obligations, i.e. obligations of participants with respect to each other, as well as to the standing by participants to demand of other participants that they do their bit, in line with the point of the joint act, and to rebuke them when they do not. Here, then, is an initial and decisive characterization of the normativity proper to legal orders, that is, to the legal *ought*. True,

[26] Ricœur, *Oneself as Another*, 121.

[27] See Margaret Gilbert, repr. *On Social Facts* (Princeton, NJ: Princeton University Press, 1992), 168.

[28] Alfred Schütz, *The Phenomenology of the Social World*, repr., trans. George Walsh and Frederick Lehnert (London: Heinemann Educational Books 1976), 165.

[29] It is not surprising that Schütz develops an aggregative view of 'we-experiences' in his phenomenology of the social world, as he explicitly embraces Max Weber's methodological individualism both in the cited book and in his posthumous book, *The Structures of the Life-World*. To this extent, the notion of a common world as a *social* world remains underdetermined in statements such as the following: 'The world of the We is not private to either of us, but is our world, the one common intersubjective world which is right there in front of us'. See Schütz, *Phenomenology of the Social World*, 171.

[30] Gilbert, *On Social Facts*, 411.

not all joint action generates legal rights, nor, for that matter, legal sanctions. But, I submit, no sense could be made of *legal* rights, entitlements, obligations, and responsibilities, nor of legal sanctions, in the absence of joint action, that is, absent forms of action in which a manifold of individual agents take up the first-person plural perspective of a 'we acting together'.

While Gilbert holds joint action, beliefs, attitudes and the like to be constitutive of a 'plural subject' or social group, I find it helpful, in view of an exploration of the selfhood proper to *legal* collectives, to distinguish, with Pettit, between joint action and group agency. Action by group agents is, on Pettit's reading, a subset of joint action: there could be no group agents absent the joint action of a plurality; but a plurality becomes a group agent when the plurality not only acts together but also monitors the consistency over time of its joint action in view of attaining the group's common goals or, more generally, actualizing the normative point of its action. In the same vein, a group agent emerges when individuals are entrusted with overseeing that the group's judgements and actions remain more or less consistent over time. This condition involves (re)specifying along the way, and when the situation so requires, the normative point of the group's action. An example could be a guided group visit to a city in which the guide, in consultation with the group members, and bearing in mind weather conditions and construction activities in key touristic areas of the city, has to decide which places to visit, and when, over the course of several days. If an 'integrated collectivity will be the same self as that collectivity at an earlier time just to the degree that it still owns or endorses the judgments, intentions and actions of the earlier', then the emergence of collective self-identity over time is linked to the emergence of the aforementioned conditions of group agency.[31] *Nous maintiendrons*.

So, a group agent is a necessary condition for a legal collective; on its own, joint action does not suffice. But group agency, while necessary, is not a sufficient condition for legal collectivity. In our guided group visit to a city, members of the group who are unhappy with the itinerary mapped out by the guide can always go their own way; or it may even be the case that consultation between the guide and the tourists shows such polarization of views about what places to visit, and when, that the group effectively disbands into smaller groups, each of which goes its own way. In contrast to such situations, a collective legal agent involves a *structure of authority* whereby certain individuals, acting on behalf of the group, (i) monitor joint action as concerns its normative point and consistency over time, and (ii) take steps to uphold joint action when its normative point is breached or when the consistency of joint action over time is otherwise undermined or imperilled.[32] This, as I read him, is what Kelsen alludes to when noting that the legal regulation of behaviour must be mediated by a legal authority, regardless of whether authority is exercised by all or some members of the

[31] Pettit, *A Theory of Freedom*, 118.

[32] Significantly, Bratman's analysis of shared intentional action and shared cooperative action, akin in some ways to Pettit's account of joint action, explicitly focuses on cases in which there are no structures of authority. See Michael Bratman, *Faces of Intention: Selected Essays on Intention and Agency* (Cambridge: Cambridge University Press, 1999), 94, 110.

collective, or even only one.[33] I would add that I construe the 'monitoring' of joint action in a very broad sense, which includes not only one or other form of judicial decision-making but also, in at least some legal collectives, the enactment of *general* legal norms oriented to promoting, recalibrating, etc. the normative point of joint action in a changing context.[34]

In short, the difference between collective legal agents and other kinds of group agents turns on how *questions* about joint action are dealt with: we are witness to a legal collective when questions about the normative point of joint action; about the rights, obligations, entitlements, and responsibilities that arise in the light of that normative point; about the consistency of participatory agency with regard to the normative point of joint action; and, finally, about the consequences that follow from inconsistency therewith, are not left over to the collective's members to decide separately for themselves In a legal order, these and related questions, especially if they are the source of conflict, are settled by authorities who act on behalf of the group as a whole, such that dissenters are bound by that decision and can, in principle, be forced to comply with it. By contrast, if the members of a group cannot resolve a question with respect to a choir, or a joint letter of protest or a team, one or more of them can simply stop singing in the choir, walk away from the team or refuse to sign the joint letter of protest. Notice, in this context, that, besides monitoring group action, a structure of authority involves *upholding* it, i.e. taking steps on behalf of the group to maintain the adherence of individual behaviour to the normative point of group action. Physical coercion is one of the ways, but not necessarily the only way, through which legal authorities seek to uphold group action.[35] Legal collectives, as compared to other plural subjects, tend to have a robust collective self-identity over time. Indeed, the consistency of joint legal action over time does not only hinge on the mutual commitment of at least *some* members of the collective to continue engaging in joint action in a way that is consistent with its past action; this *putative* mutual commitment is also backed up by authoritative monitoring and enforcement in the event of questions about joint action that need to be addressed. The ongoing process whereby the members of a collective engage in authoritatively monitored and enforced joint action is what I call a *legal practice*. And, when referring to joint action hereinafter, I will take it to mean authoritatively mediated and upheld joint action.

Consider, again, the second scenario of chapter 1. I indicated that the attempted theft involves a twofold interruption: theft suspends our understanding of *ourselves* as doing the *same* over time, namely engaging in sales transactions

[33] 'The legal authority commands a certain human behavior, because the authority, rightly or wrongly, regards such behavior as valuable for the human legal community. In the last analysis, it is this relation to the legal community which is decisive for the legal regulation of the behavior of one individual to another'. Kelsen, *Pure Theory of Law*, 32 (translation altered).

[34] Here is where law as a form of collective 'planning' comes into the picture. See, e.g. Shapiro, *Legality*, 118 ff.

[35] This is the strong institutional sense in which legal collectives 'are subjects such that those who compose them are *forced*, qua members of a collectivity, to think of it in the first person plural'. Pettit, *A Theory of Freedom*, 118 (emphasis added).

in conformity with mutual normative expectations about this kind of behaviour. On the one hand, theft suspends our self-understanding as engaging in the *same* activity. At one level this is a qualitative mode of identity that pertains to a sequence of singular joint acts: although these acts are all different and capable of being individuated, they are the same in that each of them is a sales transaction. But the 'sameness' I have in mind pertains primarily to the legal community that remains the same over time in and through those joint acts, to the collective which can be *re*-identified—or not—insofar as the joint actions of buyers and sellers continue to meet mutual normative expectations about the who, what, where, and when of sales transactions: *idem*-identity, in Ricœur's turn of phrase. On the other hand, *ipse*-identity is interrupted when, in the course of ordinary sales transactions, the party-goer is arrested at the exit of Lafayette. The theft interrupts what is deemed to be our mutual commitment to coordinate our behaviour in a certain way over time: we, as the members of a group, *ought* to interact thus, and not otherwise.

This analysis suggests that a legal order is a subject-relative and limited, albeit more or less transformable, unity of subjective, temporal, spatial, and material (meaning) relations. In the course of legal behaviour, the legal order remains more or less inconspicuous and taken for granted: clients enter, buy and leave the food department in the ordinary way, such that what are taken to be mutual expectations about how they ought to orient themselves in that place remain undisturbed. Each sales transaction between Galeries Lafayette and a client fits into a unity of relations deemed to be shared by buyers and the seller, in which each party knows who ought to do what, where, and when. The fact that a legal order is a *subject-relative* unity of relations means that both sameness and selfhood are quietly at work in this scenario: in the course of legal behaviour, all the clients move into, around, and out of Lafayette in such a way that the capacity of these clients to view *themselves* as part of the *same* group, the members of which ought to and effectively do interrelate in a certain way, remains in the background, as the more or less unquestioned presupposition of joint action. The orderliness of the legal order shared by buyers and sellers remains hidden from view, as does its subject-relativity. As a buyer, I know how one ought to enter Lafayette, how one ought to leave, and what goes on from there, e.g. that I 'ought' to take a tram, a car, a bus, walk to another ought-place, etc. And even if I do not know all the ought-places which can be connected to Lafayette, or how I ought to enter them after leaving Lafayette, I can in principle accommodate these places and passages between places into my understanding of a more encompassing legal order as an interconnected unity of ought-places. In its unobtrusiveness, an order is 'the' legal order, rather than 'our' order. Illegality interrupts this state of affairs. On the one hand, it renders obtrusive the legal order as *order*, i.e. as an interconnected distribution of relations: theft does not fit into the mutual normative expectations about who ought to do what, where, and when in this concrete situation, thereby rendering those mutual normative expectations explicit as such. On the other hand, the theft also renders those mutual normative expectations explicit as *our* expectations. It discloses us as a *group*, the members of which are deemed to be mutually committed to behaving in certain ways, and not in others. The appearance of the legal order as a *unity* of relations is *eo ipse* its appearance as a *subject-relative* unity of relations: as 'our' order.

By the same token, the qualification of an act as illegal effectively *reaffirms* legality and, therewith, collective identity in both its modes. When confronted with the breach of the spatial boundary that separates the food department of Lafayette from the street, a client in the queue might mutter under his or her breath, 'Clients ought to pay at the check-out point before leaving the store!' Also the arrest of the would-be thief reaffirms legal boundaries. This reaffirmation of legality, and of the boundaries of the legal order, entails the reaffirmation, even if only implicit, of the two poles of identity deployed by a legal order: 'Our behaviour ought to remain the *same!*'; 'We ought to continue viewing *ourselves* as the members of a group who coordinate our behaviour in a certain way!' And, finally, this reaffirmation of collective identity as sameness and selfhood is also the reaffirmation of a legal order in which appropriate actors ought to behave in the appropriate ways and in the appropriate places and times. One could say that this reaffirmation seeks to confirm that what illegality reveals as 'our' order is *the* order, that is, the order that holds for all.

3.3. COLLECTIVE SELF AND ALTERITY

The entire thrust of the foregoing section is directed to laying bare the internal connection between legal boundaries and collective identity. On the one hand, collective identity, in the sense of *idem*-identity, requires boundaries: there could be no collective character, no possibility of re-identifying a collective as remaining more or less the same over time, if there were no boundaries. On the other hand, legal boundaries require collective identity in the sense of *ipse*-identity: absent the assumption, authoritatively monitored and upheld, that there is a joint commitment concerning who ought to do what, where, and when with a view to realizing the normative point of acting together, there could be no legal boundaries, nor, for that matter, a legal order. So much for section 3.2. The aim of the present section is to take the concept of legal order one step further, showing why and how the internal connection between boundaries and legal orders entails that legal orders are *limited,* in the sense described in chapters 1 and 2. If revealing the internal connection between boundaries and legal order turns on elucidating collective identity, explaining why legal orders are limited requires introducing the contrasting terms for collective identity as sameness and as selfhood.

To see why, let me begin by introducing a three-step argument which summarizes the foregoing discussion, and which I will develop more fully in the course of the following pages. First, no legal order is possible absent the first-person plural perspective of a 'we' in joint action. Secondly, there can be no participant agency by a manifold of individuals, whether two or indeterminately many, absent a normative point of joint action: that which our joint action ought to be *about*. Acts draw their meaning as legal acts—selecting a product, paying for it, etc.—from their inclusion in an interlocking web of acts oriented to realizing a normative point. Thirdly, there can be no normative point in law absent a *closure.* This closure is material, to the extent that it not only indicates what action ought to be about, but also *what* action is called for to realize a normative point. It is also personal, determining *whose* action is called for; spatial, establishing *where* action is called for; temporal, indicating *when* it is called for. If who ought to do what, where, and when is intelligible by reference to the normative point of joint action, conversely these four dimensions of legal action give concrete shape to its normative point, even though—and this is crucial—they need not exhaust the spatial, temporal, subjective, and material conditions under which the normative point of the apposite joint act can be realized.

What does closure achieve? An answer to this question leads straight to collective identity and its contrasting terms. Following Ricœur, I have distinguished between two poles of identity: sameness (*idem*) and selfhood (*ipse*). Although Ricœur elaborates on these from the perspective of individual identity, collective identity also involves sameness and selfhood. Sameness can be parsed into numerical and qualitative identity. The former concerns unicity or oneness, such as in the expression 'one and the same'; its contrasting term is plurality, as when one refers to two or more things. The latter refers to extreme resemblance; its contrasting term is dissemblance or difference, as when 'a' is said to be different to 'b'. The second pole of identity is selfhood. It involves the capacity of agents to view themselves in the first-person perspective as the bearers of certain beliefs and the authors of certain actions. Selfhood bespeaks the first-person plural perspective when individuals refer to themselves as members of a group and to the group's intentions and actions by using indexicals such as 'we', 'us', 'our', and 'ours'. The contrasting term for selfhood is, according to Ricœur, other than self—alterity or otherness.

So, returning to our question, closure, as concerns quantitative sameness, brings about numerical identity by giving rise to *one* legal order, which stands in contrast to two or more legal orders. As concerns qualitative sameness, closure gives rise to a legal collective which is different to other legal orders, and which can itself change, becoming different over time. Notice that theories of legal pluralism appeal to both forms of *idem*-identity. On the one hand, and trivially, at issue is a plurality of legal orders, many rather than one: the contrast to quantitative identity. On the other, and no less trivially, at issue are different legal orders which 'co-exist' in a single spatio-temporal context: the contrast to qualitative identity. Importantly, however, the notions of plurality and difference presupposed by theories of legal pluralism also apply, for example, to a basket of assorted fruits, including pears, apples, and bananas. Here also, there is a plurality of 'entities', and each of these 'entities' is different to the others. To put it another way, oneness and plurality, resemblance and dissemblance, are contrasts which are applicable to all things in a very broad sense of the term 'thing', which includes bodies, events, acts, persons, and the like.

Yet sameness and its contrasts by no means exhaust what closure brings about. Indeed, it is primarily selfhood and otherness which arise from a closure. To see why, compare the closure which gives rise to a legal collective with the act of, say, cutting a pie into two. Trivially, the two pieces are simply different to each other and to the agent who divvies up the pie. The closure which gives rise to a legal order obeys an entirely different logic: *it includes and excludes*. Indeed, inclusion and exclusion are *actor*-categories, categories which make sense from a first-person perspective. So, on the one hand, closure as inclusion gives rise to a legal collective as an agent. Closure makes it possible for a manifold of individuals to view themselves as a group, the members of which ought to act jointly. In a word, closure not only gives rise to collective identity as sameness but also to collective identity as ipseity: to a *collective self*. In contrast to the act of cutting a pie into two, inclusion is a *self*-inclusion. On the other hand, and this second 'effect' is internally connected to the first, closure gives rise to a domain of *our own*. The emergence of collective selfhood goes hand in hand with the emergence of an own space, the unity of places we call ours; an own time, the unity of events we call our history; an own content, the unity of participant acts we call our joint acts; an own subjectivity, the unity of individuals we call our members.

If all of this goes into collective self-inclusion, what is excluded therefrom? What is the contrasting term for collective *self*-inclusion? In a preliminary formulation, collective self-inclusion goes hand in hand with *other*-exclusion, that is, with the exclusion of 'other than self' (Ricœur). But this remains a highly abstract formulation which casts little or no light on what is 'other than self' with respect to legal collectives.

Things get more concrete if we bear in mind that self-closure includes what the collective will call *law*, whereas it excludes what becomes *non-law* to the collective. By non-law I do not mean other kinds of normative order; I mean simply what falls beyond the pale of a collective's legal order. Law, for the collective, is on this side of the closure; non-law on the far side. Here again, there is a fundamental disanalogy between a collective self-closure and cutting a pie. Whereas in the latter the two pieces are interchangeable *qua* pieces of *pie*, the inclusion of law and exclusion of non-law is *asymmetrical* in at least four decisive ways. First, the divide is drawn from *one* of the two sides in the very process of giving rise to both, rather than from a third position: *we* include ourselves as a legal order and exclude the rest as non-law. By laying down the broad lines of joint action and its normative point, and this means determining who ought to do what, where, and when, the closure that gives rise to a legal collective is only concerned with establishing what will count for *us* as law; it says nothing, and can say nothing, about what lies beyond the compass of joint action and its normative point: non-law. The divide is asymmetrical in a second way, as well. What self-closure does is to indicate, at least minimally, what is legally *important* or *relevant* to the collective, i.e. what is the normative point which joint action seeks to realize. This also applies when closure establishes which acts are prohibited within the legal collective, for this amounts to a negative formulation of what it deems to be important and relevant. Consequently, both legal and illegal behaviour fall under the heading of 'law', from the perspective of the collective. By contrast, non-law is *all the rest*. It is the collective's *other*, in a very broad sense: other than self, to borrow Ricœur's vocabulary.

It would be a mistake to assume that the 'other' of a legal collective includes nature, for all joint action by a legal collective deploys a certain understanding of the physical world, an understanding which is incorporated, whether explicitly or implicitly, into the normative point of joint action. For example, joint action by a sea-faring collective will be quite different to that of a sedentary, agriculturally-oriented collective, as will joint action under *lex constructionis* to that by the Fédération Internationale de Football Association (FIFA); but in each case, joint action presupposes a certain orientation towards and understanding of the physical world. Non-law is a residual (rather than negative) category because it encompasses everything that is irrelevant and unimportant with a view to realizing the normative point of joint action by a given collective. Hence the closure which separates law from non-law does not involve 'picking out' and describing what falls beyond the compass of law; for non-law would then cease to be a residual category. In other words, a legal collective never entirely 'knows' what it relinquishes to its domain of non-law; no 'decision' can be taken about everything which closure abandons to non-law. This means that non-law is the domain over which a legal collective exercises no control. All a legal collective can do with respect to this domain is to declare tracts of it to be relevant and important, thereby drawing these into the ambit of law, or to declare unimportant and irrelevant what had been part of the legal order, thereby relinquishing it to the domain of non-law. Hence a third asymmetry: law is *preferred* to non-law. Obviously, this is not to say that non-law is 'unimportant' for law in the sense that there could be law in the absence of non-law. The opposite holds: absent non-law there can be no law.

These considerations on law and non-law, relevance and irrelevance, importance and unimportance, resonate with Husserl's descriptions of a *Heimwelt*—a home-world—which he sometimes contrasts to an outer world—an *Außenwelt*. In an important passage of his posthumously published notes on the phenomenology of intersubjectivity, he formulates this contrast in the form of a question: 'Does not the world as an environing life-world, hence as a practical environing world, have an unpractical horizon, a [domain of the] unexperienced and unexperienceable, which is not merely "out of bounds" (*ausser Spiel*) practically (which would already be practical), but rather a horizon that is not at all in question for praxis?'[36] Notice that the passage turns on two distinctions that are complementary but irreducible to each other. On the one hand, a home-world distinguishes between actions which are in and out of bounds, while comprising *both*. In effect, not only is this distinction of paramount practical interest, but it is also what can be questioned (*in Frage kommende*) in the course of a practice. The distinction between legality and illegality, as behaviour that is in and out of bounds, is a specification of this general feature of a home-world. On the other hand, the home-world has an external horizon which separates it from what Husserl calls an 'irrelevant outside': 'the practical interest is within (*Drinnen*)'.[37] As concerns law, this irrelevant outside, which lies beyond the pale of practical interest because it has been excluded from what is germane to joint action by a

[36] Edmund Husserl, *Zur Phänomenologie der Intersubjektivität* (The Hague: Martinus Nijhhoff, 1973), 431. For an excellent overview of these important studies, see Klaus Held, 'Heimwelt, Fremdwelt, die eine Welt', *Phänomenologische Forschungen* 24 (1991), 305–337.

[37] Husserl, *Phänomenologie der Intersubjketivität*, 431.

legal collective, is the domain of non-law. Hence a fourth asymmetry between law and non-law: inside is preferred to outside.

We advance a step further if we reformulate the notion of self-closure as giving rise to the first-person preferential distinction between *order* and *non-order*. The distinction is a first-person distinction in that legal orders have the form of legal collectives whereby a manifold of individuals act together over time. The distinction is preferential in that non-order functions as the residual domain of what is unimportant to a given collective. I speak of 'non-order', finally, rather than of *dis*order, because, for the reasons indicated above, the latter is the privative form of legal order. In contrast with disorder, non-law comprises the ambit of the *un*ordered.[38]

Various aspects of this preliminary characterization of the unordered require further analysis at this stage. The first is that the distinction between legal (dis) order and the unordered, as described heretofore, is not the massive distinction between legal (dis)order 'in general' and the unordered 'in general'. Instead, it refers to the distinction between a concrete legal order and what is unordered with respect to *that* legal order. Indeed, the unordered is a *relational* concept through and through: if the unordered is what falls beyond the scope of joint action by a legal collective, then different legal collectives will have different domains of the unordered. Notice that this includes 'overlapping' legal orders, in which the domain left unordered by a legal collective can be occupied by other legal collectives.

Second, and closely related to the first aspect, the unordered is, from the first-person plural perspective of a legal collective, a legal void. Husserl speaks, in this context, of home-worlds as having an 'empty outside' (*leeren Draussen*).[39] Whereas a legal order has 'the structural form of a filled spatio-temporality', its unordered outside constitutes an '"empty" spatio-temporality'.[40] Yet, although empty from the perspective of joint action by a collective, the domain of the unordered makes room for *other* legal orders, *other* collectives which organize themselves as legal orders. Returning to our earlier observation, if the unordered is the 'other' of a collective self, then the other of a legal collective includes its *others*, that is, other legal collectives. This shows, on a collective level, the equivalent of the contrast between a personal self and its others, for which the French reserve the term *autrui*, and the Germans *die/der Andere*. But whereas contemporary philosophy has dedicated remarkable attention to the fundamental structures of intersubjectivity between individual persons, the paucity of philosophical enquiries into the fundamental structures of intersubjectivity as concerns (legal) collectives is no less remarkable.[41] One such fundamental structure, or so I argue, is the

[38] Bernhard Waldenfels, *Order in the Twilight*, trans. David J. Parent (Athens, OH: Ohio University Press, 1996), 3.

[39] Husserl, *Phänomenologie der Intersubjektivität*, 431.

[40] Husserl, *Phänomenologie der Intersubjektivität*, 236; 139.

[41] See, amongst others, Michael Theunissen, *The Other: Studies in the Social Ontology of Husserl, Heidegger, Sartre and Buber*, trans. C. McCann (Cambridge, MA: The MIT Press, 1984). While Waldenfels has advanced a compelling objection to philosophical attempts to level down the strange to the other, he focuses almost exclusively on otherness and strangeness as concerns non-institutionalized forms of

divide between a legal order and its domain of the 'unordered'. The inclusion of a collective self is paired to the exclusion of the unordered, which makes room for other collective selves, hence other first-person plural perspectives, each with its own normative point to be realised by joint action under law. What counts as unordered, from the perspective of a given legal collective, is populated by other legal collectives, both established and emergent.

A third feature concerns the divide between legal order and the unordered. In effect, this divide is not posited *separately* from the boundaries that determine who ought to do what, where, and when. To the contrary, the divide between legal (dis)order and the unordered runs along *each* of the boundaries whereby a collective establishes who ought to do what, where, and when. Indeed, each boundary drawn by a legal collective establishes what it deems to be important and relevant, partitioning it from what is unimportant and irrelevant. But because the unordered is a residual category, and as such *opaque* to joint action by a given legal collective, the divide between legal (dis)order and what is left unordered functions differently than boundaries within a legal order. On the one hand, boundaries join and separate elements *within a unity*, such that, for example, selecting products one wants to purchase in a food store demands understanding that and how the store's check-out points mark a spatial boundary separating the food store from other places within a unity of places and joining it thereto. On the other hand, while the divide between legal order and the unordered runs along these check-out points, as it does along all other spatial boundaries of the apposite legal order, it does not join and separate places in the way boundaries do. Whereas places within a legal order are reversible in that, under the conditions dictated by joint action, a legal agent can move from one to the other and back, there is no such reversibility between legal order and the unordered. In short, the divide between a legal order and its unordered is a *limit*. A limit marks the discontinuity and asymmetry between legal (dis)order and its correlative domain of the unordered. *Limits are neither legal nor illegal* because the distinction between the legal and the illegal presupposes spatial, temporal, subjective, and material boundaries which join and separate dimensions of behaviour within the unity of a legal order. Everything that has been said earlier about limits and about frontiers, as the spatial limits of legal orders, finds its conceptual justification in the distinction that a collective must draw between legal (dis)order and the unordered.[42]

intersubjectivity, largely neglecting how they could be distinct phenomena from the first-person plural perspective of collectives. One of the aims of this book is to redress this omission.

[42] There are some similarities among the distinction between legal (dis)order and the unordered, as I am describing it here, and the systems-theoretical distinction between a system and its environment. But my account seeks to articulate the distinction between legal (dis)order and the unordered in terms of the contrast between the first-person plural perspective of a collective self and alterity, a perspective that systems theory has purged *ab initio* from the difference between system and environment. See to this effect my article, 'We and Cyberlaw: Constitutionalism and the Inclusion/Exclusion Difference', *Indiana Journal of Global Legal Studies* 20, no. 2 (2013), (forthcoming).

3.4 IMPLICATIONS AND CAVEATS

Sections 3.2 and 3.3 laid out the essentials of a concept of legal order which, I hope, can explain in a systematic and integrated fashion the features of law illustrated in the first two chapters of the book. In particular, they offer a theoretical explication of the two fundamental theses outlined in section 1.5, namely that a legal order appears from the first-person perspective as a concrete normative order that is (i) organized as a spatial, temporal, subjective, and material unity, and (ii) limited in space, time, subjectivity, and content. These two central features of legal orders can be conceptually justified if one parses the first-person perspective of a legal collective into collective identity as sameness and selfhood and their respective contrasting terms: plurality/difference and alterity. These two sections form the conceptual core of Part I, although the model remains incomplete, not least because I have yet to incorporate the notions of strangeness and fault lines. This will have to wait for a fuller discussion of a-legality in Part II. But before turning to these and related issues, the remainder of this chapter is dedicated to consolidating the findings of the model of legal order as developed thus far. Here is a set of aspects that require further attention.

A first point concerns the traditional question of legal theory. As noted at the outset of this chapter, the central question that drives Western legal theory concerns the criteria that allow of distinguishing law from other kinds of normative order. I argued that the preeminence of this question has systematically blocked a discussion about the relation between boundaries/limits and legal order. By contrast, or so I anticipated, the question about the individuation of legal orders leads directly to this relation. This by no means implies, however, that our enquiry should or can elude the traditional question of legal theory. My wager was that the latter would resurface in the process of thinking through the relation between individuation and legal boundaries. This wager has been borne out by the analyses of section 3.3. In effect, the reader will have noticed that the question about the distinction between law and other kinds of normative order has been addressed when specifying the notion of legal collectives. The decisive step is to recognize that the concept of law can be profitably approached in terms of the first-person plural perspective. In the view I am defending, if making sense of the individuation of legal orders requires delving into collective identity as sameness and selfhood, then *legal* collectives, in contrast to other collective agents, are characterized by structures of authority that monitor and uphold the consistency over time of what should count as joint action. Importantly, I do not claim that the concept of legal order I am espousing is a-historical, if nothing else because an enquiry into legal orders is historically situated, not only because it focuses on the problem of order in general and of legal order in particular, but also because it does so from the perspective of the *contingency* of legal orders. It is the contingency of legal orders that comes to the fore in the three-way distinction between legality, illegality, and a-legality. I will return to this in Part II.[43]

[43] For those who view globalization as an invitation and opportunity to move beyond the Euro-centrism that has plagued much of comparative studies in law, my focus on legal order and ordering in the course of this book will be disappointing because it builds a Western slant into its field of enquiry from the

Second, the account of legal order outlined above deliberately casts a very wide net. While it no doubt includes state legal orders, it is by no means limited thereto. My thesis is that we do well to understand legal orders as a particular way of organizing and securing collective identity as sameness and selfhood over time. I submit that this approach to the concept of law accommodates the entire range of postnational and transnational legal orders, such as *lex mercatoria*, ICANN, the International Organization for Standardization, and multinationals, as well as other forms of law. Notice, in this respect, that the model cuts across the distinction between public and private collectives: also private 'schemes' of self-regulation involve collective identity as sameness and selfhood. A multinational such as Shell is a good example, as we have seen in chapter 2. A further example is the collective composed of international construction companies and their (state) clients, who engage iteratively in joint action—large construction projects—governed by model contracts and by arbitrators who monitor and uphold the normative point of joint action.

Certainly, the qualification of certain transnational legal orders as private forms of self-regulation suggests that they are removed from the sphere of *politics*. Yet if politics involves, at a minimum, the ongoing process of questioning and articulating what is deemed to be the normative point of a collective, hence what is common to its members, then the enactment and amendment of model contracts, and the arbitral awards that authoritatively settle disputes about the normative point of sectoral joint action, are already political acts. There can simply be no collective agency without questions and decisions about what is to count as joint action by the respective group—a politics of joint action. More provocatively, private self-regulation, transnational or otherwise, is already *public*, if 'public' refers to a sphere of presupposed

very start. Patrick Glenn, for example, argues that the concept of a legal order or system 'is clearly and exclusively associated with western (and derived) Soviet legal theory'. See H. Patrick Glenn, *Legal Traditions of the World*, 2nd edn. (Oxford: Oxford University Press, 2004), xxv. I wholeheartedly agree with him that an enquiry into legal orders (and their boundaries, limits, and fault lines) is historically situated, by dint of focusing on the problem of *order* in general and of *legal* order in particular. There is a very strong case to be made for the claim that the modern concern with order stems from what Hans Blumenberg calls the 'disappearance of order' (*Ordnungsschwund*) leading over the epochal threshold from the Middle Ages into modernity. In the face of the extreme pressure to which the theological sharpening of the problem of contingency submits Western humanity's interpretation of itself and its relation to the world, the Scholastic solution of the 'transitive' conservation of the world by God is no longer either plausible or acceptable, and is reoccupied in modernity by 'intransitive' conservation, that is, self-conservation or self-preservation. This epochal transformation has a profound implication for the modern conception of order: the ordering of society becomes a *self*-ordering. No less importantly, the problem of the *ground* of legal orders, and the boundaries they draw, becomes acute in light of the contingency of social order in all its manifestations: on what grounds may a legal order include and exclude forms of behaviour? This question will attract our full attention in the final chapter of this book. By asking whether legal orders are at all thinkable absent boundaries, limits, and fault lines, I readily concede that my questioning is firmly situated within the broader historical horizon of Western modernity and the conceptual and normative problems it calls forth. Yet if my questioning is rooted in this historical situation, it also turns back on it to critically interrogate key aspects of the conceptual framework that has governed the modern conception of legal order. The further question is whether Glenn's preferred notion of 'tradition' is any less rooted in the conceptual framework spawned by modernity than the notion of legal order; *quod non*. But that is another matter. See Hans Blumenberg, *The Legitimacy of the Modern Age*, trans. Robert Wallace (Cambridge, MA: The MIT Press, 1985), 137–138. For a discussion of the political and legal implications of this epochal transition, see my article, 'Collective Self-Legislation as an *Actus Impurus*: A Response to Heidegger's Critique of European Nihilism', *Continental Philosophy Review* 41, no. 3 (2008), 323–342.

commonality absent which joint action would not be possible. What is really meant by the qualification of legal orders as modes of 'private' self-regulation is that they are relatively insulated from broader contestation of and debate about their normative point and, with it, about their boundaries. It is in this sense, for example, that Teubner notes that the consolidation of structures of authority in *lex mercatoria* may lead to its politicization, whereby 'the internal structures and processes of the law-creating mechanism—the law-making bodies in international private associations and the composition and procedures of arbitration boards—come under public scrutiny and debate'.[44] These were, of course, the kinds of issues raised by the environmental activists who occupied the Brent Spar oil rig; but these were also the issues posed by the *chômeurs* in Galeries Lafayette, who sought to expose the French legal order as a form of 'private' self-regulation, as advancing *particular* interests rather than the common interest. We must postpone a fuller discussion of a-legality until Part II; but we can already anticipate that the 'politicization' of transnational schemes of private self-regulation is part and parcel of the more general problem of how a-legality reveals a limit of a legal order by disrupting a given correlation between collective identity and legal boundaries and evoking another possible correlation thereof.

A third point worth noting turns on the weak structures of authority prevalent in some kinds of emergent legal orders. It was argued in section 3.2 that a crucial element of legal collectives, which assures them of a relatively robust identity as compared to other kinds of group agents, is that they deploy structures of authority which settle conflicts about the who, what, where, and when of behaviour in a more or less consistent fashion. It is this feature of legal collectives which may be found wanting in some emergent forms of legal order. Teubner comments, in this respect, that *lex mercatoria*, at least for the time being, 'consists of episodes with rather weak communicative links'.[45] In particular, the new merchant law's 'arbitration bodies are likewise strong in producing episodes [i.e. awards] and weak in linking them up with one another'.[46] Nonetheless, he adds, the global *lex mercatoria* does seem to be developing 'institutionalized linkages of its episodes', whereby 'a certain normative consistency' over time is assured by its 'increasing reliance on mutual observation and adaptation of arbitration bodies and by the increasing use of the "Big Three" in international commercial arbitration', namely the International Chamber of Commerce, the Iran-United States Claims Tribunal, and the International Centre for Settlement of Investment Disputes.[47] It remains to be seen to what extent

[44] Teubner, 'Global Bukowina', 22. See also Gunther Teubner, *Constitutional Fragments: Societal Constitutionalism and Globalization* (Oxford: Oxford University Press, 2011), 114–123.

[45] Teubner, 'Global Bukowina', 20.

[46] Teubner, 'Global Bukowina', 20. In line with this assessment a recent study asserts that 'the *Lex Mercatoria* is now being built through precedent...Arbitrators work to generate just decisions, but they are also careful to insist that decisions in equity are possible only if anchored in general principles...Arbitrators...have a corporate interest in making the law that governs international commerce clear, transparent, and available to future disputants. Giving reasons for their decisions, and publishing them, allows them to do both'. See Stone Sweet, 'The New *Lex Mercatoria* and Transnational Governance', 642–643.

[47] Teubner, 'Global Bukowina', 20.

lex mercatoria as a whole succeeds in going beyond its current, relatively weak structures of authority. But at least for some economic sectors the emergence of structures of authority based on mutually observing and adapting arbitration bodies, which settle conflicts on the basis of model contracts that function as the standards for the sector, are sufficiently consolidated to speak of legal collectives, the members of which iteratively engage in authoritatively monitored and enforced joint action.

The general lesson to be drawn from *lex mercatoria* is that the resilience of legal boundaries co-varies with the variable resilience of collective identity. Importantly, the resilience of legal boundaries does not amount to their 'impermeability'. Resilience concerns the extent to which legal boundaries join and separate behaviour in ways that are more or less consistent over time. The general point should be clear: the emergence of a legal order hinges on the capacity of the apposite collective to stick, by and large, to what are deemed to be its prior commitments about the who, what, where, and when of behaviour, when affronting novel situations. The stabilization/destabilization of legal boundaries is linked to a collective's capacity to monitor and maintain joint action in the face of conflict, i.e. to the emergence/decline of structures of legal authority. These structures of authority are a necessary condition for resilient legal boundaries and for sustaining collective identity over time. For this reason it is appropriate to speak of the *individuation* and *de-individuation* of legal orders; their individuality over time—their identity—is a matter of degree, not an all or nothing state. Unless a certain threshold is reached, whereby it is minimally clear for participant agents and for others who ought to do what, where, and when over time, there is as yet no legal order.

Finally, I propose to view the concept of a constitution as a first-person plural concept. To see why, it is instructive to look at Kelsen's conceptualization of a constitution. As he sees it, 'the essential function of a constitution consists in governing the organs and the process of general law creation, that is, of legislation'; he adds that constitutions 'may determine the content of future statutes...in that they prescribe or preclude certain content'.[48] This characterization of a constitution alludes to the two main functions of constitutions, namely empowerment and restraint. I will concentrate, for the time being, on empowerment, returning to restraint later in chapter 7.

Indeed, constitutions include rules that empower legal behaviour in the sense of behaviour that is commanded, prohibited, or permitted. While correct as far as it goes, this account of empowerment presupposes, without explicating, the first-person plural perspective of empowerment. A first step in this direction is taken by noting that constitutions empower by determining who ought to do what, where, and when. This includes law-making by authorities who issue general and individualized legal norms, who are as much empowered in the form of determinations of who ought to do what, where, and when as the addressees of the legal norms they enact. The passage to constitutional empowerment as a first-person plural concept is clinched when one recognizes that constitutionalization has the structure of a *collective self-empowerment*. I mean here

[48] Kelsen, *Problems of Legal Theory*, 64.

self-empowerment not in the sense of empowerment by a collective self but rather the empowerment *of* a collective self. A constitution empowers a collective self in that it opens up a realm of joint action under law. And this entails opening up the first-person plural perspective: 'we together'. The notion of collective self-empowerment as empowerment by a collective self, as captured in the canonical declaration 'we the people', is, however, a strictly derivative, and in no sense necessary, feature of a constitution as a first-person plural concept. Indeed, constitutions can have another source; for example, they can be viewed by the members of a collective as having a divine provenance, and, as such, empowering them to engage in authoritatively mediated and enforced joint action. So, not the source of collective empowerment, but rather collective empowerment as such renders constitutions a first-person plural concept.

An important implication hereof is that constitutions are *concrete*, to the extent that they structure a legal order as an interconnected distribution of ought-places, times, subjects, and act-contents which draws its (putative) unity as a legal order from the normative point for the sake of which a manifold of individuals are deemed to engage in joint action. A constitution perforce includes a (default) determination of what joint action under law is most fundamentally about, although this determination need not be enunciated in a written document. Absent a determination of the normative point of joint action, constitutional empowerment would be meaningless, and there could be no interconnected distribution of ought-places, times, subjects, and act-contents as a concrete legal order. Accordingly, to understand them as a free-standing set of rules is to engage in an abstractive process that disengages these rules from the joint action which they structure. By the same token, what determines the *unity* of a manifold of rules as comprising a single constitution is not merely the fact that those rules happen to be assembled in a written document, nor that they are treated as a systematic whole by jurists and authorities. Instead, a constitution is a unity of rules insomuch that these rules articulate the structural unity of joint action under law. The (putative) unity of a constitution both depends on and gives form to a plural subject.

This defence of a constitution as a first-person plural concept needs to be taken one step further, however, if it is to get to the heart of what is at stake in a constitution, either conceptually or normatively speaking. To the extent that constitutions legally empower a collective to engage in joint action, they establish what is to count as *our* joint action. A constitution structures decisions about what, in the final analysis, will count as *our* (authoritatively mediated and enforced) joint action. Certainly, the constitution does not stand separate from the first-person plural perspective it contributes to structuring. A set of rules will only establish what is to count as our joint action if those rules are viewed by its addressees as *our* constitution. But what I would like to emphasize at this point is that a constitution structures the ongoing legal process of inclusion in and exclusion from a collective self. Most fundamentally, a constitution structures the authoritatively mediated process of law-making whereby the limit between a collective self and other than self is redrawn. Succinctly, *a constitution is the master legal rule for inclusion in and exclusion from a legal order.*

Notice that the scope of this concept of a constitution is very broad. It is by no means limited to state constitutions. By my account, a host of other collectives have constitutions, including First Nations; the United Nations; certain regimes of human rights such as the European Council; the European Union; multinational corporations; functionally differentiated collectives, such as ICANN, the International Organization for Standardization and the like; the WTO; the Catholic Church. If the first-person plural concept of legal order which I have been concerned to espouse is very capacious, so also is the corresponding concept of a constitution. In this sense, a first-person plural concept of the constitution strongly supports the view that statehood and constitutionalism are not necessarily co-referential terms.[49] I would be happy to go further and defend the view that what is new to our current situation cannot be that we have moved 'beyond' state-centred constitutionalism, simply because there have always been non-state constitutions, in the sense noted above.

3.5 EXCLUSIVE TERRITORIALITY AFFIRMED

Separate and fuller attention is required for a key aspect of the broader debate about legal order in a global setting, a debate in the course of which terms such as 'postnationalism', 'transnationalism', and 'denationalization' have been coined in the effort to pin down what is new to law, once the paradigm of state / international law forfeits its preeminent role in regulating behaviour. Whatever their differences, there are two general assumptions that are the unquestioned point of departure for most, if not all, contemporary analyses of what is novel to law in a global setting: the inside / outside distinction and exclusive territoriality have been exposed as merely contingent features of legal order.

The first of these assumptions has been rebutted, and I have little more to say about it hereinafter. Let us turn, instead, to the second assumption. Theories of legal pluralism in a global setting have insisted time and again that exclusive territoriality is only characteristic of states, and that the emergence of overlapping legal orders in our global era exposes this feature of state law as thoroughly contingent. Sassen, for example, articulates what has become the self-evident and unquestioned assumption of a wide range of sociologies and legal theories of globalization when referring to 'the territorial sovereign state, with its territorial fixity and exclusivity'.[50] I have no quarrels with the view that we are witness to a process of legal pluralization. The model of legal order I have been at pains to develop is entirely consistent with this view. More pointedly, I have sought to put into place a comprehensive conceptual framework for understanding how legal orders are structured, such that both state law and overlapping legal orders are at

[49] See Neil Walker's articles, 'Taking Constitutionalism Beyond the State', *Political Studies* 56 (2008), 519–543, and 'The Idea of Constitutional Pluralism', *Modern Law Review* 65, no. 3 (2003), 317–359. For a forceful defence of a necessary correlation between statehood and constitution, according to which the waning role of the states ushers in the twilight of constitutionalism, see Martin Loughlin, 'In Defence of Staatslehre', *Der Staat* 48, no. 1 (2009), 1–28, and 'What is Constitutionalism?', in Petra Dobner and Martin Loughlin (eds.), *The Twilight of Constitutionalism?* (Oxford: Oxford University Press, 2010).

[50] Sassen, *Territory · Authority · Rights*, 21.

all possible. To this extent, my endeavour runs parallel to and endorses contemporary accounts of legal pluralism and pluralization. But need we accept the further assumption that the emergence of legal pluralism amounts to the collapse of collective claims to exclusive territoriality?

In a certain sense, the point made by theories of legal pluralism is perspicuous and convincing: what has changed, when the link between state and law is relaxed, is that a number of legal orders can come to *co-exist*—in fact, have always co-existed—in a given spatio-temporal context. On this reading, the co-existence of legal orders in a given spatio-temporal context is inimical to the claim to exclusivity raised by state law. The insight is certainly correct as far as it goes; when construed in this way, exclusive territoriality and overlapping territorialities are indeed disjunctive terms. But this sense of exclusiveness does not exhaust the term's scope if we bear in mind, in line with chapter 2, that the term 'overlap' conveys the idea that different collectives with different understandings of what defines them as legal spaces can share all or part of a geographical surface. In other words, the existence of overlapping legal orders is consistent with a claim to exclusivity raised by *each* of the respective collectives with respect to *its* legal space. From the first-person plural perspective, such claims to exclusivity are expressed in references to 'our' space, 'our' land and the like. That legal collectives raise claim to a space as their 'own' resonates with Pettit's observation that selfhood, in the first-person plural perspective, involves the capacity to use indexicals such as 'we', 'us', 'our', and 'ours'.[51] Such references are reflexive in character: exclusiveness boils down to a first-person plural perspective claim, namely, the claim that the members of a collective are entitled to jointly establish who may circulate—and how—in a certain distribution of ought-places. In other words, the first-person plural perspective, absent which there can be no legal order, entails that the collective's members are deemed to be mutually committed to authoritatively monitoring and upholding, with respect to both members and non-members, the spatial boundaries that indicate where certain behaviour ought or ought not to take place.

This claim is the minimal content involved in referring to a space as a collective's 'own' territory. I grant that a reference to 'our' territory is contrastive, and only at issue when the self-reference of a collective is called into question, and thereby made explicit. This is typically what happens in boundary conflicts between overlapping legal orders in a global setting. But the experience that makes this collective self-reference possible, and which triggers the claim to exclusivity, is by no means limited to boundary conflicts between overlapping legal orders. It is already discernible in the behaviour by a member of a collective that breaches normative expectations about where behaviour ought to take place, as in the second scenario of Galeries Lafayette. The qualification of behaviour as misplaced amounts, as we have seen, to an *affirmation* of the boundaries which differentiate and interconnect a manifold of ought-places into a spatial unity. In the same way, it is an affirmation of the mutual commitment

[51] Pettit, *A Theory of Freedom*, 116–117.

to upholding those spatial boundaries over time: *here*—and not there—is where this kind of behaviour ought to occur in *our* community. If, as argued heretofore, every legal order is perforce a spatial order, i.e. a differentiated interconnection of ought-places, then exclusiveness is an ingredient of law as a spatial order because exclusiveness is simply another way of saying that legal order is only possible by dint of a collective claim about where certain forms of behaviour ought—and ought not—to take place.

It is this fundamental understanding of exclusiveness which is manifested, for example, in the references to 'our land' in the anguished message posted on the homepage of the Kgeikani Kweni (First People of the Kalahari):

> We are the Bushmen of the Central Kalahari Game Reserve, Botswana. Together with our children, we number around 1,000 people. The government has forced us off our ancestral land, and we now live in resettlement camps. Since being relocated we have problems we never knew before: drinking, violence, HIV/AIDS. Many of us are dying in the camps. When we try to hunt or gather we are arrested and sometimes tortured. In December 2006 we had a historical victory in the Botswana courts. The judges ruled that our forced relocation from our beloved land was unlawful, and that we have the right to go back and hunt there as we have always done. However, despite the judgment, the government won't let us hunt and is stopping us from using the water borehole on our land. It has also refused to help us with transport home. Because of this, most of us have not yet been able to return.[52]

This exclusiveness is moreover at the heart of the no less agonized cry of the U'wa when referring to their land:

> The *riowa* has condemned us to live like strangers in our own land, he has herded us into precipitous terrains very close to the sacred cliffs whence our chief Guicanito and his tribe sprang [into the abyss] to save the[ir] honour and dignity in the face of the ferocious advance of the Spaniard and the missionary.[53]

This exclusiveness also underpins a statement in the introduction to Communication 459 of 1998, in which the European Commission delineates the main contours of an action plan to implement the Area of freedom, security and justice (AFSJ) enacted in the Treaty of Amsterdam:

> The concept enshrines at European Union level the essence of what *we* derive from our democratic traditions and what *we* understand by the rule of law. The common values underlying the objective of an area of freedom, security and justice are indeed longstanding principles of the modern democracies of the European Union.[54]

[52] See: <http://www.rinoceros.org/article9826.html> (accessed on 13 February 2013). To belabour an insight of chapter 2: also nomadic groups, *pace* Deleuze and Guattari, deploy an exclusive relation to land, albeit one that is very different to that of state collectives. Reasons of space preclude widening these considerations to include a discussion of the Jewish Diaspora, amongst others.

[53] 'Carta de los U'wa al hombre blanco'.

[54] European Commission, Communication 459/98, 'Towards an area of freedom, security and justice', in *Bulletin of the European Union* 7/8 (1998), 152 (emphasis added).

The Commission effectively claims that the AFSJ gives legal expression to Europe as a common place; that 'we, Europeans' can call this place 'our own' by virtue of shared values; that 'we, Europeans', acting jointly, are entitled to determine the conditions under which third-country nationals may enter, remain in, and must leave the AFSJ, and the conditions under which the circulation of persons, goods, services, and capital may take place therein.

The *content* of claims to exclusive territoriality in these and all other legal orders varies in line with the different normative points of the apposite orders. There is, for instance, a considerable difference between how Pintupi groups in the Western Desert of Australia establish whether someone may become part of their group and acquire rights to their land, and how the European Union determines whether third-country nationals may take up residence in the EU. For Pintupi groups, 'the content of ownership rights [involves] the "right to be asked"...such requests are unlikely to be refused, although permission might be overtly denied or withdrawn from *personae non gratae*'.[55] Notice the preferential distinction between inside and outside, and between members and non-members: in 'one's own country one does *not* have to ask'; by contrast, 'to live in another person's country requires that one must defer to him as the "owner." Visitors are freely extended rights to use resources, but in decisions about where to go, or how to deal with disputes, they are clearly second-class citizens'.[56] For the EU, by contrast, authorization to enter and take up residence in the EU is geared, amongst other things, to the protection and realization of an internal market. But in both cases there is a claim to exclusive territoriality, in the sense that those *within*—the members of the collective—claim that they are entitled, as a group, to authoritatively monitor and enforce whether outsiders may enter, and how circulation should proceed within the interconnected unity of ought-places they call their own.

By the same token, if a territory is defined as a distribution of ought-places to which a collective lays claim as its own, then territory is not merely a species of the spatial unity of legal orders but its generic name. It is in this sense of the term that Saskia Sassen views 'territory' as a 'transhistorical constant' of societies, together with authority and rights: TARs. If this generic interpretation of territoriality has escaped the attention of contemporary sociologies and legal and political theories of globalization, it is largely because the meaning of 'exclusive territoriality', no less than that of 'overlap', remains taken for granted. To belabour the point, the kind of exclusivity claimed by state collectives, which in principle precludes the co-existence of other legal orders within the physical dimension of their territories, is responsible for the precarious condition of the Kgeikani Kweni, U'wa, Roma and many other communities scattered across the face of the earth, which were in existence long before the emergence of the state.[57] And it is certainly against the background of the violence spawned by this

[55] Fred R. Myers, *Pintupi Country, Pintupi Self: Sentiment, Place and Politics among Western Desert Aborigines* (Washington, DC: Smithsonian Institution Press, 1986), 156.

[56] Myers, *Pintupi Country*, 156.

[57] Recent legal studies on Romani law offer precious indications about how Romani collectives organize themselves spatially by drawing a preferential distinction between inside and outside. See, amongst

kind of territorial exclusivity that theories of legal pluralism celebrate the declining traction of state law on behaviour. But this does not warrant the conclusion that the uncoupling of law and state ushers in the 'formation or evolution of particular global systems...that require neither territoriality nor exclusivity', as Sassen and many others would have it; it means that 'denationalization', to use Sassen's preferred term, heralds a *pluralization* of collective claims to exclusive territoriality. The emergence of a manifold of collective claims to exclusive territoriality is a condition of possibility of legal pluralization (and of the conflicts to which pluralization can give rise), not its antithesis.

But we can take a step further in showing that claims about the deterritorialization of legal orders remain state-centred. For the concept of exclusive territoriality I am defending suggests the need to operate an important transformation in the legal doctrine about state territoriality, a transformation which I can only point to here, without developing in any detail. Indeed, there is nothing in the concept of state territoriality which hinders assigning it a global reach. In some respects, states already are or can become *global states*. I have in mind what the legal doctrine calls the 'extraterritorial' validity and application of state legislation, e.g. legislation about human rights. The point I would want to make here is that the reference to 'extraterritoriality' in such cases is misleading. When a state or a 'regional' collective, such as the EU, claims global validity for legislation which governs certain kinds of behaviour, it simply includes to that effect the entire globe within its territory, in the sense noted above: the spatial unity with respect to which the members of a collective are deemed to be mutually committed to authoritatively monitoring and upholding the spatial boundaries that indicate where certain behaviour ought or ought not to take place. What is decisive is the capacity of the state to exercise *effective control* over agents who act in its (global) territory, which follows from the insight that legal order presupposes the authoritative monitoring and upholding of joint action.[58]

To sum up, a claim to exclusive territoriality is the spatial explication of the identity of legal collectives. Putting it more pointedly and more provocatively: 'non-exclusive territoriality' is an oxymoron; 'exclusive territoriality', a pleonasm. This is, in a nutshell, the upshot of the pivotal proposition of the topography of legal order outlined at the end of chapter 2, and which I formulated as follows: The preferential differentiation between inside and outside is linked to the first-person plural perspective: by closing itself as an inside with respect to an outside, a community is deemed to lay claim to a space as its own, and vice versa.

others, Walter Weyrauch and Maureen A. Bell, 'Autonomous Lawmaking: The Case of the Gypsies', *Yale Law Journal* 103, no. 2 (1993), 323–399, and Walter Weyrauch et al. (eds.) 'Symposium on Gypsy Law (Romaniya)', *American Journal of Comparative Law* 45 (1997), 225–289. I am indebted to Morag Goodwin for these and other bibliographical references on Romani law.

[58] For a careful and innovative exploration of the problem of effective control and jurisdiction with regard to the 'extraterritorial' application of human rights law, see Daniel Augenstein and David Kinley, 'Beyond the 100 Acre Woods: Navigating the Jurisdictional Jungle of Extraterritoriality, Multinational Corporations and Human Rights Violations', in D. Bilchitz and S. Deva (eds.), *Human Rights Obligations of Business: Beyond the Corporate Responsibility to Respect?* (Cambridge: Cambridge University Press, 2013).

3.6 AN ENLARGED FIRST-PERSON PLURAL PERSPECTIVE

If, contrary to what is taken for granted by legal and political theorists and by sociologists of globalization, emergent non-state legal orders necessarily organize themselves in terms of the inside / outside distinction and as territorial orders, what significant transformation of legal order, if any, is captured by terms such as 'postnationalism', 'transnationalism', or 'denationalization'? If the inside / outside distinction and exclusive territoriality are not contingent features, but rather constitutive features of legal order as such, what changes in how legal orders are or can be structured when the state / international law paradigm begins to lose its hold?

I take my cue from Neil Walker's discussion of the structure of overlapping legal orders peculiar to law in a global setting. Indeed, some of the forms of legal overlap that have emerged with globalization attest to 'an inherently "relational" element in the self-understanding and self-definition of the nonstate entity—a sense that its normative purpose and its effectiveness alike are dependent on the cultivation of a network of relations with other entities'.[59] Notice how this observation invokes collective selfhood, when referring to 'self-understanding and self-definition', as well as alterity—i.e. other than collective self—when referring to 'other entities'. As I read Walker, the question about the innovations that lead beyond state law should be sought in how overlapping legal orders structure their interaction.

In addressing this wide-ranging issue I will limit myself to the two most developed forms of overlap, which Walker dubs 'institutional incorporation' and 'system recognition'. The EU is thus far the only mature example of institutional incorporation, in which 'the host normative order makes general provision for the normative decisions of an external agency to be incorporated and, to that extent, to be treated as authoritative within the host normative order'.[60] System recognition is a less radical form of systemic interconnection because there is no general institutional mechanism enjoining recognition 'in the host system on the terms dictated by the other system. Nevertheless, the relationship of unilateral or mutual recognition is formalized by the host on a systemic level and, as such, is understood as in some way intrinsic to the self-definition of the host system'.[61] Examples include transnational human rights law, transnational trade law, and transnational criminal law. How, if at all, do these two forms of overlap modify the strong correlation between the identity of legal collectives and the boundaries of their legal orders? Walker advances the core of a response to this question when observing that institutional incorporation and system recognition institutionalize a 'relational' understanding of collective identity: they introduce a relation to other legal orders within the ongoing process of determining the

[59] Neil Walker, 'Beyond Boundary Disputes and Basic Grids: Mapping the Global Disorder of Normative Orders', *International Journal of Constitutional Law* 6, nos. 3–4 (2008), 381.

[60] Walker, 'Beyond Boundary Disputes and Basic Grids', 379.

[61] Walker, 'Beyond Boundary Disputes and Basic Grids', 380. The other three forms of systemic interconnection explored by Walker are 'normative coordination', 'environmental overlap', and 'sympathetic consideration'.

apposite collective's identity over time. On Walker's reading, what is new is not that legal collectives take into consideration other collectives in the course of articulating and pursuing their normative point; after all, this was no less the case during the heydays of the state-centred paradigm of law. In general, our joint interest, as a legal collective, is best served in the long run if we pursue it in a way that gives (some) consideration to the interests of other legal collectives. Bert van Roermund makes this general point as follows:

> As an agent, I have an overriding interest in putting my interests (as preferences) to the test of what is 'other-than-me' (reality) to see what they are worth (as stakes), for instance for self-preservation. The same goes for the collective self and its self-preservation, i.e. the continuation of shared intentional activity over time.[62]

What is new is rather the *institutionalization* of this relation, such that the normative point of the 'foreign' legal collective is, as Walker puts it, 'intrinsic to the self-definition of the host system'. This is achieved, for example, through direct effect and the preliminary reference mechanism, in the case of the EU, and through enforcement of arbitral awards through state authorities, in the case of *lex mercatoria*.

To explore how the institutionalization of overlap structures collective self-individuation in a novel way, let us first turn to the 'institutional incorporation' of the EU into the legal orders of its Member States. What we see happening is that Member States are to take up the first-person plural stance of a legal collective—the EU—as concerns a circumscribed range of interests and goals, whereby conflict about those interests and goals, and about joint action thereunder, is in principle settled by European authorities, including the European Court of Justice (ECJ). This means that the EU has a collective identity, in the twofold sense of sameness and selfhood. Its sameness over time—its collective 'character'—is linked, first and foremost, to the realization of an internal market, the normative point of which includes the 'sustainable development of Europe based on balanced economic growth and price stability, a highly competitive social market economy, aiming at full employment and social progress, and a high level of protection and improvement of the quality of the environment'.[63] Collective selfhood, for its part, comes clearly to the fore if Article 1(1) of the Treaty on European Union (TEU) is reformulated in the first-person plural perspective: 'By this Treaty, the High Contracting Parties establish among [*ourselves*] a European Union, hereinafter called "the Union", on which the Member States confer competences to attain objectives [*we*] have in common'. Crucially, however, the first-person plural perspective of the EU does not simply subsume the first-person plural perspectives of its Member States. On the one hand, the principle of specific competence attribution means that the Member States retain areas of exclusive competence vis-à-vis the EU. On the other, and more importantly, there may be issues which fall under the first-person plural perspectives of both

[62] Van Roermund, 'First-Person Plural Legislature: Political Reflexivity and Representation', 244.

[63] Article 3(3), Treaty on European Union.

the EU and a Member State in a way that calls forth a fundamental conflict about legal boundaries and collective identities.

A good example of such conflictive situations is *Grogan*, the well-known abortion information case, in which the ECJ was requested, by way of a preliminary ruling procedure, to establish whether Irish law prohibiting the distribution of information about abortion clinics situated in other Member States fell foul of European Community law.[64]

Consider, first, how *Grogan* unleashed a conflict of collective identities. Article 40.3.3 of the Irish constitution, as amended in 1983, 'acknowledges the right to life of the unborn' and enjoins the state 'as far as practicable, by its laws to defend and vindicate that right'. Accepting the legality of the activities of the defendants in *Grogan* would amount to breaching Ireland's collective identity, or so the Irish government insisted: as sameness, because the prohibition of abortion is a distinctive feature of its collective character over time; as selfhood, because the Irish collective has consistently lived up to its commitment to prohibit abortion: 'abortion has always been prohibited in Ireland'.[65] Articles 30, 39, 46, and 55 of the European Community Treaty, in force at the time of *Grogan*, allow for derogation from the free movement of goods, persons, and services between the Member States of the EC, amongst other things, on grounds of public policy. The problem, however, is that the discretionary exercise of the public policy reserve by a Member State, when one of its 'fundamental interests'[66] is imperilled, can itself constitute a challenge to the collective identity of the EC. This is not surprising inasmuch as invoking the public policy reserve implies derogating from one of the four market freedoms, each of which constitutes a 'fundamental interest' of the EC. For this reason, the ECJ has consistently reviewed the invocation of public policy by Member States to safeguard the identity of the Community legal order; that is, it authoritatively monitors and upholds the Member States' joint commitment (*ipse*-identity) to realizing an internal market (*idem*-identity). Not surprisingly, the defendants in *Grogan*, officers of three university student associations in Ireland, invoked the EC Treaty and the case-law of the ECJ to argue that accepting the Irish government's view that abortion was not a service, and as such did not fall under EC law, would entail a fundamental breach of the EC's identity.

The conflict of collective identities in *Grogan* goes hand-in-hand with a conflict about legal boundaries. From the first-person plural perspective of Ireland, its territory is an ought-place in the sense of a place in which abortion and the distribution of information about abortion clinics outside of Ireland ought not to take place. This ought-place is linked to an ought-time, succinctly captured in the assertion that 'abortion has *always* been prohibited in Ireland'. Accepting the legality of the defendants' behaviour would amount to breaching Ireland's collective history, i.e. a limited temporality that both specifies Ireland as a collective and distinguishes it from other collectives. Qualifying the distribution of information about abortion is necessary, or so the Irish government claims, to preserve Ireland as a unitary time-space. Yet the unfettered distribution of information in

[64] Case C-159/90, *Grogan* [1991] ECR I-4685 ff.

[65] Case C-159/90, *Grogan* [1991] ECR I-4986.

[66] Case 30/77, *Regina* v. *Pierre Bouchereau* [1977] ECR 2014.

any given Member States about services available in other Member States contributes, from the first-person plural perspective of the EC, to defining the internal market as a spatial unity, as a single distribution of ought-places. The ECJ formulated this principle as follows in an earlier ruling: 'consumers resident in one Member State may travel freely to the territory of another Member State to shop under the same conditions as the local population. That freedom for consumers is compromised if they are deprived of access to advertising available in the country where purchases are made'.[67] The unfettered distribution of information about services is also indispensable to the temporal unity of the EC, to the articulation of past, present, and future as a collective process of realizing an internal market: the EC as a *time-space*. Analogous boundary conflicts ensue regarding the material and subjective dimensions of the case, as seen from the points of view of Ireland and the EC.

These considerations mesh well with the analysis of spatial overlap in chapter 2. Indeed, what is the nature of a boundary dispute between the EU and its Members States, *spatially* speaking? In what sense is a dispute about the distribution of competences between the EU and its Member States a dispute about spatial boundaries? As soon as one refers to spatial boundaries in this context it becomes tempting to ask whether there is a spatial boundary that separates and joins the EU and its Member States, and, if so, whether the EU is 'outside' of its Member States, or whether the Member States are 'outside' of the EU. Patently, this is a pseudo-conundrum. As the distinction between inside and outside is always relative to a collective and to a normative point, the real question is whether a specific form of human behaviour is to be regulated in the European legal order, in the legal orders of the Member States, or jointly. Disputes about the spatial boundaries of overlapping legal orders are disputes about which of the orders is to establish *where* certain behaviour ought or ought not to take place. Analogously, disputes about the temporal boundaries of overlapping legal orders are disputes about which of the orders is to establish *when* certain behaviour ought or ought not to take place, not merely in the sense of calendar time but rather in terms of the collective history in which the behaviour ought to be situated. In effect, what renders the distribution of information about abortion legal or illegal is not the calendar date in which that behaviour takes place but rather the collective history to which it is assigned: the realization of an internal market or the realization of a collective which views the right to life of the unborn child as one of its fundamental values.

In short, *Grogan* triggered a conflict in which the identity and legal boundaries of one overlapping collective could only be maintained, or so it seemed, by breaching the identity and legal boundaries of the other collective. The ECJ dealt with this quandary by declaring that, while abortion was indeed a service under Community law, as claimed by Grogan and his co-defendants, the link between the distribution of information about abortion and the appropriate services carried out in other Member States was too 'tenuous' to qualify as a restriction

[67] Case C-362/88, *GB-INNO-BM* [1990] ECR I-686.

upon the freedom to supply services within the terms of the EC Treaty. The ECJ thereby abandoned the behaviour of the defendants to the legal order of Ireland, allowing the Irish High Court to qualify this behaviour in a way that upheld the identity and legal boundaries of the Irish collective. At the same time, however, by holding that abortion is a service which falls within the scope of European law, the ruling moved to uphold the identity and legal boundaries of the European collective. Accepting the Irish government's claim that abortion did not constitute an economic activity would have seriously compromised the identity and legal boundaries of the EC. To borrow Pettit's turn of phrase, acceptance by the ECJ of the Irish government's claim would have raised questions as to whether the EC can really 'claim to be seriously committed to its alleged purpose'.[68] But staving off this serious form of inconsistency came at a price: the argument employed by the ECJ to justify that there was no restriction upon the freedom to provide services was clearly inconsistent with its former case-law and, more generally, with the normative point of realizing an internal market. But although the price to be paid for defusing this conflict was to compromise the full effect of the freedom to provide services, the ECJ surely banked on being able to redress this problem, at a later stage and in a less controversial case, formulating anew the rule about information pursuant to the four freedoms in a way that was consistent with the normative point of realizing an internal market.

Grogan is a good example of identity and boundary conflicts that arise between overlapping legal orders in what Walker calls 'institutional incorporation'; how does it stand with overlap in the form of 'system recognition'? One of the paradigmatic examples of system recognition is transnational human rights law. By a felicitous coincidence, at the time of writing this book the European Court of Human Rights (ECtHR) delivered a judgment in *A, B and C* v. *Ireland*, in which the Court had been asked to determine whether the prohibition of abortion under Irish law fell foul, amongst other things, of the right to privacy of the applicants under Article 8 of the European Convention on Human Rights (ECHR).[69] The Court held that the right to privacy of the third applicant was breached because her rights under Irish law were uncertain and unclear in seeking an abortion when she believed that her pregnancy was life-threatening. But the Court rejected the claims of the first and second applications under Article 8, pointing to an important transformation of Irish law: if the Eighth Amendment to the Irish Constitution (1983) laid down the right to life of the unborn child in Article 40.3.3, the Thirteenth and Fourteenth Amendments (1992) subsequently limited the scope of the prohibition of abortion by authorizing travel to another state to have an abortion and access to information about abortion lawfully performed in other states. (Notice, incidentally, that these amendments belatedly brought Irish law into line with EC law; they are a good example of the two-way interaction between overlapping legal orders.) Under these circumstances, or so the Court

[68] Pettit, *A Theory of Freedom*, 112–113.

[69] *A, B and C* v. *Ireland*, 25579/05 [2010] ECHR 2032 (16 December 2010), available at: <http://hudoc.echr.coe.int/sites/eng/Pages/search.aspx#{"fulltext":["A","B and C v. Ireland"],"documentcollectionid2":["GRANDCHAMBER","CHAMBER"],"itemid":["001-102332"]} > (accessed on 9 May 2013).

held, Irish law 'struck a fair balance between the right of the first and second applicants to respect for their private lives and the rights invoked on behalf of the unborn', which fell within 'the margin of appreciation accorded in that respect to the Irish State'.[70]

Significantly, the majority decision of the Grand Chamber was contested by the dissenting opinion of six judges. In their sharply worded view, the dissenters opined that the majority decision erred in its assessment of the margin of appreciation enjoyed by Ireland. The case-law of the Court, or so they argued, has consistently held that the margin of appreciation is narrowed when there is European consensus on a matter touching upon a human right, as in the case at hand. In particular, there is a broad European consensus that more weight should be assigned to the right to life, health, and well-being of the mother than to the right to life of the foetus. Accordingly,

> it is the first time that the Court has disregarded the existence of a European consensus on the basis of 'profound moral views'. Even assuming that these profound moral views are still well embedded in the conscience of the majority of the Irish people, to consider that this can override the European consensus, which tends in a completely different direction, is a real and dangerous new departure in the Court's case-law.[71]

By allowing the moral views of the (alleged) majority of the Irish people to trump the European consensus, the Court compromised the normative point of the Council of Europe, which the dissenters spell out as follows: 'to gradually create a harmonious application of human rights protection, cutting across the national boundaries of the Contracting States and allowing the individuals within their jurisdiction to enjoy, without discrimination, equal protection regardless of their place of residence'.[72]

True, Ireland's European Convention on Human Rights Act of 2003 conditioned the effect of certain provisions of the ECHR to their being 'subject to the [Irish] constitution'. In all probability, a ruling by the ECtHR that had declared Ireland in breach of its obligations under the Convention as concerned the first and second applicants would have led no further than an internal and non-binding declaration of 'incompatibility' between Irish law and the Convention. But the dissenting opinion can be read as claiming that the price paid by the majority ruling in accommodating the Act of 2003 was too high, certainly with regard to the precedent that was being set with regard to other signatory states: the majority ruling of the Court involves a serious breach of the Council of Europe's collective identity and boundaries. As concerns boundaries, the harmonization of human rights protection, even though it has some limits, aims to create a unitary legal space. By holding that Irish law satisfied the proportionality test, the Court breached how spatial boundaries are to join and separate the contracting states over time: joining by way of the harmonization of human rights protection; separating by way of narrowly construed exceptions to harmonization. Moreover,

[70] *A, B and C* v. *Ireland*, 50 (the page number as per the internet version of the ruling).

[71] *A, B and C* v. *Ireland*, 63. [72] *A, B and C* v. *Ireland*, 63.

harmonization speaks to a temporal unity, in which past, present, and future are construed as the ongoing process of 'humanizing' the legal orders of the signatory states, a temporal unity which is also breached by the 'real and dangerous new departure in the Court's case-law'. As concerns collective identity, the harmonization of human rights protection, together with its exceptions, gives legal shape to the enduring commitment of the Council's signatory states to jointly enact (*ipse*-identity) equal standards of human rights protection for individuals within their jurisdictions, 'regardless of their place of residence' (*idem*-identity). Both forms of collective identity, of collective permanence in time, are compromised by the majority ruling, or so aver the dissidents.

The parallel between *Grogan* and *A, B and C* v. *Ireland* is clear. In both cases, the institutionalization of overlap requires each of the overlapping collectives to take into account the collective identity and legal boundaries of the other collective(s) in the course of regulating itself. 'Taking into account' means, in this context, an enlarged first-person plural perspective. It remains a *first-person* plural perspective because what is at stake is realizing the normative point of a collective through self-regulation. This involves a political judgement about what counts as the normative point of joint action, and the extent to which the collective can be inconsistent with its prior commitments in any given situation without seriously undermining its collective identity and legal boundaries. Upholding the identity and boundaries of a legal collective in the long term may well require its authorities to judiciously breach them in discrete situations: breaking agreements to keep them. But it is an *enlarged* first-person plural perspective because upholding the collective's identity and its legal boundaries over time demands doing so in a way that grants the other, overlapping collective at least some leeway to maintain its own identity and legal boundaries. The interaction between overlapping legal orders is by no means a symmetrical process, not least because it is more or less uncertain how the authorities of the other legal collective will respond to the decisions of an authority about the identity and legal boundaries of the collective it represents. It is also asymmetrical because conflicts of identity and boundaries may have different weights for the respective collectives in any given case, such that a judgement by one of the collectives that is inconsistent with its prior commitments does not compromise its identity and legal boundaries as significantly as would happen with the other collective. Finally, while there may be mutual dependency of the overlapping legal collectives, one of the two collectives may be more dependent on the other, either structurally or in a given case, such that it may be more or less forced to defer to the other's identity and boundaries in case of conflict.

The purport of these considerations about overlap is general; they also explain, for example, what is at stake in state enforcement of the new merchant law. The public policy exception, which every state holds in abeyance when considering whether to enforce an arbitral award, neatly illustrates what I have called the enlarged first-person plural perspective of overlapping legal orders. On the one hand, the exception seeks to safeguard the state against what its authorities deem to be critical breaches of its collective identity and boundaries; on the other, it is an exception to be invoked judiciously, such that the state in principle defers to arbitral awards and the collective identity and boundaries of the sectoral collective.

To sum up and insist on the central thesis that flows from my analyses, the institutional overlap of legal orders does not loosen the internal connection between boundaries and collective identity. This internal connection provides for continuity between state and non-state law when the former can no longer claim to be the paradigm of legal order. But the institutional overlap of legal order also points to an important discontinuity in how legal orders are structured. By means of 'institutional incorporation' and 'system recognition' a collective institutionalizes a relation to alterity in the ongoing process of referring to itself as a concrete normative unity. More exactly, concern for the identity of another collective or collectives is integrated into the practice of collective self-identification. Assuredly, this need not be the only structural innovation leading beyond the state-centred paradigm of legal order. Moreover, it may remain an open question whether this is the decisive innovation which justifies the use of terms such as 'postnationalism', 'transnationalism', or 'denationalization'. But it does suffice to give conceptual and empirical purchase to the claim that a significant (constitutional) transformation has been operated in how legal orders are or can be structured.

It is fitting to conclude this chapter with an observation that prepares the transition to Part II. The aim of this chapter is, as noted at its outset, to address—or at least to begin to address—the problem of the individuation of legal orders. I have argued that focusing on the problem of collective identity and its contrasting terms is a good way of getting a handle on the problem of individuation. Granted, the first-person plural model of legal order outlined in sections 3.2 and 3.3 remains faithful to the primarily *static* account of the relation between boundaries/limits and legal order that Part I has been concerned to unveil. Nonetheless, it has also become increasingly clear that a static account of collective identity ends up by abolishing itself: insofar as collective identity must be sustained over time, in the face of questions about what is to count as legal and illegal behaviour, it is the outcome of a *process* of boundary-setting. In fact, a rigorously static analysis of legal order is impossible: it would not have been possible to draw and illuminate the distinction between legal boundaries and limits, in chapter 1, unless the process of setting legal boundaries that was already underway were interrupted by a-legality. Consequently, individuality leads into individuation, identity into identification. We must now begin to scrutinize this process, bringing the structural analysis of Part I to a close and inaugurating the genetic account of legal order to be pursued in Part II. This genetic exploration will allow us to introduce the notion of normative fault lines into our systematic model of legal order.

PART II

LEGAL ORDERING

Part I contends that no legal order can be such unless it is limited: in space no less than in time; in content as much as in subjectivity. Limits are constitutive features of the concept of legal order. The assumption that global legal orders expose the inside / outside distinction as a contingent, state-bound feature of law turns out to be a particularly powerful manifestation of state-centred thinking about law. Whereas the distinction between domestic and foreign legal orders is indeed historically contingent, the closure that gives rise to the contrast between a collective's own legal space and strange places is constitutive for any conceivable legal order. Parallel considerations apply to the temporal, subjective, and material boundaries of legal orders. From this fundamental perspective legal globalization is merely a distraction.

This insight has considerable implications for contemporary legal and political theories, which have taken for granted that the emergence of non-state law calls for a drastic reorientation of our conceptual and normative assumptions about law and politics. The change of direction elicited by this conceptual and normative reorientation is anticipated by expressions such as 'global democracy', 'world constitutionalism', 'global justice', and the like. Yet, in light of our analyses, these expressions can no longer mean democracy beyond limits, nor constitutionalism beyond limits, nor, finally, justice beyond limits. To the contrary, inclusion and exclusion hold unabated sway in the global setting of law. More pointedly, inclusion and exclusion continue to hold sway not merely *de facto*—as the blemishes of the *globalisation manquée* emerging before our eyes—but rather *de jure:* as a condition in the absence of which no legal order, no democracy, no constitutionalism, global or otherwise, would be possible.

Although legal orders are necessarily limited, this obviously says nothing about whether limits can be shifted in the process of transforming boundaries, nor how boundaries *ought* to be transformed and limits shifted. Part II seeks to address these conceptual and normative issues. If Part I is structural in its approach to legal order, Part II is genetic in style: it approaches legal order as an order*ing*. In contrast to Part I, which treats legal order as an *ordo ordinatus*, Part II treats it as an *ordo ordinans*. This shift will allow me to introduce the category of normative fault lines, which has been kept in reserve in the course of Part I. In short, what interests me now is to provide a concrete account of the emergence of legal orders and their boundaries, limits, and fault lines, while also exploring whether the conditions that govern the emergence of legal orders shed light on legal normativity, in particular whether there are criteria which govern how legal boundaries ought to be set. I will develop this broad range of issues by way of an analysis of legal boundary-setting, for it is in the course thereof that legal ordering takes place. Crucially, it also renders visible the internal connection between legal ordering and legal rationality, a connection to which Part II constantly attends.

4

A Genealogy of Legal Ordering

Shifting from a structural to a genetic perspective requires, most generally and abstractly, passing from the conceptualization of legal order to that of legal ordering; from boundaries as set to boundary-setting; from collective identity to collective identification. If we follow the timeworn terminology of the legal doctrine it would be natural to turn from law as made to law-*making;* from law as enacted to the *enactment* of legal norms. While it might seem attractive to begin with law-making, the disadvantages of doing so outweigh the advantages. On the one hand, law-making consists of the authoritative positing of legal norms, whether general (e.g. statutes) or individualized (e.g. judicial rulings). In the same way that Part I eschews those reductive approaches which view a legal order as the unity of a manifold of legal norms, so also we now need to put into place a conceptual framework that could bring out into the open how and why legal ordering is primarily a specific way of ordering space, time, subjectivity, and content as a concrete (albeit putative) normative unity. On the other hand, we need a conceptual framework that is sufficiently comprehensive to include all forms of legal ordering, hence all operations in which legal boundary-setting takes place. While law-making is an important vehicle for legal ordering, it by no means exhausts the latter's scope. Finally, it goes without saying that we need a conceptual framework that is sufficiently general to describe how ordering takes place in the wide range of legal orders discussed in Part I, including but not limited to state law, international law, *lex mercatoria,* multinationals, cyberlaw, and the European Union.

Inasmuch as joint action allowed us to introduce a structural account of legal orders that is concrete and general, it seems sensible to stick to it when considering legal ordering. In particular, I want to begin by pinpointing and describing the basic operation of ordering that takes place in legal acts, before showing how illegal acts precipitate disorder and a-legal acts intimate an emergent legal order. My analysis turns on the thesis that 'intentionality', in a phenomenologically inspired sense of the term, is the basic operation of ordering—and rationality—deployed by legal acts. I am aware that this move repeats the expository strategy deployed in chapter 1, which began with legality, moved on to illegality, and ended with a-legality. As was the case in chapter 1, this strategy renders the forthcoming account of legal ordering vulnerable to the censure that it favours legality and illegality to the detriment of a-legality. The objection would be that approaching legal ordering by way of acts that conform to legal norms amounts to relinquishing any strong sense of novelty. For how could we understand the emergence of legal orders and their boundaries at all if our enquiry takes its point of departure as a legal order that has already been established, and as boundaries that have already been set? I leave this question in suspense for the time being, if nothing else because this chapter is organized in such a way that it works its way towards a rebuttal of this objection in its final section.

4.1 INTENTIONALITY AND LEGAL ORDERING

Let us get started by focusing on the notion of a legal act, which I take to comprise all kinds of acts that contribute to pulling off joint action by a legal collective. The idea is to build up the notion of a legal act in a way that adumbrates how ordering takes place in the ordinary course of joint action under law. The present section takes an initial step in this direction, arguing that acts in the ordinary course of joint action under law deploy the basic operation of *intentionality*. The first scenario of Lafayette introduced in chapter 1 will provide the material for illustrating how legal acts are intentionally structured. But it is justified, I believe, to assume that the model of legal ordering outlined hereinafter is sufficiently capacious to accommodate the wide range of legal orders explored in Part I, as it draws on the intentional structure of joint action at the heart of each of these legal orders.

If Kelsen's theory of the spheres of validity provided us with an initial *aperçu* as to why legal orders might be bounded in space, content, time, and subjectivity, so also his claim that legal norms are 'schemes of interpretation' provides a first foothold concerning the problem of legal ordering, albeit it that Kelsen's claim needs to be developed in a direction quite different to the general thrust of his approach to legal order. At the outset of the *Pure Theory of Law* Kelsen notes that the specifically legal meaning of an event 'comes by way of a norm whose content refers to the event and confers legal meaning on it; the act can be interpreted, then, according to this norm. The norm functions as a scheme of interpretation'.[1] Accordingly, Kelsen draws a distinction between acts and their meanings. On the one hand we have an 'act perceptible to the senses'; on the other 'there is a specific meaning, a sense that is, so to speak, immanent in or attached to the act or event'.[2] For instance, '[p]eople assemble in a hall, they give speeches, some rise, others remain seated—this is the external event. Its meaning: that a statute is enacted'.[3] This example calls attention to the fact that legal meanings make it possible for a complex chain of discrete acts to appear *as* a legislative act. A second example: 'a man dressed in robes says certain words from a platform, addressing someone standing before him'. Here again, something (an act) appears *as* something: 'This external event has as its meaning a judicial decision'.[4] Yet a third example: 'a merchant writes a certain letter to another merchant, who writes back in reply. This means they have entered into a contract'.[5]

[1] Kelsen, *Problems of Legal Theory*, 8.
[2] Kelsen, *Problems of Legal Theory*, 8.
[3] Kelsen, *Problems of Legal Theory*, 8.
[4] Kelsen, *Problems of Legal Theory*, 8.
[5] Kelsen, *Problems of Legal Theory*, 8.

This succinct description of norms as schemes of interpretation has a far more general scope than what first meets the eye. It points to a fundamental structure of the relation to reality deployed in perception, practical activity, desires, imaginative projections, and the like. Husserl calls this structure 'intentionality'. According to Husserl, although intentions are always directed toward their object, the intended object appears with this or that determinate meaning. He distinguishes, accordingly, between the '*object as it is intended*' and the '*object ... which is intended*'.[6] Heidegger builds on and transforms the notion of intentionality when elucidating understanding as the structure of practical activity oriented to the manipulation of things: the disclosure of '*something as something*'.[7] I cannot dwell here on the development and mutations of this cardinal concept in the history of phenomenology. The single question that interests me, with a view to clarifying the operation of intentionality at the heart of legal acts, is the following: What characterizes the relation whereby something is disclosed *as* something in law?[8] I will develop an answer to this question that steers clear of a number of controversial issues surrounding the phenomenological notion of intentionality, such as Husserl's account of transcendental subjectivity. And while my account of a legal act draws heavily on Heidegger's explorations into understanding and interpretation, I also want to steer clear of the reception of Heidegger's thinking in philosophical hermeneutics in general, and theories of legal interpretation in particular. Thus, rather than speak of a phenomenology of legal intentionality, it seems prudent to refer to the forthcoming analyses as a phenomenologically *inspired* account thereof.[9]

So, returning to our question, what characterizes the relation whereby something is disclosed *as* something in law? Most importantly, the term 'as' introduces what Waldenfels calls a 'significative difference'.[10] This means, first, that intentionality is a 'unity in difference', a unity which ruins any dualistic view of the relation between the self and reality. This unity in difference is also constitutive of legal acts. Consider the *Grogan* ruling by the European Court of Justice: there is not, first, an act (abortion) with the meaning of a delict, which is subsequently

[6] Edmund Husserl, *Logical Investigations*, vol. 2, trans. J.N. Findlay (London: Routledge & Kegan Paul, 1970), 578 (emphasis in the original).

[7] Heidegger, *Being and Time*, 189 (emphasis in the original).

[8] In the forthcoming I draw on the phenomenological notion of intentionality, rather than on the notion of intentionality developed by theories of collective intentionality of analytical provenance, because the former allows me to develop the notions of boundaries, limits, and thresholds in a more direct way than the latter.

[9] Remarkably, the few contributions to a phenomenology of law pay little or no attention to the role of intentionality in the sense of the disclosure of 'something as something' in law, despite the capital importance thereof for phenomenology—and for law, as I attempt to show hereinafter. See, e.g. Sophie Loidolt, *Einführung in die Rechtsphänomenologie* (Tübingen: Mohr Siebeck, 2010); Simone Goyard-Fabre, *Essai de critique phénoménologique du droit* (Paris: Klincksieck, 1972); Paul Amselek, *Méthode phénoménologique et théorie du droit* (Paris: Pichon, 1964); Gerhart Husserl, *Recht und Zeit* (Frankfurt: Klostermann, 1955); Gerhart Husserl, *Recht und Welt* (Frankfurt: Klostermann, 1964); Adolf Reinach, *Zur Phänomenologie des Rechts: Die apriorischen Grundlagen des bürgerlichen Rechts* (Munich: Kösel Verlag, 1953).

[10] Bernhard Waldenfels, *Spielraum des Verhaltens* (Frankfurt: Suhrkamp, 1980), 129; Bernhard Waldenfels, *Bruchlinien der Erfahrung* (Frankfurt: Suhrkamp, 2002), 28–30.

connected to the first-person plural perspective taken up by members of the Irish collective; rather, to disclose the act as a delict is to take up the first-person plural perspective of the Irish collective, in the same way that to disclose the act as a service is to take up the first-person plural perspective of the European collective. Second, intentionality is not only a unity in difference but also a 'difference in unity'. Relations to reality have an intentional structure when *mediated* by meanings, including legal meanings; legal relations to reality are *indirect*, like all intentional relations. On the one hand, 'meaning cannot be reduced to a part of reality'; contrary to what some brands of realism would have us believe, 'the experienced is not something that is purely given'. On the other hand, and certain strands of idealism notwithstanding, 'reality cannot be reduced to a moment of meaning; what is experienced is not something purely produced (*Gemachtes*)...'[11] Were what is given in legal intentionality merely a legal construct, it would not be possible to distinguish between something which is the object of legal intentionality and the object as intended. Here again, *Grogan* illustrates this important point: the distribution of information about abortion clinics (the intended object) can appear as legal, from the perspective of EU law, by dint of being ancillary to a service, and as illegal, from the perspective of Irish law, by virtue of facilitating or abetting a delict (the object as intended).

Kelsen's choice of the term 'interpretation' to characterize this intentional relation could be misleading. Many scholars use the term to refer to the process of eliciting the meaning of legal norms, especially textually anchored norms, as occurs in doctrinal studies or in judicial rulings such as *Grogan*. In this vein, Hans-Georg Gadamer's philosophical hermeneutics, including his theory of judicial interpretation, favours the explicit attempt to elicit (legal) meanings when he describes interpretation as the act of 'understand[ing] something as something'.[12] But the compass of legal intentionality is far broader than the process of eliciting the meaning of legal norms. It already takes place at the level of *practice*, in the fundamental sense of practical involvement with others and with things, such as when I grab a bag of potatoes from a shelf in a food store and then move on to pay for it at the check-out point. By the same token, legal intentionality need not be explicit. In taking the bag from the shelf, on my way to the check-out point, I am already disclosing it *as* a product I will be purchasing, even if I do so more or less blindly, without explicitly disclosing it in the form of this-as-a-product. Analogously, when handing over the money for the potatoes, what I do counts *as* a payment, even though I or others do not explicitly view it in the form of this-as-a-payment.[13] A legal act, in the form of practical involvement with things

[11] Waldenfels, *Spielraum des Verhaltens*, 130.

[12] Hans-Georg Gadamer, 'Text and Interpretation', in Diane P. Michelfelder and Richard E. Palmer (eds.), *Dialogue and Deconstruction: The Gadamer-Derrida Encounter* (Stony Brook, NY: SUNY Press, 1989), 29.

[13] Heidegger makes this point as follows: 'that which is explicitly understood... has the structure of *something as something*... In dealing with what is environmentally ready-to-hand by interpreting it circumspectively, we "see" it *as* a table, a door, a carriage, or a bridge; but what we have thus interpreted need not necessarily also be explicated by making an assertion which definitely characterizes it'. Heidegger, *Being and Time*, 189.

and others, is, in this account, far more than simply a possible object of legal interpretation; first and foremost, it is itself a mode—the *primordial* mode—of legal interpretation, if we take legal interpretation to mean the disclosure of something as something.[14]

By contrast, legal interpretation as the explicit elucidation of the meaning of legal norms is a derivative activity. More precisely, this form of interpretation inaugurates a theoretical attitude towards a legal order, which sets in when one breaks off one's practical engagement with the world, as mediated by legal meanings, to render thematic legal norms and their real referents—to elicit their legal meaning. On this reading, the lay person who inquires about the legal meaning of some act or event is already engaged in a theoretical attitude, no less than the advocate, the legal scholar or the jurisprudent, each of whom is, in his or her own way, a professional legal theorist. Bourdieu notes, in this respect, that '[t]he abstract and transcendent norm of morality and of law doesn't affirm itself expressly until it ceases to inhabit practices in their practical state... The most fundamental principles [of a practice] can only remain in an implicit state as long as they are taken for granted'.[15]

This insight returns us to chapter 1, where I had noted that contemporary legal theory usually focuses on the unity of legal orders as the unity of a manifold of legal norms (in a broad sense that includes rules and principles). This focus, I argued, is reductive, to the extent that it systematically neglects the concrete unity of the law, that is, law's appearance as a spatial, temporal, subjective, and material unity. We can now add that the reduction of the unity of a legal order to the unity of a manifold of norms goes hand-in-hand with the restriction of legal interpretation to the interpretation of norms. To recover the primordial meaning

[14] Strikingly, the operation of intentionality at the heart of legal interpretation remains beyond the purview of some of the most influential contemporary contributions to the theory of legal interpretation. Dworkin's theory of legal interpretation is a good example of this. True, he grounds legal interpretation in practices. But legal interpretation *begins*, in Dworkin's account, when the point of a practice is called into question: legal interpretation is the interpretation *of* a legal practice. On the reading I espouse, legal intentionality is already at work in each of the myriad acts that make up a legal practice, and prior to situations that question its point: the interpretation of a legal practice presupposes and moves on the ground of legal practices *as* joint intentionality. Raz, for his part, argues that the interesting question for legal theory is *why* we engage in legal interpretation. While this question certainly is pertinent in the narrow sense of interpretation embraced by Raz, it loses its differentiating purport entirely when what is at stake is illuminating the operation of intentionality that defines legal interpretation as *interpretation*, a structure it shares with *all* domains of intentionality. At this fundamental level, the question 'why (legal) interpretation?' has no answer in the form of a reason that could shed new light on the nature of law; the only way to answer it is to point to what might be called the *Faktum* of intentionality. See Ronald Dworkin, *A Matter of Principle*, repr. (Oxford: Clarendon Press, 2001), 119–117; Dworkin, *Law's Empire*, 65–68; Joseph Raz, *Between Authority and Interpretation* (Oxford: Oxford University Press, 2009), 223 ff.

[15] Pierre Bourdieu, *Esquisse d'une théorie de la pratique*, repr. (Paris: Seuil, 2000), 300. Heidegger has coined the distinction between 'readiness-to-hand' (*Zuhandenheit*) and 'presence-at-hand' (*Vorhandenheit*) to characterize two different ways of relating to tools. In the first, the 'toolness' of the tool remains unthematic and taken for granted in the process of being used in a practical activity. In the second, the 'toolness' of the tool is rendered thematic precisely when *useless*, e.g. when missing, damaged, etc. Drawing on this distinction one could say that the interruption of legal practices, when a legal norm or institution appears as *inapplicable* to the situation at hand, means that the norm or institution forfeits its readiness-to-hand, appearing instead as presence-at-hand. Practice gives way to theory. See Heidegger, *Being and Time*, § 16.

of law as a concrete normative unity one must rescue the primordial sense of interpretation as practical involvement with things and others.

In short, I propose to introduce the distinction between legal understanding and legal interpretation as a way of capturing this important point. Both operations deploy the basic structure of intentionality: they disclose something as something. But there is also a difference. As concerns legal *understanding*, the intentional structure of legal acts is part and parcel of practical involvement with others and with things, such that the disclosure of something as something—say, this-bag-of-potatoes-as-a-product—remains implicit and taken for granted. At stake are the more or less anonymous, both pre- and post-reflexive forms of social interaction to which I referred in section 1.2. As concerns legal *interpretation*, the intentional structure of legal acts is rendered explicit when individuals break off their practical involvement with things and others to take up the theoretical stance of eliciting legal meanings, that is, of eliciting the meaning of a legal practice. The shift from a practical to a theoretical attitude involves an important transformation of agency: if, in the course of the former, the legal order remained more or less unobtrusive as the background condition for the agents' activities and plans (we are buying victuals to throw a party), legal interpretation interrupts those activities and plans as *individual* plans and activities, such that agents come to view themselves as clients, the food shop as a specific kind of ought-place (a place where certain forms of behaviour are authorized and others not), and so forth. In short, legal interpretation involves taking up a properly legal point of view, whereby the meaning of a legal practice becomes thematic as such and is the object of interpretation.[16] I will return to this distinction in section 4.5; for the moment, I want to flesh out more fully its common root, namely, the general structure of legal intentionality.

4.2 DISCLOSING SOMETHING AS SOMETHING*

The act whereby someone picks up a bag of potatoes on his or her way to pay for it at the check-out point illustrates, I argued, the canonical formulation of legal intentionality as the 'disclosure of something as something'. But this example and the broader scenario in which it takes place suggest that the formulation is too abridged. Nothing can appear as legally meaningful unless it does so within a space and time, *which also appear as legally meaningful*. In other words, the indirect character of legal intentionality includes the *where* and the *when* of what is disclosed. Turning first to space, something does not only appear somewhere, but *as* somewhere. To disclose a bag of potatoes as a product is also to disclose the space in which it is located *as* a food store, that is, as the ought-place that belongs together with buying that product. The operation of intentionality at work in the appearance of space as a legal space is also apparent in the examples Kelsen marshals to drive home his point that legal norms are schemes of interpretation. Indeed, 'people assemble in a hall', such that some 'stand' and others 'remain

[16] This conception of the legal point of view is very different to that proposed by Raz in his article, 'Kelsen's Theory of the Basic Norm', reprinted in Raz, *The Authority of Law*, 137–143.

seated'. Viewing an act as a legislative act is inseparable from its appearance *as* taking place in an ought-place, e.g. a parliamentary or congressional building. Look at Kelsen's second example: 'a man [speaks] from a platform, addressing someone standing before him'. The act of passing judgment appears *as* taking place in a courthouse. Then again, 'a merchant writes...*to* another merchant, who writes *back*...' The adverbs 'to' and 'back' speak to different places within a single distribution of ought-places in which certain acts, when taken together, count *as* a contract.

In the same way, something appears not only somewhen, if I may put it that way, but *as* somewhen. To understand grabbing a bag of potatoes as a product involves inserting this act in the meaningful sequence of acts that makes up buying a product: a person has entered the food shop, picks up the bag now, and will move on to the check-out point. Also Kelsen's examples make legal sense to the extent that they can be viewed as fitting into a temporal interconnection of legal acts. 'People [first] assemble and [then] give speeches, some rise [while] others remain seated': the meaningful sequence of actions counts as pulling off a legislative act. 'A man speaks [now] from a platform [after the pleadings have taken place, and before the man is taken to jail]': to say that an act is a judgment is to view it as inserted within the sequence of acts that make up a criminal procedure. Finally, [after] preliminary correspondence between the two, 'a merchant writes [now] to another merchant, who [later] writes back': the two acts appear as the signing of a contract because they fit into a temporal whole that counts as the negotiation, closing, and fulfilment of a contract. In terms of what Waldenfels dubs the 'significative difference', this entails, on the one hand, that space and time are not given immediately but rather mediated through legal meanings, and, on the other, that space and time cannot be simply reduced to how they manifest themselves in any given legal practice. How places and times are disclosed as ought-places and ought-times within a certain legal practice does not exhaust their possible normative meanings.[17]

But the canonical formulation of intentionality needs to be unpacked further if it is to provide a more complete account of legal intentionality. While 'the disclosure of something as something' fits no less comfortably with disclosing a document as a cheque or a building as a courthouse than it does with the perception of things (Husserl) or their practical manipulation (Heidegger), this formulation is too crude to accommodate the distinction between the subjective and material spheres of validity of legal norms: someone is disclosed *as* a buyer (an ought-subject) and *as* selecting a product to be bought (an ought-content). Here again Kelsen's examples illustrate this point. 'People assemble in a hall, they

[17] This crucial point escapes Kelsen entirely. On his reading of legal interpretation, that behaviour appears as legally meaningful requires distinguishing between two elements: on the one hand, 'an act or series of acts—a happening occurring at a certain time and in a certain place, perceived by our senses: an external manifestation of human conduct'; on the other, 'the legal meaning of this act'. Space and time are 'conditions' for legal interpretation in Kelsen, not part of reality as intended. See here the positivistic core of Kelsen's thinking about legal interpretation, which explains why he could not understand that the spatial and temporal spheres of validity of legal norms are perforce limited. See Kelsen, *The Pure Theory of Law*, 2.

give speeches, some rise, others remain seated…' Certain persons are disclosed *as* members of parliament and *as* enacting a statute. 'A man dressed in robes says certain words from a platform, addressing someone standing before him'. Someone is disclosed *as* a judge and *as* passing judgment. Finally, 'a merchant writes a certain letter to another merchant, who writes back in reply'. Someone is disclosed *as* a contracting party and *as* closing a contract. As was the case with space and with time, the 'significative difference' characteristic of legal intentionality entails that legal subjectivity and the content of legal acts are never given immediately, but rather always indirectly, mediated through legal meanings. In short, a more complete formulation of legal intentionality is this: the disclosure of something as someone, as somewhat, as somewhere, and as somewhen. This formulation is rather cumbersome; a more tractable formulation is the following: *the disclosure of something as something**.[18]

Thus far, I have focused on the structure of legal intentionality in terms of the subjective, material, spatial, and temporal dimensions of an individual act. But this is still only part of the picture. No single act would be legally meaningful unless it pointed beyond itself to other ought-subjects, ought-contents, ought-places, and ought-times. Something appears as something* only insomuch that it appears within a *referential unity*. This was, of course, the upshot of the scenarios we discussed in chapter 1, when arguing that the unity of a legal order presents itself as a differentiated interconnection of places, times, subjects, and contents. It is not otherwise with Kelsen's examples of norms as schemes of interpretation, even though he does not draw this conclusion. For example, a statutory enactment is only meaningful as such in connection with other acts by other subjects (e.g. elections by citizens and executive actions by administrative organs who must implement the statute); the place in which the statute is enacted must refer beyond itself to other ought-places if it is to be viewed as a parliamentary building (e.g. polling stations, courts, jails, administrative buildings); the time in which it occurs must refer beyond itself, both into the past and the future, if it is to make temporal sense in the law (e.g. elections, the swearing in of the members of parliament, the administrative implementation of the law).

Accordingly, to disclose something as something* is also always to *co*-disclose the fourfold referential unity in which that something is given. This co-disclosure is not merely ancillary to what is first and foremost the disclosure of something* in particular. Instead, co-disclosure in legal intentionality involves the *prior* disclosure of an order, which functions as the horizon whence something can be grasped as something*. Picking up a bag of potatoes and walking towards the check-out point to pay for it, on my way to throwing a party with my friends, would not be possible unless I already co-disclose the fourfold dimensions of the legal order in which such an act makes sense. What Heidegger has to say about the relation between the ready-to-hand (e.g. a hammer in use) and a world holds also for the relation between a legal act and the apposite legal order: 'In anything ready-to-hand the world is always "there". Whenever we encounter anything,

[18] I will use the asterisk, in the forthcoming, as shorthand for the four dimensions or boundaries of legal orders.

the world has already been previously discovered, although not thematically'.[19] Hence, the disclosure of something as something* involves the co-disclosure of a legal order, in the specific sense of a 'whole of involvements'[20] organized in terms of the normative differentiation and interconnection of the what, who, where, and when of legally significant acts. In other words, disclosure is always also the co-disclosure of the *unity* of ought-places, ought-times, ought-subjectivities, and ought-contents whence something can appear as something*. Legal norms could not orient behaviour unless their four 'spheres of validity' function, most fundamentally, as *horizons of meaning:* for something to be given in the law as something* it must point beyond itself, in the form of ought-references, to other elements of each of these four spheres of validity.

4.3 WE [OUGHT TO] JOINTLY DISCLOSE SOMETHING AS SOMETHING* IN-ORDER-TO-φ

A further element must be integrated into our analysis of legal intentionality: what appears as something* in a legal order appears from a *first-person plural perspective*. Take *Grogan*: an act appears as a delict from the first-person perspective of the Irish collective. This perspective is not merely accessory to legal intentionality; changing the first-person plural perspective also changes how the object is intended: the act appears as a service from the first-person perspective of the European collective. The same goes for each of the examples put forward by Kelsen: it would not be possible to disclose something as a legislative act, as a judicial ruling, or as a contract unless one takes up the appropriate first-person perspective. This insight returns us, once again, to the phenomenological concept of intentionality: something appears as something *to* someone.

To *whom* does something appear as something, in the course of legal intentionality? The foregoing analyses acknowledge without reservations that there could be no legal intentionality absent the first-person *singular* perspective of the actors who participate in a legal practice. It is an individual who, driving his or her car into a slot reserved for the employees of a corporation, views him or herself *as* someone (an ought-subject: employee), his or her act *as* somewhat (an ought-act: parking), the slot *as* somewhere (an ought-place: a parking lot) and *as* somewhen (an ought-time: commencing work); and so forth. As the example shows, this first-person singular perspective is an ingredient of individuals' legal *self*-understandings. In the same way that I can make legal sense of what someone else is doing when parking a car in front of the corporation's headquarters, so also when it is *I* who does so.

Crucially, however, legal intentionality is never merely the aggregation of a manifold of first-person singular perspectives. This point is important because it allows us to introduce a corrective to phenomenological accounts of the 'intersubjectivity' of intentionality. For example, Husserl shows that perception cannot be merely one-sided or unilateral; awareness that at any given moment perception

[19] Heidegger, *Being and Time*, 114.

[20] 'Bewandtnisganzheit', in Heidegger, *Being and Time*, 118 (translation altered).

only discloses one side of an object goes together with co-awareness that there are others who (can) disclose other sides of the same object; in this sense, perception is multilateral.[21] Despite its acuity, this account of the intersubjective character of intentionality goes no further than what Gilbert nicely calls 'we both' or, if there are more than two observers, 'we each'. By contrast, legal intentionality comes into its own when intersubjectivity takes on the form of 'we together'.[22] When disclosing something as something*, an individual engages in what Margaret Gilbert calls participant agency—action as part of a plural subject. Although it is in each case an individual who parks his or her car in front of the corporation's headquarters, he or she does so as a participant in joint action, i.e. on the understanding, however inarticulate, that, under the given circumstances, we, the legal collective in which he or she partakes, ought to treat the apposite act as one to which he or she is entitled, that is, an act that fulfils shared expectations about who ought to do what, where, and when. A fuller description of the operation of intentionality constitutive of legal acts would be, therefore, the following: the disclosure of something as something* from the perspective of a 'we' in joint action. To the extent that such disclosure is also always the co-disclosure of the referential unity whence it is intelligible who ought to do what, where, and when, a collective is the correlate of a legal order. In their involvement with others and with things, individual participants in a legal practice orient themselves spatially, temporally, subjectively, and materially by actualizing, however implicitly and even anonymously, the first-person plural perspective of a 'we' in joint action.

To carry further our picture of legal intentionality we need to sketch out more fully how it is connected to joint action. The *point* of joint action is pivotal in this respect. It is not difficult to see how the point of joint action fits into the structure of legal intentionality: 'we jointly disclose something as something* *in-order-to-φ*', where 'φ' counts as the normative point of joint action. Legal intentionality has

[21] In Dan Zahavi's words, '[p]rovided that the subject as subject is directed towards objects, provided that every experience of objects is characterized by the [horizonal] appearance of the object, where a certain aspect is present and the others are absent, and provided that this [horizonal] intentionality, this interplay between presence and absence can only be accounted for phenomenologically through a reference to a plurality of possible subjects, the consequence is, that I in my being as subject is referred to Others, regardless of whether I experience them concretely or not, regardless of whether they actually exist or not'. Dan Zahavi, 'Husserl's Intersubjective Transformation of Transcendental Philosophy', repr. in Rudolf Bernet, Donn Welton, and Gina Zavota (eds.), *Edmund Husserl: Critical Assessments of Leading Philosophers*, vol. 4 (London: Routledge, 2005), 366.

[22] Parallel misgivings apply to Heidegger's characterization of human existence as 'being-with' (*Mitsein*) and of the world as 'with-world' (*Mitwelt*). This characterization remains too general to capture the specificity of the first-person plural perspective of a 'we' in joint action. To lay bare the features of intersubjectivity proper to the first-person plural perspective, Heidegger would have had to develop an 'analytic of collective *Dasein*', substituting his famous analysis of the cobbler wielding a hammer in the workplace for the analysis of a *group*, the members of which act together in the workplace. (See Heidegger, *Being and Time*, 95 ff; 118–119). This is not to say, however, that phenomenology is entirely destitute of descriptions of joint action, as shown by Schütz's description of making music together; but the specificity of joint action is not really worked out therein. See Alfred Schütz, *On Phenomenology and Social Relations* (Chicago: Chicago University Press, 1970), 214–216. This *lacuna* may explain, in any case, why there is a dearth of properly phenomenological accounts of legal order and ordering, that is, of accounts that take their point of departure as the operation of intentionality deployed in joint action under law.

a point.[23] I put a bag of potatoes into a pannier and walk towards the check-out point in-order-to-buy-it; this 'in-order-to' of my act is its legal point. Obviously, this point is nested, from the perspective of the individual, in higher-order points of the action, e.g. I am buying this product in-order-to throw a party. And the points of kinds of joint acts are also nested, from a collective perspective, in the normative points of more general legal institutions to which those joint acts contribute.

Importantly, 'in-order-to-φ' comprises, but is not restricted to purposes. 'Point includes purpose, but can refer to any motive, value or reason that can be given to explain or justify the practice from the point of view of the actor'.[24] Notice, however, that the point of a legal practice need not be something which participant agents explicitly have in mind when acting. To the contrary, the habituality of legal practices, whereby the joint action becomes 'second nature' to actors, is a constitutive feature of legal intentionality in the mode of legal understanding. The point of a legal practice becomes the object of explicit attention when the theoretical attitude sets in, when that which agents understand themselves and their fellow participants as doing together is interrupted. This is the moment at which legal understanding yields to legal interpretation, such that the point of a practice begins to function, in Twining's words, as a 'motive, value of reason that can be given to *explain* or *justify* the practice...' Prior to the explanatory or justificatory function of point comes its pre-reflexive and pre-predicative orienting function.

Furthermore, while Twining correctly notes that the point of a legal practice involves the first-person perspective, at stake is the first-person *plural* perspective: the point of a legal practice appears when one takes up the perspective of the group agent. When I place the bag of potatoes in the pannier, and look around to see where the check-out points are situated, my act refers to acts by other actors, with whom I act *together*, e.g. the employee at the check-out point, whom I expect to act in accordance with the point that informs my act, and who, conversely, expects that I act in accordance with the point guiding his or her act. That *we jointly* disclose something as something* requires that each of us contribute to realizing the point of a joint act in the appropriate way. That there are *appropriate* forms of participant agency is a compact way of saying that the point of a joint act determines who *ought* to do what, where, and when. We are on familiar terrain here, having noted in chapter 3, with Gilbert, that joint action gives rise to mutual obligations, entitlements, and the like, such that participant agents have special standing to demand of their fellow agents that they do their bit in the joint act, and to rebuke them and hold them responsible, if they do not.

Here, then, is a preliminary approximation to the operation of legal intentionality. By way of legal acts 'we [ought to] jointly disclose something as something*

[23] My account of the point of joint action modifies and generalizes Heidegger's description of the 'equipmentality' of equipment: 'Equipment is essentially "something in-order-to..." [*etwas-um-zu*]'. Heidegger, *Being and Time*, 97.

[24] Twining, *General Jurisprudence*, 110. For a strongly purposive reading of point see Dworkin, *Law's Empire*, 55–59.

in order-to-φ'. The brackets around 'ought to' signal that, in the ordinary course of a legal practice, what agents do and what they ought to do run over into each other; only when the point of the act becomes problematic do 'ought' and 'is' fall apart.

The time is ripe to wrap up this section by showing how a study of legal intentionality clinches a transition from legal order to legal ordering. In what way does legal intentionality contribute to a theory of legal ordering?

The shortest and most direct answer is that *to act legally is to disclose something as something*, and to disclose something as something* is to order*. Indeed, legal acts display the elemental achievement of legal ordering because to order in the law is to determine, whether in general or in particular, who ought to do what, where, and when in a way that is consistent with the normative point of the corresponding first-person plural perspective of a 'we acting together'. Notice the ubiquity of legal ordering. The operation of intentionality is manifest in law-making, not least in the enactment of general norms, such as statutes, model contract forms for international construction projects, European regulations and directives, internal regulations of multinational corporations, etc. In all these cases, legal acts order by assigning a place, time, subject, and content to a *kind* of act. Legal ordering also takes place in individualized law-making, such as an administrative decision or judicial ruling. But the legal ordering that takes place in joint action is by no means restricted to law-making. Legal ordering is already at work in the myriad legal acts whereby individuals are practically involved with things and with others. Legal ordering occurs at the mundane level of purchasing a ticket before stepping onto the platform of a train station, and not merely because it is part and parcel of a contract. To the contrary, a contract is one of the possible forms of legal ordering because it presupposes the operation of intentionality common to all legal ordering. In fact, those mundane forms of practical involvement with others and things make up the bulk of legal ordering, even though the ordering that takes place therein usually remains largely implicit and veiled to the participants. Purchasing a train ticket, driving a car into a parking lot, putting up a fence around a site in the framework of an international construction contract under the aegis of *lex constructionis*, operating a machine on an oil rig out in the North Sea and buying and downloading music from cyberspace are 'mundane' examples of legal ordering because all legal acts are mundane in the fundamental sense noted above, namely a joint assignment of something as something* in a *world*.

Yet a further implication of legal acts as acts of legal ordering becomes apparent if we remember that chapter 1 described legal order as a 'ready-made' differentiated interconnection of elements. The foregoing analyses suggest that differentiating and interconnecting is what legal acts *do:* in the very move by which a legal act differentiates by picking out something (even if it is a class of things or acts, as in the enactment of a statute) and disclosing it as something*, it also interconnects by referring this something beyond itself, to other elements with which it belongs in the fourfold referential unity of a legal order. From this perspective, the modern doctrinal contrast between 'customary' law and 'posited' law is derivative. Their common root is the 'posing' of law in the form of a *disposing* of space, time, subjectivity, and content. Legal acts, *qua* intentional acts, *arrange* each of these four dimensions, and all of them together, each time around. This is why it could be asserted, in chapter 1, that behaviour is not only in space but also 'spaces'; that it not only occurs in time but also 'times'; that it not only presupposes subjectivity but also 'subjectifies'; that it not only takes its cue from the content of legal norms but also 'materializes'. All of this is what defines the operation of legal intentionality as an ordering. In short, ordering—a joint disposing that differentiates and interconnects by disclosing something as something* in-order-to φ—characterizes legal acts *qua* intentional acts. This ordering achievement of legal acts remains concealed if, with Kelsen, one banishes them, as acts, to the domain of 'natural events' which are only amenable to causal explanation, sociological or otherwise.

4.4 WE [OUGHT TO] JOINTLY DISCLOSE SOMETHING AS SOMETHING* ANEW IN-ORDER-TO-φ

This preliminary account of legal ordering has an important limitation, however: it examines the operation of intentionality deployed by a single legal act in isolation from its insertion in a legal practice. Yet legal acts do not come alone; they take place in the course of legal practices. The insertion of acts in legal practices is an integral part of the structure of legal intentionality, hence of legal ordering. How? Why? Here again, Kelsen's characterization of legal norms as 'schemes of interpretation' offers the clue, provided another aspect of his insight is brought into focus. Thus far I have sought to clarify legal norms as schemes of *interpretation*. But what does it mean that legal norms function as *schemes* of interpretation?

The 'schematic' character of legal norms is linked to the anticipatory structure of intentionality, to their 'horizonality', which Ludwig Landgrebe explains as follows in his introduction to Husserl's *Experience and Judgment*:

> Every experience has its own horizon... This implies that every experience refers to the possibility... not only of explicating, step by step, the thing which has been given in a first view... but also of obtaining, little by little, as experience continues, new determinations of the same thing.[25]

The horizonal character of intentionality involves an 'aiming-beyond' something as given, which *anticipates* how it might be given in further experience (its 'inner horizon') and how it might stand in relation to other things or acts (its 'outer horizon').[26]

Although Husserl is primarily concerned with elucidating the horizonality of perception, his analyses are also pertinent to legal acts. For example, before entering a

[25] Edmund Husserl, *Experience and Judgment: Investigations in a Genealogy of Logic*, Ludwig Landgrebe (ed.), trans. James S. Churchill and Karl Ameriks (London: Routledge & Kegan Paul, 1973), 32.

[26] '[T]his aiming-beyond... is also an aiming-beyond the thing itself with all its anticipated possibilities... to other objects of which we are aware at the same time... This means that everything given in experience has not only an internal horizon but also an infinite, open, *external horizon of objects cogiven*'. Husserl, *Experience and Judgment*, 33.

food store, the members of a legal collective *anticipate in a general way* who ought to do what, where, and when if one wants to purchase vegetables, even though the specifics of going about this particular act still need to be sorted out with respect to the concrete situation of Lafayette. The members of the community of international construction companies anticipate in a general way who ought to do what, where, and when in the event that a construction firm and a client enter negotiations for a turnkey project, even though the specifics of the particular project need to be hammered out in the course of the negotiations. This anticipating-in-general-who-ought-to-do-what-where-and-when is, most fundamentally, what defines legal norms as *schemes* of interpretation, as schemes that provide normative orientation in the course of practical involvement with things and others.

The anticipating-in-general proper to legal schemes bears on the temporal structure of legal acts. Although each legal act is 'new' in the minimal sense that it has features that individuate it with respect to any prior act, each such act also reiterates earlier legal acts of the same kind. Someone buys a ticket for a fast train between A and B and steps onto the platform—like others before him or her. This may be the first time ever that someone actually buys a ticket for a fast train (e.g. the first fast train pressed into service); but this novelty presupposes a more fundamental continuity with previous instances of, say, a contract of carriage, which this new act carries forward and transforms. For this reason legal intentionality discloses something as *something**, i.e. as a *kind* of legal act: this document as a 'train ticket', this train station as 'the point of departure of a contract of carriage', this person as a 'passenger', now as the 'time of departure', etc. *Qua* schemes of interpretation, legal norms anticipate what will be disclosed in the form of a 'typical generality'.[27] As such, they open up a 'realm (*Spielraum*) of possibilities',[28] such that new acts can appear as further specifications of the scheme (e.g. the first fast train service 'falling under' a contract of carriage and determining it in a different way to other contracts of carriage).

So, although each act *qua* legal act is unique in a number of ways, what renders it more (and less, as we shall see) than a singular event is that it projects itself into the future by re-iterating a legal meaning and the four kinds of boundaries that define an act as a legal act. When someone parks his or her car in the slot assigned to the employees of a corporation, his or her act is, at each step, a *reiterative anticipation* of the normative dimensions of the kind of legal act at issue, hence of the boundaries that determine an act as an instance of something*. The anticipatory structure of legal intentionality involves the iteration and iterability of legal meanings, whereby an indeterminate number of acts can be disclosed as instantiations over time of a kind of legal act that ought to take place, as captured in the technical expression 'something*'. Legal understanding is *re*-understanding, *re*-cognition; legal interpretation, *re*-interpretation. A fuller formulation of legal intentionality is, therefore, the following: we [ought to] jointly disclose something as something* *anew*. This returns us to the initial question about legal ordering: to order, by way of legal acts, is to *re-order*. Legal ordering has the structure of a reiterative anticipation and is, as such, an ordering anew.

[27] Husserl, *Experience and Judgment*, 36. [28] Husserl, *Experience and Judgment*, 32.

This insight casts light on the internal connection between legal acts and legal practices, in particular why the operation of intentionality proper to legal acts cannot be grasped in isolation from legal practices, nor the latter independently of the former. Indeed, a phenomenologically inspired reading of Kelsen's insight that legal norms are *schemes* of interpretation boils down to this: that legal acts take place in the course of legal practices means that legal acts are structured as a reiterative anticipation; that legal practices unfold by way of legal acts means that a practice denotes the re-ordering process whereby we jointly disclose something as something* anew in-order-to-φ.

The idea that legal norms, as schemes of interpretation, open up a 'realm of possibilities' deserves closer consideration. Modal logic, according to which a logically possible proposition is a proposition that can be asserted together with its negation, without implying a logical contradiction, is of little assistance in conceptualizing legal possibility, and not because it embraces a 'technical' notion of possibility or because it focuses on propositions. The problem is that modal logic abstracts from possibility as a *practical* concept. The legal doctrine comes closer to the mark, even though it nowhere addresses the problem of possibility as such, and even though it conceals the primordial manifestation of legal possibility in the very move by which it reveals it. Indeed, the legal doctrine already points the way towards a practical notion of legal possibility when it draws up classifications of rights, obligations, and the like. Think, for example, of the law of obligations, which distinguishes, on the received doctrinal view, between obligations with respect to contract, unjust enrichment, management of the property of another, the reception of the thing not due, and tort. In turn, contractual obligations are either innominate or nominate, where the latter are parsed into sales, gift, lease, carriage, loan, employment, and so forth. These doctrinal classifications effectively map legal possibilities as species of legal acts falling under more generic forms thereof. What gets lost in this doctrinal approach, yet is the self-evident presupposition of all such classifications and charts, is that legal possibilities are primordially possibilities from the *first-person perspective*, both individual and collective. They are first-person repertoires of involvement with others and with things, whereby certain agents occupy certain places at certain times when acting in certain ways. In other words, legal possibilities are primarily *my own* possibilities, the range of ways in which I can orient myself when acting in a legal order; hence, my legal possibilities are also my possible *self*-understandings as a legal agent. Moreover, to the extent that these possibilities arise in the framework of my participation in joint action, they are *our own* possibilities, the possibilities available to us, the members of a collective, when acting together in the course of legal practices. In this sense, legal possibilities are legal *com*-possibilities.

Husserl uses the expression 'capacity' (*Ver-möglichkeit*) to refer to this first-person sense of possibility, as something I can do.[29] At first glance, 'legal capacity', as in the capacity of natural and legal persons to make binding amendments to

[29] Husserl, *Experience and Judgment*, 32. See, amongst others, Edmund Husserl, *The Crisis of European Sciences and Transcedental Phenomenology*, trans. David Carr (Evanston, IL: Northwestern University Press, 1970), § 47.

their rights, duties, and obligations, is the legal manifestation of 'capacity' in the first person. But the better term is *empowerment* or *authorization*. My range of legal possibilities is the range of that which I am authorized or empowered to do by legal schemes.[30] There is, accordingly, an internal link between legal possibilities and boundaries: *if legal possibilities establish who is authorized or empowered to do what, where, and when, legal boundaries are the boundaries of empowerment*. Boundaries are the temporal, spatial, subjective, and material constraints of legal capacity. The expression '*ultra vires*' is never merely metaphorical. Relatedly, and returning to modal logic and its definition of logical possibility, non-contradiction does indeed play a role in legal possibility. But legal possibility speaks to a *practical* form of non-contradiction: one cannot enter into a contract of sale and also expect to receive something as, say, a gift. In short, *qua schemes* of interpretation, legal norms enable individuals, 'capacitate' them as it were, by authorizing a range of legal acts as to their who, what, where, and when.

Importantly, by opening up a realm of legal possibilities, legal schemes go hand-in-hand with the closing down of other normative possibilities, a feature of legal order to which we alluded in the opening chapter of this book. The possibilities which are closed down are not merely forms of action which are declared illegal, for these are legal possibilities with a negative sign. As a normative order, legal order counts in advance with the possibility of acts in breach of who ought to do what, where, and when. Instead, at issue are forms of acting which are *incompossible* from the point of view of joint action. This is just what the *chômeurs* sought to show with the *autoréduction*: the food shop of Lafayette cannot, without contradiction, be both a place for engaging in the sale *and* donation of victuals. More precisely, the *autoréduction* intimates an act that is incompossible with the extant order because it is neither a donation nor a sale, while conjoining contradictory features of both. *Qua* schemes, legal norms empower and disempower, enable and disable. Accordingly, legal schemes of interpretation are conditions of possibility of legal acts. They are also conditions for the meaningfulness of acts as legal acts and, to that extent, also conditions of the *self*-understanding of a legal collective and its members. *What is intelligible in our legal order is what is possible as our joint action, and vice versa*. Whence a fuller formulation of the notion of a legal practice: to act legally is to orient oneself within and to actualize *anew* the 'realm of possibilities' made available by legal schemes; to orient oneself within this realm of possibilities, disclosing something as something*, is to understand oneself *anew* as a participant in a legal collective.

We take yet a further step if we note that the anticipating-in-general deployed in legal intentionality comprises the four spheres of validity of legal norms themselves. These are the most general conditions governing a legal order as a 'realm of possibilities'. Certainly, the range of acts authorized by a legal order may vary over time; assuredly, the range may be different to, and even incompatible with,

[30] This sense of authorization or empowerment resonates with Kelsen's account thereof, according to which '"to authorize" (*ermächtigen*) means, in the context of a legal order, to confer the power to create law'. Nonetheless, it should be noted that legal empowerment as a form of practical possibility remains beyond the pale of his analysis. Kelsen, *Pure Theory of Law*, 118.

the realms of possibilities opened up/closed down by other legal orders (e.g. the distribution of information about abortion clinics in *Grogan*). But regardless of how any act might be disclosed as something* in a given legal order, legal intentionality requires anticipating that any conceivable act is organized in such a way that it can fit into and reiterate the fourfold referential unity of a legal order. Not only acts which actually appear as possessing a legal meaning, but also acts which *could* appear in a legal order with this or that meaning, must appear as the concrete articulation of a who, what, where, and when, because these four dimensions determine the horizonal structure of a legal order as a 'totality of typification' (*Totalitätstypik*).[31] If schemes of legal interpretation configure a realm of possibilities, and in this sense condition legal possibilities, then the four spheres of validity of legal norms are the most general conditions of legal possibility and intelligibility; they are, properly speaking, the concrete a priori of legal ordering.

4.5 ORDERING AND RATIONALITY

Sections 4.1 to 4.4 sought to lay bare the structure of legal ordering as the operation of intentionality deployed in legal acts. Although I have concentrated primarily on the prosaic act of someone picking up a bag of potatoes on his or her way to paying for it at the check-out point of a food shop, analogous descriptions could be made for participant acts in any one of the other kinds of legal orders discussed in Part I, such as multinationals, *lex constructionis*, cyberlaw, the European Union, and nomadic collectives. The operation of intentionality is the common root of *all* legal ordering. The present section consolidates the findings of these sections by adumbrating what is perhaps their cardinal implication: the internal connection between legal ordering and legal rationality. I shall argue that while a legal act is the name a legal collective gives to behaviour that counts as *objective* for it, and in that sense as rational, an illegal act counts as *subjective* for it, hence as irrational. By contrast, a-legality speaks to behaviour which calls into question the *distinction* itself between objectivity and subjectivity, as drawn by a legal collective. In other words, by questioning what a legal collective calls an (il) legal act, a-legality challenges what the collective holds to be (ir)rational.

To get our bearings it may be helpful to briefly contrast the account of legal rationality outlined hereinafter to a wide range of contemporary accounts of practical rationality. According to these accounts, practical rationality is 'reason-giving' about or the 'justification' of norms of action in an argumentative process. Whatever the further presuppositions and assumptions which might be made, and which delimit in advance what a wide variety of authors are prepared to call rational 'dialogue', 'deliberation', 'discourse', or whatever, most contributions to this field of enquiry take for granted that practical rationality is the toing and froing between discussants, whereby each demands of the others that they come up with mutually acceptable grounds for the norms or standards

[31] Husserl, *Experience and Judgment*, 36.

which are to guide their actions. Succinctly, practical rationality is usually defined as the argumentative grounding of norms of action.[32]

This approach, whatever its merits, is both abstract and reductive. Abstract, because it focuses on a legal order as a set of norms, bracketing legal order as a concrete normative whole organized as an interconnected distribution of spatial, temporal, subjective, and material dimensions. Reductive, because the standard approach has legal rationality beginning when a norm of action is questioned, whereas rationality is no less effectual in the ordinary course of joint action under law. To parry these abstractive and reductive moves, I propose to explicate the concept of legal rationality implicit in the operation of intentionality deployed by joint action under the law: to intend is to objectify, and to objectify is to order. The section follows a two-pronged strategy. For the first, it parses objectification into three interlocking components: disclosing something as something* anew; we jointly; in-order-to-φ. For the second, it peruses the transformations of these interrelated components that take place in legality, illegality, and a-legality. The distinction between legal understanding and legal interpretation will prove helpful when clarifying the different modalities of legal rationality.

(a) *Legality*. Someone enters the proverbial food shop, selects a bag of potatoes, pays for it at the check-out point and leaves to continue with his or her daily chores. However humdrum, this act illustrates the main features of legal rationality in the pre-and post-reflexive mode of understanding. Let me show how it illustrates each of the three aspects into which its complex structure has been analysed.

Consider, first, the disclosure of something *as* something* anew, which already points to the basic achievement of rationality: something is *objectified*, inasmuch as it is revealed as having a legal meaning, e.g. a contract of sale. Importantly, what is objectified, when something is disclosed as *something**, is more than only an actor's behaviour. The asterisk signals that the objectification which takes place in the operation of understanding has spatial, temporal, subjective, and material dimensions. One acts rationally, in the mode of understanding, when one (an ought-actor) does what one ought to, where one ought to, and when one ought to. And this means that a legal act is rational in that it objectifies space, time, subjectivity, and content, *all at once and together*. My behaviour is objective, in the example, to the extent that I know how I ought to make my way around in the food shop, what kinds of things I may do there, when I should engage in certain acts with others, and so forth. This four-dimensionality of legal rationality is entirely lost from view in argumentative approaches that focus exclusively on the justification of the propositional content of legal norms. Conversely, we can already surmise that all 'justification' and 'reason-giving' concerning the

[32] The contributions to this field of enquiry are numerous, and include, amongst others, Rawls' idea of public reason, Habermas' theory of communicative rationality, Pettit's theory of freedom as discursive control, Alexy's procedural theory of legal argumentation, Perelman's new rhetoric, Toulmin's theory of argumentation, and MacCormick's account of the justification of judicial decisions.

propositional content of norms of action ultimately aim to establish who ought to do what, where, and when.

Crucially, as follows from the analysis of section 4.3, the objectivity of legal acts is four-dimensional in another sense, too: something can only be objectified, disclosed as something*, if it is disclosed *together with* other places, times, subjects and act-contents. The act of picking up a bag of potatoes and dropping it into the pannier before walking to the check-out point is objective to the extent that it *points beyond itself* in each of these four dimensions. The act is rational by dint of coming about in the appropriate ought-place, which, in turn, draws its meaning as an ought-place (i.e. the shop floor) from its linkage to other ought-places; by dint of coming about at the appropriate ought-time (i.e. after walking into the food store and before leaving it); etc. An act is legally objective or rational inasmuch as it leads away from itself, towards the *whole* of relations in which it is embedded and whence it draws its meaning—an order. A legal act in the mode of understanding fits into *the* order, in the singular. Notice, furthermore, that, in the mode of understanding, the objectivity of the act we have been describing presupposes that the whole of relations which condition its objectivity is *inconspicuous* as such. What allows me and others to understand my act as going about buying a product, and to view this act as legal, is that it takes place against the background of a fourfold interconnected distribution of ought-places, ought-times, ought-subjects, and ought-acts which remains beyond normative question.

To conclude this first aspect of legal rationality in the mode of understanding, notice that picking up a bag of potatoes and walking toward the check-out point to pay for it is to engage in an act *anew*. In this way, each new act, despite its uniqueness, stabilizes itself, surviving the evanescence of its occurrence. As noted in section 4.3, legal acts are embedded in legal practices, whereby each legal act points beyond itself, into the past and into the future, in the form of a reiterative anticipation. An act acquires objective status by projecting itself into the future, re-iterating what are deemed to be mutual expectations about who ought to do what, where, and when.

A second aspect of legal rationality in the mode of understanding turns on '(we) jointly'. Indeed, to disclose something as something* in the ordinary course of joint action is to reveal it as possessing a normative meaning others understand and share, such that what is disclosed as something* has an *intersubjective* consistency and subsistence over time. For it is not only I who views my behaviour as selecting a product I want to purchase, and who anticipates that the employee at the check-out point and I will engage in a certain sequence of interlocking acts (registering the product, paying for it, etc.), such that I am entitled to subsequently walk out of the store with the bag of potatoes. Other clients and employees in the food shop will also understand me as going about buying products, in the same way that I understand others as clients and employees who are going about the same kind of activity, etc. That is to say, the objectivity of the act presupposes that it *points beyond itself* to a manifold of acts by other individuals, with which it meshes together into a joint act, even though this joint act need not be, and generally is not, conspicuous as such. Indeed, there need be no explicit awareness of the fact that *we* are engaging in this act together; this is simply how 'one' goes about this kind of legal act. The parentheses in '(we) jointly' signal the pre- and post-reflexive anonymity of joint action in the mode of understanding, and to which we alluded in chapter 1.

There is a third aspect of a legal act in the mode of understanding which is important to securing its rationality. An act is rational, in the mode of legal understanding, when the members of a collective can view it as a participant act by dint of being in accordance with what they take to be, however pre-reflexively, the normative point of joint action.[33] In the same way that the objectivity of a legal act requires that it refer anew to an interconnected distribution of ought-places, ought-times, ought-subjects, and ought-acts, as well as to a collective, so also it must refer beyond itself toward a normative point, whence a manifold of acts appear as interconnected into a joint act which gives rise to entitlements and obligations between the participants. Once again, objectivity has the structure of something *pointing beyond itself*: something is disclosed as something* *in-order-to-φ*. The normative point of a legal act remains more or less inconspicuous in the mode of understanding; it is that which is taken for granted in the course of a legal practice.

Let me spell out some implications of this analysis of legal rationality in the mode of understanding before moving on to illegality:

(i) 'Knowing how' one ought to go about buying a bag of potatoes need not involve 'knowing that' one ought to do so, in a broad sense that includes explicit awareness of each or even any of the three aspects of objectification we have discussed hitherto. The rationality of acts in the mode of legal understanding is an embodied rationality, a 'knowing how' that is *prior to all reason-giving or justification*.

(ii) Gilbert notes that obligations in the course of joint action have a directed or relational character: in the course of participating in joint action I owe something to others, to which they have a correlative right, and they enjoy standing to demand that I comply and to rebuke me if I do not act accordingly. The relational character of legal obligation can be parsed, accordingly, into the three kinds of relations I have noted: to a collective, to a legal order, to the normative point of joint action. It is in this threefold relational sense that behaviour, as legal behaviour, is in *accordance* with the law. Moreover and crucially, in the normal course of a legal practice 'is' and 'ought' run over into each other: everything* is at it should be, and everything* should be as it is. The practically possible is actual, and the actual is what is practically possible.

(iii) Any account of legal rationality as the discursive or argumentative grounding of the propositional contents of norms of action is a reductive abstraction

[33] Taylor makes this point as follows: 'the practices which make up a society require certain self-descriptions on the part of the participants. These self-descriptions can be called constitutive. And the understanding formulated in these can be called pre-theoretical [in the sense] that it does not rely on theory. There may be no systematic formulations of the norms, and the conception of man and society which underlies them. The understanding is implicit in our ability to apply the appropriate descriptions to particular situations and actions'. Taylor, *Philosophy and the Human Sciences*, 93.

that loses sight of the *experiential basis of all legal grounding*. Indeed, this experiential basis is none other than the threefold referentiality of legal acts I have been concerned to adumbrate. That legal acts are objective, in accordance with the law, means that they are grounded; that they are grounded means that they refer beyond themselves in each of the three ways described heretofore: to a collective, even if in a pre-reflexive stance; to an interconnected distribution of times, places, subjects, and act-contents—an order; to the normative point of joint action, which they contribute to realize. These are *the three grounds of legal acts*; all discursive or argumentative 'reason-giving' and 'justification' which aim to ground the propositional content of norms of action are oriented, at bottom, to showing whether and how behaviour actualizes these references.

(iv) A further remark concerns the connection between rationality and *legal order*. Succinctly, *if to objectify is to ground, then to ground is to order*. Indeed, to order, as I indicated in an earlier section of this chapter, is to assign a place, a time, a subject, and a content to behaviour, in line with what are deemed to be (our) mutual expectations about who ought to do what, where, and when in-order-to-φ. This threefold assignment or disposing, which is the threefold grounding I have been concerned with elucidating, amounts to the basic *rational* achievement of joint action as an ordering. Legal rationality, on this reading, consists in a setting-into-order, or more precisely, a resetting-into-order.

(v) I noted in chapter 3 that a constitution structures the first-person plural perspective of a manifold of individuals who engage in authoritatively mediated and enforced joint action for the sake of φ. Spelling out this idea more fully, a constitution comprises rules for decisions about the threefold ground of behaviour as behaviour that is legal, hence objective or rational: (i) who is authorized to impute acts to a collective as its own acts and to uphold them as such; (ii) what is to count as the who, what, where, and when of joint action; and (iii) what is to count as the normative point of joint action. In this sense, *a constitution is a rule of legal rationality*; it is a default setting of what ought to count as legal (ir)rationality from the perspective of the members of a collective.

(vi) A final observation concerns the relation between rationality and *collective identity* over time. In a nutshell, legal behaviour is rational, in the mode of understanding, in that it secures the continuity over time of a collective. Behaviour that reiterates mutual expectations about who ought to do what, where, and when reiterates collective identity as selfhood and as sameness: it reiterates our mutual commitment to act together—selfhood over time; it also reiterates what* we are committed to doing jointly—sameness over time. And, although I will have a lot more to say about this in chapter 6, legal behaviour reiterates the *legal boundaries* of the collective by reiterating collective identity as selfhood and as sameness. Legal rationality as a resetting-into-order is the practice of resetting-legal-boundaries.

(b) *Illegality*. Security guards have nabbed someone attempting to steal cans of foie gras from the food shop. To describe the act in this way is to qualify it as *subjective*, as *irrational*. What renders this act subjective in terms of the intentional structure of legal rationality? What I seek to uncover is the concrete experience which remains concealed when it is said that illegal behaviour is irrational because it cannot be justified in terms of a mutually endorsable norm of action. What is the concrete experiential basis of what would otherwise remain a purely abstract form of negation when one speaks of behaviour as 'ir-rational'? The answer is, in a nutshell, that an act is legally subjective if it *stands out as isolated* in the three ways indicated heretofore. The privative or negative characterization of an illegal act as irrational concerns a specific interruption of the threefold reference of behaviour we must now turn to consider. Quite simply, the interruption of a legal practice takes on the form of its *suspension*: an act ought not to refer to the collective, to an order, and to a normative point.

Let us begin with '(we) jointly'. The negativity of ir-rationality means, concretely, that, when attempting to steal the foie gras, the individual and his or her act ought not to stand for the group and its joint action. Our gaze comes to rest squarely on the would-be thief, who, when being taken away by the security guards, becomes conspicuous as isolated from other clients because stealing the cans of foie gras is not an act we ought to attribute to ourselves as part of our joint act. It is not an act *we* ought to authorize or empower, hence not an act that is objective by dint of its collective ownership. Yet more forcefully, it is an act we ought *not* to call our own, if other acts are to count as being part of our joint action. It is an act, but ought not to be viewed as a participant act; this, concretely, is what it means that legal irrationality involves the *breakdown of intersubjectivity*. Importantly, if joint action in the mode of legal understanding is pre-reflexive in that actors need not explicitly take up the first-person plural perspective when acting, this perspective now becomes *reflexive*: who qualifies an act as illegal views him or herself and others, including the would-be thief, as part of a group, the members of which ought to act in certain ways—and not in others. The pre-reflexive, more or less anonymous, 'one acts' gives way to the reflexivity of '*we* ought to act' in this way (and not in that way). The group becomes conspicuous as such. Accordingly both the illegal act and the collective become conspicuous in the form of their discordance. Subjectivity or irrationality is the experience of *conspicuous discordance* in which the negation of the attributability of the act to the collective involves the latter's reaffirmation as the group to which participant acts should be attributed.

Second, the illegal act stands out alone because it ought not to point beyond itself to the fourfold web of ought-relations which separate and join together those engaged in joint action. This means, on the one hand, that the act does not reiterate what are deemed to be mutual expectations about who ought to do what, where, and when in the given circumstances. The act stands out alone because it is not embedded in the reiterative structure of a legal practice: not *anew*. On the other hand, the act stands out alone because the process of understanding the act (as buying foie gras) by relating it to an interconnected distribution of ought-places, ought-times, ought-subjects, and ought-contents retrospectively breaks down when the security guards collar the culprit and take him away. The fourfold co-referentiality required to disclose something as something* is interrupted, such that the act ought not to fit into the order. In the same movement by which the act comes to stand out alone, so also the interconnected distribution of places, times, subjects, and act-contents becomes conspicuous as the web of relations from which the act ought not to have isolated itself. Here again, the subjectivity of an act speaks to the experience of *conspicuous discordance*: the appearance of the act as isolated, as irrational, goes hand-in-hand with the appearance of an order that is reaffirmed as *the* order, in the singular.

Third, an illegal act is subjective, irrational, because it ought not to take place if the normative point of joint action is to be realized. In other words, the act, in our example, stands out alone because it misses the (normative) point of a contract of sale; as a result, it cannot be understood, together with a manifold of other acts, as part of what we ought to do to pull off a joint act in-order-to-φ. So the irrationality of illegal behaviour speaks, once again, to the experience of *conspicuous discordance*: the normative point of joint action comes out into the open as 'that for the sake of which' the act ought to have taken place, but does not, such that both the act and the normative point draw our attention.

Consider some implications that follow from this account of legal irrationality:

(i) A concrete analysis of illegality shows why argumentative theories which focus exclusively on practical rationality as the justification of norms of action are reductive. The charge that illegal behaviour is irrational or subjective is not only, and certainly not in the first instance, a claim about the propositional content of norms of action. Irrationality in the law speaks most fundamentally to the interruption of the three references which lends an act an objective status. An act is deemed to be illegal or irrational because it is *ungrounded*, which means that it does not reiterate references to an order, to a collective, and to a normative point. Accordingly, 'reason-giving', as the argumentative justification of norms of action, is a late apparition, which kicks in, if at all, when legal understanding has been interrupted. In the same way, and regardless of how we describe the discursive justification of the propositional contents of norms of action, what is most fundamentally at stake therein is restoring the *experience* of legal behaviour as being relational—grounded—in each of these three ways.

(ii) In illegal behaviour 'is' and 'ought' fall apart in such a way that how things ought to have come about is reaffirmed in the face of what has happened. Furthermore, this reaffirmation already prepares the way for re-establishing the threefold reference of an act as a legal act. 'He ought to go to jail!', exclaims one of the clients, who watches the shoplifter being taken away. This exclamation, perhaps corroborated at a later stage by a judicial ruling, encapsulates the threefold move whereby the act, which had stood isolated, is reintegrated into the domain of objectivity and rationality. The exclamation introduces a reference to the collective: we ought to (jointly) convict him; a reference to the order: the assignation of a what (e.g. privation of liberty), where (jail), when (after conviction, and for the duration of the sentence), and who (a convict), all of which are inserted in the legal order from which the illegal act has isolated itself; finally, a reference to a normative point: in-order-to uphold property rights. The process of (re) setting-into-order has already begun.

(iii) In the same way that legal behaviour in the mode of understanding is rational because it reorders, so also illegal behaviour is irrational because it *disorders*. By becoming isolated, an act appears as not-in-legal-order, as the disruption of legal order.

(iv) Finally, illegal behaviour is irrational because it interrupts collective identity over time, in its two poles: sameness and selfhood. On the one hand, who ought to do what, where, and when is not reiterated—the act is no longer the *same* as earlier joint acts, although it ought to be. On the other, the illegal act does not reiterate mutual expectations about joint action, although it ought to; the commitment of a manifold of individuals to acting together—the permanence of a collective *self* over time—is interrupted. An illegal act is irrational, on this reading, because it arrests collective identity as a principle of temporal permanence. And this entails that behaviour is subjective or irrational because it breaches legal boundaries which the collective has committed to honouring over time.

(c) *A-Legality*. I now turn to examine how a-legality questions the way in which a collective draws the distinction between rationality and irrationality. What interests me, once again, is to elucidate the experiential basis of how a-legality questions this distinction.

Consider, to begin with, the reference to a collective: we jointly. A legal act is objective in that participant agents ought to refer it to the collective as its own act, as an act which is empowered or authorized. Illegal behaviour is subjective in that participant agents ought not to refer it to the collective as its own act; these are acts which ought not to be empowered or authorized. A-legality has a more complex structure. On the one hand, it partakes of legality or illegality, such that it ought or ought not to be ascribed to the collective. The *autoréduction* is, arguably, an act of extortion under French law, hence an act that ought not to be authorized by or attributed to the collective. On the other hand, the *autoréduction* raises the claim that the act ought to be authorized by—hence referred to—a collective which is *other* than the collective which would qualify the act as extortion. Notice the difference between (il)legal and a-legal behaviour: the former speaks to acts which are objective—or subjective—because they do—or do not—mesh into what are deemed to be the mutual expectations we ought to endorse; the latter, by contrast, renders the group conspicuous by questioning whether what are deemed to be the mutual expectations of its participants ought to be what allows a plurality of individuals to view themselves as a group. Accordingly, a-legality challenges how a collective has drawn the distinction between rationality and irrationality by questioning which acts are acts that we ought and ought not to ascribe to ourselves as *our* joint act and, more radically, *whether* there is a collective to which acts ought to be ascribed.

If a-legal behaviour questions the reference to collectivity, so also it questions the reference to the normative point of joint action. Such is the stake of the *chômeurs'* action. On the one hand, the *autoréduction* misses the point of transactions in food shops such as Galeries Lafayette; it does not refer to or realize their normative point as articulated by the extant legal order. Amongst other things, the act is not oriented to realizing the principle 'to each according to their means'. On the other hand, it points beyond itself to another normative point, which, the *chômeurs* claim, ought to be realized by joint action, e.g. the principle 'to each according to their needs'. So a-legal behaviour renders conspicuous that for the sake of which a manifold of individuals act jointly, but not as what ought to be reaffirmed but rather as what ought to be *otherwise*. A-legality challenges how a collective has drawn the distinction between objectivity and subjectivity by questioning that for the sake of which we ought and ought not to act jointly.

Finally, a-legal behaviour also questions who ought to do what, where, and when if a manifold of individuals are to act jointly. Here again, the *autoréduction* reveals that mutually interfering references are at work in a-legality. On the one hand, the act points beyond itself to the whole of ought-places, ought-times, ought-persons, and ought-contents in which it comes about. Amongst other things, the qualification of the act as extortion implies the reaffirmation of the food shop as a specific kind of ought-place, in which certain acts are empowered and others are debarred. On the other hand, the act points beyond itself to an interconnected distribution of ought-places, ought-times, etc. *other* than the extant order. A-legality challenges how a collective has drawn the distinction between rationality and irrationality by questioning the fourfold web of relations in which behaviour ought to be inserted and from which it ought not to detach itself.

In short, *pluralization* is the key to a concrete, non-reductive account of the disruption of legal (ir)rationality by a-legal behaviour and situations. A-legality denotes the experience of a pluralization that strikes at each of the three references which determine behaviour as legally objective or rational. First, the one group, to which participants understood themselves as belonging in the course of joint action, gives way to *intersubjective estrangement*. Second, what had been taken to be the same legal order in the form of behaviour that fits what each participant deems to be shared expectations about who ought to do what, where, and when, gives way to a plurality of normative orders, to *mutually interfering* ways of organizing the time, space, subjectivity, and content of joint action under law. Third, a-legality throws joint normative expectations about joint action out-of-joint, such that what* our action is about loses its straightforwardness, giving way, to a lesser or greater degree, to disorientation that is interpersonal as much as it is spatial and temporal. The pluralization of joint action, so described, characterizes the experience whereby the boundaries of a legal order manifest themselves as a *limit* beyond which other legal orders and other rationalities are possible or actual. Hence, 'legal pluralism', when defined from the observer's perspective as the co-existence of legal orders in the same spatio-temporal context, is a derivative characterization of plurality. It presupposes the primordial experience of legal pluralization, which is also an experience of the pluralization of legal rationalities. While events such as the *autoréduction* may be chronologically posterior to the emergence of legal pluralism in the sense indicated by Twining, they are anterior in the order of conceptual and ontological dependency, inasmuch as a-legality reveals the correlation between the pluralization of legal orders and the pluralization of collective selves.

A number of implications follow from this insight:

(i) By interrupting the normal course of a legal practice, the *autoréduction* can be seen as raising the following question: What* ought our joint action to be about? Notice how this question calls attention to the threefold grounding of behaviour: what* *our joint action* ought to be about—the reference to a collective; *what** our joint action ought to be about—the reference to an interconnected distribution of ought-places, times, subjects, and contents; what* our joint action ought *to be about*—the reference to the normative point of joint action. This is the practical question to which legal collectives respond when setting boundaries, even if, as we shall see in chapter 6, boundary-setting involves, to a lesser or greater extent, a responsive framing of the question raised by a-legality.

(ii) A distinction was drawn, in section 4.1, between *practical* engagement with things and persons and the *theoretical* engagement which sets in when such practical engagement is broken off to become the explicit object of normative investigation. The former was referred to as understanding; the latter, as interpretation. On this reading, legal interpretation arises when legal ordering in the mode of understanding gives way to the theoretical attitude inaugurated by the question, what* ought our joint action to be about? Legal interpretation, in its fundamental sense, is the activity of engaging this question, which arises when the immediacy of behaviour in the pre- and post-reflexive mode of understanding is interrupted. All legal interpretation, narrowly defined as the elucidation of legal meanings, in particular of textually embodied legal meanings, presupposes and is at the service of this central question.

(iii) In this fundamental sense of the term, the lay person, no less than the legal authority that enacts individualized or general norms (e.g. a judge or legislator) and the legal scholar, is called on to engage in legal interpretation when a legal practice is interrupted. Such was the case with the *autoréduction*, which forced the clients and management of Lafayette to deal with the question concerning what* joint action ought to be about under the circumstances at hand. Legal interpretation, for the clients and the management of the food shop, involved concretely responding, in one way or another, to the question raised by the *autoréduction*. This suggests that a rich conception of legal rationality, one that could integrate legality, illegality, and a-legality, demands thinking through the nature of the interplay between question and response which arises between the a-legal transgression of legal order and collective responses thereto by way of boundary-setting. This interplay will attract our attention in chapters 5 and 6.

(iv) The interruption of joint action wrought by the *autoréduction* highlights an important presupposition of argumentative conceptions of legal rationality. Remember that the *chômeurs* unfurled banners with slogans and accosted the clients and management of Lafayette, explaining the point of their action and seeking to win them over for their cause. More fundamentally, the conceptualization of legal argumentation as 'reason-giving' or as the 'justification' of legal norms gets started when the ordinary course of a legal practice is interrupted by a situation or behaviour that renders joint action questionable. In other words, theories of legal argumentation focus on legal rationality in the theoretical, reflexive stance towards a legal practice which I have dubbed legal interpretation. The highly stylized argumentative scenarios imagined by theorists of legal argumentation, in which a discussant demands that other individuals justify the norms governing their course of action, are abstractions rooted in the practical question raised by concrete behaviour such as the *autoréduction*.

(v) Like illegality, so also a-legality interrupts collective identity over time, in its two modes of sameness and selfhood. With regard to sameness, who ought to do what, where, and when is not reiterated: the act is no longer the *same* as earlier such joint acts. With regard to selfhood, a-legal behaviour does not reiterate mutual expectations about joint action: the mutual commitment of a manifold of individuals to acting together is interrupted, and with it the permanence of a collective self over time. The qualification of an act as illegal entails reaffirming collective identity as sameness and selfhood, and taking the appropriate steps to re-establish it. A-legality, by contrast, calls into question *what** might be the content of mutual commitment and, to a lesser or greater extent, *that* there is a mutual commitment at all which joins together a manifold of individuals into a group agent. With varying degrees of intensity, the very *existence* of a collective is at stake each time that a-legality challenges what* joint action by its members ought to be about. This entails that a-legality is not simply irrational by dint of interrupting collective identity over time; instead, a-legality raises the question what is to count as (ir)rationality, and thereby whether there ought to be a collective that subsists over time, and how it ought to be organized to be able to subsist over time.

4.6 BACK TO THE 'FIRST' CONSTITUTION

The thrust of the foregoing section can be summarized as follows: behaviour that counts as legal for a collective is behaviour that it views as objective or rational because it is in accordance with the threefold ground of joint action under law; illegal behaviour, by contrast, is behaviour a collective views as subjective or irrational insofar as it is discordant with the threefold ground of joint action under law; a-legality speaks to behaviour that no longer falls neatly on either side of the divide between objectivity and subjectivity because it calls this divide into question, hence what a legal collective calls (ir)rational behaviour.

Before examining a-legality at any greater length, a prior issue has been dealt with, which remains hitherto unaddressed. In effect, the analysis of legal ordering I have developed assumes that there is *already* joint action under law, such that an individual act can appear as legal or illegal, as objective or subjective. To show how the objectivity (or subjectivity) of an individual act as a *legal* (or illegal) act can be assured, namely, by realizing (or not realizing) the threefold reference to a collective, to a legal order and to the normative point of joint action, I have taken for granted that there is already a legal order, that there is already a legal collective and that there is already a normative point of joint action under law. But what about the legality of what is deemed to be joint action under law and its threefold ground? And what about the legality of the first constitution, as a master rule that establishes what is to count as our legal order? This is, of course, the question about the *origin* of joint action under law, hence the *origin* of the distinction between legality and illegality, and of the boundaries which shape this distinction, as drawn by a legal collective.

Notice how this ties into what has been said about the structure of legal intentionality, in which legal norms, as 'schemes of interpretation', involve collective *anticipations* of who ought to do what, where, and when in-order-to-φ. If legal anticipations speak to the future, to how something* ought to be disclosed, then the source of the normativity of these anticipations, hence of norms as legal norms, has to be sought in the *past*, in the fact that joint action under law has the form of a *reiterative* anticipation. While I have taken for granted that legal acts have a reiterative structure, no account has been given of how a legal order emerges at all, such that the reiterative anticipation deployed in legal ordering can get going. Once again the question about the origin of joint action under law, about the origin of the distinction between legality and illegality, comes into view. In short, we must now turn to a *genealogy* of legal ordering and rationality, and with it to a genealogy of legal normativity. Gilbert obliquely broaches this problem, when indicating that action is participant action when it 'rightly' can be ascribed to a collective as part of the interlocking set of individual actions required for the realization of a joint act.[34] The question about the objectivity of legal intentionality is, at least in part, the following: under what conditions can an act *rightly* be ascribed to a collective as its *own* act?

This question leads directly to a key institutional dimension of legal practices: the authoritative monitoring and enforcement of joint action. As noted in chapter 3, this feature of legal practices concerns how legal collectives deal with questions that arise about joint action: about its normative point; about the rights, obligations, entitlements, and responsibilities to which it gives rise; about the consistency of individual acts therewith; about the consequences that

[34] Gilbert, *On Social Facts*, 422.

follow from breaching it. Such questions are characteristically settled by legal authorities *who act on behalf of the group as a whole*, such that dissenters are bound by their decisions and can, in principle, be forced to comply with them. Yet this 'institutional' solution to the problem of the objectivity of legal acts only postpones it: what guarantees that legal authorities decide *rightly* whether acts which are brought to their attention count as legal acts, that is, as acts which ought to be attributed to the collective?

If the problem of objectivity leads over to that of the attribution of an act to a collective as a whole, the problem of attribution gives way to the problems of representation and authorization—of *authorized representation*. It is instructive to briefly look at how Gilbert deals with these problems in her account of plural subjectivity. When describing group representation she appeals to 'the idea of a group as a whole accepting that one thing is to count as something else. A certain individual's or small group's deciding is to count as our* deciding, and so on'.[35] Group representation, as she sees it, is 'authorized representation' if and when the group as a whole accepts that one or more of its members decide or act on behalf of the whole. Notice, first, that this restricted modality of authorized representation presupposes a broader modality thereof, which encompasses *all* participant agency. In effect, Gilbert's characterization of representation as 'one thing counting as something else' holds for *all* interlocking acts that make up a joint act: while each of those is the act of individuals, they are not merely individual acts: they count as part and parcel of a collective act to the extent that they can 'rightly' be attributed to the collective as a whole. To view an act as a *legal* act is to claim that it counts as a legal collective's *own* act. Because collective action takes place through participant agency, a representational *claim* is necessarily built into legal acts as intentional acts. Given this broad sense of authorized representation, it is clear that the task of authorized representation in the restricted sense is to monitor and enforce joint action: it establishes whether a particular act or type of acts may be attributed to the collective, that is, whether it can rightly be held that '*we jointly* disclose something as something*'. A judge would be exemplary for authorized representation that decides whether a *particular* act is legal* (or illegal*); an organ entrusted with the enactment of general rules would be exemplary for establishing whether a *type* of act is legal*. But once again the problem of an infinite regress looms large: what warrants the representational claim raised by who decides whether an act or type of act is legal*? For, to revisit the quandary, acts that monitor and enforce joint action under law raise a prima facie claim to their own legality*.

In Gilbert's account, acceptance allows of blocking infinite regress: representation is authorized if and when we as a whole accept that 'a certain individual's or small group's deciding is to count as our* deciding, and so on'. Acceptance certainly has an important role to play in representation, as we shall see in the next section, but it cannot stave off the infinite regress. For it raises the same problem about membership which confronts all versions of social contract

[35] Gilbert, *On Social Facts*, 207. Gilbert uses the asterisk to signal, roughly, forms of group action and intentions.

theory: whose acceptance counts as acceptance by a member of the collective? A certain circularity becomes visible: if 'we as a whole' must authorize representation, the opposite also holds: there can be no 'we as a whole' absent representation. The plural subject is *perforce* a represented subject. The number of members of a social group makes no difference, in this respect: it also holds for groups composed of two individuals: the group as a unity is represented by each of its members who engages in participant agency. Waldenfels summarizes in a trenchant manner what by now has become a well-established criticism of social contract theory and all of its ramifications and permutations: 'A "we" [cannot] say "we"... A political group only finds its voice by way of spokespersons, who speak in its name and represent it *as a whole*'.[36] On this strong reading, representation is more than simply allowing something to count for something else, as Gilbert proposes; it means that something present counts for something *absent*. In re-presentation something present refers to something absent—*anew*.

The 'anew' of representation is at work in legal intentionality, whereby something is disclosed as something* anew. Legal acts are a reiterative anticipation of who ought to do what, when, and where from the first-person perspective of a 'we', or so I argued. Hence the question about the objectivity of legal acts, about their status as *legal* acts, is elicited by their very structure, which cannot 'anticipate-in-general' without reiterating or representing 'we as a whole'. But here is the snag: we as a whole, must be represented; it is perforce absent. There is no moment of an original presence which could guarantee either *that* we are a whole, joined together by a point of shared action, nor *what** our joint action ought to be about. Legal intentionality involves a representational *claim* in this twofold, strong sense. Ultimately, the questions about the legality of legal intentionality and about the legality of legal ordering are inseparable from the question about the *origin* of a legal order and its rationality, of the conditions that govern how the distinction between legality and illegality is drawn 'to begin with'.

Enter Kelsen. One of Kelsen's outstanding and enduring contributions to legal theory is to have realized that the problem of legal objectivity—of what makes acts into legal acts—is inseparable from the problems of representation and attribution, and that these problems come to a head in the question about the origin of legal orders. His approach to this question is perhaps best illustrated by a passage in the second edition of the *Pure Theory of Law*, in which he introduces the idea of the state as an acting subject:

> If the state is presented as an acting subject, if it is said that the state has done this or that, the question arises which is the criterion according to which certain acts performed by certain individuals are attributed to the state, are qualified as acts or

[36] Bernhard Waldenfels, *Verfremdung der Moderne: Phänomenologische Grenzgänge* (Essen: Wallstein Verlag, 2001), 140. See also Bert van Roermund, *Law, Narrative and Reality: An Essay in Intercepting Politics* (Dordrecht: Kluwer Academic Publishers, 1997), 145 ff; Bonnie Honig, 'Between Decision and Deliberation: Political Paradox in Democratic Theory', *American Political Science Review* 101, no. 1 (2007), 1–17; Sofia Näsström, 'The Legitimacy of the People', *Political Theory* 35, no. 5 (2007), 624–655; Jacques Derrida, 'Declarations of Independence', *New Political Science* 15 (1986), 7–15. For a particularly incisive analysis of the representation of 'we' in the framework of post-apartheid South Africa, see Carrol Clarkson, 'Who are "We"? Don't Make Me Laugh', *Law and Critique* 18, no. 3 (2007), 361–374.

functions of the state, or, what amounts to the same, why certain individuals in performing certain acts are considered to be organs of the state.[37]

If we allow the 'state' to function, in this passage, as a stand-in for a legal collective, Kelsen avers that the acts of legal collectives are the acts of their organs. The law, he correctly argues, can only make sense of collective agency in terms of legal acts. Accordingly, a legal act is the act of an individual which may be attributed to a collective: 'the problem of the state as an acting person... is a problem of attribution'.[38] Kelsen's introduction of the notion of attribution allows him to link acts, *qua legal* acts, to representation. In effect, attribution has a representational structure: 'the essence of an organ is that it "represents" the state'.[39] The quotation marks do not convey conceptual qualms about the appropriateness of qualifying the acts of officials as representational acts but rather signal Kelsen's willingness to extend representation beyond its traditional domain of parliamentary representation: to attribute an act to the state is to claim that an organ's act *stands for* the act of a collective. This notion of an organ corresponds, evidently, to the broad notion of authorized representation noted above.

Representation is intimately related to a second essential feature of legal acts: *empowerment*. To attribute an act to a collective—to view it as a legal act—implies that the act is authorized by a higher-level norm. Hence attribution has a regressive structure: one moves from a legal act to the norm that authorizes it, and so on. Crucially, this regression is not infinite: relations of empowerment lead back to a 'first constitution', enacted by an assembly or an individual. But, by definition, who enacts the first constitution cannot be empowered to do so by a norm of positive law. Thus 'the assembly referred to in the historically first constitution, by adopting this constitution establishes itself—according to this constitution—as the Constituent National Assembly provided for by the constitution'. This, he immediately adds, is tantamount to the 'self-creation of the organ concerned', that is, a self-empowerment.[40] As Kelsen recognizes, self-empowerment is a contradiction in terms; a first constitution, an oxymoron.

If, as noted earlier, empowerment or authorization is the legal manifestation of practical possibility, then Kelsen's insight points to a paradox at the heart of legal possibility: self-empowerment is, as it were, the im/possible origin of legal possibilities. I say 'im/possible' because the act which opens up a realm of legal possibilities and closes down others is neither legally possible nor impossible, but rather an act that gives rise to the distinction itself between the legally possible and impossible. More generally, Kelsen unveils a paradox at the heart of the law: ultimately, the legality of legal acts cannot be established from within the legal order itself; but because the law can only think of acts as legal acts, an act can only initiate a legal order if it is retroactively interpreted as an authorized or empowered act. In other words, no legal order can ground its own objectivity,

[37] Kelsen, *Pure Theory of Law*, 291.

[38] Kelsen, *Pure Theory of Law*, 297.

[39] Kelsen, *Allgemeine Staatslehre*, 310.

[40] Kelsen, *Pure Theory of Law*, 154–155.

nor how it draws the distinction between objectivity and subjectivity, rationality and irrationality; only retroactively can the act that gives rises to the distinction itself between objectivity and subjectivity appear as objective, valid. Again, and in a final formulation of the paradox: the act of legal *ordering* par excellence, namely the act which inaugurates a legal order, and which lends all further acts the status of (il)legal acts, is neither legal nor illegal; only retroactively can it be viewed as authorized or empowered: as an act of *legal* ordering. Such is the function of the basic norm, the *Grundnorm*.[41] In the same way, the act which inaugurates a form of legal rationality, by both posing and answering the practical question, 'What* is our joint action about?', is itself neither rational nor irrational.

4.7 THE PARADOX OF REPRESENTATION

The Kelsenian paradox demands that we scrutinize afresh joint action under law as an intentional act. As transpired in the course of our explorations, legal acts disclose something as something* *anew*. This means that legal acts have the form of a reiterative anticipation. The generality of anticipation-in-general turns on the re-iteration of 'we as a whole'. Now the crucial problem is to make sense of the origin of a legal order if legal acts have a reiterative structure. For, one might want to object, the inaugural act of a legal order cannot, by definition, be reiterative. Otherwise, how can it mark a *beginning*? If one accepts that legal orders have a beginning it would seem that one must also acknowledge that legal orders emerge through acts in which a collective is immediately present to itself *as a whole*. Re-presentation, re-iteration, would follow up on—and be subordinate to—this immediate and founding self-presence, a self-presence that can be renewed at any moment in the further career of the collective. The objection would resolve the ambiguity hidden in the word 'anew' into a stark and irreducible opposition: 'new' and 'again'. On the one hand, there is the ordering act that gives rise *to* a legal order; on the other, there is ordering *within* a legal order. The compass of the legal acts as intentional acts would be limited to the latter; legal intentionality presupposes, but cannot explain, the former: novelty in a strong sense.

This, in substance, is the objection of *originalism*—the view that there is or can be a simple opposition between presence and representation, between an originating act and its reiterations. Originalism is particularly enticing because it seems to address two problems that remain outstanding in a phenomenologically inspired concept of legal intentionality. The first is that the opposition between presence and representation augurs clean ruptures, in which an emergent legal order can break entirely with the past, by revolutionary means or otherwise—or so we are told. The second is the problem of the objectivity of legal orders, as sharpened by the problem of representation. After all, if we as a

[41] I readily accept that this interpretation of the function of the *Grundnorm* is considerably removed from the neo-Kantian interpretation thereof which, according to many Kelsen experts, Kelsen himself favoured. My aim is not, however, to provide an exegesis of Kelsen but rather to probe the philosophical significance of the problems he identified and struggled with.

whole are irredeemably absent, what could guarantee that an act is legal because it is grounded in a collective, in an order and in a normative point? More generally, what could guarantee that acts are *(il)legal** acts; that legal* acts are *our* acts; that legal boundaries are *our* boundaries; that the constitution is *our* constitution?

It pays, therefore, to examine whether and in what sense the origin of a legal order can be conceptualized as a reiterative anticipation. In particular, does the Kelsenian paradox suggest that the emergence of a legal order is governed by a paradox of representation?

An incident that took place in the European Social Forum in Florence in November 2002 offers a revealing glimpse into the conditions that govern the emergence of legal order. Indeed, the Forum of Florence witnessed the effort of a revolutionary faction to marginalize an institutional faction composed primarily of NGOs. 'Our movement is not reformist; it is radical', declared Vittorio Agnoletto, former spokesman of the Genoa movements and member of the International Committee of the World Social Forum, thereby forgetting the charter of principles of Porto Alegre, which stipulates that the Forum is an 'open meeting place', and that 'no one is authorized to express . . . positions that claim to be those of all participants'.[42] Notice the dilemma: a space remains open only if no claim is made in the name of a whole; but without such a claim, no alternative political and legal order can be founded. The price of 'radical openness' in politics is that no joint action is possible. Unless the multitude becomes a unity in action, unless it ceases to be a multitude and becomes a collective subject, it cannot constitute itself as a political community, by revolutionary means or otherwise.

Crucially, Agnoletto's invocation of a 'we', when referring to 'our movement', reveals a remarkable equivocity that goes to the heart of the origins of legal collectives. On the one hand, there is no first-person plural perspective in the absence of an act that effects a *closure* by seizing the political initiative to assert: (i) *that* there is a collective of individuals joined together in action by a common point; (ii) *which* point joins together a manifold of individuals into a collective; and (iii) *who* belongs or can belong to the collective. Each of these aspects surfaces, however incipiently, in Agnoletto's claim: (i) we already exist as a movement; (ii) a determination of what the movement ought to be *about* (radical transformation) in a way that excludes other interpretations of the movement's point (reform); (iii) those who share the point of the movement (radical transformation), and are prepared to engage in joint action consistent with this point, are welcome as members; others—the reformists—are not. So, although foundational acts elicit a presence that interrupts representational practices, this rupture does not—and cannot—reveal a manifold of individuals immediately present to itself as a *whole*. 'We jointly' emerges through an act that summons it into being as a bounded collective. Far from marking a moment of pure spontaneity or activity, in which a collective acts in the strong sense of enacting a legal order

[42] Laurence Caramel, 'Forum de Florence: offensive de la gauche radicale', *Le Monde*, 16 November 2002. Cited in Henri Maler, 'Le Monde en quête de "phénomène de société" ', on the website of Observatoire des Médias ACRIMED: <http://www.acrimed.org/article811.html> (accessed on 12 May 2013).

ex novo, Agnoletto's invocation of a 'we' reveals a primordial *passivity* at the heart of collective activity: instead of originating a legal order through a joint act, the collective is originated by an inaugural act that is not a joint act. See here collective self-constitution as the constitution *of* a collective self through the enactment of a legal order.

On the other hand, Agnoletto's speech-act also reveals that who would institute a collective must claim to act in the name of the collective, that is, must claim to act as an *authorized representative*: he not only speaks about but also on behalf of 'our movement'. Moreover, the would-be representative claims to act on behalf of what is *already* a collective. The representative claims to re-present, re-iterate, 'we as a whole'. But clearly this invocation is not sufficient to summon a collective into being. The putative representational act that originates a collective would *empower* or *authorize* individuals as members of a community, seeking to wrest a realm of legal possibilities for joint action from the background of anonymous and pre-reflexive forms of sociality that constitutes the social domain. But this would-be empowerment—this emergent possibility of legal possibilities—only comes about if individuals retroactively identify themselves as the members of a collective by exercising the powers granted to them by that inaugural act. The representational claim and the realm of legal possibilities it opens up depend on the addressees who, by jointly disclosing something as something* anew in-order-to-φ, render the putative representation an authorized representation. This, returning to Gilbert, is the way in which 'acceptance' plays a role in authorized representation. Notice the inverted asymmetry: if the necessary intervention of a spokesperson who acts on behalf of a whole discloses an irreducible passivity in joint action, a no less irreducible passivity is inscribed in the act which would originate a collective: this act depends on the 'uptake' by its addressees if it is to succeed. See here collective self-constitution as the constitution of a legal order *by* a collective self.

Hence, Agnoletto's assertion gives the nay to a simple opposition between presence and representation. Representation has a paradoxical structure because an act can only *originate* a community by *representing* its origin. Everything *begins* with a *re*-presentation. More precisely, an act can only originate a collective if it succeeds—and as long as it succeeds—in representing an original collective, an original normative point and an original interconnected distribution of ought-places, times, subjects, and act-contents. In other words, an act can only originate a collective by claiming to represent its original answer to the practical question, What* ought our joint action to be about? The proximity with the Kelsenian paradox of origins, in particular the retroactivity whereby a founding act is disclosed as legal, comes into view. Indeed, the inaugural act of a legal order can only be viewed retroactively—and ever provisionally—as its inaugural act. A collective is never present to itself at its own foundation.

The paradox of representation reveals that, while operating a rupture, the inaugural act of a legal order has the structure of an intentional act: *it anticipates by reiterating*. When Agnoletto exclaims, 'Our movement is not reformist; it is radical', he anticipates-in-general, even if the contours of what is to come in the way of an emergent legal order remain highly—but not completely—tenuous and dependent on uptake by its addressees. This anticipation-in-general is, moreover, the putative representation of 'we as a whole', even if no longer of the collective it seeks to overturn: we are already a collective with a shared point whence we will progressively disclose who ought to do what, where, and when. In this sense, then, the inaugural act is no different to legal acts that follow it. But notice two important implications that follow from this. The first is that even though Agnoletto's act deploys the operation of intentionality, it is by definition not an act of *collective* intentionality, which, on the reading I have proposed heretofore, is an ingredient of *legal* intentionality. As a result, and this is the second implication, also the legal acts that follow from the inaugural act involve a *putative* representation, a *putative* act of legal intentionality. More generally, the conditions that govern the emergence of a legal order stamp their ambiguity on *all* the legal acts deployed in the course of a legal practice: legal orders are *putative* legal orders. And this is why 'we are a collective' is always a *claim* to this effect raised by someone: 'we are (deemed to be) a collective'.

I would add two caveats to this general insight. The first is that it is not necessary that the closure which gives rise to a legal collective spell out who ought to do what, where, and when from the very beginning; the fourfold closure of a legal order will typically come about more or less gradually, more or less in piecemeal fashion. The incident at the European Social Forum of Florence shows that Agnoletto's claim to represent a 'we' invokes a normative point that enables him to draw an initial distinction between those who belong and those who do not, leaving what are initially more or less inchoate temporal, subjective, and material boundaries of the would-be collective to be determined at a later stage of its career. The closure of a legal collective does not take place at one blow; closure is an *emergent* closure. The second is that this feature of closure only draws its full significance for legal collectives when couched in the form of a paradox: a closure that takes place as a 're-closure'. We will examine this paradox in chapter 6, when revisiting the problem of identification as a collective re-identification.

In any case, the deconstruction of the simple oppositions that drive originalism as a metaphysical programme clears the way for a host of new questions. To begin with, it raises the question about ruptures, namely whether and how it makes sense to conceptualize inaugural acts as opening up a future that is not in one way or another the reiteration of the past. Furthermore, if all foundation is *re*-foundation, then, conversely, are not all acts 'within' an established legal order in one way or another also *founding* acts? Might legal acts be ordering acts, not merely because they assign a place, time, subject, and content to action, but also because these dimensions are never simply settled in advance? Would not legal acts have to establish, each time anew, what counts as legal*, given that the 'we as a whole' they would reiterate is irrevocably absent? Is not 'anew', in the disclosure of something as something* anew, irreducibly ambiguous, such that it means both 'again' and 'new', even though the weight of one or the other of these two aspects can vary, such that pure novelty and pure repetition are ideal types that can be approximated but never fully actualized? If such is the case, how could we nonetheless conceptualize novelty and novel possibilities, hence the *emergence* of legal orders and their boundaries?

4.8 THE A-LEGAL ORIGINS OF (IL)LEGALITY

These and a number of other questions will require our extended attention in the coming chapters. For the moment, and to conclude this chapter, I wish to zero in on how the paradox of representation impinges on the legality of legal acts. At issue is not only the objectivity of legality and the subjectivity of illegality but also the objectivity of the *distinction itself* between legality and illegality. Look again at Agnoletto's invocation: 'Our movement is not reformist; it is radical'. It brings about a *closure* that is supposed to *already* have taken place. In the very act of positing boundaries, Agnoletto claims that his act re-presents boundaries which already have been set: the paradox of representation returns in the form of a paradox of boundaries: to set *new* boundaries, an act must succeed in *re*-setting them.

Now, 'success' speaks to both efficacy and validity. These are not simply disjunctive terms, as Radbruch notes: 'Law is not valid *because* it can be effectively enforced, but rather it is valid *when* it can be effectively enforced, *because* only then can it guarantee legal certainty'.[43] Kelsen adds that a complete correspondence between efficacy and validity is not necessary nor even possible, as this would render the distinction meaningless: 'when one can assume that something will necessarily take place, one has no need to order that it happen'.[44] At the same time, unless the closure which gives rise to joint action is successful, i.e. efficacious to a certain extent, no collective has emerged and stabilized itself sufficiently for there to be a valid legal order. But validity cannot be collapsed into efficacy: 'The question of the validity of any particular norm is answered within the order by recourse to the first constitution, which establishes the validity of all norms'.[45] Here, once again, is the rub. The inaugural act which gives rise to the distinction between legality and illegality (it is not difficult to imagine how illegality would be configured if one utters 'radical, not reformist'), is neither legal* nor illegal*. In other words, and despite the possible 'success' of an inaugural act, in the sense of its efficacity, the conditions governing the emergence of (il) legality* cannot guarantee the objectivity of the distinction itself, as drawn in the apposite order, nor the objectivity of the order's boundaries.

So what I want to say is this: the inaugural act of a legal order is the inverted image of the a-legality that irrupts into a legal order in its later career. If the latter speaks to acts which contest the distinction between legality and illegality as drawn by a legal order, the former concerns the non-legal emergence of the distinction itself. The correlation between the two is no coincidence. Agnoletto's

[43] Gustav Radbruch, *Rechtsfilosofie*, 2nd edn. (Heidelberg: C.F. Müller, 1999), 83. Although I cannot discuss this problem here, I wonder whether the analysis of social 'typicality' developed by Schütz and Luckmann is sufficiently refined to avoid collapsing validity into efficaciousness or normality, at least as concerns legal orders. Once again, the shortcomings of a conception of intersubjectivity in terms of 'we both' or 'we each' become apparent. See Alfred Schütz and Thomas Luckmann, *The Structures of the Life-World*, vol. I, trans. Richard M. Zaner and J. Tristam Engelhardt Jr. (Evanston, IL: Northwestern University Press, 1973), 229–242.

[44] Kelsen, *Problems of Legal Theory*, 60.

[45] Kelsen, *Problems of Legal Theory*, 62 (translation altered).

invocation illustrates that there can be no joint action that is not *limited* joint action; all joint action requires a more or less determinate point that provides orientation for establishing who ought to do what, where, and when. 'We as a whole' is perforce a limited whole. Hence the anticipation-in-*general* that guides the inaugural act of a legal order and all further ordering within the legal order is a *limited* generality. No anticipation-in-general without inclusion, and also no anticipation-in-general without exclusion—literally. As a result, the distinction between legal (dis)order and the unordered, to which collective self-inclusion and the exclusion of other than self gives rise, is a thoroughly ambiguous achievement. On the one hand, it would be a mistake to view exclusion merely as a 'privation' of legal order; first and foremost, exclusion is a positive achievement of joint action under law. *Closure is a necessary condition for disclosure.* In effect, the disclosure of something as theft, testament, trust, or whatever, presupposes the normative distinctions introduced by legal meanings and, ultimately, the closure that separates legal (dis)order from the unordered. Closure is indispensable for normative orientation by the members of a collective; in its absence, they would not know how they ought to act as participant agents. On the other hand, the operation of normative inclusion and exclusion implies that, in the very act of revealing an event as legally significant, joint action under law effects a normative reduction of what it reveals. *Disclosure is necessarily a normative closure of the interpreted.* Legal intentionality reveals and conceals, actualizes a normative meaning by eliding other possible meanings: the 'significative difference' (Waldenfels) is also what I would call a *normative* difference.

This casts the 'jointness' of joint action in an ambiguous light. When discussing legal acts as intentional acts I have taken for granted that there is a common point shared by participants, even if not rendered explicit, and which allows them to keep track of each other's actions and to work together towards realizing it. In a word, I have taken for granted the *reciprocity* of joint action. But joint action, as it turns out, is kick-started by a unilateral act: someone must take the initiative to say 'we' on behalf of the we. Thus a unilateral *command* is ensconced in the multilaterality of joint action under law as one of its conditions of possibility. To this extent, a unilateral command has a positive significance for law, and not only the negative meaning of what is arbitrary, as is so often taken for granted by contemporary political and legal theories. But the ambiguity that governs the unilaterality of foundational acts, that is, the non-reciprocal origin that lies 'behind' a legal order, returns from 'ahead' in the form of non-reciprocal—unilateral—acts that interrupt the joint disclosure of something as something*, hence that call into question 'expectations of expectations' (Luhmann). This is what the *chômeurs* did, when what seemed to be an ordinary and entirely 'mundane' act suddenly and retroactively revealed itself as extra-ordinary and extra-mundane, as an act that turned joint action against itself to show that what is impossible in the legal order they interrupted is possible in another. At one level, expectations are disappointed by someone's action. At a more fundamental level, however, what a-legal action calls into question is whether we ought to entertain expectations about each other's expectations, and what* these expectations ought to be. The conditions that give rise to joint action entail that reciprocity under the aegis of the common point of joint action is always a putative reciprocity. This putative reciprocity explodes, when a-legal behaviour arises, into a *double* or even a *multiple asymmetry* of perspectives.

As a consequence, a-legality *ex post* during the career of a legal order is the counterpart to the a-legality *ex ante* of inaugural acts: because a legal order cannot guarantee the objectivity of how the legal / illegal distinction has been drawn at its inception, it cannot guarantee that future action ought to be grasped as either legal* or illegal*. Also, the im / possibility of the inaugural act returns in the form of im / possible action, action which intimates practical possibilities other than what I / we are authorized to do in the course of joint action under law. *The inaugural closure that gives rise to the boundaries of a legal order also assures that these can manifest themselves as limits.* Finally, in the same way that the act that inaugurates a legal order is neither legal nor illegal, so also, as we have seen in chapters 1 and 2, the limits of the legal order it brings forth are neither legal nor illegal.

Let me wind up this chapter by noting that these considerations on the paradox of representation begin to make good on a promise made to the reader in chapter 1. When introducing the three scenarios played out in the Lafayette of Rennes I acknowledged that an expository strategy that begins with the scenario of legality, then passes on to illegality, and ends up in a-legality, opened itself up to the charge of being partisan to the *status quo*. In particular, it seemed to favour legality and illegality to the disadvantage of a-legality. By extension, the claim that legal orders are perforce limited would be a surreptitious plea for 'ownness' and identity at the expense of strangeness and novelty. A phenomenologically inspired theory of joint action under law would provide conceptual legitimation to the claim that the boundaries of a legal order are *our* boundaries, boundaries that we *own* as a collective, and therefore are entitled to uphold and modify as we see fit.

I am well aware that critical vigilance is required with respect to these and related problems. But critical vigilance cannot mean that we avoid conceptualizing legal acts as partaking of a species of joint action, merely because the first-person perspective of a legal collective favours ownness, unity, identity, and the like. To refuse to engage these terms because they are politically and philosophically 'suspect' is to relinquish the conceptual tools in the absence of which we cannot even begin to make sense of legal boundaries and limits. Rather than turning our backs on concepts that then simply continue to do their work behind our backs, the task is to invert the order of analysis, showing how legality and illegality might be dependent on a-legality, and familiarity on strangeness, hence that *the first-person plural perspective always comes second*. In fact, it never entirely 'arrives'. What I have sought to do in this chapter is to show that it is not possible to remain within the domain of legality and illegality, hence of legal unity, if one thinks through to its end the question about the origin of this distinction. Very concretely, and returning to the expository strategy of chapter 1, what I have sought to show in the present chapter is that one cannot grasp what goes into the (il)legality of grabbing some tins of foie gras from a shelf in a food shop without also stumbling upon what makes it possible that grabbing those tins can become an a-legal act. Yet more pointedly, what today qualifies as legal for a collective is the result of a normalizing process leading back to an a-legal act, to a transgression of legal boundaries. This insight effectively carries forward, albeit in inverted fashion, Schmitt's central thesis about the concreteness of legal orders: 'We know that the norm presupposes a *normal* situation and *normal* types . . . A norm . . . only masters a situation insofar as this situation has not become entirely *abnormal* and as long as the normally presupposed type has not disappeared'.[46] Yes; but legal normality is the outcome of a process of normalization that has its inception in the abnormal. *In the beginning was a-legality.* And as the a-legal interpellates us from a second-person position, the second person comes earlier than the first. For the same reason, 'us' is prior to 'we', that is, the object of an act prior to being the subject thereof. Radicalizing a phenomenologically inspired reading of joint action under law reveals that a-legality is at the source of the distinction between legality and illegality, hence that strangeness is folded into ownness, pluralization into unification, differentiation into identification, disintegration into integration, and the second person into the first. When we push our enquiry in this direction, the questions I raised earlier return in all their relevance and urgency: are acts simply *(il)legal** acts? Are legal* acts simply *our* acts? Are legal boundaries simply *our* boundaries? Is the constitution ever simply *our* constitution?

[46] Schmitt, *Über die drei Arten des rechtswissenschaftlichen Denkens*, 19, 20.

5

A-Legality

The moment has arrived for an in-depth analysis of a-legality. Thus far, Part I has offered a preliminary description of its main features within the framework of a structural analysis of legal order. Just enough was said about a-legality to undergird the thesis, essential to Part I, that legal orders are necessarily limited because joint action by a legal collective presupposes a closure that is spatial, temporal, subjective, and material. While this fourfold closure may remain more or less concealed in the ordinary course of a legal practice, a-legality brings it into view. Subsequently, chapter 4, the introductory chapter to the account of legal ordering in Part II, argued that the conditions which govern the emergence of a legal order, hence the distinctions between legality and illegality, objectivity and subjectivity, rationality and irrationality, are also the conditions which explain why legal collectives are always exposed to the possibility of a-legality, which questions how these distinctions are drawn. We need to deepen this genetic account, examining in greater detail how a-legality questions a legal order and how a collective responds thereto in the ongoing process of setting legal boundaries. The present chapter delves into a-legality; chapter 6, into boundary-setting. The main problem we will confront in this chapter is whether a-legality is something more and other than the not-yet-(il)legal. The key to this problem is also the key to the distinction between limits and fault lines.

5.1 ESTRANGEMENT

Deepening our understanding of a-legality requires looking further at how the closure which gives rise to a collective calls forth the possibility of a-legality. In turn, this requires carrying forward and radicalizing the exploration of collective identity and its contrasting terms, in particular the contrast between selfhood and other than self, as outlined by Ricœur.

The main idea sketched out in sections 3.2 and 3.3 was that closure brings about the inclusion of a collective self and the exclusion of other than collective self. As *inclusion*, closure gives rise to a collective self, whereby a manifold of individuals are to view themselves as a group agent in-order-to-φ. Accordingly, closure includes a realm of practical possibilities as the range of acts available to us, the members of a collective, when acting together in the course of joint action under law: legal com-possibilities. Law opens up practical possibilities by empowering certain actions and empowering indeterminately many—but not infinitely many—ways of connecting these actions to each other (paying for a tram ride, going into the Lafayette food department, taking home the victuals in a cab, etc.). Legal possibilities, in the sense of normative empowerments, call forth the possibility of illegality, that is, behaviour in breach of what is legally empowered. On this reading, a legal order is concrete because it actualizes a determinate realm of practical possibilities, in the twofold sense of certain legal possibilities and certain possibilities of illegality. As *exclusion*, the closure which inaugurates a legal collective relegates everything that is beyond the pale of joint action and its normative point to the residual domain of the unordered. In the same way that closure, by including, gives rise to a 'filled' spatio-temporal unity inside, so also, by excluding, it gives rise to an 'empty spatio-temporality' outside (Husserl). Although empty from the perspective of the legal collective, this empty outside makes room for *other* practical possibilities that are deemed irrelevant, unimportant, in light of joint action by the members of a legal collective. The unordered comprises a surfeit, rather than a dearth, of practical possibilities, yet a superabundance of possibilities that have been levelled down to the status of the irrelevant and unimportant, as the price that must be paid if there is to be any legal empowerment at all. Consequently, the closure which gives rise to a legal order as a realm of practical possibilities cannot empower without also disempowering, cannot capacitate without incapacitating.

In short, and summarizing the findings of sections 3.2 and 3.3, the closure of a legal collective gives rise to the limit between legal (dis)order and the unordered. This limit joins and separates collective selfhood and other than self: a legal collective and its other(s). But alterity is a far broader category than *strangeness,*[1] the domain of a-legality. What is specific to otherness-as-strangeness in the form of a-legality?

Before getting started, let me indicate right away that my approach to the problem of strangeness is circumscribed in two decisive ways. First, I approach strangeness as it appears in the framework of *legal* ordering, which is why I have introduced the notion of a-legality. This approach by no means exhausts either the phenomenon of strangeness or how it manifests itself as such with respect to other kinds of orders. In fact, it may well be one of the peculiarities of legal ordering that it cannot accommodate the full spectrum of the experiences of strangeness.[2] Second, my aim in introducing the category of a-legality, as the legal manifestation of otherness-as-strangeness, is to explain why the three-way distinction between boundaries, limits, and (as we shall now see) fault lines is constitutive for legal orders and legal ordering. I will not be discussing those aspects of a-legality which might fall beyond the pale of a study of the relation between legal orders and their boundaries, limits, and fault lines.[3]

[1] This is Waldenfels' main criticism of Ricœur's book, *Oneself as another*. See Bernhard Waldenfels, 'The Other and the Strange', *Philosophy and Social Criticism* 21 (1995), 111–124. My account of collective self-closure is indebted to this article, as well as to Waldenfels' earlier article, 'Experience of the Alien in Husserl's Phenomenology', *Research in Phenomenology* 20 (1990), 19–33.

[2] Waldenfels explores an 'ecstatic' strangeness of the self and a 'diastatic' strangeness that arises between me and others, and which are different to the strangeness of the (legally) extra-ordinary, as manifested in a-legal behaviour and situations. See Bernhard Waldenfels, *Bruchlinien der Erfahrung*, 174 ff, 205 ff.

[3] It should be clear, in any case, that 'a-legality', as I will conceptualize and illustrate it, has little or nothing to do with the politically inert sense of strangeness as the 'unknown', to which Habermas appeals when defending 'an abstract form of civic solidarity among strangers who want to remain strangers'. See

Notice, at the outset, that a-legality is not equivalent to the unordered, although there could be no a-legality in the absence of the latter. Whereas both terms of the distinction between legality and illegality fall under the first term of the contrast between legal (dis)order and the unordered, it would be a mistake to equate a-legality to its second term. Indeed, a-legality concerns behaviour and situations that, having being relegated to the sphere of what a legal collective views as irrelevant and unimportant, *emerge* therefrom to question what a concrete collective calls legal (dis)order. By questioning how a legal order sets the *boundaries* that give shape to the distinction between legality and illegality, a-legality challenges how a concrete legal collective draws the *limit* between legal (dis)order and the unordered. Typically, a-legal behaviour and situations would amount to only a fraction of everything that falls under the residual category of the unordered.

This preliminary determination of the phenomenon of a-legality calls forth a possible objection. If the limit between legal (dis)order and the unordered is most fundamentally at stake in a-legality, it may seem a distraction to have insisted in the foregoing chapters that a-legality challenges the *boundaries* of (il)legality. Would it not have been better to state that a-legality directly questions the *limit* between legal (dis)order and the unordered? No, and for good reasons. If the unordered is what stands beyond the pale of joint action by a legal collective, as that to which law has no direct access because it is irrelevant and unimportant to the collective, then what has been relegated to that domain can only manifest itself *indirectly*, that is, as a modification of what counts as (il)legal behaviour.[4] Because the limit between legal (dis)order and the unordered runs along each of the boundaries drawn by a legal collective, rather than separately from these, it only appears, as a limit, in behaviour and situations which call these boundaries into question. And this means that a-legality can only indirectly disrupt how a legal collective partitions what is relevant from what is irrelevant, what is important from what is unimportant. To call these legal boundaries into question is to intimate other possibilities, i.e. other ways of drawing the boundaries that establish what is legally important and relevant, and what is not. A-legal behaviour is behaviour in which the unordered manifests itself within the legal order as another possible ordering of behaviour which interferes with the realm of practical possibilities made available by the legal collective it questions—about which more later.

Furthermore, (il)legality can be challenged from *both* sides of the disjunction, and not only by questioning what counts as illegal. In particular, (il)legality can be

Jürgen Habermas, 'Legitimation through Human Rights', in Pablo de Greiff and Ciaran Cronin (eds.), *Global Justice and Transnational Politics* (Cambridge, MA: The MIT Press, 2002), 206.

[4] This resonates well with Laclau's discussion of the notion of the limit of a system of signification: 'if limits could be signified in a direct way, they would be internal to signification and, *ergo*, would not be limits at all...[I]f what we are talking about are the limits of a *signifying system*, it is clear that those limits cannot themselves be signified, but have to *show* themselves as the *interruption* or *breakdown* of the process of signification'. See Ernesto Laclau, *Emancipation(s)*, repr. (London: Verso, 2007), 37. See also the analysis of antagonism, equivalence, and difference, as well as the associated notion of a 'constitutive outside', in Ernesto Laclau and Chantal Mouffe, *Hegemony and Socialist Strategy: Towards a Radical Democratic Politics*, 2nd edn. (London: Verso, 2001), 122–134, and Chantal Mouffe, *The Democratic Paradox* (London: Verso, 2000), 13.

disrupted from the pole of *legality*, as when, in the face of a decree by the Serbian government prohibiting persons from gathering together in public places, people took massively to the streets to 'walk their dogs' in the period leading up to the downfall of Milosevic's regime.[5] Moreover, the challenge to (il)legality need not be deliberately directed to contest how the legal collective draws the distinction between what is important and what is unimportant. A-legality is not limited to 'activism' in general nor to 'direct action' in particular, where the latter is defined as action explicitly channelled by individuals or groups towards realizing social or political goals in ways other than those authorized by the legal order. For this reason I generally refer to a-legality in terms of behaviour and situations, rather than of action. A good example is the enactment and progressive sharpening of environmental regulations in the face of behaviour that was initially viewed as legal because, for many legal collectives, environmental concerns initially lay beyond the pale of the normative point of joint action. Such concerns were unimportant and, as such, belonged to the domain of the unordered; environmentally destructive behaviour *emerged* as a question for legal collectives, even though such behaviour did not intend to contest what counted as legal behaviour—to the contrary. Notice how even in this and analogous cases, such behaviour emerges from the domain of what I called the *unordered*, although it is initially disclosed as legal, and therewith as standing within the legal order.

In the same way that the domain of the unordered is relational, that is, unordered in relation to a particular and concrete legal order, so also a-legal behaviour. It makes no sense to pose the question about a-legality as though there are specific kinds of behaviour that are a-legal *as such*, independently of any given legal order, and which anyone could inventory and describe. A-legal behaviour concerns a concrete legal collective because it challenges how *that* legal collective draws the distinction between legality and illegality. So instead of asking, 'What is a-legal?', a question for which no general answer is possible, we need to ask, 'What is the mode of appearance of a-legality?' In other words, how does behaviour appear as more and other than merely legal or illegal, and to whom? Only the latter question allows us to identify and describe the general features of a-legality, while also respecting that a-legal behaviour only manifests itself as such in relation to members of a concrete legal collective.[6] This mode of appearance is what I have sought to grasp with the compound term 'a-legality'. On the one hand, the relational character of a-legality is captured in the reference to a-*legality*. Here, legality comprises both terms of (il)legality as drawn by a concrete legal collective: something appears as relevant and important from the perspective of the legal collective, hence as more or less legal or illegal. On the other,

[5] I owe this wonderful example to Ivana Ivkovic, a doctoral student at the Department of Philosophy of Tilburg University, which she marshalled to expose my one-sided focus on illegality in an earlier account of how a-legality questions the legality/illegality disjunction.

[6] Insofar as a legal order involves the *authoritative* mediation and upholding of joint action, authorities must be among those 'to whom' an act appears as a-legal, as they are those who, in the final instance, are to decide about a-legality when setting the boundaries of (il)legality. This institutional dimension of authority is a decisive feature of legal intentionality in general and of a phenomenology of a-legality in particular.

the 'a' of *a*-legality does not merely mean the negation of law, for that would be legal disorder: the privative manifestation of legal order. Instead, it speaks to other ways of ordering behaviour as being important and relevant, *despite* having been levelled down to what is unimportant and irrelevant for the legal collective.

These general considerations on legal order and the unordered, and on the indirect mode of appearance of a-legality, mesh well with what Husserl calls the experience of strangeness, and which might perhaps be better captured with the term *estrangement*. In this vein, a legal order partakes of the structure of a *Heimwelt*, a world which is 'already known, already familiar',[7] such that in principle one knows who ought to do what, where, and when, even if this practical knowledge is ever incomplete and amenable to further completion. The operation of intentionality proper to joint action under law, as sketched out in chapter 4, seeks to capture this idea, for it is by 'jointly disclosing something as something* anew in-order-to-φ' that individuals understand themselves as legal actors and understand the legal order in which they participate. In contrast with the familiarity of a home-world, in which actors comprehend what they ought to do, Husserl observes that 'the strange is first of all the incomprehensible strange' (*unverständlich Fremdes*). And he immediately adds that 'of course, anything, however strange, still has a core of what is known, for otherwise it could not be experienced at all, not even as strange'.[8] While Husserl introduces these considerations about estrangement in the framework of a discussion of what one might call cultural strangeness, they also apply to the experience of estrangement which arises as a modification of legal intentionality. I refer to a 'modification' of legal intentionality to point to the two features of a-legality. On the one hand, behaviour could not be strange for a legal order unless the distinction between legality and illegality, as drawn by that order, in some way applies to it: a-*legality*. In other words, behaviour that emerges from the domain of the unordered does so *as* something*. To repeat Husserl's turn of phrase, a-legal behaviour 'still has a core of what is known, for otherwise it could not be experienced at all, not even as strange'. But, on the other hand, the disclosure of something *as* something* does not grasp what behaviour claims to be *about*. The disclosure of something as (il) legal* misses its (normative) point, which is not only 'other' than that anticipated by legal intentionality but also a normative point the realization of which *interferes* with joint action under law: *a*-legality. Legal intentionality is arrested. This is crucial. If the domain of the unordered incorporates the entire range of 'other' possibilities which have been excluded from joint action, a-legality questions a concrete legal collective by demanding the realization of practical possibilities which *block* or *obstruct* the realization of the practical possibilities made available by a legal order. So, for example, the *autoréduction* appears both as more or less illegal (arguably a case of extortion) and as demanding the actualization of practical possibilities which interfere with the possibilities made available by contracts of sale under French law (the blockage of the check-out points). To sum up, a-legal behaviour is both inside and outside the legal order: inside, because

[7] Husserl, *Phänomenologie der Intersubjektivität*, 430.

[8] Husserl, *Phänomenologie der Intersubjektivität*, 432.

accessible as legal or illegal behaviour; outside, because inaccessible in terms of that behaviour's normative point. This is, on a preliminary reading, the legal mode of what Husserl calls strangeness: 'accessibility in its genuine inaccessibility, in the mode of incomprehensibility'.[9]

Several features of a-legality merit further exploration here. First, a-legal behaviour brings about a certain 'occupation' (*Besetzung*), as Husserl puts it, of the domain of the unordered, which is initially an 'empty spatio-temporality'.[10] With this occupation, the limit between a 'filled' inside and an 'empty' outside is punctured. The outside ceases to be opaque, intimating a place that is *else*where; a time that is *else*when; actors who are *else*whom; a form of behaviour that is *else*what. This is what happened, to return to our example, with the initiative of the *chômeurs*. The food shop and its environs appeared initially as 'filled' to the extent that it was a seamless distribution and interconnection of legal places that exhausted where one could orient oneself when participating in a joint act. For many clients, the *autoréduction* depleted the fullness of this legal region, intimating an ought-place which demands actualization, but which can only be actualized in another distribution of ought-places because it is incompatible with the extant distribution of ought-places made available by the legal order. In the same way, whereas joint action attested to the fullness of time, in which there is an appropriate time for each participant act and sequences of acts (entering the food shop, selecting products, queuing up at the check-out point), the *autoréduction* stripped legal temporality of its plenitude, intimating an ought-time and sequence of times that have no 'right' time within the interconnected distribution of ought-times made available by joint action. Comparable depletions of the fullness of a legal order by a-legality also held for how the order configures the subjectivity and the content of legal acts. In short, a legal order can appear as 'full' only as long as the unordered appears as 'empty'.

An additional feature of a-legal behaviour that merits consideration is its *irruptive force*. I deliberately speak of 'irruption', rather than of 'eruption', because a-legality reaches a legal order from what was initially the opaque domain of the unordered. The 'practical interest within' (Husserl) is interrupted from without. Note that this is also the case when a-legality comes about in what a legal collective calls its own space, such as with the *autoréduction*: the strange need not be foreign, nor the foreign strange. The term irruption—which means to break in or to break through—evokes the element of *force* in a-legality. Its 'force' speaks, on the one hand, to unmediated power, that is, to the actualization of practical possibilities which are not empowered by the legal collective. This actualization of unforeseen practical possibilities goes hand in hand with a certain depletion of empowerment within the legal order—a certain *powerlessness* of participant agents—to the extent that who engages in a-legal behaviour not merely does what he or she ought not to do, but does something *other* than what lies within the range of practical possibilities made available by joint action. And it speaks, on the other, to constraint upon the legal collective, which is *forced* to deal, in one

[9] Husserl, *Phänomenologie der Intersubjektivität*, 631.

[10] Husserl, *Phänomenologie der Intersubjektivität*, 139.

way or another, with the unforeseen practical possibilities with which a-legality confronts it, even if only to ignore them. To borrow Alfred Schütz's formulation, 'Not to answer is also an answer'.[11] Two far-reaching implications follow from the 'forcefulness' of a-legality. If having to deal with a-legality means having to establish how the limit between legal (dis)order and the unordered must be drawn, hence having to determine what counts as collective *self*-ordering, then, in a sense very different to that envisaged by Rousseau, the individuals who compose a legal collective are 'forced to be free'. Xenonomy—not merely heteronomy—is inscribed in collective autonomy: necessarily, not merely in fact. Moreover, being forced to deal with a-legality means having to lay down what counts as the legal boundaries defining who ought to do what, where, and when. In a word, a-legality forces (what thereby becomes) us, the legal collective, to establish what counts as *our* boundaries. But if 'we' are forced to do this, in response to a-legality, then 'our' boundaries are something we never fully have under our control or own: *we owe our boundaries to others*. To repeat an earlier formulation, the first-person plural perspective comes second, and the second-person perspective, first.

Moreover, irruption connotes unexpectedness, surprise. For if a legal collective cannot 'know' in advance what it abandons to the domain of the unordered, thereby relinquishing control over the latter, this is the domain whence the unexpected can irrupt into a legal order. A-legal behaviour catches agents participating in joint action by surprise, as happened with the *autoréduction* in Galeries Lafayette, because it reveals as relevant and important what joint action by a legal collective has levelled down to the domain of the irrelevant and unimportant. Whereas a legal order marks out the domain of what can be expected, because to order is to re-order in the form of a reiterative anticipation, the unordered is the domain whence something appears to the members of a legal collective which they could not anticipate because it does not simply reiterate what has gone before it. Consequently, a-legal behaviour is extra-ordinary and ex-temporaneous.

The unexpected character of a-legality points to yet a further feature of its irruptive force: the *asymmetry* between legal (dis)order and a-legality. We have already discussed how the self-closure that gives rise to a legal collective involves an asymmetry whereby (dis)order is preferred to the unordered, what is important to what is unimportant, inside to outside. Self-closure calls forth a second asymmetry, or more exactly, a double asymmetry, which becomes manifest when a-legality irrupts into a legal order. On the one hand, the unordered, as the domain over which a legal collective has no control, is also the domain which *precedes* legal order. Precedence does not have the meaning, in this context, of a merely temporal sequence whereby an a-legal act is followed up by its legal qualification. A-legality precedes the legal order in that it is what the legal collective cannot anticipate, that which does not meet legal expectations concerning what is to come about, and in that sense always comes too early. This is precisely what is at stake in the 'foreclosure' of possibilities by a legal order, where 'foreclosure'

[11] Alfred Schütz and Thomas Luckmann, *The Structures of the Life-World*, vol. II, trans. Richard M. Zaner and David J. Parent (Evanston, IL: Northwestern University Press, 1989), 71. See also Waldenfels, *Antwortregister*, 241.

means both closing down and closing in advance. On the other hand, the response of the members of a collective to a-legality is no less asymmetrical. To see why, consider the *autoréduction*. What was striking about the situation which emerged when the *chômeurs* blocked the check-out points is the ambiguity it generated. While some of the clients and participants in the blog that emerged in the wake of the incident were sympathetic to the *chômeurs'* cause, many of the clients of Lafayette and some of the bloggers felt that the *chômeurs* exercised duress, thereby perpetrating an illegal act. In short, for some of the actors involved in the event, the act appeared as a-legal; for others—perhaps most—as simply illegal. So whether an event is a-legal, and how it calls into question the limit between legal (dis)order and the unordered, is established *retroactively*, in the responses it calls forth, in particular in the course of authoritative boundary-setting. Here then is the double asymmetry: the precedence of a-legality is coupled to the retroactivity of the responses it calls forth.[12] This double asymmetry will be examined at greater length in chapter 6.

5.2 THE NORMATIVE COMPLEXITY OF A-LEGALITY

A-legality, I have been arguing, involves an incompatibility between, on the one hand, practical possibilities as actualized in a legal order (a-*legality*), and, on the other, practical possibilities the actualization of which are demanded by certain behaviour and situations (*a*-legality). In fact, interference, rather than incompatibility, is the better term, for at issue is the blockage or obstruction of bodily behaviour in a realm of practical possibilities. The references to 'interference' and to 'other' practical possibilities remain underdetermined. Indeed, a distinction must be drawn between practical possibilities which could be actualized in a legal order as falling within the range of a collective's *own* possibilities, on the one hand, and, on the other, practical possibilities that *exceed* the range of practical possibilities available to a collective, that is, which surpass the range of ways in which a legal collective can order who ought to do what, where, and when in-order-to-φ. This distinction needs further elaboration and illustration, as it is central to my account of a-legality, not least because it will allow me to introduce, in due course, the notion of a normative fault line.

Before examining this distinction more fully it is important to be on guard against two pitfalls. The first is the assumption that a-legal behaviour or situations fall neatly into either of the two sides of the distinction. The normative claim raised by a-legality is complex, I argue, because it *conjoins what is practically possible and impossible* for a collective, even though one or the other of these two dimensions may be more prominent in any given situation. A normative claim that only revealed possibilities that are the collective's own possibilities, or possibilities that definitively exceed what it could actualize, are ideal types which

[12] See Jacques Derrida's radicalization of Freud's notion of *Nachträglichkeit* (the *après coup*) as the 'supplement of origin' in *L'écriture et la différence* (Paris: Seuil, 1967), 314. See also Waldenfels on precedence (*Vorgängichkeit*) and retroactivity (*Nachträglichkeit*) in *Antwortregister*, 262–263, and the associated notion of a 'temporal diastase' in Waldenfels, *Bruchlinien der Erfahrung*, 173–175.

a-legal behaviour and situations can approximate but never entirely realize. I propose, therefore, to speak of the 'weak' and 'strong' *dimensions* of a-legality, instead of 'weak' and 'strong' *modes* thereof. The second pitfall is the assumption that there is a neat repertoire of possibilities given in advance to a collective as its own possibilities, and a host of other possibilities which it could in advance discount as exceeding its own possibilities. Which possibilities are a collective's own possibilities, and which surpass these, only becomes apparent retroactively, *après coup*, in authoritatively mediated responses to a-legality, even though the precedence of a-legality entails that a collective never merely has at its disposition which possibilities are its own and which are not. I will return to this point in section 5.3 and when discussing the precedence of a-legality and the retroactivity of boundary-setting in the course of chapter 6.

The weak dimension of a-legality confronts a collective with a *provisional* interference to joint action under law, whereby extant legal empowerments are obstructed by other practical possibilities the realization of which is demanded in light of the normative point of joint action. At issue here is behaviour or situations which a collective discloses as illegal* (or legal*), but which it ought to disclose as legal* (or illegal*) in-order-to-φ, or so it is claimed. To this extent, a-legality challenges the collective disclosure of something as legal*, *rather* than as illegal*; or as illegal*, *rather* than legal*. This ties up with what has been said in chapter 4 about the threefold reference of joint action, namely: (i) the reference to a collective; (ii) the reference to a legal order that lays out who ought to do what, where, and when; (iii) the reference to the normative point of joint action. In effect, the weak dimension of a-legality obstructs the three references in such a way that they become problematic. A gap appears between how these references are realized and how they could be realized. As a result this threefold obstruction confronts the collective with the practical question, what* ought our joint action to be about? This means that a-legality, in its weak dimension, appears as what irrupts into a legal order from the domain of the unordered, yet which is in principle *orderable* by it. Thus the weak dimension of a-legality does not fundamentally question the capacity of a legal collective to order the unordered because the normative issue concerns whether something ought to be disclosed as legal* or as illegal*. This dimension of a-legality intimates, accordingly, other practical possibilities than those which have been actualized as legal empowerments, but which nonetheless remain within the realm of the collective's *own* legal possibilities. Conversely, possibilities appear as our own possibilities to the extent that 'we' can disclose something as what ought to become *either* legal* *or* illegal*. In two words, this dimension of a-legality concerns *unordered orderability*. The interference or obstruction of joint action under law manifests itself as temporary: a-legality is the-not-yet-(il)legal. This returns us to what was said at the end of section 4.4 about the internal correlation between practical possibility and legal intelligibility: what is intelligible (and we can now add: orderable) in a legal order are the collective's own possibilities, and vice versa. The weak dimension of a-legality not only raises the practical question—What* ought our joint action to be about?—but this appears as a question to which the collective can respond by resetting the boundaries of (il)legality, thereby shifting the limit between legal (dis)order and the unordered.

By contrast, the 'strong' dimension of a-legality denotes a normative claim that resists apportionment under *both* terms of the legality/illegality disjunction. Whereas in its weak dimension a-legality questions that it has been apportioned to one of the terms rather than the other, the strong dimension of a-legality concerns a normative challenge that a legal collective cannot accommodate either as legal* or as illegal* by reformulating the terms of joint action under law. Both terms of the disjunction miss the point—indeed, miss the normative point—whence a-legal behaviour questions joint action by a legal collective. More is certainly possible for a legal collective than the realm of practical possibilities it has actualized and rendered available to participant agents in the form of legal empowerments. But the strong dimension of a-legal behaviour attests to possibilities that are incompossible with the range of possibilities accessible to the legal collective in-order-to-φ. It bursts the threefold reference to (i) a legal collective, (ii) the legal order which lays out who ought to do what, where, and when, and (iii) the normative point of joint action. At issue is a normative claim that registers as legal or illegal, yet to which *we cannot relate* in its own terms; it betokens a practical possibility we cannot view as our own because it is incompossible with what* our joint action is about. Strongly a-legal behaviour denotes what definitively cannot be said and done in a legal collective, hence what can only be said and done in another legal collective.

This does not entail, however, that the first-person plural perspective of the collective and the second-person perspective intimated by the strong dimension of a-legal behaviour are incompossible in their *entirety*: there will be 'sectors' of behaviour which are compatible with both perspectives, and others which are not. *Grogan* is a good example of this, as the practical incompossibility between the Irish and EU legal orders was limited to abortion and ancillary activities thereto.[13] Accordingly, if, in its weak dimension, a-legality denotes a normative claim to the extent it is unordered but orderable, in its strong dimension it denotes this claim to the extent that it is *unordered and unorderable.* It resists inclusion in its own normative terms within the realm of legal empowerments made available or which could be made available by the apposite legal collective. At issue is a normative claim that is *definitively* extra-ordinary and ex-temporaneous to the collective it challenges, that is, a claim that is normatively inaccessible because it is impossible for us to realize it as a legal empowerment, and vice versa. In short, the strong dimension of a-legality challenges the boundaries of a legal collective in a way that exceeds the question to which it can respond by resetting its legal boundaries: what* is our joint action about?

It may be helpful to illustrate these ideas with some examples, repeating the caveat, lodged at the outset of section 1.2, that every 'illustration' also *frames* a

[13] Talk about the 'clash of civilizations' or other 'mega-clashes' gets it right and wrong: right, in that there are practical incompossibilities which can become apparent across collectives; wrong, in the assumption that these practical incompossibilities concern the collectives in their entirety.

situation in a certain way, rather than others. The first example seeks to illustrate behaviour in which the weak dimension of a-legality is predominant; the three examples thereafter illustrate the predominance of the strong dimension of a-legality.

Let us first examine Brazil's *Movimento dos trabalhadores rurais sem terra* (MST), the Landless Workers Movement, an example of a-legality I briefly discussed in chapter 2. It is worthwhile quoting in full how its 'official' website describes the movement:

> The MST carries out long-overdue land reform in a country mired by unjust land distribution. In Brazil, 1.6% of the landowners control roughly half (46.8%) of the land on which crops could be grown. Just 3% of the population owns two-thirds of all arable lands. Since 1985, the MST has peacefully occupied unused land where they have established cooperative farms, constructed houses, schools for children and adults and clinics, promoted indigenous cultures and a healthy and sustainable environment and gender equality. The MST has won land titles for more than 350,000 families in 2,000 settlements as a result of MST actions, and 180,000 encamped families currently await government recognition. Land occupations are rooted in the Brazilian Constitution, which says land that remains unproductive should be used for a 'larger social function'. The MST's success lies in its ability to organize and educate. Members have not only managed to secure land, thereby food security for their families, but also continue to develop a sustainable socio-economic model that offers a concrete alternative to today's globalization that puts profits before people and humanity.[14]

The passage amounts to a description of the MST as a collective in joint action. What is their joint action about? What is its normative point? In the face of unjust land distribution in Brazil, the MST seeks to redress this situation by occupying unused land and, on the basis of the social function of property, as enshrined in the Brazilian constitution, to obtain land titles for the dispossessed.

This description of the MST land occupations and their other actions, such as the occupation of the offices of public institutions and multinationals, blockades of roads and railroads, and the like, presents it as an example of a-legality. Indeed, by occupying unused land they breach property rights, such that their act appears as illegal from the first-person plural perspective of the Brazilian collective. Whence a-*legality* (in the broad sense of behaviour that is either legal or illegal, ordered or disordered). Yet to simply disclose their occupation as illegal is to miss its normative point, or so the MST claims; their aim is to highlight other practical possibilities, as concerns who ought to do what, where, and when, than those made available by Brazilian law. Accordingly, their land occupation is also an 'occupation', as Husserl phrases it, of what was initially an opaque outside. If the spatio-temporal configuration of the Brazilian legal order was 'filled', at the outset of the MST's activities, such that there were proper places for all and at all times, this spatio-temporality is depleted of its fullness by the MST's occupation (*Besetzung*) of an 'empty outside', which points to other practical possibilities,

[14] Site of the MST, <http://www.mstbrazil.org/?q=about> (accessed on 13 February 2013).

to another spatio-temporal configuration of the Brazilian legal order which interferes with the extant legal order. Whence *a*-legality. The MST advocates the empowerment of its disempowered members. But because empowerment is not simply about granting them land rights which already accrue to the legally empowered, but about redefining the criteria for land ownership, the MST is powerful in that its land occupations reveal what current legal empowerment does not achieve but can and ought to achieve, or so they claim. See here a conceptual justification of André van der Walt's insight, cited in chapter 2, that 'to think about property in the margins also implies taking note of the strong positions that sometimes feature in the margins, particularly when they are founded on direct rejection of or confrontation with the dominant property regime'.[15] Those 'strong' positions attest to what I called the irruptive *force* of a-legality.

Importantly, as the website notes, the MST demands that the Brazilian authorities *recognize* the land rights of its members. In this vein the website also refers to 'long-overdue land reform' and to 'unjust land distribution'. According to the site's description, the members of the MST seek 'full citizenship' in the Brazilian collective; having been marginalized by the default answer of Brazilian property law concerning what* joint action ought to be about, they demand to be included in relations of legal reciprocity, such that action can again become joint action, that is, action by 'we' as a *whole*. The MST claim that another configuration of who ought to do what, where, and when in the Brazilian legal order is available to the collective as one of its *own* possibilities, a possibility which ought to be actualized in view of realizing the collective's normative point and restoring the unity of the collective. What the current default setting of Brazilian property law discloses as illegal* behaviour ought to give way to its disclosure as legal*.

These considerations suggest that the challenge to the legal/illegal distinction, as described by the site of the MST, is weak: it evokes a form of *unordered orderability*. 'Unordered' because their land occupations intimate practical possibilities that had been relegated to the sphere of the irrelevant and unimportant by the Brazilian legal order; 'orderable' because the new configuration of space, time, subjectivity, and content they demand can be rendered consistent, or so they claim, with what the collective views as relevant and important, in terms of the Brazilian constitution. Granted, the demands of land redistribution by the MST have often been rebuffed, and often violently, by landowners as much as by the government. But the demand for recognition raised by the MST, as described by the site, does not pose a fundamental challenge to the Brazilian collective.

Yet, one should be wary of assuming that the weak dimension of a-legality exhausts the normative claim raised by these land occupations. To begin with, the logic of closure applies to the MST itself: no joint action without inclusion and exclusion. What kind of behaviour has been marginalized within the MST, such that the site can present land occupation as being consistent with the normative point of the Brazilian collective, as laid down in Article 184 of the Constitution?

[15] Van der Walt, *Property in the Margins*, 243.

Need we take for granted that all those who participate in land occupation under the flag of the MST would explain and justify their action in the way described on the site? A further reason for being wary is the site itself, which is addressed to the 'friends' of the MST. One of the drop-down boxes on the site reads 'Getting involved'. *Who* do they want to involve? Who counts as a 'friend' of the MST? If involvement is, as Husserl points out, always 'practical interest within', what is it that the description pushes out into the domain of the irrelevant and unimportant? What is it that goes unsaid? The description itself provides an indirect answer, when it claims that the aim of land redistribution is to achieve 'food security' for the MST's members, within the broader aim of developing 'a sustainable socio-economic model that offers a concrete alternative to today's globalization that puts profits before people and humanity'. What has been pushed out is forms of questioning the legal/illegal divide which cannot be accommodated within this socio-economic and anthropocentric understanding of joint action, a self-understanding which allows the MST to view itself as seeking recognition within the Brazilian collective, and a self-understanding with which its 'friends' can identify and 'get involved'. This is the domain, I conjecture, whence the strong dimension of a-legality could irrupt in the form of land occupations which cannot be accommodated by the Brazilian legal collective.[16]

So much for the weak dimension of a-legality; while the examples could be multiplied, land occupation by the MST suffices, I hope, to clarify the structure of normative claims insofar as they challenge the disclosure of something as legal* *rather* than as illegal*, or as illegal* *rather* than as legal*. By contrast, the strong dimension of a-legality arrests legal intentionality in a more radical way: behaviour appears as (il)legal but has a normative point that definitively eludes *both* terms of the disjunction.

Occupation, in the twofold sense of occupation of an ought-place within a unity of ought-places that configures a legal space, and occupation of an 'empty outside', inaugurated the May 1968 events in Paris, as well. The occupation of the Sorbonne, on 14 May, and the subsequent general wildcat strike in which workers across France occupied factories, train stations, post offices, and the like, ushered in one of the exemplary manifestations of the strong dimension of a-legality: insurrection. The radical challenge to the French legal order did not come from the unions, who sought to negotiate better conditions for their constituencies with the government, while also seeking to undermine the general wildcat strike. Nor did it come from the Communist Party, which in its own way sought to contemporize with the De Gaulle government. Both challenges spoke to a-legality in its weak dimension. Radical questioning came from the workers who, refusing to accept the authority of either the unions or the political parties, both of which had vested interests in the

[16] There are indications that the MST harbours aspirations leading back to millenarian revolt movements in the northeast of Brazil, most notably the revolt that gathered around the figure of Antonio Conselheiro. See Euclydes da Cunha, *Rebellion in the Backlands*, trans. Samuel Putnam (Chicago, IL: University of Chicago Press, 1944). The epigraph of Vargas Llosa's magnificent novel about Conselheiro and the revolt at Canudos ably captures the nature of the struggle: 'The Antichrist was born to govern Brazil but the Counselor is come to deliver us from him'. See Mario Vargas Llosa, *The War of the End of the World*, trans. Helene Fane (New York: Faber and Faber, 2004).

continuation of the extant legal collective, sought to overthrow the state and directly take over the economy.[17]

I will not discuss those events any further here. Instead, I would like to draw on and modify Kelsen's remarkable analysis of a legal revolution with a view to highlighting the cardinal features of the strong dimension of a-legality. The setting he imagines is the attempt by a band of revolutionaries to overthrow a monarchy and install a republican form of government:

> If the revolutionaries succeed, the old system ceases to be effective, and the new system becomes effective, because the actual behaviour of the human beings for whom the system claims to be valid corresponds no longer to the old system but, by and large, to the new system. And one treats this new system, then, as a legal system, that is to say, one interprets as legal acts the acts applying the new system, and as unlawful acts the material facts violating it. One presupposes a new basic norm, no longer the basic norm delegating lawmaking authority to the monarch, but a basic norm delegating lawmaking authority to the revolutionary government. If the revolutionaries were to fail because the system they set up remained ineffective... then the initial act of the revolutionaries would be interpreted not as the establishing of a constitution but as treason, not as the making of law but as a violation of law.[18]

I will bracket Kelsen's invocation of the basic norm, which has been discussed in chapter 5. What is important here is that such settings call into question joint action by a legal collective in an extreme way: the contested legal collective and the emergent legal collective cannot co-exist; they are incompossible, not merely in terms of certain practical possibilities available to the one but definitively excluded by the other, but as collectives. In effect, whereas a-legality in its weak dimensions reveals other possibilities as a collective's own possibilities, and which allow for shifting the divide between legal (dis)order and the unordered, a fundamentally different picture emerges with the overthrow of a legal collective. Kelsen's analysis reveals that the insurrection leading up to a revolution precipitates what might be called 'interpretative incommensurability'. The problem is not that the act of the revolutionaries cannot be understood within the legal order they attempt to overthrow; it is that their act can only be interpreted as treason or sedition: as illegality pure and simple. The act's intelligibility within the legal order—as treason—goes hand in hand with the act's radical unintelligibility—as constitution-making—within the same order. Conversely, the revolutionary interpretation of the act of overthrowing a legal order cannot be other than constitution-making, without betraying its claim to being the founding act of a legal order. 'The proletariat is "either revolutionary or nothing"'.[19]

Kelsen's account of insurrection as interpretative incommensurability suggests that no encompassing point of view can bridge the interpretative abyss

[17] See René Viénet, *Enragés and Situationists in the Occupations Movement*, trans. Loren Goldner and Paul Sieveking (New York: Autonomedia, 1992). Available on the website of the Situationist International at: <http://www.cddc.vt.edu/sionline/si/enrages.html> (accessed on 13 February 2013).

[18] Kelsen, *Problems of Legal Theory*, 59.

[19] 'Address to All Workers, Enragés-Situationist International Committee, Council for Maintaining the Occupations', trans. Ken Knabb. See <http://www.cddc.vt.edu/sionline/si/address.html> (accessed on 13 February 2013).

between treason and constitution-making; no dialectic succeeds in integrating a revolutionary act into the legal order. To interpret the act of revolutionaries as constitution-making, instead of as treason, is not to widen the scope of legality by exploiting the practical possibilities of the legal collective they aim to overturn; it is to step *out* of one legal order and *into* another. Which brings us back to one of the central insights of chapter 4: the bounds of legal intentionality and intelligibility are the bounds of what is practically possible for a legal collective. The interpretative abyss separating treason and constitution-making illustrates the radical unintelligibility that characterizes the strong dimension of a-legality: what cannot be said and done in one legal order can only be said and done by entering another order. To view the insurrection in May 1968 as constitution-making, in that it sought to organize council power and economic self-rule by workers councils, is to go, like Alice, through the looking glass.

An important case in the broader debate about multiculturalism and minority rights yields a second illustration of the strong dimension of a-legality. I have in mind the well-known *Quebec Secession Reference*, by the Canadian Supreme Court.[20] The central question the Court was called on to consider in this reference was 'whether Quebec has a right to *unilateral* secession' (§149). The Court rejected such a right. Although the Court did not say so explicitly, it effectively contended that a putative right to unilateral secession is an oxymoron. To invoke a *right*, whatever its nature, is to presuppose relations of political and legal reciprocity with those who must honour the right, or so the Court argued; yet the very idea of *unilateral* secession is incompatible with the reciprocity that must have been presupposed in the act of claiming a *right* to secession. A province that would claim a right to secede or to modify the terms of Confederation, without discharging its obligation to negotiate with the other interested parties as established by the Constitution, effectively engages in a performative contradiction, as it both affirms and denies a 'reciprocal obligation', as the Court put it.

But what is the origin of these reciprocal obligations? The Court's answer to this question is, in fact, the linchpin of the Reference: 'Confederation was an initiative of elected representatives of the people then living in the colonies scattered across part of what is now Canada. It was not initiated by Imperial *fiat*' (§34). So the agreement whereby the delegates enacted the Confederation was a representational act and, as such, an authorized initiative and, by extension, an authorized agreement. No less importantly, although the delegates were deemed to represent a *differentiated* unity when founding the federation, they represented, first and foremost, a differentiated *unity*—a 'unified country', to borrow the Court's turn of phrase in another passage of the reference. 'At Confederation, political leaders told their respective communities that the Canadian union would be able to reconcile diversity with unity' (§43). In this way, the Court eludes—and elides—the thorny problem of the emergence of legal reciprocity itself. The

[20] *Reference re. Secession of Quebec* [1998] 2 S.C.R. 217–297. Citations refer, in the main text, to the sections of the Reference. For a detailed analysis of this Reference, see my article, 'Recognition as Domination: Constitutionalism, Reciprocity and the Problem of Singularity', in Neil Walker, Jo Shaw, and Steven Tierney (eds.), *Europe's Constitutional Mosaic* (Oxford: Hart, 2011), 205–230.

problem is intimated when the Court acknowledges—as acknowledge it must—that the Canadian federation was born from an *initiative*. In effect, can we make sense of an 'initiative' at all without introducing an element of unilaterality into foundations? As noted at the end of chapter 4, the initiative to found a polity is always seized, while also presupposing what it would bring about: unity. Can it be seriously argued—not least in light of the acts of conquest that remain beyond the compass of the Court's historical reconstruction of Confederation—that the initiative to found the Canadian federation rests on the prior joint commitment of all those who would be bound by reciprocal obligations to act together into the future in view of promoting their common good?

We will return to discuss the non-reciprocal emergence of reciprocity in chapter 7. Notice, for the moment, that this problem strikes at the heart of the Court's reasoning in at least three ways. First, if there is no unilateral right to secession, because this amounts to an oxymoron, can this argument not be turned against the Canadian Constitution itself? Indeed, do rights and 'reciprocal obligations' under the Constitution not lead back to a foundational act which, to the extent that it is unilateral, is incapable of generating rights and 'reciprocal obligations' for all who fall under its rule? Second, can the Court simply brush off as 'unsound' (§75) the argument that 'the same popular sovereignty that originally led to the present Constitution must... also permit "the people" in their exercise of popular sovereignty to secede by majority vote alone'? (§75) Can the Court really claim that 'our national existence [is] seamless in so many aspects'? (§96) The third difficulty concerns, finally, the Court's own authority to issue a reference about the unilateral secession of Quebec. Can it avoid being both party and judge in the reference? For the decisive problem arising from contestation by Quebecer secessionists is not how their cultural distinctness could obtain constitutional recognition, such that the Court and the other federal authorities could be reasonably held to represent them as a particular group partaking of 'the whole people'; it is that the Quebecer secessionists reject being represented as part of 'the whole [Canadian] people'. For them, recognition of their rights under the Canadian constitution is a form of domination.

In short, the Quebecer denunciation of recognition under the Canadian constitution evinces a concept of 'difference' that resists neutralization and pacification through the 'politics of difference' advocated by a recognition-based theory of constitutionalism. At stake is a 'difference'—a claim to group distinctness, cultural or otherwise—that is not merely a manifestation of particularity within a more encompassing generality, whether realized or realizable, but rather a form of difference that obdurately resists inclusion in a given circle of legal reciprocity. In a word, at stake is a strong manifestation of *strangeness*. Crucially, given that the genesis of political community always depends, to a lesser or greater extent, on unilateral acts—on 'initiatives', as the Canadian Supreme Court puts it—that get legal reciprocity going, those claims cannot simply be written off as 'unreasonable' or 'anarchic', other than at the price of concealing the an-archic origins of political community. The Court's reasoning obliquely attests to a moment of 'an-archy' that inhabits all and sundry legal orders. In the same way that the initiatives that give rise to a polity, differentiating it from what become its others, can never be fully included within its legal order, so also there are subsequent claims to difference that resist inclusion within this order—on principle, and not merely in fact. The stalemate that arises between, on the one hand, the Canadian rebuke that the Quebecer secessionists fall prey to a performative contradiction, and, on the other, the Quebecer objection that Canadians beg the question when they demand that Quebec present its claim as a constitutional claim, is exemplary for the strong dimension of a-legality: to qualify the challenge as legal or illegal, or to establish the criteria under which it would be the one or the other, is to miss what the Quebecer secessionist claim is about. They challenge the applicability of *both* terms of the distinction because they deny *ab initio* the authority of the Canadian Constitution.

This is not to deny that the reference covered hitherto untrammelled ground in responding to Quebecer secessionist aspirations. Arguably, the reference set a new milestone in how a collective can respond to the secessionist challenge. In this sense the Quebecer challenge also displayed a weak dimension to which the Court was sensitive in its response. Nor is it to deny that these aspirations raised considerable normative problems of their own, as attested to by the strong resistance to secession by the vast majority of non-French speaking Quebecers—including First Nations—as well as by many French-speaking Quebecers. The logic of self-closure is once again at work: the unilaterality which marks the emergence of the Canadian federation, and which secessionist aspirations contest, would reappear with the emergence of an independent Quebec. But this leaves the basic point about the strong dimension of a-legality unperturbed: the challenge addressed to the Canadian federation by the secessionists reveals possibilities that surpass the possibilities available to the Canadian collective as its own possibilities because they cannot be accommodated in the practical question to which it can respond by shifting the limit between legal (dis)order and the unordered: what* ought *our* joint action to be about? The challenge of unilateral secession could not but be qualified as illegal.

Let me present a third instance of a-legality in a way that favours its strong dimension. When Anders Behring Breivik made his first public appearance in the criminal proceedings brought against him for the killings in the centre of Oslo and on the island of Utøya on 15 July 2011, his first words were, 'I am the commander of the Norwegian Resistance Movement and of the Order of the Temple. I refuse to accept [the authority] of the court because it has received its mandate from institutions which support an ideology of hatred and multiculturalism'. He added: 'I concede the deeds, but deny that I am guilty'.[21] He subsequently refused to recognize the legitimacy of the ruling by the Oslo District Court that condemned him to preventive detention, but indicated he could not appeal the decision as this would amount to recognizing the court's authority to judge him.

[21] Cited in 'Norwegischer Attentäter: Richter unterbrechen wirre Breivik-Tirade', in *Spiegel Online*, 14 November 2011, <http://www.spiegel.de/panorama/justiz/norwegischer-attentaeter-richter-unterbrechen-wirre-breivik-tirade-a-797587.html> (accessed on 13 February 2013).

On the one hand, by dint of bringing criminal charges against Breivik, the Norwegian legal collective discloses his act as legally relevant and important, with a view to qualifying it as legal* or illegal*. On the other hand, Breivik acknowledges that while his deed is not legal under Norwegian law, he denies that it is illegal. Indeed, he can only be found guilty of an illegal act, or so he claims, if one accepts the 'ideology of hatred and multiculturalism' that animates the normative point of joint action by the Norwegian collective. His acts are neither legal nor illegal, or so he claims: they challenge the normative point on the basis of which the Norwegian collective draws the distinction between legal and illegal behaviour. No less than the judges who sit in court, Breivik understands himself as representing the Norwegian collective when presenting himself as commander of the Norwegian Resistance Movement. But his is the appeal to a Norwegian collective that is in contradiction with the practical possibilities made available for participant agency by the extant legal order. If, to borrow Twining's expression, a normative point includes any 'motive, value or reason that can be given to explain or justify [a] practice', then Breivik offers a justification of his deed by appealing to the normative point of an emergent collective which is incompossible with the liberal Norwegian collective on whose behalf the judges will decide about the (il)legality* of his deed. Significantly, the reporter of *Spiegel Online* who covered the proceedings noted that 'it sounds as though he spoke from another world to the advocates, judges and almost two hundred observers'. The precise formulation would have been a *strange* world, a strange world ensconced in what members of the Norwegian collective call their own world. The farmhouse in which Breivik appears to have written his manifesto and prepared the bomb which exploded in the centre of Oslo, and the island of Utøya, during the killing of the youth group of the Norwegian Labour Party, attest to an 'occupation' in the twofold sense of the term noted above. The strangeness of the Norway Breivik claims to represent manifests itself in the experience of unintelligibility burdening the survivors present in the court: 'What kind of person is that, what goes through his head?'[22] The title of an article published in *The Guardian* neatly captures the ambiguous emotive responses called forth by strangeness: 'Norway awaits Anders Breivik trial with mixture of revulsion and fascination'.[23]

Let me conclude this section by noting that it is tempting to shrug off these three examples—insurrection, secession, terrorism—as largely irrelevant and unimportant in light of the day-to-day operation of most legal orders the readers of this book would presumably be involved in. In comparison with the kinds of quotidian conflicts in which we are engrossed in the course of legal practices, the strong dimension of a-legal behaviour is of largely marginal importance. The practical question—What* is our joint action about?—captures all our attention. Further examples, such as the contestation of *lex constructionis*, state law

[22] Gerald Traufetter, 'Ein fast unerträglicher Auftritt', *Spiegel Online*, 14 November 2011, <http://www.spiegel.de/panorama/justiz/attentaeter-breivik-vor-gericht-ein-fast-unertraeglicher-auftritt-a-797671.html> (accessed on 13 February 2013).

[23] James Edmonton, 'Norway awaits Anders Breivik trial with mixture of revulsion and fascination', published in *The Guardian*, 13 April 2012, <http://www.guardian.co.uk/world/2012/apr/13/anders-breivik-trial-norway> (accessed on 13 February 2013).

and international law by the U'wa, as discussed in chapter 2, only seem to reinforce this impression. Yet, far from being an objection, the foregoing analyses suggest that to disparage or belittle these examples as marginal is to reveal practical involvement in the very kinds of legal collectives for which such behaviour is unimportant or irrelevant, hence marginal, until such time as a-legality suddenly comes near, catching us by surprise. More pointedly, there is no uninvolved site whence examples of a-legality can be proffered and accepted as such—or rejected. A theory of legal order that would take seriously the first-person plural perspective cannot exempt itself from adopting that perspective when attempting to reveal the different ways legal orders can be called into question.

5.3 FAULT LINES

The time has come to introduce the concept of a normative fault line into our model of legal order. It should by now be clear that I have been deploying an incremental expository strategy. I began with a characterization of legal *boundaries*, showing that law orders behaviour by setting its spatial, temporal, material, and subjective boundaries. I then proceeded to show that legal boundaries cannot join and separate ought-places, ought-times, ought-subjects, and ought-act contents absent the (putative) unity of a legal order. Now, there can be no unity of a legal order, global or otherwise, unless the legal order is *limited*, that is, unless it opens up a realm of practical possibilities—legal empowerments—by closing down others. Importantly, limits are not separate from boundaries: each of the boundaries of a legal order can manifest itself as its limit when behaviour or situations reveal those boundaries as excluding practical possibilities the collective actualization of which is demanded by such behaviour or situations. This entails, amongst other things, that any spatial boundary of a legal order can manifest itself as one of its frontiers, as was the case with the check-out points at the Lafayette food department in the course of the *autoréduction*.

This is where our enquiry has taken us. Because I had not yet fully developed the notion of a-legality, no further step could be taken to render the structure of boundaries more complex. The distinction that has been introduced between the 'weak' and 'strong' dimensions of a-legality allows us to take two further, decisive steps. On the one hand, the weak dimension of a-legality—i.e. a-legality as the not-yet-(il)legal—clarifies why limits can be *shifted* in the responsive process of (re)setting the legal boundaries of a collective. The extant setting of the (il) legal distinction by way of boundaries that determine who ought to do what, where, and when appears as being no more than a default-setting of joint action under law, that is, one amongst a range of possible settings available to the collective to realize the normative point of joint action. By recalibrating legal boundaries, in response to the weak dimension of a-legality, a collective actualizes its *own* possibilities. To the extent that a collective responds to a-legality by reconfiguring the legal/illegal distinction—i.e. with a new setting of who ought to do what, where, and when—it shifts the limit between legal (dis)order and the unordered, either incorporating into joint action what had been deemed unimportant, or abandoning to the domain of the unimportant what it had deemed important. Limits betoken legal boundaries insofar as they are *contingent*, hence tranformable, from the first-person plural perspective of the corresponding collective.

On the other hand, the 'strong' dimension of a-legality is critical to understanding why the distinction between boundaries and limits does not suffice to grasp either the structure of legal orders or the dynamics of legal ordering. In its strong dimension, a-legality no longer summons a collective to shift the limit between legal (dis)order and the unordered; it lays bare a *fault line* between what a collective can order—the orderable—and what it cannot order—the unorderable. As is the case with limits, so also the fault lines of a legal order run along each of its boundaries. The distinctive feature of fault lines is that, unlike limits, they cannot be shifted; they must be *overstepped*, and in being overstepped lead over from one legal collective into another. To repeat an earlier insight, what cannot be said and done in one legal order can only be said and done by taking leave of that legal collective and entering another. The practical possibilities intimated by the strong dimension of a-legality, and which interfere with the range of practical possibilities available to a legal collective, can only be realized as our own possibilities if one adopts *another* first-person plural perspective. To accede to the normative demand raised by the strong dimension of a-legality is to take a one-way ticket across a normative fault line. A fault line marks the *end* of a legal collective in the spatial and temporal senses of the term: a place and a time beyond which it can no longer exist.[24] If a collective emerges through an act that is im/possible because it opens up a realm of practical possibilities and closes down others, the collective has to reckon throughout its career with the possibility of incompossibilities that bring legal ordering to an end. In contrast to contingent limits, fault lines signal both a *practical necessity* for the collective—a legal boundary that a collective cannot posit otherwise if it is to subsist as the same and as a self—and an *existential contingency*, to the extent that it is confronted with forms of joint action which interfere, as incompossible, with its continued subsistence as the same and a self.

It is tempting to ask, 'How do the members of a collective know that they are jointly confronted with a fault line?' But this question is in fact a variation on the question 'What is a-legal?', and which I earlier rejected. Instead, the question we need to ask is this: what is the *mode of appearance* of the strong dimension of a-legality? How do legal boundaries manifest themselves as fault lines?

The question is especially urgent in light of the Hegelian objection, which runs as follows: how can there be an experience of a fault line at all unless one has already gone *beyond* the fault line, thereby overcoming it as a fault line? Indeed, how can we transcend a fault line unless what lies beyond it belongs to the domain of what are already in principle our own possibilities?[25] In line with this objection, fault lines would collapse into limits, and a-legality would be no more than the not-yet-(il)

[24] If I may be allowed a pun in German, the strong dimension of a-legality intimates, however obliquely, what is *Jenseits* and *Jenzeits* the collective it calls into question.

[25] This is a paraphrase of Hegel's polemic with Kant about the nature of a limit. In response to Kant's thesis that there are limits to human cognition, Hegel retorted that to be aware of a limit one must already be beyond that limit: '[T]he very fact that something is determined as a limitation implies that the limitation is already transcended'. See Georg Friedrich Wilhelm Hegel, *Science of Logic*, trans. John Niemeyer Findlay (London: Allen & Unwin, 1969), 134.

legal—its weak dimension. A-legality would be provisional: it would enjoy no independent status with respect to (il)legality, as, over time and given favourable circumstances, the extraordinary is always reducible to legal (dis)order. A general theory of legal order and ordering can make do with boundaries and limits; fault lines are superfluous. More pointedly: to claim that fault lines are a constitutive feature of legal orders is to indulge in the reification of collective identity and legal boundaries.

To address this set of issues it is first necessary to deal with the following problem: how is it that the strong dimension of a-legality can appear as a *normative* claim? For, after all, the problem is that the normatively unorderable is that to which the collective is and must remain normatively indifferent, that is, that which it cannot view as important and relevant in light of its normative point. How, then, can that to which the collective is normatively indifferent manifest itself as a normative claim to the collective? As an *exception*. For behaviour or a situation could not manifest itself as an exception to a legal order unless it registers normatively; otherwise, it would be something of which the legal collective could take no notice: it could not even register as an exception. But, putting aside the meaningless and misleading triviality that 'the exception confirms the rule', what is the mode of appearance of an exception to a legal collective? Schmitt hits the nail on the head when he avers that '[t]he exception is that which cannot be subsumed; it defies the general codification'.[26] Bear in mind that the translation falls short of adequately conveying the German expression with which Schmitt refers to the exception (*die Ausnahme*), namely *sie entzieht sich*, which means that the exception 'defies', 'eludes', and 'exceeds' a legal order, all at once. So the specific mode of appearance of the strong dimension of a-legality as a *normative* claim is that of a claim that is in defiance of, withdraws from, and exceeds the normative point of joint action whence places, times, subjects, and act-contents derive their ought-character. It is in this sense, specifically, that fault lines can only reveal themselves *indirectly* to a legal collective.

Granted, limits also reveal themselves indirectly, as I have explained in section 5.1. Both limits and fault lines partake of the general structure of a-legality, which, as the extra-ordinary, can only appear indirectly, in the form of what questions the *boundaries* of a given legal order. But there is a fundamental difference between the modes of appearance of a limit and of a fault line. Whereas limits bespeak a gap between extant legal empowerments and those practical possibilities which are unrealized but realizable by the collective, normative fault lines mark the gap between the practical possibilities accessible to a collective and practical possibilities which are inaccessible to it. As a result, an exception manifests itself as a normative claim that resists a collective's qualification of it as either illegal or legal, yet which, on an authoritative assessment, the collective cannot but (continue to) qualify as illegal, rather than as legal; or that it cannot but (continue to) to qualify as legal, rather than as illegal. It is because of this definitive incompossibility that the exception questions legal boundaries in a way that does not allow of shifting the limit of legal (dis)order; an excessive normative claim

[26] Carl Schmitt, *Political Theology: Four Chapters on the Concept of Sovereignty*, trans. George Schwab (Cambridge, MA: The MIT Press, 1985), 13 (translation altered).

entails that we, as a collective, have reached the end of our normative tether. Each of the three illustrations of the strong dimension of a-legality advanced in section 5.2 shows authorities as having to reaffirm legality unconditionally: as far as here, and no further. Moreover, as the constitutional deadlock between the Canadian Supreme Court and the Quebecer secessionists shows with particular clarity, normative fault lines manifest themselves, argumentatively speaking, in the circular reasoning, the *petitio principii,* whereby normative challenges to joint action can only be met by presupposing its normative point. Now, a circular reasoning marks the *end* of reason-giving, of justification, of dialogue, of rational grounding. It is in this way, returning to the Hegelian objection, that fault lines can manifest themselves indirectly, as marking the end of a legal collective's normative tether, while not collapsing into a limit that reveals the gap and tension between extant legal empowerments and those practical possibilities that a collective could actualize as its own.

It is important to avoid the assumption that boundaries appear, in the face of a-legality, 'either' as limits 'or' as fault lines. This disjunctive reading would dissolve the normative complexity of a-legality, uncoupling its two dimensions, respectively the 'weak' and the 'strong', into two modes of a-legality. As noted earlier, a-legality has a complex normative structure that conjoins possibilities that a collective could realize and other possibilities that exceed its compass. For this reason, boundaries manifest themselves as being *both* limits and fault lines, albeit that the predominance of the one or the other is variable, depending on the a-legal challenge. As a result legal boundaries manifest themselves, *qua* limit, as more or less (but never only) *contigent* and, *qua* fault lines, as more or less (but never only) *necessary*. In some cases, such as in the claims of the MST, boundaries appear preponderantly as limits which can be shifted. In other cases, for which the killings in the centre of Oslo and the island of Utøya are exemplary, boundaries approximate a pure normative fault line in which authorities reaffirm unconditionally the extant setting of (il)legality.

Does this account of fault lines not boil down to the reification of collective identity and legal boundaries? It would if, as mentioned at the outset of 5.2, fault lines required that there be a perspicuous stock of possibilities given in advance to a collective as its own possibilities, and a raft of other possibilities which it could in advance discount as surpassing what it could realize. But no such prescience is available to a collective's members and authorities. On the one hand, as Schmitt correctly recognizes, the exception cannot be codified in advance; a-legal behaviour and situations catch us flat-footed, thwarting the reiterative anticipations governing the normal process of legal ordering whereby something is disclosed as something*. Nor, on the other hand, is it possible to codify in advance how a legal collective ought to respond to the exception. Which possibilities are a collective's own possibilities, and which surpass these, only becomes apparent retroactively, *après coup,* in the authoritatively mediated responses to a-legality. What is decisive for the thesis that fault lines are constitutive elements of legal orders is that a collective never merely has at its disposition which possibilities are its own and which possibilities exceed the compass of what its members can do jointly.

The objection may nonetheless be raised that the reification of collective identity and legal boundaries has already set in the moment one draws the distinction between a collective's own possibilities and those which exceed it. But, to repeat the point illustrated by the constitutional deadlock between the Canadian Supreme Court and the secessionist Quebecers, the distinction comes to the fore in the face of the circular reasoning by which a collective would neutralize and domesticate excessive normative claims. Furthermore, it pays to articulate the metaphysical thesis that underpins this objection. Indeed, the objection that reification can only be averted if legal ordering is, at least in principle, the progressive transcending of limits in the direction of an ever greater inclusiveness presupposes that legal collectives are a favoured vehicle of the 'transition of the finite into the infinite'.[27] Acknowledging that normative fault lines necessarily belong to the concept of legal orders does not entail the reification of collective identity and legal boundaries; it does entail, however, a strong thesis about the finitude of legal collectives. I will have something more to say about the ontology of legal collectives in chapter 6, and about the normative implications that follow therefrom in chapter 7.

This reading of the exception also needs to be defended against the reductive implications that Schmitt attaches to his insight. Indeed, his further characterization of the exception deprives it of its normative ambiguity, collapsing it into a challenge to public order that requires neutralizing or destroying the source of the challenge. This is not to say, however, that there is no connection between the strong dimension of a-legality and public order. Indeed, if one brackets the interminable doctrinal debate about the nature and modalities of public order, this much seems clear: in its fundamental manifestation, public order concerns challenges to the conditions required for the continued existence of a legal collective as the same and as a self. Construed thus, public order is not limited to 'states', any more than are challenges to public order. It is constitutive for all and sundry legal orders. These considerations bring the problem of authority back into the picture. I noted in section 3.2 that legal orders involve authorities who (i) monitor joint action as concerns its normative point and consistency over time, and (ii) take steps to uphold joint action when its normative point is breached or when the consistency of joint action over time is otherwise undermined or imperilled. We can now develop this insight more fully: the determination of what counts as a challenge to public order is part and parcel of the authoritative monitoring and upholding of joint action under law. To this extent, a first-person plural concept of legal order and legal ordering supports Schmitt's insistence on assigning a central role to public order in his theory of law.

But acknowledging that the exception can manifest itself in the form of a challenge to the continued existence of a legal collective as the same and as a self is not to say that this is the primordial mode of appearance of the exception. Schmitt's reductive move is at its starkest in the passage in which he argues that 'the exception, which is not codified in the existing legal order, can at best be

[27] Hegel, *Logic of Science*, 136.

characterized as a case of extreme peril, a danger to the existence of the state, or the like. But it cannot be circumscribed factually and made to conform to a preformed law'.[28] Notice how the ambiguity of the exception, which is at once resistance to, and withdrawal from, inclusion in a given legal order, is levelled down to what poses an extreme danger to or imperils the existence of that collective, and which calls for exceptional measures in the form of action addressed to neutralize or destroy it.

We have reached the heart of the debate with Schmitt: the relation between a-legality and enmity. Schmitt's uncompromising thesis about the friend/enemy distinction as the constitutive political distinction is well known. In his words, the political enemy is 'the other, the stranger (*der Fremde*); and it is sufficient for his nature that he is, in a specially intense way, existentially something different and strange, so that in the extreme case conflicts with him are possible.'[29] And he adds that it is up to the participants to decide 'whether the otherness of the stranger in the concrete conflict at hand means the negation of one's own form of existence and therefore must be repulsed or fought to preserve one's own extant form of life'.[30] I concede that, in the same way that there is a connection between the exception and public order, so also there is a relation between the stranger and the enemy. Schmitt is no doubt right in arguing that political enmity is one of the possibilities called forth by the normative closure required for joint action under law. But it is by no means constitutive of strangeness, as he suggests. I would say that there is a strict parallelism between Schmitt's reduction of the exception to an acute challenge to public order that requires neutralization or destruction and his reduction of the stranger to the enemy. Otherness-as-strangeness, as revealed in the strong dimension of a-legal behaviour, betokens what is exceptional vis-à-vis a given legal order, i.e. what definitively resists inclusion in what counts as legal (dis)order for that collective. Assuredly, this excessive normative claim *interferes* with the realization of the collective's normative point. Herein resides the condition whereby otherness-as-strangeness can take on the form of political enmity.[31] But the interference wrought by a-legality is not *eo ipse* an existential threat to a legal collective. In the same way that the kind of measures taken to address a situation of public order do not exhaust the exceptional measures by which a legal collective can respond to the strong dimension of a-legality, so also war does not exhaust how a legal collective can respond to what appears as irreducibly alien to its practical possibilities.

As a result, Schmitt's famous thesis about sovereignty needs to be revised in three related ways. First, sovereignty is a *fault line concept*, rather than a

[28] Hegel, *Logic of Science*, 6.

[29] Carl Schmitt, *The Concept of the Political*, expanded edn., trans. George Schwab (Chicago, IL: University of Chicago Press, 2007), 27 (translation altered).

[30] Schmitt, *The Concept of the Political*.

[31] While I share Waldenfels' reservations about the move to equate strangeness and enmity, I disagree with his thesis that 'enmity stands for . . . the refusal of hospitality (*Gastfreundschaft*)', at least as concerns law. See Bernhard Waldenfels, *Hyperphänomene: Modi hyperbolischer Erfahrung* (Frankfurt: Suhrkamp, 2012), 314.

'boundary concept' (*Grenzbegriff*).[32] If fault lines mark the end of legal ordering in a temporal and spatial sense, then they also mark the end of the unity of a legal order. Sovereignty is all about what ultimately—i.e. in the end and at the end—counts as legal unity in the face of irreducible political plurality. Second, to decide whether a fault line has been encountered is not only—and certainly not most primordially—to decide who is an enemy and how the enemy is to repulsed or fought; it is to determine what exceptional measures might be appropriate to deal with what exceeds the collective's own possibilities. Third, whether one has come up against a fault line and how it should be dealt with is not merely a 'decision', in Schmitt's sense of the term. True, a normative fault line is never fully independent of the authoritative measures taken to deal with what lies beyond it; but which possibilities are a collective's own possibilities and which are not never only stands at the disposition of authoritative determinations to this effect. We will return to this last point at greater length when examining, in chapter 6, the hiatus between the precedence of a-legality and the retroactivity of boundary-setting.

I wrap up this section by drawing out two further features of a-legality, and which merit separate mention. Both turn on the problem of inclusion and exclusion, brought about by the closure which gives rise to a legal collective.

What I have called the weak dimension of a-legality calls attention to closure as the problem of *exclusion*. In this, it sheds light on the conceptual underpinnings of a wide range of normative theories of law and politics, which focus on the exclusion brought about by closure, and which aspire to secure a greater inclusiveness for law in the face of what it has unjustly excluded. But the prior question is this: how is a greater inclusiveness at all possible? How is it at all possible that a collective can become more inclusive, integrating into the legal order what it had marginalized? Part of the answer resides in the fact that there could not be a greater inclusiveness unless more were possible for a collective than the possibilities it has actualized as legal empowerments. The default-setting of a legal order actualizes certain possibilities, while marginalizing other ways by which it could realize the normative point of joint action. A collective can integrate what it had unjustly excluded, in terms of its own normative point, by tapping into a narrower or broader range of practical possibilities as its *own* possibilities. Conversely, the inclusion of what had been excluded can only appear as what a collective *ought* to do if it is something the collective *can* do—if inclusion actualizes one of the collective's own possibilities.

This insight requires revising the analysis of closure offered in sections 3.3 and 5.1, where it was asserted that closure brings about a self-*inclusion*. To leave it at that would be reductive: a-legality could not confront a legal collective with possibilities that are its own unless closure is a self-*exclusion* as much as it is a self-inclusion. What has been excluded in *self*-exclusion is other practical possibilities which are our *own*, that is, other ways of establishing who ought to do what, where, and when with a view to realizing the normative point of our joint act.

[32] Schmitt, *Political Theology*, 5 (translation altered).

To secure a greater inclusiveness is, therefore, to actualize one of the possible ways in which we can act together.

It is fair to say that securing a greater inclusiveness in response to the closure that gives rise to a legal collective has been the principal aim of most contemporary normative theories of law. In that sense, they are theories that seek to deal with the problem posed by the weak dimension of a-legality; they take for granted that legal boundaries function as limits—and nothing more. What remains beyond the purview of these theories, yet which is brought into stark focus by the strong dimension of a-legality, is the problem opposite to that of bringing about a greater inclusiveness. Indeed, they are impervious to situations in which *inclusion is the problem signalled by a-legality, not its solution.* Sensitivity to this problem requires acknowledging that fault lines are an ingredient of legal order. The U'wa do not demand to be included in the Colombian legal order, nor in *lex constructionis,* classical international law or *ius gentium*. Their inclusion in these legal orders is what they reject. Those Quebecers who would secede are not requesting recognition of their rights as a 'distinct minority' under the Canadian constitution: they reject being treated as a minority because they realize all too well that political plurality has already been subordinated to legal unity when one asks how constitutionalism could regulate the process whereby minority groups raise claims to cultural recognition. The Irish collective, as represented by the Irish Supreme Court, rejects that it be included in the EU for the effect of establishing the legal status of abortion or acts abetting abortion. The workers who sought to exercise economic self-rule in the form of workers' councils did not seek to obtain more rights under French law; their inclusion in the French legal order was what many viewed as the problem, and motivated their attempt to overthrow it in May 1968. The attacker of the Danish cartoonist who lampooned the prophet Muhammad did not seek to have his rights to privacy, to freedom of religious expression, or what not protected; he attacked inclusion in a collective in which aniconism is not law and, by extension, a collective in which religion is a manifestation of cultural identity, rather than the law of God. What goes under the name of 'secessionist' movements is but one instance of the strong dimension of a-legality, although perhaps it would be more correct to say that a-legality confronts every legal collective with multifarious figures of secessionist aspirations, whether tumultuous or halcyon, heeded or ignored.

These considerations suggest that my initial depiction of the structure of closure needs to be revised a second time. If self-inclusion is paired to *self-exclusion*, so also closure ensures that other-exclusion is paired to *other-inclusion*, more precisely to the inclusion of strangeness. The strange is ensconced in what 'we' call our own legal order. Oneself as *strange*, and not merely 'oneself as another', as Ricœur would have it.

All of this adds up to the insight that a legal collective is the unremitting integration and disintegration of joint action; an ongoing process of unification and pluralization. And, crucially, it suggests that legal boundaries are not merely disjunctive in their role of including and excluding, as is overwhelmingly taken for granted in contemporary legal and political theory. Yes, legal boundaries include and exclude; but what a-legality shows is that *legal boundaries include by excluding, and exclude by including*. This will be of decisive importance in the conclusion, when discussing, and bidding farewell to, universalism and particularism as projects that could offer normative orientation for legal orders in a global setting.

5.4 CIVIL DISOBEDIENCE

Before turning to the concluding section of this chapter, it is appropriate to pause and briefly consider how the normative complexity of a-legality sheds light on the problem of civil disobedience. Does a theory of a-legality do anything more than provide an extended conceptual analysis of civil disobedience? Does it have anything to say that has not already been said countless times by liberal theories of law and politics? Yes, or so I argue. To justify this claim I will focus on John Rawls' classic interpretation of civil disobedience as espoused in his *Theory of Justice*. While it is by no means the only contribution to the topic, it does provide a particularly lucid and lucent account that allows of identifying similarities and differences between civil disobedience and a-legality. His theory is well known and has been extensively discussed, so I will limit myself to discussing those aspects which are most relevant to the aforementioned question.

Civil disobedience, as Rawls defines it, is 'a public, nonviolent, conscientious yet political act contrary to law usually done with the aim of bringing about a change in the law or policies of the government'.[33] As the definition indicates, acts of civil disobedience are overtly illegal acts; but their aim is to contest how the law draws the distinction between legality and illegality. In that minimal sense, they are a-legal acts. Importantly, acts of civil disobedience are acts which, despite being illegal, presuppose fidelity to the constitutional order. They are acts whereby a minority attempts to persuade the majority that the distinction between legality and illegality, as drawn in the extant legal order, is in breach of the 'common sense of justice'[34] undergirding the constitution, and which renders minority and majority parts of a single collective: a *whole*. Civil disobedience seeks to show that, as it stands, legislation is in contradiction with its necessary presupposition if it is to be binding on all, namely, the equality of the members of the collective. Accordingly, and this is the crux of Rawls' argument, by engaging in acts of civil disobedience 'we are appealing to others to reconsider, to put themselves in our position, and to recognize that they cannot expect us to acquiesce indefinitely in the terms they impose upon us'.[35] In short, the act of civil disobedience demands that reciprocal relations be reinstated, in line with the underlying principle of justice that makes of that collective a society of equal and free citizens. Rawls adds that not all forms of inequality justify engaging in acts of civil disobedience. Indeed, 'it seems reasonable, other things equal, to limit it to instances of substance and clear injustice . . .'.[36] Additionally, civil disobedience

[33] Rawls, *A Theory of Justice*, 364. See also 'The Justification of Civil Disobedience', in Samuel Freeman (ed.), *Collected Papers* (Cambridge, MA: Harvard University Press, 1999), 176–189.

[34] Rawls, *A Theory of Justice*, 366.

[35] Rawls, *A Theory of Justice*, 382.

[36] Rawls, *A Theory of Justice*, 372.

is only justified when earlier attempts to bring around the majority to acknowledging the injustice of legislation have fallen on deaf ears, and there is no hope that pursuing these ordinary channels will sway it. In any case, Rawls notes, 'it is important that the action be properly designed to make an effective appeal to the wider community'; 'care must be taken to see that it is *understood*'.[37] Notice that the reference to 'understanding' an appeal ties in directly with everything that has been said heretofore about understanding and intentionality, even though Rawls nowhere discusses this operation as such.

Philip Pettit develops this point more fully, showing that a lot more is at stake in effective (or perhaps one should say 'responsible') civil disobedience than good craftsmanship. On his reading, politics requires that disaffected minorities exercise pragmatism in their demands, given that 'there are reasonable differences of opinion which political argument must try to reach across'. Alluding to claims raised by radical environmentalist groups, Pettit adds that political pragmatism

> requires those who are committed to various political causes to be able to articulate the concerns they want the state to take up in terms which others can understand and internalize. Unless the devotees of a cause are prepared to do this, they cannot reasonable expect their fellow citizens to listen, let alone to go along.[38]

Political pragmatism goes to the very heart of the problem of civil disobedience, as described by Rawls, Pettit, and others. For what about those situations in which formulating the claim in a way that (something) can be 'understood' (as something*) by the majority would require stripping it of the very normative point which those who engage in an illegal act are concerned to make? And what about those cases in which a normative claim falls on deaf ears by virtue of the normative *indifference* with which it is met, inasmuch as what is claimed is held to be unimportant and irrelevant, i.e. not a matter of 'substance', as Rawls would have it? At this point, a-legality manifests itself, to borrow Emilios Christodoulidis' trenchant expression, as the 'objection that cannot be heard'.[39] Pettit's advice to disaffected minorities to exercise pragmatism surely falls prey to a *petitio principii*: only those arguments count as 'reasonable' and worthy of being 'listened' to which postulate the rationality of anthropocentrism, which is what radical environmental politics challenges. Does the confrontation between the votaries of radical environmental politics and their fellow citizens presuppose conditions of reciprocity such that, provided they are sincere, the former cannot but acknowledge that their position must bow to 'the force of the better argument'?[40] The contrast between 'reasonable differences of opinion' and an opinion

[37] Rawls, *A Theory of Justice*, 376 (emphasis added).

[38] Philip Pettit, *Republicanism: A Theory of Freedom and Government*, repr. (Oxford: Oxford University Press, 2002), 136. Notice, once again, the reference to 'understanding'.

[39] Emilios Christodoulidis, 'The Objection that Cannot be Heard: Communication and Legitimacy in the Courtroom', in Antony Duff et al. (eds.), *The Trial on Trial, Vol. 1: Truth and Due Process* (Oxford: Hart, 2004), 179–202.

[40] Jürgen Habermas, *The Theory of Communicative Action*, vol. 1, trans. Thomas McCarthy (Boston, MA: Beacon Press, 1981), 25.

that falls outside the scope of the reasonable has the structure of inclusion and exclusion proper to a closure: it is drawn from one of the two poles—the pole that claims reasonableness for itself—but claims to be able to speak on behalf of *both* poles. The pragmatic admonition to be reasonable, to couch demands in ways that can be understood by the majority if one would have it listen and perhaps be swayed, illustrates the neutralization and assimilation of the strange which go hand in hand with the invocation of reciprocity as the justifying principle of civil disobedience.

By bringing Rawls, Pettit, and Habermas to bear on this issue, I wish to signal that this is not merely an ancillary quandary confronting civil disobedience, a problem a wide range of normative theories of law and politics still need to come to grips with, but which otherwise leaves their conceptual core largely intact. It is a quandary that goes to the very heart of the notion of practical rationality animating their accounts and justifications of civil disobedience. Whatever the differences between these normative theories—and differences there certainly are—they develop a concept of practical rationality that relies on the principle of reciprocity. To borrow Rawls' expression, they are theories dedicated to dealing with 'injustices *internal* to a given society'.[41] Habermas' appeal to a 'world internal politics' (*Weltinnenpolitik*) is but the global extrapolation of the assumption that justice and injustice are about assuring relations of legal reciprocity *within* a collective.[42] For these theories, an outside has but a provisional status, as that which can be integrated into the legal order, provided those who stand inside and outside negotiate the terms of joint action 'in good faith'.[43] In a word, they collapse a-legality into the not-yet-(il)legal, into what is not-yet-legally-understood-but-understandable: unordered orderability. Who, having contested the (il)legal divide, continues to resist integration into the legal order, acts unreasonably or in 'bad faith', and need not be taken seriously, either by the legal collective or by political and legal philosophy. Indeed, who, in his or her right mind, would refuse to be treated as an equal and free citizen of the collective? Well, those struck by forms of injustice in which the unequal is treated as equal. I will return to the problem of reciprocity in chapter 7.

5.5 CHAOS

It seems fitting to bring this chapter to a close with a short reflection on the relation between a-legality and chaos, which in its everyday usage means a state of utter confusion. It is by no means my intention to trace the history of this concept and its different meanings. What interests me is to provide an interpretation of the relation between chaos and legal order in light of the concept of a-legality outlined heretofore. A number of the salient meanings of chaos are germane

[41] Rawls, *Theory of Justice*, 371 (emphasis added).

[42] Jürgen Habermas, *The Inclusion of the Other: Studies in Political Theory*, trans. Ciaran Cronin and Pablo de Greiff (Cambridge: Polity Press, 2005), 128 (translation altered; the expression was coined by C.F. von Weizsäcker).

[43] Rawls, *Theory of Justice*, 373.

to this endeavour: Hesiod's characterization of chaos as the yawning abyss that separates earth and heaven at creation; the Platonic/Stoic view on chaos as the undetermined and formless—the unordered; Aristotle's conceptualization of chaos as an empty space; and the interpretation of chaos as possibility, which brings together thinkers so disparate as Nicholas of Cusa and Nietzsche.[44]

The problem of the relation between legal order and chaos was implicitly introduced at the very beginning of this chapter, when I argued that the closure that gives rise to a legal collective includes legal (dis)order and excludes the *unordered*, the 'formless' in the sense of that which has no legal meaning because it is beyond the pale of joint action by a collective: chaos as an 'empty' space-time. Importantly, however, and in contradistinction to the demiurgic understanding of chaos as pure matter awaiting a form to be imposed on it by an agent, we have seen that the unordered is the domain of superabundant practical possibilities: chaos as possibility. There is nothing particularly mysterious about this. The surfeit of possibilities ensconced in the unordered is linked to what Waldenfels calls the 'significative difference' which structures legal intentionality: something is disclosed as something*—*rather than as something else*. Legal intentionality can only disclose by closing, reveal by concealing, which means that legal ordering always goes hand in hand with the marginalization of possibilities that can reappear at a later stage to disrupt legal order. In other words, the structure of legal intentionality ensures that legal order has never left chaos behind. To put it somewhat paradoxically, legal order has never left chaos behind because chaos reaches it from ahead as that which precedes legal order. In effect, chaos precedes the reiterative anticipations of legal ordering as the *unexpected* which catches participant agents by surprise, confusing and disorienting them. It is in this sense that a-legality is more or less 'chaotic', in the everyday meaning of the term. Moreover, a-legality emerges into the legal order from the domain of the unordered; one could even say that a-legality *immerges*, as it irrupts more or less forcefully into a legal order, throwing joint action out-of-joint. It immerges into the law from across a divide that marks the discontinuity between legal order and the opaque domain of the unordered; in this sense, and harking back to Hesiod, a-legality is 'abyssal'.

The emergence of a-legality brings us, finally, to the heart of the relation between chaos and legal order. If, from the first-person plural perspective of a legal collective, chaos manifests itself in its acute, existential form as a state of emergency, then emergency is not merely a 'state' that is declared by the sovereign in response to the chaos which threatens to engulf a legal order. The state of emergency *is* the emergency—or immergency—of a-legality from the domain of the unordered. The state of emergency marks the point at which a-legality announces itself as the ultimate possibility confronting the legal collective: that it can cease to exist.[45]

[44] For a historical overview of this concept, see Marina Kurdzialek's entry on 'Chaos' in Joachim Ritter et al. (eds.), *Historisches Wörterbuch der Philosophie*, vol. 1 (Darmstadt: Wissenschaftliche Buchgesellschaft, 1971), 980–984.

[45] For an excellent discussion of the radical facticity of collectives, which she develops from a Heideggerian perspective, see Nanda Oudejans' dissertation, *Asylum: A Philosophical Inquiry into the International Protection of Refugees* (Oisterwijk, Netherlands: BOXPress BV, 2011).

Carl Schmitt, when discussing the constituent power of the people in a democracy, notes that 'the nation can change its forms and give itself continuously new forms of political existence... It can be the "formless formative capacity" '.[46] Regardless of what Schmitt has to say about the nation, the notion of the 'formless forming' (*das formlos Formende*) aptly captures the idea that a-legality immerges from the unordered domain of superabundant possibilities into legal order. Although Cornelius Castoriadis does not mention Schmitt by name, there can be little doubt that he had this passage in mind when describing 'the social' as what

> is given as the structure—indissociable form and content—of human ensembles, yet which goes beyond any given structure, an ungraspable productive element (*un productif insaisissable*), an unformed forming element, something that is always more and always other. It is something that can be presented only in and through the *institution*, but which is always infinitely more than the institution, since it is, paradoxically, both what fills in the institution, what is formed by it, what continuously overdetermines its functioning, and what in the final analysis founds it: creates it, maintains it in existence, alters it, destroys it. There is the social as instituted, but this always presupposes the social as instituting.[47]

In the closing pages of his book, Castoriadis returns to this feature of the social, rejecting the view that the social is ever either merely chaotic in the sense of a material waiting to have a form impressed on it by a demiurge, or merely ordered in and of itself as a system of essences. Institutions, he notes, impose order 'on an initial stratum of the given which unceasingly lends itself to this; but which also never is, and never can be, only *that*...'.[48] He refers to this mode of being of what is taken up in an order, but never exhausted by it, with the remarkable term 'magma'. A-legality is the irruption of social magma into a legal order.

[46] Carl Schmitt, *Constitutional Theory*, trans. Jeffrey Seitzer (Durham, NC: Duke University Press, 2008), 129.

[47] Castoriadis, *The Imaginary Institution of Society*, 112.

[48] Castoriadis, *The Imaginary Institution of Society*, 462 (translation altered).

6

Setting Legal Boundaries

This chapter completes the descriptive account of legal ordering initiated in chapter 4 and carried forward in chapter 5. The reader will remember that chapter 4 sought to lay the groundwork for a concrete and non-reductive account of legal ordering centred on the intentionality of joint action. Chapter 5 sought to clarify how a-legality interrupts legal ordering, distinguishing between the weak and strong dimensions thereof. While both chapters indicate that collectives respond to a-legality by setting their boundaries, it remains unclear how, precisely, legal boundaries are set. We must now address this *lacuna*. The problem to be dealt with in this chapter is twofold. On the one hand, it is necessary to get a handle on how, in response to a-legality, boundary-setting can *transform* legal collectives. Transformative boundary-setting responds to what is *orderable* in the normative claim raised by a-legality; it involves shifting the limit between legal (dis)order and order. On the other hand, we need to understand the nature of boundary-setting which gives rise to a novel collective by breaking out and away from an extant collective. Inaugural boundary-setting is the obverse of what remains *unorderable* by a collective in the normative claim raised by a-legality; it marks the passage across a fault line leading from one first-person perspective into another one. I propose to address these issues by exploring how boundary-setting takes place in the course of collective self-identification. A discussion and appraisal of how collectives can respond to the strong dimension of a-legality is postponed till chapter 7.

6.1 THE IDENTIFICATION OF A COLLECTIVE AS A THING

It should not be surprising that I have chosen to clarify boundary-setting by way of an enquiry into collective self-identification. If, as shown in chapter 3, the structural account of the boundaries and limits of legal orders required introducing the concept of collective identity or individuality, a genetic account, oriented to showing how legal ordering takes place in the course of boundary-setting, requires inspecting the process of collective identification or individuation. In turn, this demands looking at identification both in terms of sameness and of selfhood, together with the contrasting terms of each of these poles of identity/identification. Accordingly, let us begin our exploration into collective identification with sameness, *idem*-identity, that is, at the level at which the identification of a collective is no different to the identification of, say, a stone, a tree, or an event. For, in a very broad sense of the term 'thing', legal collectives are things or entities one can speak about and identify. While there is a first-person plural perspective on identification to which we will turn in a moment, it cannot be the only perspective thereon. Manifestly, other persons than agents who participate in joint action can identify the apposite legal collective, as well; no less manifestly, participant agents can also take on the stance of an observer to identify it in this way.

Peter Strawson deals with just this problem in *Individuals*. He notes at the outset of the book that the world is populated by a host of particulars, such as material bodies, events, actions, people, shadows, and the like, about which speakers can make identifying references when talking with others. To identify something, Strawson notes, means to pick out 'which member, or members of [a] class' someone is talking about.[1] Under what conditions can a hearer identify what individual the speaker is referring to? In a nutshell, he answers,

> [w]e can make it clear to each other what or which particular things our discourse is about because we can fit together each other's reports and stories into a single picture of the world; and the framework of that picture is a unitary spatio-temporal framework, of one temporal and three spatial dimensions. Hence, as things are, particular-identification in general rests ultimately on the possibility of locating the particular things we speak of in a single unified spatio-temporal system.[2]

The location of particular things has its core in demonstrative identification, in which speaker and hearer are able to directly pick out the particular referred to from 'the entire range of particulars now sensibly present'.[3] Individualizing operators, including demonstratives ('this', 'that'), personal pronouns ('I', 'you'), adverbs of place ('here', 'there') and adverbs of time ('now', 'yesterday', 'tomorrow'), play a crucial role to this effect. Strawson adds that although not all particulars can be demonstratively identified, they can be identified by a description that links the particular to a particular which can be demonstratively identified, which, to repeat his turn of phrase, is 'sensibly present' to speaker and hearer. We will return to this point later.

Although Strawson does not refer to collectives in general, nor specifically to legal collectives, his account can be made to extend to them: also legal collectives are particulars; and also legal collectives can be identified. True, it may be quite difficult to identify any given legal collective. But, from the point of view of Strawson's account, it is clear that the most general conditions for the identification of a legal order must be the same as those which hold for all other particulars. Indeed, and regardless of whether we live in a world composed of few or many legal orders, it would not be possible for interlocutors to talk about individual legal orders absent a single spatio-temporal framework that allows of identifying them.

Decisively, this spatio-temporal framework, in which everything must have its place and time, allows for a 'community of experience'[4] such that it makes no difference who engages in the process of identifying legal collectives. More specifically, it makes no difference whether who identifies a legal collective is one of its members

[1] Strawson, *Individuals*, 16.

[2] Strawson, *Individuals*, 38.

[3] Strawson, *Individuals*, 19.

[4] Strawson, *Individuals*, 29.

or, say, a jurisprudent or a sociologist of globalization. 'It is a single picture which we build, a unified structure, in which we ourselves have a place, and in which every element is thought of as directly or indirectly related to every other; and the framework of the structure, the common, unifying system of relations is spatio-temporal'.[5] The place we 'have'—'our own place', as Strawson also puts it—amounts to the place one happens to 'occupy' or 'possess' within that system of spatial relations.[6] For this reason, 'place', 'position', and 'location' are terms Strawson uses interchangeably. In the account of spatiality espoused by Strawson, being a 'possessor' of a place amounts to having a location, to being a 'space-taking thing'.[7] While the location of each particular thing must be unique, for otherwise it could not be identified, its uniqueness is determined in terms of the spatial relations it entertains with all other particulars—and nothing more. In the background of this description of the spatio-temporal framework of identification lies the mathematical idealization of space as a three-dimensional continuum that is homogeneous and empty.[8] Not surprisingly, Strawson refers to maps and mapping as vehicles for spatial identification. This interpretation of place and of space explains why it makes no difference who identifies a legal collective, and whether what one identifies is a legal collective or, say, a material body. When identifying ourselves as a legal collective, by referring to our own place, we do the very same thing as when one points out to someone the place where a boulder is located or where an event occurred.

Analogous considerations apply to the system of temporal relations, ordered as dates in calendar time: 'we, the speakers, the users of the dating and placing systems...'.[9] Here again, it makes no difference who speaks and who listens, as calendar time provides a common temporality that makes possible 'identification in history'.[10] On this reading, history is a single, infinite, and segmentable temporal continuum, sequentially organized as a before and an after, rather than as a temporal arc spanning a past, present, and future.[11] As such, calendar time makes it possible to identify legal orders by indicating, even if more or less roughly, their beginning and/or their end in time. As calendar time is also the time in which everything comes about and exists, it is possible to identify everything in a way that relates it temporally to all other things and events. Accordingly, if our own place is simply the place one happens to occupy, and which is related to all other

[5] Strawson, *Individuals*, 29. [6] Strawson, *Individuals*, 25. [7] Strawson, *Individuals*, 54.

[8] As Ströker puts it, things located in the space of intuition, whence the idealization leading to mathematical space begins, are 'removed from their context of utility, they stand extricated from any functional relationship with other things. An isolated entity there and yonder has its location merely as a "position" in space completely external to it; an accidental, arbitrarily exchangeable somewhere no longer having any relationship to the thing itself'. See Ströker, *Investigations in Philosophy of Space*, 85–86. See also Edmund Husserl's essay, 'Idealization and the Science of Reality—The Mathematization of Nature', in Husserl, *The Crisis of European Sciences and Transcendental Phenomenology*, 301–314.

[9] Strawson, *Individuals*, 30. [10] Strawson, *Individuals*, 18.

[11] But, as Ricœur rightly notes, calendar time involves the collective mediation of cosmic time, as a calendar requires an axial event which marks the beginning of time. This event is axial by dint of its extraordinary collective importance and significance, which already involves a first-person plural perspective on time. See Paul Ricœur, *Time and Narrative*, vol. 3, trans. Kathleen Blamey and David Pellauer (Chicago, IL: Chicago University Press, 1990), 104 ff, and Émile Benveniste, 'Le langage et l'expérience humaine', in Benveniste et al. (eds.), *Problèmes de langage* (Paris: Gallimard, 1966), 3–13.

places in the single spatial framework, so also our own history is simply that interval of datable time in which a legal collective happens to exist, and which stands in temporal relations of a before and an after with respect to all other legal orders, things, and events.

Theories of legal pluralism appeal to this interpretation of identification and of spatio-temporality, even if it remains largely implicit and taken for granted in their accounts. Consider, to this effect, Twining's terse characterization of legal pluralism: 'normative and legal orders co-exist in the same time-space context'.[12] What the legal sociologist does is to demarcate a spatial domain and a temporal period within this all-encompassing framework, e.g. Europe in the period from 1990 to 2011, then to identify and describe the different legal orders that have co-existed in that space and period of time. If pressed about the confines of Europe, the legal sociologist demarcates it by fiat: the spatio-temporal context is arbitrary. Conversely, to identify a legal order is to indicate where it is located in the spatio-temporal context demarcated by the theorist, and, by implication, in the single spatio-temporal framework common to all things, persons, events, and processes. In line with this interpretation of space, legal pluralists and sociologists of globalization stress the importance of 'mapping law' and 'scales' of law, with a view to identifying particular legal orders.[13] Indeed, by varying the 'scale' one varies the spatial context of the legal collectives one is talking about, moving from the sub-national to the national, regional, and global. There is in principle no problem with expanding the largest scale, taking it from the planetary to the 'interplanetary' or—why not?—the 'intergalactic', even if these remain practically meaningless possibilities for the foreseeable future.

The single spatio-temporal framework to which Strawson refers is indeed a basic condition for all possible identification. But although there could be no identification of legal collectives in its absence, this does not mean that this single spatio-temporal framework, as described by Strawson, is what allows for the identification of a legal collective *as* a legal collective. Indeed, do the members of a collective do nothing more, when referring to a place as their own place, and to a history as their own history, than identify themselves in terms of a three-dimensional spatial location and a temporal segment in calendar time? Whereas the own place of a thing is simply the place where it happens to be, the own place of legal behaviour is the place where it *belongs*—where it ought to come about. Whereas the own time of a thing is simply the segment of calendar time in which it happens to exist or come about, the own time of legal behaviour is the time to which it *belongs*—when it ought to come about. And this means that, in the same way that the connection between place and behaviour is internal, so also between time and behaviour. In short, the spatio-temporality of a legal collective, *qua collective*, is the space and time of joint action, not the spatio-temporality of things, even though the former supervenes on the latter. In this vein, the entire thrust of the foregoing chapters has been to show that the

[12] Twining, *General Jurisprudence*, 70.

[13] See Twining, *General Jurisprudence*, 269 ff; de Sousa Santos, *Toward a New Legal Common Sense*, 417 ff; Sassen, *A Sociology of Globalization*, 18–23, 238–240.

strong sense of possessiveness involved in referring to our own place and our own history presupposes collective selfhood, whereby a manifold of individuals view themselves as a group that engages in joint action. This objection effectively echoes Ricœur's criticism of Strawson's theory of identification: 'identifying oneself' is not merely 'identifying "something"'.[14] But I will develop this objection in a way that is quite different to that proposed by Ricœur. Indeed, while I share Ricœur's conviction that Strawson's approach to identification neutralizes identity as selfhood to the benefit of identity as sameness, Ricœur's subsequent development of this criticism leads him to abandoning the discussion of identification as concerns its spatial and temporal dimensions. Yet these dimensions require closer scrutiny if we are to make sense of the identification of a collective as the identification of a collective *self*. Moreover, and crucially, neither Strawson nor Ricœur examine identification as the problem of identifying a *collective* self.[15]

6.2 THE IDENTIFICATION OF A COLLECTIVE AS A SELF

Strawson notes that to identify something is to identify its unique place and time, that is, the place and time that are its own, and which distinguish it from all other things. Referring to spatial identification, he observes that the 'identification and distinction of places turn on the identification and distinction of things; and the identification and distinction of things turn, in part, on the identification and distinction of places'.[16]

While this passage refers to the identification of things, it provides a clue as to how the identification of a legal collective as a self is possible: in connection to the identification of legal place, at least in part. Now, to identify a legal place is to single out a specimen of a certain kind of ought-place; 'the parking lot is over there', says the pedestrian to the driver who has pulled over to ask where he or she may park his or her car. Certainly, the response does not, of itself, involve the identification of a legal collective. The pedestrian might well have responded, '*one* parks the car over there'; by contrast, it would sound odd to respond, '*we* park cars over there'. Accordingly, and in line with the analysis of intentionality outlined in chapter 4, there is an anonymous, pre- and post-reflexive form of joint action which precedes and succeeds the identification of a legal collective as a self, namely joint action in which mutual expectations about how one ought to act and that one acts as a participant agent are not the object of explicit attention; one simply interacts with others, more or less blindly; I called this social interaction in chapter 1. The identification of a collective as a self is a late apparition,

[14] Ricœur, *Oneself as Another*, 27.

[15] The possibility of identifying a collective as a thing and as a self leads back, ultimately, to the forms of embodiment of agents which Husserl calls, respectively, *Körper* (body object) and *Leib* (lived body). See Edmund Husserl, *Ideas Pertaining to a Pure Phenomenology and to a Phenomenological Philosophy*, vol. II, trans. Richard Rojcewicz and André Schuwer (Dordrecht: Kluwer Academic Publishers, 1989), 165 ff. Although I cannot develop this theme here any further, it confirms the thesis, noted earlier in this book, that a theory of legal order as a concrete normative order must take seriously the embodied condition of participant agency in joint action.

[16] Strawson, *Individuals*, 37.

so to speak, which kicks in when, in our example, the ought-character of a legal place is called into question. The pedestrian says, '*one* parks the car over there, but bear in mind that parking is only free from 8 PM to 6 AM'. 'Why?', asks the driver. 'Well', replies the pedestrian, '*our* city council has introduced paid parking to increase its revenues'. Collective self-identification requires, thus, that someone take up the *reflexive stance* of a participant agent *qua* participant agent; someone must see him or herself and other agents as participating in joint action. Returning to a basic distinction of chapter 4, the identification of a legal collective as a self arises when understanding gives way to interpretation. While this reflexive stance can be triggered by conflict, the example shows that this need not be the case; it suffices that, in one way or another, the ought-character of behaviour is called into question. These considerations are analogous to Strawson's description of thing-identification, which only arises when hearer and speaker are communicating *about* something to which they are oriented as the object of their discourse.

It follows from this analysis that the identification of a collective as a self comes about through the *attribution* of an act to the collective as its own act. On the one hand, there is no collective self absent a series of interlocking acts by participant agents; it is the acts of these agents which are located and locatable in the space and time of collective action (and of things). But, on the other hand, these acts, although performed by participant agents, are acts of the collective, e.g. *we* (together) are pulling off a parking contract. Importantly, space and time are not simply a pre-condition for the attribution of acts to a collective: they are part and parcel of what is attributed to it as what it owns. For if an act is the collective's own act inasmuch as it is performed by someone—a participant agent—who is authorized to do so (the 'who' and the 'what' of joint action), so also the attribution of an act to a collective requires that it take place where and when it ought to, that is, in the place and time assigned to it by the collective in light of the normative point of joint action. After all, who is the 'we' to whom an act would be attributed, that is, who is *identified* as the agent? Well, the group of individuals who are committed to comporting themselves in a certain way in a certain kind of place, and so forth, in-order-to-φ.

Notice how the threefold reference which is constitutive of legal intentionality comes back into the picture: (i) the reference to a collective, as the owner of behaviour; (ii) the reference to a legal order that lays out who ought to do what, where, and when; (iii) the reference to the normative point of joint action. Collective self-reidentification, we can now see, is the explicit actualization of this threefold reference. The identification and distinction of a collective self requires being able to identify and distinguish legal places, times, subjects, and act-contents, which, in turn, requires being able to identify and distinguish the normative point of joint action.

Moreover, attribution—identification—can come about in what I have called first-order joint action, such as when the pedestrian, in response to the question of the driver, responds, 'our city council ...'. In this sense, the identification of a legal collective as a self is a ubiquitous feature of legal practices. But, crucially, identification also takes place in second-order joint action, when, in case of conflict or otherwise, certain legal organs *authoritatively* attribute an act to a collective—or not. An authoritative judgement about the legality or illegality of behaviour always involves an authoritative identification of a collective, hence an authoritative actualization of the threefold reference of legal intentionality: *we* countenance this (kind of) act by this (kind of) person at this (kind of) place and time in-order-to-φ. The parenthetical interpolations mark the difference between individual rulings and the issuance of general norms, both of which fall under second-order identification. For reasons noted in chapter 3, second-order identification is crucial: legal collectives are collectives in which certain organs are empowered to monitor and uphold joint action, even against those who would disagree, thereby sustaining collective identity over time. Self-identification by legal collectives is always, in the final instance, the authoritatively mediated and enforced self-attribution of an act as (part of) a joint act, even though this second-order identification is usually held in reserve in the course of legal practices. Conversely, a legal collective falls apart, ceases to subsist in time, in the absence of structures of authority that can reidentify it over time.

A further step is taken towards clarifying the difference between thing-identification and self-identification if one scrutinizes the linkage between identification and distinction, a linkage Strawson discretely introduces in the passage cited at the outset of this section, and which Ricœur fleshes out more fully as follows: 'to *identify* and to *distinguish* constitute an inseparable verbal pair. In order to identify it is necessary to distinguish, and it is in distinguishing that we identify'.[17] Now, the identification of a collective self requires distinguishing it from *other than self*, not from things. Paraphrasing Ricœur, in order to identify ourselves as a collective self it is necessary to distinguish ourselves from other than self, and it is in distinguishing ourselves from other than self that we identify ourselves as a collective self. As we have seen in chapter 3, the distinction between collective self and the rest comes about through a *closure*. Hence, identification and distinction are the two sides of closure: identifying a collective as a self and distinguishing it from other than self requires including legal (dis)order and excluding the unordered, hence including what is important and relevant and excluding the rest as unimportant and irrelevant. As this last dimension makes clear, identification and distinction are not neutral events: to identify a collective self, distinguishing it from other than self, is to introduce a *preferential* distinction: legal (dis)order is preferred to the unordered, and the collective self to other than self.

Consequently, *qua* self, a legal collective is 'in' space and time in a way that is irreducible to how things—including collectives, when viewed as things—are 'in' space and time. Indeed, 'in-ness' speaks, in the former case, to the limit between a legal order and its domain of the unordered, such that realizing the normative

[17] Paul Ricœur, *The Course of Recognition*, trans. David Pellauer (Cambridge, MA: Harvard University Press, 2005), 25. This conceptual pair is what legal theorists have in mind when formulating the question about the nature of law, and what distinguishes it from other forms of normative order, as the identity question. The point I am making is that the collective self-identification and distinction from other than collective self is conceptually and chronologically prior to this interpretation of the 'identity question' about law. See to this effect section 3.1.

point of joint action by a legal collective requires a *spatio-temporal discontinuity* between collective self and other than self. This is the point of the distinction between borders and frontiers. Whereas there can be no borders, as *legal* boundaries, absent a spatial continuity within which different ought-places are differentiated and interconnected (i.e. classical international law), frontiers mark the spatial limit of a legal order, hence a discontinuity and an asymmetry between inside and outside. Certainly, a legal collective can act as a participant agent in a higher-order legal collective, e.g. the Member States of the European Union, of the World Trade Organization or, for that matter, of the United Nations. In such cases, there is a spatio-temporal continuity that joins together all members of the higher-order collective. But this kind of spatio-temporal continuity is necessarily paired to a spatio-temporal discontinuity with respect to what lies beyond the pale of joint action of the higher-order legal collective and, as a consequence, of the legal collectives that compose it. The case of the U'wa, discussed in chapter 2, aptly illustrates that, even in the case of global law, such as *lex constructionis*, the 'community of experience' (Strawson) required for collective self-identification is perforce *limited*, in space as much as in time.

These considerations remain, however, quite abstract. How, concretely, do the identification and distinction of legal collectives come about? Consider Strawson's comment about the reliance of thing-identification on 'space-taking things'. As he explains it, the identification of things requires that they occupy or take space, or can be related to things which occupy or take space. Everything remains the same and everything changes when we pass from a 'space-taking thing' to a 'space-taking self'. Here also, an 'occupation' or 'taking' is required, if the identification of a legal collective as a self is to be possible, but now in the intransitive verbal form: we stake out a place as *our own* in identifying *ourselves*, and vice-versa. In a nutshell, self-identification begins as a closure that distinguishes between collective self and other than self, and closure comes about through a taking: the self-identification of a collective literally *takes place*. Self-identification and self-emplacement are two sides of the same coin.

This insight resonates with Carl Schmitt's reflections on the notion of *nomos*. Schmitt's interpretation of *nomos* relies on the idea that law is, as he puts it, a 'unity of order and emplacement'.[18] What is of interest in his interpretation of *nomos* is not so much the concrete spatiality of legal order—something Schmitt has surprising little to say about—as his analysis of the act that founds a legal order by emplacing it: *nemein*. He notes that this Greek verb is usually taken to mean a sequence of acts whereby an initial act of division and distribution (*teilen*) is followed by exploitation, i.e. a productive use and possession of what has been divided and distributed (*weiden*). This interpretation, as he sees it, neutralizes the political content of *nemein*. For the sequence of acts that compose it begins earlier, with a taking (*nehmen*): 'in the same way that distribution precedes exploitation,

[18] *'Einheit von Ordnung und Ortung'*. See Carl Schmitt, *The Nomos of the Earth in the International Law of the Jus Publicum Europaeum*, trans. G.L. Ulmen (New York: Telos Press, 2003), 42 (translation altered). See my article 'Give and Take: Arendt and the *Nomos* of Political Community', *Philosophy and Social Criticism* 32, no. 6 (2006), 785–805.

a taking precedes distribution. Not the distribution, not the *divisio primaeva*, but a taking is what comes first'. For, he adds, 'no human being can give, distribute and apportion without taking'.[19] This primordial act is an appropriation, a 'taking of land' (*Landnahme*). An act that seizes land, an *occupation*, founds the law both internally and externally: internally, by making room for the allocation of entitlements and obligations, as well as for their 'exploitation'; externally, by distinguishing a political community from other political communities. No less importantly, *land*-taking underscores the fundamental difference between the spatialities of thing-identification and of collective self-identification. The latter speaks to lived space, hence to beings for whom identification has an existential dimension in the strict sense of the term: collective self-emplacement discloses space as a condition for sustaining *life*.[20]

We'll return in a moment to critically examine Schmitt's account of land-taking. For the moment, I want to retain and defend the idea that there can be no identification of a legal collective as a self in the absence of a taking, of an occupation that effects a closure which distinguishes it from other than self, and which prepares the way for a 'filled' inside—'distribution' and 'exploitation'—over and against an 'empty' outside. As we have seen in chapter 5, Husserl refers to the 'occupation' (*Besetzung*) of an empty outside. But this should not blind us to the fact that the closure which gives rise to a legal collective and its 'filled' space is itself the outcome of an occupation, albeit an occupation that, for many, has ceased to be experienced as such and becomes the taken for granted and familiar space a collective calls its 'own'. The 'Occupy Wall Street' movement both questioned the occupation of the world by capitalism and how it 'filled' space and time, and sought to take land, when it occupied Zuccotti Square in New York, promptly re-baptizing it as Liberty Square. The example is particularly apposite for it shows that unless an emergent collective manages to emplace itself in a space it claims as its own, and which is irreducible to the places of extant collectives (whence the new name of the square), it cannot identify itself as a novel collective. This internal correlation between self-identification and place-identification is conspicuous in the Declaration of the Occupation of New York: 'We, the New York City General Assembly occupying Wall Street in Liberty Square ... urge you to assert your power ... [to] exercise your right to peaceably assemble; occupy public space; create a process to address the problems we face, and generate solutions accessible to everyone'.[21] Notice how the Declaration's generalizing shift from

[19] 'Nomos-Nahme-Name', in Carl Schmitt, *Staat, Großraum, Nomos: Arbeiten aus den Jahren 1916–1969* (Berlin: Dunker & Humblot, 1995), 573–591. See also 'Nehmen/Teilen/Weiden', in Carl Schmitt, *Verfassungsrechtliche Aufsätze aus den Jahren 1924–1954*, 4th edn. (Berlin: Duncker & Humblot, 1958), 489–504. Schmitt's etymology of *nemein* and *nehmen* is probably spurious, but what is important is the conceptual point he makes.

[20] Referring to the land question, van Roermund notes that land is 'the sum-total of the conditions of my being in a permanent metabolism (as Marx would say) with the world around me'. See Bert van Roermund, 'Migrants, Humans and Human Rights', in Hans Lindahl (ed.), *A Right to Inclusion and Exclusion? Normative Fault lines of the EU's Area of Freedom, Security and Justice* (Oxford: Hart, 2009), 171.

[21] <http://www.nycga.net/resources/documents/declaration/> (accessed on 13 February 2013). For a good write-up on the origin and future of Occupy Wall Street, see Mattathias Schwartz, 'Pre-Occupied: The Origins and Future of Occupy Wall Street', *The New Yorker*, 28 November 2011.

'we' to 'you' to 'we' is paralleled by an implicit generalizing shift from Liberty Square to Liberty World. Interestingly, the occupation went far beyond a sit-in; all kinds of activities have been organized, aiming to show alternative ways of acting together to pull off economic transactions: distribution and exploitation, as Schmitt would put it. Indeed, it is only to the extent that the primordial land-taking consolidates itself as distribution and as exploitation that a collective really emplaces itself, closing itself into a 'filled' spatio-temporality (Husserl) that can be identified as a collective self in joint action over and against an 'empty' outside. It remains to be seen whether the Occupy movement can bring about this consolidation, organizing itself as authoritatively mediated and upheld joint action under law, or whether it will remain a largely virtual 'we'. Its prospects, at the time of writing this book, do not seem particularly promising.

Notice the corollary that follows from the insight that land must be taken if collective self-identification is to be possible. Indeed, the Occupy movement shows that the closure that gives rise to a novel collective always involves, to a lesser or greater extent, *an act of conquest*. In this sense it is no different to the conquest that gave rise to Canada, or to which an independent Quebec would give rise, any less than to the element of conquest involved in the emergence of multinationals and all other manifestations of 'global law'. Collective self-identification involves a closure that, if successful, imposes and consolidates itself over and against extant legal collectives. Land must be taken if a novel collective is to identify itself, which means that to a lesser or greater extent it must be seized, taken away, from extant collectives in the form of a novel unity of ought-places in which at least certain forms of behaviour cease to fall under the aegis of the former. Collective self-identification is never an innocent undertaking, not even when a movement seeks to oppose capitalism by emplacing itself in what it comes to call Liberty Square.

The identification of legal collectives that takes place from a detached observer's perspective presupposes, on this account, the first-person plural perspective on identification, *but not vice versa*. It is tempting to assume that it is primarily the legal taxonomist engaged in mapping legal orders in a global setting who 'need[s] to find a way to individuate them'.[22] Yet the individuation of legal collectives is first and foremost what participant agents themselves do in the course of joint action. *The primordial mode of the identification of a legal collective as a self is self-identification by its members,* even if, as we have seen at the end of chapter 4, self-identification begins as the identification *of* a collective self rather than as identification *by* a collective self. In any case, until self-identification gets started, or when it breaks down, there is not yet, or no longer, a collective self that can be identified from the relatively detached perspective of an observer.

The priority of collective self-identification over detached forms of identifying collectives entails furthermore that the former takes place as a response to the practical question geared to establishing from a first-person plural

Available at: <http://www.newyorker.com/reporting/2011/11/28/111128fa_fact_schwartz> (accessed on 13 February 2013).

[22] Twining, *General Jurisprudence*, ch. 15 (only available on the Internet site of the book), 20.

perspective who ought to do what, where, and when in-order-to-φ. Indeed, *collective self-identification is required when members of a collective are confronted with the practical question: 'what* ought our joint action to be about?'* This casts fresh light on what was said about legal interpretation in section 4.5. By articulating what* our joint action ought to be about, legal interpretation is the vehicle of collective self-identification. To respond to this practical question, setting the boundaries of who ought to do what, where, and when, is to interpret who we are, and this means to identify ourselves as a collective and to distinguish ourselves from what is other-than-us. All of this gets lost in conventional accounts of practical rationality when construed in terms of 'collective self-determination'.

These considerations need to be pushed yet a step further to get to the heart of self-identification as a response to the practical question confronting collectives. If identifying a collective self involves distinguishing it from other than self and vice versa, then, ultimately, it is *the limit between legal (dis)order and the unordered which is the practical stake of collective self-identification*. The practical question about the point of joint action is whether a collective should include as important and relevant—as part of legal (dis)order—what has been excluded as unimportant and irrelevant—as unordered—or, conversely, whether it should push out into the domain of the unimportant and irrelevant what had been deemed to be important and relevant. Collective self-identification turns, therefore, on two questions. The first: ought what* has been excluded from law to be included therein? The second: ought what* has been included in law to be excluded therefrom?

We will grant detailed consideration to the nature of this 'ought' in chapter 7. For the moment it suffices to note that these questions can only arise because, as noted earlier, the closure that gives rise to a legal collective is something more and something other than the inclusion of self and the exclusion of other than self. On the one hand, there is no self-inclusion that is not also a self-*exclusion*; closure actualizes collective possibilities at the price of excluding other possibilities which can retroactively appear as its own possibilities. On the other, there is no other-exclusion that is not also other-*inclusion*, as becomes apparent retroactively. More pointedly, there is no other-exclusion that does not involve the inclusion of strangeness: the strange need not be foreign. In a word, self-identification calls forth the possibility of self-*misidentification*. If the identification of things can misfire, so also the identification of a collective as a self: 'Not in our name!' Notice that the slogan can be read in two ways: 'Not in our name, although this ought to be the case'; and 'In our name, although this ought not to be the case'. Both speak to forms of misidentification in the course of joint action by a legal collective. Legal authority, in the sense of authoritative decisions about joint action and its normative point, is, ultimately, (putative) empowerment to identify a collective in the face of first-order questions about identification and misidentification.

6.3 FROM IDENTIFICATION TO REIDENTIFICATION

Using Strawson's analysis of identification as a foil, I have sought to evince the basic structure of collective self-identification, linking it to the closure which gives rise to the distinction between self and other than self. Importantly, his analysis of identification spills over into an account of reidentification, hence of identity over time. Strawson's question concerns the criteria or methods on the basis of which a particular can be identified 'as *the same individual* as a particular encountered on another occasion'.[23] His answer is, in a nutshell, that the reidentification of things depends on applying the same unified spatio-temporal framework on different occasions. Whatever the merits of Strawson's account of *idem*-reidentification, Ricœur's objection once again kicks in: his account of reidentification does not deal with the identity over time of a self. But while Ricœur focuses on the reidentification of a self, he limits himself to the (narrative) reidentification of a personal self. In contrast to both, what interests me is to understand *collective* self-reidentification. Everything turns on the following question: in what way does the 're' of reidentification enable—and undermine—collective identity over time?

At first glance, the relation between reidentification and the permanence in time of a collective as the same and as a self is straightforward. As concerns *idem*-identity, a legal collective remains (more or less) the same over time, and can be reidentified as such, by its members and by others, inasmuch as joint action remains (more or less) the same, which means that what are deemed to be mutual expectations about who ought to do what, where, and when remain (more or less) the same, and are fulfilled, by and large, in the course of legal practices. As concerns *ipse*-identity, a collective subsists in time to the extent that a manifold of individuals view themselves as the members of a group who act jointly and are prepared to continue upholding the group's past decisions and acts in the course of their joint action: *nous maintiendrons*. To the extent that a collective's present and future joint action honours its past commitments, a collective perdures as a self; the collective self remains identical over time: joint action displays a form of 'uninterrupted continuity'.[24] Notice that uninterrupted continuity does not concern so much what perdures in the sequence of a before and an after proper to calendar time, but rather the uninterrupted continuity of the past, present, and future of a collective, such that these are sutured together as the modes of a *single* temporal arc in the course of joint action. It is this form of permanence in time which is at the heart of reidentification as collective self-reidentification, and which remains beyond the purview of Strawson's account of reidentification as identification of 'the same individual' on different occasions.

Which closure must be reiterated, such that collective identity can be sustained over time? Well, the closure that gave rise to joint action in the first place, or so it seems. Reidentifying a collective self in the course of a legal practice would go hand-in-hand with reiterating the inaugural closure—the act of taking or occupying land—that distinguished the collective self from the rest: the unordered. By continuing to act together in the way dictated by that inaugural closure, we reiterate the boundaries that establish who ought to do what, where, and when, thereby reiterating the inaugural divide between legal (dis)order and the unordered, between what is important and relevant and what is not.

[23] Strawson, *Individuals*, 31.

[24] Ricœur, *Oneself as Another*, 117.

Yet, in light of our earlier account of the paradox of representation, this picture of collective self-reidentification is reductive. For there is no original closure which is followed up by a series of re-closures, any more than there is an original identification which is followed up by a series of reidentifications. The closure that originates a collective self, distinguishing it from other than self, *represents* an original closure: a re-closure. Schmitt would have it that 'no human being can give, distribute and apportion without taking'; the correct and paradoxical formulation would be: no human being can give, distribute, and apportion (for the first time) without re-taking. In effect, the members of a collective have no direct access to the original boundaries of the collective of which they partake, nor to what joins them together as the members of a whole; the original unity of a legal collective and its original boundaries only manifest themselves indirectly, by way of their representations. *The 're' of collective reidentification is governed by the paradox of representation.*

The European Union—initially the European Economic Community—exemplifies the link between reidentification and the paradox of representation. At first sight, the Preamble to the Treaty of Rome gives form to an act of collective self-identification: the founding states, it asserts, 'have decided to create a European Economic Community'. As contended earlier, although formulated in the third person in the Treaty, the identifying act takes place in the first person: we constitute ourselves as a European Economic Community by way of a spatio-temporal closure. Indeed, the Treaty goes on to set out the terms of joint action and its normative point, thereby setting the divide between legal (dis)order and the unordered. Each of the Schmittian elements is present in the Treaty: a land-taking (*nehmen*); a distribution of entitlements (*teilen*); their exploitation (*weiden*). In the beginning, and as the beginning, there is an act of collective self-identification, or so it seems.

Closer analysis suggests otherwise. The Preamble includes a passage that has remained well nigh unchanged in all later treaties: the signatories to the Treaty of Rome are 'determined to lay the foundations of an ever closer union among the peoples of Europe'. Commentators do not tire of emphasizing that the Preamble refers to 'peoples' in the plural, rather than to 'people' in the singular, concluding that the European Community/Union is not a federal polity.[25] But these commentators lose sight of the no less evident fact that by referring to an '*ever closer union* of European peoples', the Preamble not only posits a union as the future vanishing point of the integrative process, but also claims that there *already* was a collective spatio-temporal unity at the time of laying its legal foundation in the Treaty of Rome, a community of peoples that, by virtue of their shared values and interests, can engage in a process of legal and economic integration. So the wording of the Preamble implies that the Treaty of Rome does not *initiate* the community of European peoples; it does not take or occupy Europe, preparing the way for distribution and exploitation. The Treaty claims to *build* on a prior

[25] For a particularly emphatic defence of this position, see Joseph Weiler, 'The Fischer Debate—The Dark Side', in Christian Joerges et al. (eds.), *What Kind of Constitution for What Kind of Polity? Responses to Joschka Fischer* (Florence: European University Institute, 2000), 235–247.

closure, providing this community with an institutional setting and specific goals. The Preamble views the Europe Economic Community as carrying forward an original scission that separates an undifferentiated space into two places: Europe and the rest. The datable act of positing the European Economic Community's boundaries claims to derive from a spatial closure lost in an irretrievable, undatable past. The very act that takes land, staking out the European Economic Community as a common (internal) market over and against the rest, asserts that it re-takes, re-claims, re-occupies, Europe as 'our own'.[26]

Notice the paradoxical structuring of time (and space) which comes to the fore in the Preamble: the Treaty that effectively creates a legal collective retrojects this creation onto a past which is held to function as the origin of the new legal collective. The Treaty that gives rise to a novel legal collective transfers the birth of this order into the past, and then goes on to assert that the Treaty is but an implication of the origin. This is, then, the strong meaning of 're' in representation and in reidentification: 're' does not refer to what supervenes or follows an original present and presence, a 'here' and 'now' in which a manifold of individuals constitute themselves as a community in the plenitude of a simple presence to themselves. Instead, and paradoxically, one must say that *identification begins as a reidentification;* that to originate a collective self, by a novel identification, is forcibly to reidentify an original self to which there is no direct access.

This paradox has an implication of the greatest importance for a theory of the political uses of indexicality. This is a theme that was prepared in the first section of this chapter, when we briefly introduced Strawson's account of the identification of particulars. Indeed, although the range of individualizing operators includes definite descriptions and proper names, indexicals such as personal pronouns ('I', 'you') and adverbs of place ('here', 'there') and of time ('now', 'yesterday', 'tomorrow') play a key role in securing what he calls the 'demonstrative identification' of particulars which are, as he puts it, 'sensibly present'.[27] Now, although Strawson does not develop a theory of indexicality in terms of the self-identification of collectives, the Treaty of Rome neatly illustrates how the political use of indexicals is destabilized by the paradox of representation. The possibility of identifying 'we', the European Union, located 'here' in Europe, and enacting legislation 'now', in the light of our common past and with a view to ensuring our shared future, presupposes the invocation of a first 'we-here-now' that has no referent, i.e. that never was 'sensibly present'.[28] If, in political metaphysics, a simple present and presence are deemed to be the ultimate guarantee of the unity of a community and of the binding character of its boundaries, the Preamble to the Treaty of Rome shows us, to the contrary, that the original self of the European Community is radically absent from the act which founds it by identifying the legal collective and distinguishing it from the rest. That

[26] It should come as no surprise that the Occupy Wall Street movement presents itself as 'reclaiming our country'.

[27] Strawson, *Individuals*, 19.

[28] See my article, 'The *Anomos* of the Earth: Political Indexicality, Immigration and Distributive Justice', *Ethics and Global Politics* 1, no. 4 (2008), 193–212.

identification begins as a reidentification means that the foundation of a legal collective leads back, borrowing Merleau-Ponty's well-known insight, to 'a past which has never been a present'[29] and, we should add, to a place which has never been 'here'.

Small wonder, then, that Romano Prodi intervened at the summit of Helsinki in 1999 to ask, 'Where does Europe end?'[30] This question captures the practical nature of the problem of collective self-reidentification confronting the EU, both then and now. Whether or not to admit Turkey to the EU is but one manifestation of the practical question to which it must respond: what* ought our joint action to be about? Like every legal collective, the EU is exposed to this question by dint of the paradox which governs its emergence. And, given the internal connection between the four dimensions of a legal order, the ostensibly spatial question raised by Prodi cannot be responded to independently of the responses to questions about the who, the what, and the when, which, in being attributed to the EU, identify it as a self and distinguish it from other than self.

6.4 QUESTION AND RESPONSE

Prodi's question, 'Where does Europe end?', and the responses it might call forth, illustrates a more general point about collective self-identification that requires further attention. In effect, collective self-identification comes about in the interplay between question and response. A further clarification of the concept of collective self-reidentification requires, therefore, delving into this interplay. How, in particular, does it manifest itself in the course of acts which set legal boundaries?[31]

Notice, to begin with, that boundaries are not questioned each time around in joint action under law, which, in its normal trajectory, is largely anonymous and pre-reflexive. The closure of space, time, subjectivity, and act-content deployed in joint action usually remains a 'matter of course' for participant agents. The analysis of the first scenario in Lafayette shows that participants interact more or less effortlessly, understanding what they and others ought to be doing when engaging in joint action, thereby reiterating the default setting of the limit between legal (dis)order and the unordered, even if this limit and the first-person plural perspective whence it is drawn are in no way the object of their attention. As a result, the clients and employees of the food shop uphold extant boundaries, although their behaviour is not 'deliberately' oriented to doing so. If one can speak of responsiveness at all in the ordinary course of joint action, then it would be in the form of habitual responses to a practical question that has ceased to press itself onto participant agents as a question in need of a response. By the same token, it would be more accurate to speak of boundaries as being

[29] Maurice Merleau-Ponty, *Phenomenology of Perception*, trans. Colin Smith (London: Routledge, 1989), 242.

[30] Cited in Xavier Vidal-Folch, 'Los límites del club Europa: La futura ampliación hasta 28 países abre el debate hasta dónde llega Europa y dónde debe terminar la UE', *El País*, 14 December 1999: <http://elpais.com/diario/1999/12/14/internacional/945126012_850215.html> (accessed on 12 May 2013).

[31] My interpretation of this interplay is inspired by the foundational analyses of responsiveness developed by Bernhard Waldenfels in *Antwortregister*.

set (anonymously), rather than of a group agent as setting boundaries. Only when a situation challenges boundaries, as was the case with the initiative of the *chômeurs*, does it become clear that responsiveness is built into the structure of joint action because, quite trivially, each partial act responds to another partial act or to a situation in light of how the agents understand what* their joint act ought to be about. At the same time, the practical question—what* ought our joint action to be about?—becomes an issue demanding a response—if necessary an authoritative response—in the form of an act that *sets* the boundaries of the legal collective. The *chômeurs'* initiative interrupts the habituality of a sedimented form of responsiveness, whereby the practical question about joint action and its normative point forces itself onto the clients and employees, such that they must respond to it, in one way or another. And it is in such situations that the internal connection between collective self-reidentification and responsiveness becomes visible.

So it is necessary to flesh out more fully the concept of collective self-identification by asking how question and response are related in the course of boundary-setting, hence what it means to *set* legal boundaries.

Responses, in a first albeit reductive approach, seem to follow questions. Someone is caught stealing cans of foie gras. The ordinary flow of joint action is interrupted, such that joint action and its normative point are rendered explicit: what* ought our joint action to be about? The response to illegality takes on—or ought to take on—the form of boundary-*enforcement*. But take the case of the *chômeurs*, who block access to the check-out points, demanding that they be allowed to take victuals, including foie gras, to the unemployed standing outside. The transgression of the distinction between legality and illegality elicited by a-legal challenges to legal boundaries is responded to by acts that constitute new boundaries. A-legality calls forth, or should call forth, boundary-*constitution*.

This initial approach to the interplay between questions and responses has the merit of showing that it is important to parse boundary-setting into boundary-enforcement and boundary-constitution. But positing a simple disjunction between the two would be misguided. Indeed, if, as has been shown, all collective self-identification begins as a reidentification, then all boundary-constitution begins as a boundary-enforcement, in a broad sense of the term. Conversely, to the extent that all reidentification involves an identification, so also boundary-enforcement is also always, to a lesser or greater extent, boundary-constitution. Such is the upshot, for example, of the preamble to the Treaty of Rome. But the problem with the foregoing account of the interplay between question and answer is that it would render responses a more or less pre-programmed 'reaction' to questions which function like a 'stimulus'. It would make no sense to speak of collective *self*-identification under these circumstances, nor of legal ordering as a collective *self*-ordering, that is, as a reflexive process. Indeed, no simple sequence goes from illegal behaviour to boundary-enforcement, on the one hand, nor from a-legal behaviour to boundary-constitution, on the other. Remember, in this context, that whereas some of the clients of Lafayette saw in the *autoréduction* nothing more than an act of extortion, i.e. an illegal act, others sympathized with the *chômeurs*, and would perhaps be prepared to take up their cause, attempting to bring about a new default setting of who ought to do what, where, and when. What sense, then, are we to make of the interplay between question and answer?

Let me introduce an important distinction between two kinds of questions and responses, which is linked to the distinction between (il)legality and a-legality. First, acts of boundary-setting are responsive in that they must establish whether behaviour is legal or illegal—*derivative* questionability and responsiveness. But, secondly, boundary-setting is responsive in that it must establish whether behaviour is a-legal—*primordial* questionability and responsiveness. Boundary-setting responds to both questions, together. There are not some forms of behaviour which confront a collective with the question whether it is legal or illegal, and others with the question whether it is a-legal. Like a-legality, which manifests itself indirectly in the form of situations that question the legality/illegality distinction, so also the responsiveness of boundary-setting to a-legality is *indirect*. Because the limit between legal (dis)order and the unordered runs along each of the boundaries drawn by a legal collective, this limit only appears obliquely, in the form of situations that question how the boundaries of a collective organize the preferential distinction between legality and illegality. For this reason, the question posed by a-legality is an indirect question, a question that concerns the collective as such: what* ought our joint action to be about? In the same way, boundary-setting can only respond obliquely to a-legal situations that question the limit between legal (dis)order and legal order by reconfiguring (il)legality, i.e. by reconfiguring the boundaries establishing who ought to do what, where, and when in-order-to-φ. Boundary-setting in the course of collective self-identification is, as one might put it, a form of *indirect action*.

A further and decisive step toward clarifying the responsive structure of collective self-reidentification turns on the precedence of a-legality and the retroactivity of responsiveness. A-legality, I briefly argued in section 5.1, does not precede legal order merely in the trivial sense that there is a chronological sequence whereby first comes a question and then follows a response. A-legality precedes a legal order in the form of situations that fall outside the range of what participant agents could expect to happen in terms of the reiterative anticipation deployed in joint action. In this sense, precedence means that a-legality comes *too early*; it has already reached the participants in joint action before they can adjust to it, catching them unprepared and by surprise, leaving them more or less at a loss as to who ought to do what, where, and when.

A case in point is, of course, the initiative of the *chômeurs*: the interlocking web of acts whereby individuals enter the food shop, select the products they need, and complete their transaction at the check-out points is suddenly interrupted by behaviour that reveals practical possibilities other than those envisaged by the clients and employees of Lafayette, and which the *chômeurs* deem normatively preferable to the practical possibilities made available by extant joint action. The Occupy Wall Street movement offers another good illustration of the precedence of a-legality. *Adbusters*, a Vancouver-based anti-consumerist magazine founded by Kalle Lasn, published in June 2011 what has by now become a famous poster showing a ballerina poised on the 'Charging Bull' sculpture near Wall Street.

Above the gracious ballerina stands the stark question, 'What is our one demand?' Below the bull stands the putative answer: 'Occupy Wall Street. September 17. Bring tent'.[32] Later events have shown that the question could not be contained, that all answers, including those offered by occupiers, came too late to extinguish it; they fell short of the mark, and not merely because the question on the poster sought to whittle down the challenge posed by the occupation of Zucotti Park to a single demand. Despite a renewed invitation by *Adbusters* to the Wall Street occupiers to 'zero in on what our one demand will be', the 'Declaration of the Occupation of New York City' decried the 'mass injustice' perpetrated by the 'corporate forces' of the world and listed twenty-three grievances, ranging from illegal foreclosure processes to the creation of weapons of mass destruction. These grievances, the Declaration added, are non-exhaustive. Pressure to streamline the demands of the Occupy Wall Street movement has been brought to bear by politicians and members of the broader public, anxious to ascertain whether the movement's demands are sufficiently 'realistic' to be taken seriously. But, significantly, pressure is also generated by the very dynamic of emergent collectivity. The Declaration, issued by 'We, the New York City General Assembly occupying Wall Street in Liberty Square', urges the 'people of the world' to 'occupy public space; create a process to address the problems we face, and generate solutions accessible to everyone'. But *what* are the problems we face—'we', as 'one people, united'—and for which we—together—should generate solutions accessible to everyone? An emergent collective inevitably faces the question: what* ought our joint action to be about? And any answer to this question involves a closure that spawns its own forms of a-legality. Were the Occupy movement to become a new collective, the question that sparked it—What is our one demand?—would return to precede and disrupt it.

In short, the precedence of a-legality is the precedence of the question to which a legal order is a default response. The question 'precedes' the response in that the latter does not exhaust the former. This entails, most fundamentally, that the situations which call forth a response are never simply a legal construct, never only the outcome of an act that bestows a normative meaning on them. This bears on legal intentionality: something *reveals itself*, albeit indirectly, which does not entirely coincide with how it is *disclosed* (as something*) in the course of joint action. A-legality intimates an irreducible asymmetry in favour of questions over responses, an asymmetry which no response ever entirely catches up with. This asymmetry renders manifest the significative difference between 'something' and 'something*' as a *normative* difference: why ought legal boundaries be drawn in this way and not otherwise?

On the other hand, the responsiveness of boundary-setting is never only subordinate to what calls legal boundaries into question. Responsiveness by a legal collective never only 'follows' questionability in the twofold sense of coming 'after' and 'obeying'. Boundary-setting is retroactive in that *the question to which it responds only becomes manifest in the response itself*. Boundary-setting is responsive in that it establishes retroactively whether and how behaviour is a-legal in the

[32] <http://26.media.tumblr.com/tumblr_lsd8ucoCX91qbrgmdo1_500.jpg> (accessed on 13 February 2013).

very act of establishing what counts as legal and illegal behaviour. This is what the different responses to the *autoréduction* so clearly brought out into the open. If the precedence of questions precludes that situations are merely legal constructs, so also the retroactivity of responses precludes that situations are directly accessible with their 'original' normative meaning, and which a legal collective does nothing more than reproduce in its responses.

Consequently, and going back to our initial query, the sequence going from (il)legality to boundary-enforcement, and from a-legality to boundary-constitution, is paired to the inverted sequence: behaviour *becomes* (il)legal, albeit provisionally, when boundaries are enforced, and *becomes* a-legal when legislation constitutes boundaries, configuring in a new way who ought to do what, where, and when. To this extent, the retroactivity of responses allows acts of boundary-setting to surprise us and catch us off guard, in the same way that genuine questions have the capacity to do so. The asymmetry in favour of questions has its correlate in an asymmetry accruing to responsiveness, which is not to say that the former is 'compensated' or 'mitigated' by the latter. Instead, it speaks to an irreducible *hiatus* in between question and response.[33]

The transformation brought about by the European Court of Justice's *Van Gend & Loos* ruling (and subsequently by *Costa* v. *ENEL*) illustrates the retroactivity of responses and the precedence of questions. On the face of it, the situation about which the Court had to hand down a ruling seemed more or less routine. In terms of the default response to the practical question about the normative point of joint action by the EEC, the Court was bound to dismiss the claim raised by the Dutch transportation company. But the Court saw a question where others had not, and which only appeared *après coup* in its two rulings: what does it take to effectively realize a common market between the Member States, if the rules governing ordinary international treaties tend to impede or postpone its realization? Direct effect and the supremacy of European law are not merely the Court's answer to this question; the rulings that introduce these doctrines also reveal it as the question to which they can and must respond. One might want to conclude, following this line of reasoning, that the question to which the Court responds is subservient to its rulings. Yet the question articulated in the Court's responses by no means exhausts the question to which it responds. One indication of this was the German Constitutional Court's '*So lange*' rulings, followed up by the famous *Maastricht* judgment,[34] which, amongst others, raised the question whether the introduction of direct effect and supremacy with a view to an effective realization of the European common market should be allowed

[33] According to Nonet and Selznick, 'a responsive institution retains a grasp on what is essential to its integrity while taking account of new forces in its environment. To do so, it builds upon the ways integrity and openness sustain each other even as they conflict. It perceives social pressures as sources of knowledge and opportunities for self-correction'. This idea, which captures the core insight of Nonet and Selznick's contribution to the responsiveness of law, overlooks the precedence of questions and the retroactivity of responses, and fails to work through the conceptual and normative implications of the hiatus between question and response for a theory of legal order. See Philippe Nonet and Philip Selznick, *Law and Society in Transition: Toward Responsive Law* (New Brunswick, NJ: Transaction Publishers, 2001), 77.

[34] BVerfG, 2 BvR L 134/92 and 2159/92, 155–213. See also the Constitutional Court's more recent Lisbon ruling (BVerfG, 2 BvE 2/08 of 30 June 2009, 1).

to imperil the high level of fundamental rights protection and democratic participation afforded by Member States. Retroactively, the German Constitutional Court's rulings show that the European Court's articulation of the question to which direct effect and supremacy were an answer comes too late: the practical question to which the EEC can respond—what* ought our joint action to be about?—continues to *precede* how the different participants articulate it in the course of European integration, such that their responses never entirely catch up with it. Nor does this practical question exhaust the question raised by those who would challenge the EU as a collective.

6.5 THE HIATUS BETWEEN QUESTION AND RESPONSE

This last proviso requires further clarification and takes us to the heart of the possibilities and limitations of collective self-identification as a response to a-legality. Indeed, I have suggested on various occasions that a-legality interrupts the ordinary course of joint action, confronting a collective with the practical question, what* ought our joint action to be about? Collective self-identification has the structure of a response to this question. Yet might this practical question confronting a legal collective already have begun to *domesticate* a-legality?

The problem turns on the double asymmetry between a legal collective and a-legal behaviour. Notice that by viewing the question raised by a-legality as a question about the normative point of joint action, one already takes up the first-person plural perspective of a legal collective. One takes for granted that a-legal behaviour confronts participant agents with the question concerning the range of practical possibilities available to *us*, the legal collective. Notice, moreover, that this assumption can quickly lead to the further assumption that those who engage in a-legal behaviour *also* view themselves as participants in the collective, such that their action reaffirms them as members of the collective, and the collective as a unity, in the very process of challenging it. Hence, the place whence they challenge the legal order has no place within the distribution of ought-places made available by the legal collective, *although it ought to*. Collective self-reidentification would allow for reconfiguring the legal space of the collective so that those who have been unjustly excluded therefrom are assigned an ought-place within its compass.

In short, taking for granted that the question raised by a-legality is but the question concerning what* our joint action ought to be about does two things. First, it favours the inside vis-à-vis the outside; second, it conceals the asymmetry of this preferential differentiation, taking for granted that the questioning of joint action presupposes a more fundamental reciprocity: those who challenge joint action are participant agents, like the rest of us, who seek to redefine what we, as a *whole*, ought to call (il)legal behaviour. The *autoréduction* of the *chômeurs*, on this reading, would be the act of individuals who, seeking to bring about a just French collective, reaffirm their condition as members of that collective in the very process of challenging its default answer to what joint action ought to be about. On this rendition of what took place, the *autoréduction* would presuppose a *political relation* between the *chômeurs* and (the clients of) Lafayette, namely the relation that links participant agents in joint action, even if the normative point of that relation is the object of conflict.[35] The *chômeurs* would claim to be part of us; more exactly, they would demand to be recognized as such by their inclusion in relations of legal reciprocity. Their challenge to the collective would read: let us become what* we already are as a group, albeit potentially.

But is this necessarily what the *chômeurs* are doing? Should one take for granted that they are reaffirming their membership in the French collective when engaging with Lafayette and its clientele? Perhaps. But perhaps not, and regardless of whether they 'consciously' view their act as having one or the other meaning. Might their attempt to pass beyond the check-out points without paying for the victuals retrospectively prove to be an attempt to *leave* the French collective, to cross over into the far side of the fault line between this legal order and its domain of the unorderable, where only other joint action by another collective would be possible? Instead of transforming the French legal collective, might their contestation point to the possible emergence of a *new* collective which could engage in other joint action, with other members and with other structures of authority to monitor and uphold collective identity? Only time will tell—for the time being.

By raising this point I am not denying that the question concerning the normative point of joint action is raised in the face of a-legal behaviour; in fact, it is the question that *has* to arise for whom, taking up the first-person plural perspective of a legal collective, seeks to reorder the collective with a view to integrating what has been unjustifiably excluded from it. What I am asserting, however, is that the precedence of a-legality gainsays that the question raised by a-legal behaviour is ever simply reducible to the question to which the collective responds: what* ought our joint action to be about?

Indeed, to a lesser or greater extent, *responses articulate questions in ways that render them amenable to a response*. This leads back to what has been said in chapter 5: the response to a-legality, by way of boundary-setting, is always bound up with an authoritative assessment about which practical possibilities are the collective's *own* possibilities, regardless of whether that assessment takes place in the form of an individual norm (e.g. a ruling) or a general norm (e.g. a statute). Remember that legal collectives are collectives in which second-level organs are empowered to monitor and uphold joint action over time, even against those who would disagree. Hence if authoritative acts of boundary-setting respond to a-legal behaviour with a novel configuration of who ought to do what, where, and when in-order-to-φ, they also always establish what kinds of a-legality the collective can deal with. This is crucial: the a-legality a collective can deal with, by changing the default setting of joint action, is one which allows it to subsist as a collective self over time, that is, one which, on the authority's assessment, allows a collective to *reidentify* itself.

[35] It is significant, in this respect, that, according to Rawls, the idea of public reason, which turns on reciprocity, 'concerns how the *political relation* is to be understood'. Conversely, reciprocity presupposes that there is a relation between members of a group, which constitutes them as such. See John Rawls, *Political Liberalism*, exp. edn. (New York: Columbia University Press, 2005), 442 (emphasis added). I return to this issue when considering the notion of a hiatus at the end of this section.

Pettit's inquiry into collective selfhood and identity over time obliquely exposes what is at stake in the responsive framing of questions by collectives: '[A] group will be unable to present itself as an effective promoter of its purpose if it routinely seeks to establish consistency and coherence in the cases envisaged by renouncing one or other of its past commitments; if it never allows its present judgment to be dictated by past judgments, there will be no possibility of taking the pronouncements of such an inconstant entity seriously'.[36] If a group is to be a constant entity that can be taken seriously, it must stick, by and large, to its prior commitments, commitments that restrict the range of responsive options available to the group when affronting new challenges. Absent this relative constancy over time, there could be no collective *self*-identification nor collective identity over time as 'intertemporal respons*a*bility', as one might put it.[37] Thus far Pettit. This insight, which already bespeaks the responsive framing of questions, can be honed yet further: the *joint commitment to realizing a normative point that determines whether a collective can be 'taken seriously' also determines which challenges to that commitment can be 'taken seriously' by the collective*. What a legal collective cannot take seriously is the flip side of 'taking rights seriously'.[38] Remember the mirth and derision with which the *autoréduction* was greeted by some of the participants on the blog. What cannot be taken seriously by a collective can lead to laughter by its participants, which, as Plessner notes, speaks to the collapse of meaning in the face of a boundary situation.[39] There is, however, a second possibility, namely, that what cannot be taken seriously by a collective evokes *indifference* among its participants. The quandaries confronting a theory of civil disobedience that would exhort 'disaffected minorities' to exercise political pragmatism if they want to be listened to, couching their claims in terms the majority can understand and be moved by, return to undermine the view that question and response are the poles of a dialogue governed by the principle of reciprocity. The responsiveness available to a legal collective that would change over time, while also sustaining and reidentifying itself as a self, hides a blind spot which bursts the reciprocity of the hallowed principle of constitutional dialogue: *audi alteram partem*.[40] This blind spot intimates a question that exceeds the practical question to which a collective can respond by reordering legal boundaries; as such, it intimates an 'impractical'—or more precisely an *impracticable*—question: the unorderable.

Accordingly, the double asymmetry between the precedence of a-legality and the retroactivity of collective responses attests to a *hiatus* between the question a-legality addresses to a legal collective and the practical question to which the collective can respond. On the one hand, there could not be a hiatus unless

[36] Pettit, *A Theory of Freedom*, 112.

[37] I borrow the expression 'responsability' from Peter Fitzpatrick, *Modernism and the Grounds of Law* (Cambridge: Cambridge University Press, 2001), 76.

[38] Ronald Dworkin, *Taking Rights Seriously* (Cambridge, MA: Harvard University Press, 1978). I am grateful to Bart van Klink for having drawn my attention to this point.

[39] See section 1.4.

[40] Tully, *Strange Multiplicity*, 115. See also the references to this principle in his *Public Philosophy in a New Key*, vol. 1 (Cambridge: Cambridge University Press, 2008), esp. 151–152; 201; 291–316.

there were a *relation* between its two poles; but, on the other, there could be no hiatus unless there is also a *non-relation* between them. The strangeness of a-legality resides in this hiatus. Ultimately, the 'a' of a-legality refers to practical possibilities which remain definitively inaccessible to a collective because it can only render practical possibilities accessible to itself by raising and answering the question: what* ought *our* joint action to be about? The assimilation of the strange has already begun when one takes for granted that the question posed by a-legal behaviour is nothing other and nothing more than the question concerning what* our joint action ought to be about. As a result, the acts of boundary-setting, whereby a collective reidentifies itself by indicating who ought to do what, where, and when for the sake of φ, display a *finite responsiveness* to what questions legal boundaries, which means that those acts frame a-legal situations in such a way that these provoke the collective self with a *finite questionability*—a questionability it can deal with. And this, in turn, is to aver that a-legality confronts collective self-reidentification with *normative fault lines* that mark the end of legal ordering, as much as with limits which can be shifted by including what had been excluded or excluding what had been included. A finite questionability and a finite responsiveness are constitutive features of the ontology of legal collectives.

6.6 COLLECTIVE TRANSFORMATION

The foregoing sections have sketched out the main contours of a general theory of collective self-identification. But it remains unclear how the *transformation* of a collective over time takes place in the process whereby a collective reidentifies itself when responding to a-legality. If the 're' of reidentification is indispensable to the continuity of collective identity, in what way might it also be indispensable to its transformation? This shift of fronts evokes the problem of *change*, a problem that harks back to Aristotle. This problem is of central importance to our enquiry because, although legal collectives are forcibly limited, in time as much as in space, and personally no less than materially, this says nothing about the transformation and transformability of legal collectives and their boundaries and limits. True, there is yet a further problem about transformation that demands our attention, namely the transformation which gives rise *to* a collective, and not merely the transformation *of* a collective during its career. How would reidentification play a role in both forms of transformation, if they are different? These issues come to a head in the problem of *rupture* and its modalities: what sense can be made of transformation as the rupture of collective identity, if transformation takes place as a process of *re*-identification? I will argue that the paradox of collective self-reidentification, albeit now in the guise of a paradox of constituent power, casts new light on these issues.

It may be helpful to elaborate on an example with a view to conceptualizing legal change. I draw again on the *Van Gend & Loos* ruling of the European Court of Justice, but steering clear of the technicalities of the doctrine of direct effect and focusing, instead, on the general features of collective transformation. It may suffice to note that, by introducing direct effect, the Court empowers individuals to invoke and rely on provisions of binding European law before national courts, if those provisions meet certain conditions. In a word, private actors are empowered to act as a specific kind of political actors: market citizens.[41]

The reasoning underpinning the introduction of direct effect is of interest with a view to understanding the nature of collective transformation. The following passage is the heart of the ruling: 'The objective of the EEC Treaty, which is to establish a Common Market, the functioning of which is of direct concern to interested parties in the Community, implies that this Treaty is more than an agreement which merely creates mutual obligations between the contracting States'.[42] On the one hand, the Court claims that it exercises norm-creating power within the scope of the law: the Court as a constituted power. On the other, the Court effectively exercises power over the scope of the law, to the extent that its ruling posits the European Community not only as a community of states, but also and primordially as a community of 'market citizens': the Court as constituent power. In the very same act by which the Court claims to act within the scope of the powers conferred on it by the Treaties, it effectively acts *ultra vires*, conferring powers on individuals, enabling them to invoke direct effect, and on itself, declaring itself competent to act as a constitutional court. Remember, in this context, that both the Netherlands and Belgium had challenged the jurisdiction of the Court to deliver a preliminary ruling on an issue raised by a private person, on grounds that the question whether the norms of European Community law prevail over national law fell squarely within the jurisdiction of the national courts.

The cited consideration of *Van Gend & Loos* has the structure of innovation by transgression. If I may be allowed to play with the technical notion of an *acquis communautaire*,[43] the Court's ruling transgresses 'acquired' community in view of 'acquiring' a community. The acquired reading of the Treaty, with respect to which the ruling is both blatant transgression and daring innovation, was, of course, that the Treaty, turning the Court's own words against it, is nothing but 'an agreement which merely creates mutual obligations between the contracting States'.

Innovation by transgression has two different but interrelated aspects which require our attention here. First, *Van Gend & Loos* deploys a creativity which is irreducible to the acquired meaning of the Treaty. Although the Court's teleological reasoning is, retroactively, a possible reading of the Treaty, it is by no means, as the ECJ suggests, an 'implication' thereof. The Court's argumentation dries up long before it has been able to provide a 'sufficient reason' for its ruling. Accordingly, the Court cuts off further discussion by appealing to a *circular* reasoning. For the claim that the Treaty is more than an ordinary treaty

[41] For a good overview of the doctrine of direct effect, see Paul Craig and Gráinne de Búrca, *EU Law: Text, Cases, and Materials*, 4th edn. (Oxford: Oxford University Press, 2008), 268 ff.

[42] Case 26/62, *Van Gend & Loos* [1963] ECR 12.

[43] According to the Glossary of the European Union, the Community *acquis* is 'the body of common rights and obligations which bind all the Member States together with the European Union'. See: <http://europa.eu/legislation_summaries/glossary/community_acquis_en.htm> (accessed on 13 February 2013).

under international law only holds if one presupposes that the functioning of a Common Market is not of 'direct concern' only to the states but also to individuals, that is, only if one presupposes that the Treaty is not an ordinary treaty under international law![44] Yet it would be a grave mistake to simply write off the Court's reasoning as specious. What the circularity makes clear is that legal transformation involves a rupture which cannot be fully bridged in terms of 'deliberation' or 'reason-giving', the traditional hallmark of rationality, practical or otherwise. Against Gadamer and Heidegger, *Van Gend & Loos* shows that the 'circle of understanding' operant in legal interpretation can only be productive if it is vicious.[45] The rupture that accompanies collective transformation goes hand in hand with a rupture in legal rationality. Second, what is acquired by transgressing the established order becomes itself a part of established order. Innovation—by definition the manifestation of unorthodoxy—congeals into orthodoxy. The transgression of the acquired interpretation of the Treaty introduces a novel normative meaning that becomes available for reiterative anticipation in the ordinary course of joint action.

The innovative transgression wrought by this landmark case illustrates the basic structure of the transformation of a collective over time, and of the rupture of collective identity which accompanies it. While the paradox of constituent power points to a remarkable disorganization and reorganization of the four dimensions of legal order, I will limit myself hereinafter to the transformation of a legal collective as a spatio-temporal unity.

Remember, to begin with, that in the ordinary course of events, past, present, and future are sutured together in such a way that the past determines the where of joint action, now and into the future. Joint action under law in the mode of understanding has the structure of a reiterative anticipation: one knows what one has to do when one enters the food store to buy some victuals on one's way to a party—one does what oneself and others have done countless times in the past. By contrast, the exercise of constituent power disrupts the spatio-temporal unity of joint action. Instead of projecting the past into the future, constituent power retrojects the future into the past. Indeed, *Van Gend & Loos* anticipates what a European collective ought to be about, casting this anticipation back into the past, such that *what is held to have already taken place is what is yet to come*. This retrojective projection captures the rupture and disorganization of temporal unity that governs all new answers to the practical question about the normative point of joint action. No less importantly, it also captures the rupture and

[44] A similar circularity is at work in the crucial recital of the *Costa* v. *ENEL* judgment of the European Court of Justice: 'The law stemming from the Treaty, an independent source of law, could not because of its special and original nature, be overridden by domestic legal provisions, however framed, without being deprived of its character as community law and without the legal basis of the Community itself being called into question'. In the very process of deriving the supremacy of the Community legal order from its status as 'an independent source of law', the Court attributes supremacy to the Community legal order, thereby *instituting* it as 'an independent source of law'—and itself as the constitutional court of the European Community. See Case 6/64, *Costa* v. *ENEL* [1964] ECR 594.

[45] Hans-Georg Gadamer, *Truth and Method*, 2nd edn., trans. Joel Weinsheimer and Donald G. Marshall (London: Continuum Books, 2005), 267 ff; Heidegger, *Being and Time*, 194–195.

disorganization of spatial unity which accompanies collective transformation. Indeed, what is retrojected into the past is the European Community as a novel unity of ought-places. Whereas it had been a spatial unity in which private actors were only empowered to engage in economic behaviour in line with the so-called 'four freedoms', the signatory states are retroactively deemed to have joined into a spatial unity in which a novel kind of behaviour ought—is empowered—to take place, namely, the participation of private actors, via the preliminary reference procedure, in the political process of defining what counts as the commonality of the common market. To the extent that the initiative concerning what* our joint action ought to be about is taken up and carried forward by its addressees, space and time reorganize themselves into a novel first-person plural spatio-temporal unity that consolidates itself as the reiterative anticipation deployed by legal intentionality and the 'uninterrupted continuity' of collective identity over time—for the time being.

In short, *Van Gend & Loos* resets the boundaries of the European Community by redrawing the limit between what is important and relevant to the collective and what is not. It answers in a new way the practical question concerning what* joint action by the European collective ought to be about. And this means that it answers in a new way the question concerning the objectivity or rationality of behaviour (see section 4.5): what counts as: (i) the collective to which an act can be attributed as its own; (ii) the interconnected distribution of ought-places, times, subjects, and act-contents that constitutes the realm of practical possibilities made available for joint action under law; (iii) the normative point of joint action. If, initially, only agency by Member States had been deemed important and relevant with a view to determining the normative point of joint action by the European collective, agency to this effect by market actors is now also deemed to always have been important and relevant. What, in the inaugural closure, had been pushed out into the domain of the unordered as irrelevant and unimportant, is brought into the European legal order by way of an empowerment that grants novel rights and obligations to private actors. Who ought to do what, where, and when is determined in a new way. And this means that the transformation of the European Community has two mutually implicating aspects: the European Community *identifies* itself in a new way, *distinguishing* itself in a novel way from the rest—from the unordered domain of non-law.

The transformation of the limit between legal (dis)order and the unordered implies that the Court acted from *within and without* the European collective. That the Court acted *ultra vires* in *Van Gend & Loos* should be taken literally: in rendering its judgment, the Court stood outside of the EEC. The Court acted from a place that was not an ought-place in the EEC, i.e. a place where an act ought—is empowered—to take place. Constituent power is by definition not situated in the place which it configures as an ought-place. The Court's ruling, like all exercise of constituent power, *immerges* into a legal order from the domain of the unordered. The Court's ruling has the irruptive force of an a-legal act. It caught the participants by surprise, as something they had not and could not anticipate in terms of the realm of practical possibilities opened up by the Treaty. The Court's ruling empowers private actors and itself, introducing practical possibilities that had been marginalized, even if not explicitly, in the process of European integration. Yet the Court also claimed to act as a constituted power, and could retroactively appear as such, to the extent that it secured uptake for its innovation by these actors and the Member States, including national judiciaries in the course of preliminary reference procedures. The Court sought to reveal possibilities that could appear to participants as their *own* possibilities in the course of joint action by the European collective. Retroactively, and to the extent that private actors exercised their new powers with the acquiescence of the Member States and their judiciaries, the Court could be seen as having acted in conformity with the 'spirit' of the Treaty and its terms of empowerment, hence as located *inside* the EEC. The Court's ruling could belatedly appear to have broken an agreement to be able to keep it, thereby acting *intra vires*.

Let us consider in closer detail how the disarticulation/rearticulation of spatio-temporal unity illuminates the relation between practical possibilities and collective transformation. In effect, legal collectives change over time by actualizing practical possibilities of their own which had been excluded. Yet if the range of practical possibilities available to a collective is given in advance, then the potential vectors of collective change are predetermined from the very start. A collective's 'own' possibilities would speak, in good Aristotelian fashion, to the actualization of forms contained inchoately in the collective's point of departure. Change would be but the ex-plication—literally the unfolding or deployment—of possibilities im-plied in the origin. But then the paradox of representation would collapse into a form of originalism: the possible trajectories of a legal collective would already be laid down at its origin, and collective transformation would be no more than the repetition of these original possibilities, or the deviation therefrom. Such is, indeed, Schmitt's claim about the *Landnahme* which gives rise to a collective: 'all subsequent regulations... are either a continuation of the original basis or a disintegration of and departure from the constitutive act of land-appropriation...'.[46] Strictly speaking, there would be no novelty, nor could one speak of collective transformation as involving the *rupture* of collective identity. Importantly, this reading of the relation between change and possibility lies at the heart of all theories that would view collective transformation as a *dialectical* process, including Ricœur's. The fundamental claim of dialectical theories of collective transformation boils down to this: *to change is to become who we already are, albeit potentially*. This would be the way that collective *re*identification assures collective identity over time, while also allowing for the transformation of joint action. The dialectical movement from potentiality to actuality restages, in its own way, the Aristotelian movement leading from *dynamis* to *energeia*.

The temporal *décalage* wrought by constituent power suggests, however, a different reading of the relation between transformation and practical possibilities. The surprise, even shock, with which *Van Gend & Loos* was greeted, attests to the fact that direct effect was not a possibility that had been contemplated in advance, and which was held in reserve until such time as it would be appropriate

[46] Schmitt, *Nomos of the Earth*, 78 (translation altered).

to introduce it. In this sense, direct effect was not a practical possibility waiting to be ex-plicated as the im-plication of the Treaty, the Court's assertion to this effect notwithstanding ('The objective of the EEC Treaty... *implies*...'). Nor is direct effect a practical possibility that the Court merely reads into the Treaty, whereby the Treaty functions as the docile and acquiescent screen onto which the Court arbitrarily projects its views about the normative point of European integration. For then it would be meaningless to speak of *our own* possibilities; anything and everything would go. To succeed, the Court's initiative must show that direct effect meshes well with and enhances the repertoire of empowerments available to participant agents with a view to realizing the normative point of European integration. The innovation introduced by *Van Gend & Loos* is analogous to 'working or constitutive language' in literature, whereby 'constituted language, suddenly off center and out of equilibrium, reorganizes itself to teach the reader—and even the author—what he never knew how to say or think'.[47] *Van Gend & Loos* catches 'us', the European collective, by surprise, evincing a practical possibility 'we' knew nothing about until the ruling, yet which, *après coup*, can appear as *our own* possibility, a possibility we do well to exploit (Schmitt: *weiden*) because it provides an effective way of dealing with the problems to which European integration is a response. Only retroactively, and to the extent that the Court's initiative caught on, can European integration appear to be no more than the process of actualizing a practical possibility 'implied' in the Treaties.

To sum up, the Court's initiative to empower economic agents as market citizens must show that direct effect is faithful to—honours—the original terms of empowerment, yet an original empowerment which only becomes manifest retroactively—in the ruling that introduces direct effect. It is in this way that reidentification is at work in collective transformation: the novel identification of a collective, and of who ought to do what, where, and when for the sake of φ, comes about *après coup*. The 're' of reidentification speaks in such cases to the retrojective anticipation wrought by constituent power, that is, to collective change as the *postponement* (etymologically: 'post' + 'ponere', to place later) of collective identity, not to a 'dialectic' of self and other than self, as Ricœur and many others would have it. Inasmuch as the transformation of a legal collective involves resetting the boundaries that establish who ought to do what, where, and when, thereby resetting the limit between collective self and other than self, legal transformation comes about as the deferral or postponement of collective identity.[48]

[47] Maurice Merleau-Ponty, *Prose of the World*, trans. John O'Neill (Evanston, IL: Northwestern University Press, 1973), 14.

[48] I draw here on Derrida's notion of *différance*. Seyla Benhabib's conceptualization of 'iteration' in what she calls 'democratic iterations', and which she attributes to Derrida (wrongly, in my opinion), remains firmly anchored in the Hegelian dialectic, when she advocates 'a postmetaphysical and postnational conception of cosmopolitan solidarity which increasingly brings all human beings, by virtue of their humanity alone, under the net of universal rights'. See Seyla Benhabib, *The Rights of Others* (Cambridge: Cambridge University Press, 2004), 21; 179–180; Seyla Benhabib, 'Another Cosmopolitanism', in Robert Post (ed.), *Another Cosmopolitanism* (Oxford: Oxford University Press, 2006), 47–48.

6.7 THE EMERGENCE OF A NOVEL LEGAL COLLECTIVE

The foregoing considerations hold, arguably, for the transformation *of* a collective over time; after all, the Court understood itself as bound by the Treaty: its rulings claim to honour and uphold joint action by the European collective in the very process of transforming its terms. The Court's ruling sought to reveal and incorporate practical possibilities as the participant agents' own possibilities for their *continued* participation in joint action under law. But would not another account of transformation be demanded by the act of constituent power that gives rise *to* a legal collective? In contrast to the novelty afforded by the deferral or postponement of collective identity, the emergence of a new collective and collective identity calls for a stronger sense of novelty and rupture. Whereas *Van Gend & Loos* deployed a weak form of constituent power, the exercise of constituent power in its full sense opens up a new realm of practical possibilities that are no longer the realization of an extant collective's own range of possibilities. Can we make sense of this rupture in terms of collective self-*re*identification? Would it not demand an act of collective self-identification?

To get our bearings it may be helpful to begin by briefly considering and rejecting the powerful interpretation of rupture and constituent power recently advanced by Emilios Christodoulidis. Vigorously opposing those interpretations of constituent power—including my own—that would level it down to reformism, Christodoulidis asserts that revolutionary constituent power manifests itself as the 'pure presentation of a collectivity that calls itself to presence in a sovereign moment of immediacy, in a process of assembling itself'.[49] The claim that constituent power is the 'pure' self-gathering of a collective seeks to dissolve the paradoxes we have discussed into a simple disjunction between two terms, to then favour the first term of the disjunction: either constituent power or constituted power—so, constituent power; either presence or representation—so, presence; either identification or reidentification—so, identification. In a word, the objection amounts to a plea for originalism: there is an original 'self-assembly' in which a multitude gather together and are immediately present to themselves as a unity in action. 'At the moment of the undertaking of praxis, and it is in the modality of the present-future that praxis needs to be understood... the subject of praxis as multitude remains an "open set of relations" understood as unity in respect of a *projected* telos...'.[50] This moment of immediacy, of immediate self-identity, is the moment of 'truth', of 'unity', and of 'radical equality', all in one; *ens et bonum et verum et unum convertuntur*, as the Schoolmen would put it.

Most generally, I share Christodoloudis' worry that many, perhaps most, legal theories are bereft of an account of legal rupture to the extent that they focus primarily or even exclusively on legal transformation. My interest in highlighting the category of fault lines as irreducible to that of limits runs parallel, in some ways,

[49] Emilios Christodoulidis, 'Against Substitution: The Constitutional Thinking of Dissensus', in *The Paradox of Constitutionalism*, 195.

[50] Christodoulidis, 'Against Substitution', 197.

to his insistence on the need to recover a strong sense of rupture for legal theory.[51] Furthermore, as concerns constituent power in particular, Christodoulidis is no doubt correct to note that there can be no 'subject of praxis' unless those who compose the plural subject understand themselves as a 'unity in respect of a *projected* telos . . .'. The problem is, however, that a multitude cannot become a unity unless individuals—call them activists, militants, or what you will—seize the initiative to say what* joint action should be about in light of what* they claim we already are.[52] 'In the postmodern era, as the figure of the people dissolves, the militant is the one who best expresses the life of the multitude', Negri and Hardt tell us.[53] In addition to resistance, they further note, militancy aims to bring about 'the collective construction and exercise of a counterpower capable of destroying the power of capitalism and opposing it with an alternative program of government'.[54] Which is simply another way of saying that the militant *represents* the multitude as putative unity, retrojecting into the past a *telos* which is yet to be realized. This retrojective anticipation would allow a manifold of individuals—a multitude—to view themselves as members of a group who act together. Thus the multitude are gathered together before they can gather themselves into a unity; only retroactively, if the militants secure uptake by those they summon to act together, does the self-constitution of a collective cease to be merely the constitution *of* a collective self to become, for the time being, the constitution of a legal order *by* a collective self. The political use of indexicals is once again destabilized by the paradox of representation: the utterance, 'we assembled together here and now', leads back to a past that was never a present and to a place that was never here. Negri and Hardt's claim that 'revolutionary political militancy' is 'not representational but constituent activity' is quite simply (dis)ingenuous.

I am not merely quibbling about words, nor is my point only conceptual. Because there can be no gathering together of a multitude into a collective subject without acts that seize the initiative to include and exclude, any characterization of constituent power that either downplays or elides the closure that gives rise to joint action by a legal collective runs the risk of eliciting what it would hold at bay: 'there is no need to assume [that unity] will be policed through terror'.[55] The emergence of a novel collective always involves an element of conquest; it is never only a 'project of love'.[56] Negri and Hardt spell out in a remarkably candid way what is at stake in a theory of emergent legal collectives that would release constituent power of the paradox of representation: revolutionary political militancy today, or so they claim, 'is linked to a new world, a world that knows no

[51] See Emilios Christodoulidis, 'Strategies of Rupture', *Law and Critique* 20, no. 1 (2009), 3–36, and Emilios Christodoulidis, 'End of History Jurisprudence: Dworkin in South Africa', in F. Du Bois (ed.), *The Practice of Integrity: Reflections on Ronald Dworkin and South African Law* (Cape Town: Juta, 2004), 64–85.

[52] For an incisive criticism of Negri's theory of constituent power and militancy, see Bert van Roermund, 'Constituerende macht, soevereiniteit en representatie', *Tijdschrift voor Filosofie* 64, no. 3 (2002), 509–532.

[53] See Antonio Negri and Michael Hardt, *Empire* (Cambridge, MA: Harvard University Press, 2000), 411. Notice how the paradox of representation is secretly doing all the work in the term 'expresses'.

[54] Negri and Hardt, *Empire*, 412.

[55] Christodoulidis, 'Against Substitution', 197.

[56] Negri and Hardt, *Empire*, 413.

outside. It knows only an inside, a vital and ineluctable participation in the set of social structures, with no possibility of transcending them'.[57] 'A world that knows no outside'—I cannot think of a more compact formulation of politics as a project of totalization, nor of politics as stasis. Novelty comes, when it comes, from the outside.

But how? In what way does the novelty that gives rise to a collective differ from the novelty that transforms an extant collective? The difficulty raised by this question is to offer an answer that is neither circular nor abstract. It would be circular if one were to define emergent collectivity in terms of a novel first-person plural perspective or a novel plural subject, for then we are back at square one: what renders that perspective or plural subject 'novel'? It would be abstract to assert that a legal collective emerges with the enactment of a 'first constitution', that is, with an act of law-making that is not the exercise of a legal competence. One way of moving beyond these difficulties is to assert that a legal collective emerges by *breaking out* of an extant collective. To borrow Husserl's expression, a collective emerges when behaviour occupies and consolidates itself in what had been the 'empty outside' of joint action by an extant collective. As we have seen, the empty outside is the domain of practical possibilities which have been marginalized as irrelevant and unimportant to joint action. To occupy this outside is to open up a realm of practical possibilities which are not available to joint action within, even though the occupation takes place *inside* the collective whence it would break out of. In such cases, breaking out of a collective has the form of an occupation that irrupts into the collective. Consequently, the characterization of transformation as *innovative transgression* also holds for emergent collectivity.

In their own ways, and with different levels of intensity and success, the 'Occupy Wall Street' movement, the Quebecer secessionist movement and the insurrection of May 1968, irrupt into extant legal orders, revealing practical possibilities and forms of empowerment that are not available to the collective into which they irrupt. But the breaking out of an extant legal collective, which marks emergent collectivity, also takes place, albeit much less spectacularly, in all forms of global law. For example, the new *lex mercatoria* emerges when state law proves incapable of adequately regulating transnational commercial transactions.[58] 'Incapable' alludes here to the practical possibilities which have been marginalized by the normative point of joint action under state law. On this reading, *lex mercatoria*, or more exactly, the panoply of sectoral self-regulating collectives clustered under this general moniker, emerges by breaking out of state law, occupying the empty outside of state law by opening up a realm of practical possibilities irreducible to empowerment under state law. The occupation of the domain of transnational commerce by the new merchant law has its most visible emplacement in the headquarters of the arbitration tribunals which settle disputes between participants in transnational business transactions. The reference to arbitration tribunals is important because the occupation of an empty outside must consolidate itself if it is to give rise to a novel legal collective,

[57] Negri and Hardt, *Empire*, 413.

[58] Stein, *Lex Mercatoria*, 16 ff.

putting into place second-level organs that authoritatively monitor and uphold joint action and its normative point. The fierce resistance of state authorities and of state-centred legal doctrine to the new merchant law, at least during its initial stages, attests to the fact that 'breaking out of' state law involves, to a lesser or greater extent, an act of force. *Lex mercatoria* conquers, imposes itself; it takes land away from states and other collectives. Regardless of whether it is the object of jubilation or defenestration, legal pluralization is never a neutral event.

Moreover, each of these examples—'Occupy Wall Street', Quebecer secessionism, the May 1968 insurrection and *lex mercatoria*—shows that a legal collective emerges as a response to a question. In each of these examples, breaking out of an extant legal collective is not only to break out of its responses to the question about joint action but also to effect a rupture with the *kinds* of questions to which it can give a response, if it is to sustain itself over time as a self and as the same. Giving a twist to Pettit's account of collective identity over time, to break out of a legal collective is to 'take seriously' those very questions that cannot be taken seriously by an extant collective. This is what happened with *lex mercatoria*, inasmuch as state law could not take seriously, nor respond adequately to, the needs of merchants engaged in transnational commerce. So also the Declaration of the Occupation of New York, which urges its addressees to 'create a process to address the problems we face, and generate solutions accessible to everyone...'. Notice how 'addressing the problems we face' runs over into its inverted form: not only must 'we' (who are already a unity) determine and address those problems which extant collectives leave unresolved, but, conversely, to identify a problem is to begin to identify—to summon into being—the 'we' in joint action which could solve it. It would not be difficult to show that the same pattern governed the insurrection of May 1968, and Quebecer secessionism. It is also the pattern which drove the enactment of the European Economic Community, which emerged as a response to questions that could not be responded to by its Members States, individually considered. To press home this point one last time: the first-person plural perspective comes second, and the second person, first; us is prior to we.

6.8 COLLECTIVE DE-IDENTIFICATION

The foregoing analyses sought to illuminate how collective self-reidentification governs the emergence and transformation of legal collectives. To this effect I have taken for granted that boundary-setting and collective self-reidentification are correlative terms. Yet there is a third possibility which has escaped our attention thus far, and which moves in precisely the opposite direction: boundary-setting as a mode of *collective de-identification*. This third possibility leads back to and carries forward the discussion of the exception and public order, as outlined in section 5.3. At issue is the nature of boundary-setting when authorities claim that they confront an acute challenge to public order.

An illustration of what this concretely means are the events that took place at Italy's Lampedusa Airport Zone temporary holding centre for asylum-seekers (CPTA), when 1,787 foreign nationals, including men, women, and children, reached the island between 29 September and 8 October 2004. Amnesty

International reports that 'the Lampedusa centre ... was then closed to outside visitors, on security grounds: no public telephone was available for the use of detainees who were effectively cut off from the outside world'.[59] It goes on to state that

> it was not until 6 October 2004, some five days after requesting authorization and, 'following the return by air of more than 1,000 persons to Libya', that [UNHCR] was granted access to Lampedusa centre which it then entered on 7 October. Its preliminary evaluation was that 'the rushed methods used to sort out the incoming persons by nationality' had 'not allowed individual persons from all national groups concerned to claim asylum'.[60]

A similar incident took place in March 2005. In both cases, no lawyers, judges, journalists, members of parliament, or NGOs were allowed into the centre while it was closed off.

Not Amnesty International's reports of allegations of 'physical assault by law enforcement officers' and other personnel of the centers, not the 'excessive and abusive administration of sedative and tranquilizing drugs', not the 'unhygienic living conditions', not the 'unsatisfactory medical care', and the like are most fundamentally at stake at what took place during those events, from the perspective of the process of boundary-setting. What is essential to this effect is the status of the individuals who 'stayed' at the centre during those periods. According to the Italian government, CPTAs (*Centri di Permanenza Temporanea e Assistenza*) are

> the instrument selected to enable the provisions for the repatriation of aliens who have entered Italy illegally to be carried out more effectively ... they are also one of the key means of ensuring the effective functioning of expulsion procedures which ... is a pre-condition for the correct implementation of an immigration policy based on annual quotas.[61]

In this respect, Amnesty International has expressed serious reservations about the *detention* of asylum-seekers in CPTAs, arguing that such detention is disproportionate in the face of international standards. The Italian government has countered this critique by saying that asylum-seekers are 'held' (*trattenuti*), rather than detained, at the Lampedusa CPTA. The distinction is crucial, albeit in a way different to that intended by the Italian government. To qualify an asylum-seeker as a detainee is to recognize that he or she is *misplaced*, thus that, although illegally, he or she has entered a legal space. Entry to the Italian legal space is precisely what the holding centre at Lampedusa is designed to avoid: expulsion without even the minimal guarantees of due process counts as the 'pre-condition' for immigration policy respectful of due process.

Lampedusa lays bare the following paradox at the heart of collective self-reidentification: the founding self-closure of a collective calls forth the

[59] Amnesty International, 'Italy. Temporary Stay—Permanent Rights: The treatment of foreign nationals detained in "temporary stay and assistance centres" (CPTAs)', 31. Report published on 20 June 2005, available at: <http://www.unhcr.org/refworld/country,,AMNESTY,,ITA,,43b14cd04,0.html> (accessed on 12 February 2013).

[60] Amnesty International Report, 32.

[61] Amnesty International Report, 2.

possibility, held in suspense until the circumstances so require, of enforcing the borders of the collective's own territory by *dis*-owning part of that territory. By undoing the concrete unity of territoriality, such that, deprived of its normative dimension, what remains is its purely physical substrate, a parallel detachment takes place with respect to the asylum-seeker, who, divested of her or his status as a legal subject, becomes a human being who can lay claim to nothing more than 'the abstract nakedness of being human'.[62] In the same way that an ought-place ceases to be such, what had been legal power now comes to stand, as naked power, over and against this abstract nakedness. Accordingly, in the same move by which a legal collective dis-owns part of its territory, the collective's legal officials cease to be such in their treatment of asylum-seekers: to dis-own a place is to disavow the acts that occur therein as acts of legal officials, bringing to a halt the self-reference of a legal collective, hence the possibility of collective *self*-reidentification. That individuals were 'held' at the Lampedusa centre, as the Italian government argued, is exact: *tenes corpus* is an accurate description of the factual relation between the personnel of the centre and the individuals who populated it during the events of October 2004 and March 2005.

As concerns the EU, of which Italy is a Member State, enforcing the boundaries between an internal and an external market was deemed to require compromising the very rule of law on which the Area of freedom, security and justice (AFSJ) is premised. By suspending the rule of law, legal authorities also suspended the powers they have received to *maintain* law and order. In the course of enforcing the EU's claim to an own place, Lampedusa became unrecognizable as part of the Union's *own* place, legally speaking. One would miss the point if one were to aver that those events unmask the EU as an area of servitude, insecurity, and injustice; more radically, even the possibility of this *ex negativo* characterization disappeared because joint action under law, which could have provided the measure of such a qualification, was suspended with respect to the individuals who populated these 'non-places' and non-times.[63] European public order ultimately 'appears as the common denominator in a society based on democracy and the rule of law' by virtue of suspending democracy and the rule of law.[64]

It was noted earlier that the limit between legal (dis)order and the unordered is neither legal nor illegal, and that this can be traced back to an initial occupation—a *Landnahme*—that is itself neither legal nor illegal. Such an occupation also governs the closure of the European polity, first as an internal market, subsequently as an 'Area of freedom, security and justice'. Events such as those at the Lampedusa CPTA attest to situations in which the conditions which govern the emergence of a collective catch up with it from ahead. The invocation of an acute challenge to public order plays itself out in an act of setting boundaries,

[62] Hannah Arendt, *The Origins of Totalitarianism* (New York: Harcourt Brace, 1951), 297.

[63] Agamben refers to 'absolute non-places with respect to the law' when discussing analogous events in France. It would be more precise to note that, for the duration of these events, the respective centres were non-places and non-times with respect to asylum law. Giorgio Agamben, *State of Exception*, trans. Kevin Attel (Chicago, IL: Chicago University Press, 2005), 51.

[64] European Commission, Communication 459/98, 156.

but boundaries that are not *legal* boundaries. The taking that originates a collective manifests itself indirectly and *après coup* in what authorities deem to be acute situations of public order. *The taking whereby collective self-identification gets going has its inverted image in the abandonment wrought by acts of collective de-identification.*

It must be granted that the possibility of radical challenges to public order, i.e. to the continued existence of a collective as the same and as a self, arises together with the closure that gives rise to that collective. This harsh finding can be partially mitigated by noting, as I have done earlier, that whether or not public order is at stake in a way that calls for collective de-identification is never simply predetermined by these events; it is also, and retroactively, the outcome of an authoritative response whereby a collective's boundaries are set. But to let this caveat do all the work is to leave a crucial problem unaddressed. Collective de-individuation raises the following fundamental question: what qualifies a response as *authoritative?* Indeed, the events that took place in Lampedusa burst the formal approach I have taken to authority, which I have defined in terms of monitoring and upholding joint action under law. The problem of the *normativity* of legal orders and legal ordering becomes most acute in the face of the relation between authority and exceptional measures. To this set of normative problems we must now turn in the closing chapter.

7

A Politics of A-Legality

This final chapter turns to the long postponed problem of the normativity of legal order and ordering. The line of investigation I will be developing should not be surprising and can be introduced in a quite straightforward fashion: how *ought* boundaries to be set? And this means: what *ought* to be included, and what excluded? Indeed, that inclusion and exclusion are not merely descriptive but also—and perhaps more fundamentally—normative categories becomes immediately clear in demands for, say, a 'greater inclusiveness' or the correlative reproach that a legal order 'excludes' or 'marginalizes' individuals and forms of behaviour. The normative ring of inclusion and exclusion is just as strong in demands that certain forms of behaviour be banned, repressed, etc. All of these demands and reproaches are a pervasive feature of how individuals and groups relate to extant legal collectives, and to which these respond, in one way or another, in the course of collective self-identification. By questioning how a collective draws the preferential distinction between legality and illegality, the a-legal calls attention, on the one hand, to how the collective draws the preferential distinction between objectivity and subjectivity, rationality and irrationality. And it questions, on the other, the normativity of a legal order, or more exactly, who *ought* to do what, where, and when. So a main problem of a normative theory of legal ordering is how a collective ought to respond to a-legality. Giving a twist to what Waldenfels calls 'responsive rationality', at issue is a theory of normative responsiveness.[1] I will not be able to fully develop such a theory in the course of this chapter. I will outline the contours of a single, but crucial feature thereof, namely a politics of a-legality which indirectly acknowledges, in the process of setting boundaries, that every legal collective has a blind spot in the form of normative claims that resist integration into the circle of reciprocity and mutual recognition, yet which the collective cannot simply shrug off as specious, other than at the price of falling prey to a *petitio principii*. A politics of a-legality offers, as will transpire, an interpretation of the normativity of legal ordering that takes leave of both particularism and universalism.

7.1. INCLUSION AND EXCLUSION AS A NORMATIVE PROBLEM

This opening section of the chapter effects the transition from a descriptive to a normative account of legal ordering. It evinces the internal connection between the operation of inclusion/exclusion and the central categories which govern

[1] Waldenfels, *Order in the Twilight*, 23 ff.

so much of normative thinking about legal order and legal ordering: equality, (distributive) justice, freedom, and security. Far from being a tangentially normative issue, inclusion/exclusion is the red thread that joins together these categories; conversely, these categories illuminate different facets of the inclusion/exclusion operation as the central normative problem confronting all and sundry legal orders. Although an extended discussion of these four normative categories greatly exceeds the scope of this book, a brief analysis may suffice to support the general thesis that a study of boundaries, limits, and fault lines is not only of decisive importance to a descriptive account of legal ordering but also to a normative theory thereof.

Consider, first, the internal connection between equality and inclusion, as described by Pettit in an important passage of *Republicanism*: 'The inclusivist assumption that each is to count for one, none for more than one... already embodies a sort of egalitarian commitment: it means that the polity is required to treat people as equals'.[2] What is most interesting in this passage is the internal correlation it postulates between inclusion and equality, even though it leaves inclusion as such below the threshold of explicit conceptualization: because equality demands inclusion, and because inclusion is an agent-relative concept, legal and political equality is the name we give to identity as sameness of participants from a first-person plural perspective. Importantly, as has been argued throughout the foregoing chapters, inclusion is fourfold, comprising inclusion in the unitary space, time, content, and subjectivity of joint action. Any attempt to distinguish between 'metaphorical' and 'literal' forms of inclusion is blind to the fundamental structures of inclusion (and exclusion), absent which joint action under law would not be possible. Now, the equality that inclusion in a collective brings about has two aspects. On the one hand, inclusion makes possible equality and inequality in a derivative sense, namely, different roles and a different weighing of the importance of roles in light of the normative point of joint action under law. On the other hand, the fundamental form of equality entailed by inclusion goes hand in hand with a no less fundamental 'inequality', namely what has been excluded as irrelevant and unimportant with respect to joint action under law. Call this contrast Equality/Inequality, with capital letters. All forms of protest about (in)equality indirectly question the Inequality between legal (dis) order and the unordered. In the same way that a-legality reveals legal boundaries to be the limit of a legal order, so also a-legality reveals the intra-ordinal distinction between the equal and the unequal to be the limit between the Equal and the Unequal. In short, all claims and counterclaims about equality and inequality in the law are, at bottom, claims and counterclaims about inclusion and exclusion, hence about the boundaries, limits, and fault lines of legal orders.

It is not otherwise with justice. This follows quite naturally from the formal definition of justice, as the injunction to treat the equal equally, and the unequal unequally. Rather than rehash what I have just said about the relation between inclusion and Equality/Inequality, let me illuminate the point by reference to another, classical formulation of the principle of justice: *suum cuique tribuere*—to

[2] Pettit, *Republicanism*, 110–111.

each their own. Here again, there is an internal connection between justice and legal inclusion. To begin with, at issue is 'their own' in the sense of their own place, time, act-content, and subjectivity. Because a legal order is an interconnected distribution of ought-places, ought-times, ought-act contents, and ought-subjects, it is these four dimensions of behaviour which are distributed by acts of distributive justice. Remember that already in the first chapter I referred to a legal order as an interconnected *distribution* of places, times, subjects, and contents. It is not otherwise with retributive and commutative justice. Moreover, and crucially, it would not be possible to assign to 'each their *own*' unless a first-person plural perspective is taken up whence places, times, subjectivities, and act-contents are meted out. Now, as has been shown previously, there can be no interconnected distribution of ought-places (nor ought-times, etc.) absent a collective self-inclusion and the exclusion of other than self, hence an inclusion of legal (dis)order and the exclusion of the unordered. Consequently, all claims and counterclaims about justice and injustice in the law are, at bottom, claims and counterclaims about inclusion and exclusion, hence about the boundaries, limits, and fault lines of legal orders.

And freedom? According to its timeworn definition, freedom is self-rule. If we look at freedom as it pertains to collectives, self-rule has two dimensions. As collective self-*rule*, more precisely as collective self-*legislation*, freedom involves the collective capacity to establish who ought to do what, where, and when for the sake of φ. In other words, collective freedom involves being able to jointly set the legal boundaries that *constrain* participant agency with a view to realizing the normative point of joint action. As collective *self*-rule or *self*-legislation, collective freedom involves the reflexivity whereby a manifold of individuals jointly rule over themselves as a group. Now neither collective self-*rule* nor collective *self*-rule would be intelligible absent inclusion and exclusion. In fact, the internal connection between both dimensions turns on inclusion and exclusion: it would not be possible to establish who ought to do what, where, and when for the sake of φ absent a collective self-inclusion; conversely, collective self-inclusion takes place by way of a closure that establishes who ought to do what, where, and when for the sake of φ. Accordingly, all discussions about freedom and servitude are discussions about how boundaries (hence constraints) to individual behaviour ought to be drawn, such that individual acts can count as part and parcel of action *by* the collective as a whole. Now this is nothing other than the question about what* ought to be included in legal (dis)order and what* excluded therefrom.

And then security. Note, to begin with, that, as far as collectives are concerned, it would be a mistake to reduce insecurity to specific states of mind of the individuals that compose them, such as fear, unease, or terror. Although these psychological states are certainly an ingredient of collective insecurity, they do not clarify what constitutes it as a legal-political phenomenon. At one level, of course, insecurity registers in the form of legal disorder, hence in the form of illegal acts. This means that illegal acts create a condition of collective insecurity to the extent that they imperil the capacity of a group of individuals to order interpersonal relations in the community for the sake of φ. As such, illegality speaks to insecurity as a specific form of *groundlessness*: the illegal act is groundless because it cannot be attributed to the collective that must authorize it, although it ought to; because it stands isolated from the web of spatial, temporal, subjective, and material web of relations in which it ought to be inserted; and because it misses the normative point of joint action, although it ought to realize it. Accordingly, these three grounds remain more or less unproblematic and taken for granted in the official act that seeks to secure joint action under law by qualifying behaviour as illegal. In other words, the authoritative acts that declare certain acts to be illegal effectively reaffirm the limit between legal (dis)order and the unordered. However, there is a more fundamental, albeit indirect, manifestation of groundlessness, hence of collective insecurity, namely, one whereby a-legality challenges the very distinction between legality and illegality, as drawn by a collective. This is groundlessness or insecurity as *contingency*, which calls into question, with variable degrees of intensity, the three grounds of legal behaviour.[3] I propose, therefore, to differentiate between collective insecurity arising from primary or from secondary challenges to a legal order. Primary challenges call into question the very distinction between legal and illegal acts, as posited in a legal order; secondary challenges do not. At issue in collective security is not only sustaining the legal boundaries which establish who ought to do what, where, and when but also establishing what is to count as included in legal (dis)order and as excluded therefrom, in light of the possibility of fault lines that mark the end of legal ordering and, with it, of a collective. In short, all claims and counterclaims about security and insecurity are, at bottom, claims and counterclaims about inclusion and exclusion, hence about the boundaries, limits, and fault lines of legal orders.

This is admittedly a very brief and abstract presentation of equality, justice, freedom, and security, which would need to be fleshed out more fully and illustrated with concrete examples.[4] But, as indicated at the outset of this section, reasons of space preclude engaging at any length with these four fundamental normative categories; what has been said should suffice to make clear that there is an internal connection between each of these categories and the inclusion/exclusion operation. So in lieu of a systematic account of these normative categories we do well to focus on their unifying theme, working out more fully why the operation of inclusion/exclusion is of capital importance to a normative theory of legal ordering. The remainder of this section lays the groundwork for what later follows by formulating more precisely how the operation of inclusion/exclusion is connected to legal ordering as a normative problem.

A first avenue of approach is, of course, an exploration of the normativity of legal orders. I have been concerned to show that the practical question—what* ought our joint action to be about?—sparked by a-legality can be parsed into three aspects: the collective (our joint action); the legal order (what*); the

[3] For an excellent discussion of the modern conceptualization and experience of contingency, see Hans Blumenberg, 'Kontigenz', in Kurt Galling (ed.), *Die Religion in Geschichte und Gegenwart. Handwörterbuch für Theologie und Religionswissenschaft*, vol. III, 3rd edn. (Tübingen: J.C.B. Mohr, 1959), 1794.

[4] For a fuller development along these lines of collective (in)security and distributive justice in the framework of debates about immigration into the EU as an 'Area of Freedom, Security, and Justice', see Hans Lindahl, 'Border Crossings by Immigrants: Legality, Illegality, and Alegality', *Res Publica* 14 (2008), 117–135, and Hans Lindahl, 'Breaking Promises to Keep Them: Immigration and the Boundaries of Distributive Justice', in *A Right to Inclusion and Exclusion?*, 137–159.

normative point (to be about?). But the fourth aspect of the practical question has thus far been bracketed for expository purposes: what* *ought* our joint action to be about?

True, the problem of the normativity of legal orders and their boundaries is already prefigured by the concept of 'directed' or 'relational' obligation which flows from the notion of joint action. The reader will remember that Gilbert's insight is twofold: first, there is a directed obligation when a specific person owes another specific person or persons a particular action, hence that the latter has/have a right to its performance; second, directed obligations arise from joint commitment. 'By virtue of the existence of the commitment, and that alone, the parties have rights against each other to actions that conform to the commitment. As a result, they have the standing to demand such actions of each other and to rebuke each other for not so acting'.[5] On this plural subject reading of normativity, the legal 'ought' boils down to a species of directed obligations which are to be performed by participant agents in the course of joint action. No less importantly, and though she does not broach this issue, Gilbert's account of directed obligations affords an initial explanation of the normativity of legal boundaries. Not only are directed obligations owed to specific persons, such that they presuppose bounded membership in a plural subject, but they also concern specific ought-places, ought-times, and ought-act contents in a limited legal order. What* ought to be included in legal (dis)order and what* excluded therefrom follows from what we owe to each other as members of a collective in joint action, and vice versa.

While the notion of directed obligation is a first and decisive step towards clarifying the normativity of legal orders, it is necessary to revisit the paradoxical foundation of collectives to understand why legal normativity is, in the strict sense of the word, questionable. The insight that foundation occurs as a re-foundation, such that there is no direct access to the original closure which gives rise to a collective, can be reformulated as follows: the inaugural invocation of a 'we together', when enacting a legal order, presupposes that there is already a *prior* joint commitment by those who will be subject to the order, and which obtains concrete form in the legal rights and obligations which emanate from that joint commitment. In other words, the emergence of a legal collective rests on an initiative that claims *that* there is already a joint commitment to act together and *what** agents owe to each other when engaging in joint action under law. A-legality calls this twofold claim into question, at which point the paradox of (re)foundation kicks in yet a second time: because there is no access to the original joint commitment which is deemed to have given rise to a legal collective, so also the terms of that putative joint commitment, and the legal obligations and rights to which it gives rise, can be redefined in response to a-legality. But how *ought* its terms to be redefined? This is what renders legal ordering a normative problem. In other words, if a-legality indirectly questions how a collective has drawn the limit between legal (dis)order and the unordered, what* ought to

[5] Margaret Gilbert, *A Theory of Political Obligation* (Oxford: Oxford University Press, 2008), 147.

be included in legal (dis)order and what* excluded therefrom in the course of boundary-setting?

A second avenue of approach to legal ordering as a normative problem turns on the concept of legal rationality. The nature of its connection to the operation of inclusion/exclusion should be perspicuous in light of our earlier discussion of the topic. Indeed, to predicate of an act that it is legal is to assert that it is rational or objective by dint of realizing a threefold reference: to a collective; to a unity of places, times, subjects, and act-contents; to the normative point of joint action. Moreover, 'ought' and 'is' flow over into each other in the everyday course of joint action under law: everything is as it ought to be and everything ought to be as it is. To qualify an act as illegal is to view it as irrational or subjective because it fails to realize these three references, although it ought to. 'Ought' and 'is' fall apart, such that what ought to have come about is reaffirmed over and against what actually took place. To this extent, then, legality and illegality leave undisturbed the limit which includes legal (dis)order and excludes the unordered. By disrupting the preferential distinctions which structure the default setting of legal (dis)order, a-legality calls joint action into question: what* ought our joint action to be about? A-legality depletes the normativity of joint action, such that what* our action *ought* to be about loses its straightforwardness, giving way to normative disorientation. To say that what counts as legally rational or irrational has become problematic is to assert that what *ought* to be included in legal (dis)order, and what excluded therefrom, has become problematic.

Consequently, what is at stake in legal rationality as an ordering process is never only establishing what counts as legal and illegal behaviour. Legal rationality is also and more fundamentally oriented to establishing what* ought to be included in legal (dis)order as relevant and important and what* ought to be excluded therefrom as irrelevant and unimportant. Inclusion/exclusion is the fundamental two-faced operation of legal rationality as an ordering process. But the fundamental question confronting rationality is how this limit *ought* to be drawn, when a collective is confronted with a-legality. This is nothing other than the question about the normativity of legal order noted above. The problem confronting a theory of legal rationality as a normative theory of legal ordering is, therefore, the following: how ought we to *respond* to a-legality when setting the boundaries of a legal order? And this means: how to deal with boundaries as limits and as fault lines?

7.2 RECIPROCITY AND A POLITICS OF BOUNDARY-SETTING

Here is where the principle of reciprocity suggests itself as a way of dealing with this normative problem. Although reciprocity has surfaced on various occasions in the previous chapters, the time is now ripe to consider it at greater length. Indeed, a wide range of theories assign a central role to reciprocity when elucidating the normativity of legal order and ordering. Should we follow these theories and accept that the principle of reciprocity offers a normatively adequate account of how we ought to respond to a-legality? To clear the way for answering this question, this section examines three approaches to reciprocity. The first two defend a particularistic reading of reciprocity, i.e. a reading that situates normativity in bounded communities: communitarianism and Rawls' political liberalism; the third, a universalistic reading thereof: Habermas' discourse-theoretical version of cosmopolitanism.

Note, before turning to examine these approaches, that reciprocity is built into the very notion of joint action, inasmuch as normative expectations about who ought to do what, where, and when are deemed to be *mutual* expectations: what I ought to do as a participant agent, what I expect that you ought to do as a participant agent, and what I expect that you expect that I ought to do, are guided by what I take to be our shared understanding of what we ought to do together. We are deemed to have reciprocal expectations as to what* our joint action ought to be about, and we reciprocate in our behaviour to the extent that each of our actions meets those expectations. Participant agents can take for granted that their normative expectations match each other as long as they interact in a way that contributes to pulling off a joint act under law. When breached, these normative expectations remain mutual expectations in the sense of expectations we *ought* to share, given the normative point of joint action. For this reason, rebuking or otherwise sanctioning whoever breaches normative expectations remains within the circle of reciprocity. The problem is when normative expectations are transgressed, that is, when a-legality calls into question the putative reciprocity of joint action.

The theories of reciprocity we will be examining assume that, in such cases, it is necessary to fall back on more general normative expectations that are shared by the participants in joint action, and which allow of settling the dispute concerning what their joint action ought to be about. According to this picture, reciprocity remains the core of legal ordering, in two related ways. On the one hand, the parties to a conflict continue to reciprocate in the sense of giving reasons to each other that could justify the terms of joint action under law. On the other, they continue to reciprocate in that they must appeal to more fundamental shared normative expectations if they are to settle their differences rationally. To this extent all accounts of reciprocity presuppose the symmetry between and reversibility of the positions of the parties in conflict.

This is clearly the case in communitarianism. The 'particularism of history, culture, and membership' entails, or so Michael Walzer argues, that even if individuals are committed to impartiality,

> the question most likely to arise in the minds of the members of a political community is... What would individuals like us choose, who are situated as we are, who share a culture and are determined to go on sharing it? And this is a question that is readily transformed into, What choices have we already made in the course of our common life? What understandings do we (really) share?[6]

When conflict ensues between the members of a political community about what they ought to do jointly, they must fall back on their past, on their common culture, to sort out what ought to be their mutual normative expectations

[6] Michael Walzer, *Spheres of Justice: A Defense of Pluralism and Equality* (New York: Basic Books, 1983), 5.

into the future, such that the identity of the collective can be sustained over time. Reciprocation in the case of conflict is a mutual giving and taking of reasons oriented to establishing 'what understandings we (really) [and already, HL] share' as members of the particular community to which we belong. David Miller makes a comparable point, in his study on nationality, when noting that 'when I identify myself as belonging to a particular nation, I imply that those whom I include as my co-nationals share my beliefs and reciprocate my commitments'.[7] The 'mutual recognition' deployed by the reciprocation of commitments is only possible to the extent that there is a 'national identity', such that 'the people belong together by virtue of the characteristics that they share'—a 'national character' or 'common public culture', as Miller also puts it.[8] Reciprocation in the case of conflict is a process of mutual reason-giving between members that strives to assure the 'historical contin[uity]' of the community into the future by 'reappropriating' its past and its origin 'as our own'.[9] Responsiveness to a-legality means that the limit between legal (dis)order and the unordered ought to be set in a way that is faithful to and reaffirms the past *because it is our own past*. So Miller's thesis leads over into, or at least prepares the way for, its inverted form: we ought to include as our co-members those who share our beliefs and reciprocate our shared commitments.

The assumption that reciprocity should be understood in terms of the reappropriation of, and mutual recognition within, a shared (cultural) identity has met considerable resistance. According to its critics, this view of reciprocity effectively entrenches the dominant cultural identity, whereas it is this very identity which members of the collective seek to question. Moreover, to the extent that the contestation of legal orders inevitably calls into question what is *our own* past, the communitarian interpretation of reciprocity demands deference to certain authorities who are such because, having privileged access to the substantive core of the collective's own past, they can guarantee that boundary-setting *reappropriates* that original past, rather than alienating the community therefrom. In short, a communitarian reading of reciprocity presupposes a form of originalism, an original sphere of 'ownness' that is directly accessible and which can be—and *ought* to be—recovered in its originality in the course of boundary-setting.

John Rawls has formulated the principle of reciprocity germane to joint action (under law) in a way that seems to avoid these problems:

> [T]he question of reciprocity arises when free persons, who have no moral authority over one another and who are engaging in or who find themselves participating in a joint activity, are among themselves settling upon or acknowledging the rules which define it and which determine their respective shares in its benefits and burdens.[10]

[7] David Miller, *On Nationality* (Oxford: Oxford University Press, 1995), 23.

[8] Miller, *On Nationality*, 23, 25.

[9] Miller, *On Nationality*, 23. What MacIntyre has to say about 'desert' holds a fortiori for reciprocity: 'the notion of [reciprocity] is at home only in the context of a community whose primary bond is a shared understanding both of the good for man and of the good of that community and where individuals identify their primary interests with reference to those goods'. Alasdair MacIntyre, *After Virtue*, 3d edn. (London: Duckworth, 2007), 250.

[10] John Rawls, 'Justice as Reciprocity', in Freeman, *Collected Papers*, 208.

This formulation suggests that reciprocity comes to the fore as a normative principle when individuals seek to reach agreement about the terms of joint action, either when entering into it or when renegotiating its terms. No assumption here, or so it seems, of a shared past which circumscribes the circle of reciprocity. As Rawls further explains it, joint action 'will strike the parties as conforming to the notion of reciprocity if none feels that, by participating in it, her or any of the others are taken advantage of or forced to give in to claims which they do not accept as legitimate'.[11] Obligations, legal obligations in particular, derive their binding character from joint action that meets the criterion of reciprocity: 'their engaging in it gives rise to a prima facie duty (and a corresponding prima facie right) of the parties to each other to act in accordance with the practice when it falls upon them to comply'.[12] By settling their differences in accordance with the principle of reciprocity, and discharging their obligations under joint action that satisfies the principle, participants engage in mutual recognition; they 'exhibit their recognition of each other as persons with similar interests and capacities'.[13] Joint action that realizes mutual recognition vouches, in Rawls' view, for a 'well-ordered', i.e. a well-grounded, society. Reciprocation between all participant agents, in response to a-legality, leads to agreement concerning: (i) the collective to which behaviour should be attributed as its own; (ii) who ought to do what, where, and when; (iii) for the sake of φ. In other words, the principle of reciprocity is the normative principle that allows of establishing, directly, what ought to count as (il)legal—hence (ir)rational—behaviour, and, indirectly, what ought to be included in legal (dis)order and excluded therefrom as irrelevant and unimportant.

Rawls' further development of the concept of reciprocity, like that of communitarians, is particularist: it favours closed political collectives as a prior condition for reciprocity;[14] as a result, the closure that gives rise to a polity, including the distinction between member and non-member, is removed from the principle's scope. A wide range of cosmopolitan thinkers have vigorously opposed this particularistic reading of reciprocity. Habermas' discursive reading of practical rationality is one of the most influential cosmopolitan attempts to release reciprocity of this and related strictures. In the framework of a practical discourse among participants who are free and equal, 'everyone is required to take the perspective of everyone else, and thus project herself into the understandings of self and world of all others', or so Habermas argues. And he adds: 'from this interlocking of perspectives there emerges an ideally extended we-perspective from which all can test in common whether they wish to make a controversial norm the basis of their shared practice'.[15] Like Rawls, Habermas argues that the

[11] Rawls, 'Justice as Reciprocity', 208.

[12] Rawls, 'Justice as Reciprocity', 209.

[13] Rawls, 'Justice as Reciprocity', 212.

[14] Rawls, *A Theory of Justice*, 8; Rawls, *Political Liberalism*, 12.

[15] Jürgen Habermas, 'Reconciliation through the Public Use of Reason: Remarks on John Rawls' Political Liberalism', *Journal of Philosophy* 92, no. 3 (1995), 117. Other critical studies of Rawls' restrictive reading of the scope of reciprocity, and which seek to radicalize its universalizing potential, include Charles

key to reciprocity is the capacity of individuals to take up each other's perspectives with a view to reaching agreement on the norms of (joint) action. Unlike Rawls, Habermas stresses that reciprocity deploys an ever greater inclusiveness. Negatively formulated, reciprocity 'de-limits', in the sense that taking up each other's perspectives removes the limits of individual perspectives: 'Discourse ethics... views the moral point of view as embodied in an intersubjective practice of argumentation which enjoins those involved to an idealizing de-limitation (*Entschränkung*) of their interpretive perspectives'.[16]

Accordingly, it is no coincidence that Habermas links rationality to the problem of boundaries in general. As a desideratum, he contends, rationality is 'the injunction to complete inclusion'.[17] On this reading, the internal *telos* of rational human activity is to achieve unity in the sense of *all-inclusiveness*. This injunction does not mean that legal boundaries disappear. If pressed, Habermas and all other advocates of universalism would no doubt concede that legal orders are inconceivable in the absence of the boundaries that determine who ought to do what, where, and when. Instead, the injunction means that legal boundaries are provisional and defeasible in such a way that what a legal order has unjustifiably excluded can be progressively included therein, even if an all-inclusive legal order must be indefinitely postponed in historical time. Habermas forcefully espouses this thesis when describing what he takes to be the normative lodestar of the postnational constellation: 'solidarity with the other *as one of us* refers to the flexible "we" of a community that resists all substantial determinations and extends its permeable boundaries ever further'.[18] Reciprocity, as the rational core of legal ordering, becomes the lynchpin of a politics of inclusion. *To respond is to reciprocate, and to reciprocate is to include the other.*

On this universalistic reading of the principle of reciprocity, an all-inclusive legal order is the normative criterion that allows of establishing what ought to count as (il)legal, hence as (ir)rational. Ultimately, a collective is rational, and that means that legal obligations are fully objective and binding, if and when such obligations: (i) could be authorized by a collective composed of all members of humanity; (ii) in terms of a legal order that determines who ought to do what,

Beitz, *Political Theory and International Relations*, rev. edn. (Princeton, NJ: Princeton University Press, 1999) and Thomas Pogge, *Realizing Rawls* (Ithaca, NY: Cornell University Press, 1989). Other universalizing accounts of reciprocity include Thomas Nagel, *Equality and Partiality* (New York: Oxford University Press, 1991), Seyla Benhabib, *Situating the Self* (London: Routledge, 1992), Rainer Forst, *Contexts of Justice*, trans. John M.M. Farrell (Berkeley, CA: University of California Press, 1994), and Jeremy Waldron, '*Partly Laws Common to All Mankind*'. See also Amy Gutmann and Dennis Thompson, *Democracy and Disagreement* (Cambridge, MA: The Belknap Press, 1996), 52–94.

[16] Habermas, 'Reconciliation through the Public Use of Reason: Remarks on John Rawls' Political Liberalism', 117. For an earlier and more general formulation, see Jürgen Habermas, 'What is Universal Pragmatics?', in Habermas, *Communication and the Evolution of Society*, trans. Thomas McCarthy (London: Heinemann Educational, 1979), 3, 62–63.

[17] Jürgen Habermas, *The Postnational Constellation*, trans. Max Pensky (Cambridge: Polity Press, 2001), 148.

[18] Habermas, *The Inclusion of the Other*, xxxv–xxxvi. Notice that the idea of ever-expanding borders is informed by the Hegelian dialectic, whereby the experience of a limit is to already have moved beyond it. The metaphysical thesis of the passage from the finite into the infinite undergirds Habermas' interpretation of the postnational constellation.

where, and when (iii) for the sake of a normative point of joint action all could agree to.

But there is a latent difficulty in each of the foregoing readings of the principle of reciprocity. In its communitarian form, the problem is, as noted, whether mutual recognition can mean anything other than recognition of the dominant cultural identity. In a somewhat different form the problem reappears in Rawls, to the extent that reciprocation in the course of 'public' reasoning presupposes a prior determination of what counts as *reasonable* disagreement, absent which there could be no mutual recognition of agents 'as persons *with similar interests and capacities*' (emphasis added).[19] Despite all his protestations to the contrary, the problem also surfaces in Habermas when he would have reciprocity enable 'solidarity with the other *as one of us*'. The suspicion arises that all readings of the principle of reciprocity that postulate the reversibility of positions between the parties in conflict end up becoming strategies of assimilation of the other. A reading of reciprocity predicated on the reversibility of perspectives would transform a politics of inclusion into a politics of assimilation.

Such is the objection levelled by Iris Marion Young against what she calls liberal defences of 'liberation as the elimination of group difference'.[20] And she adds: 'if the only alternative to the oppressive exclusion of some groups defined as Other by dominant ideologies is the assertion that they are the same as everybody else, then they will continue to be excluded because they are not the same'.[21] To counter the assimilatory effects of a reading of reciprocity premised on the reversibility of perspectives, Young advocates a politics of difference based on the insight that our perspectives are 'asymmetrical and irreversible'.[22] Importantly, however, the asymmetrical and irreversible positions of parties in conflict still leave room for reciprocity, or so Young argues. A politics of difference turns on asymmetrical reciprocity, which is, in turn, the favoured vehicle of a politics of inclusion: by affirming group difference, 'there is equality among socially and culturally differentiated groups, who mutually respect and affirm one another in their differences'.[23]

Yet can reciprocity be asymmetrical if it is to be reciprocity? Can one do away with the reversibility of positions if, as Young would have it, parties are to mutually recognize and affirm each other as different with the aim of ensuring 'the full participation and inclusion of everyone in a society's major institutions'?[24] How could the affirmation of group difference become the vehicle for inclusion

[19] Rawls, 'Justice as Reciprocity', 208.

[20] Iris Marion Young, *Justice and the Politics of Difference* (Princeton, NJ: Princeton University Press, 1990), 157. Also Taylor's politics of recognition, which he contrasts to a 'politics of equal dignity', can be seen as endorsing a politics of difference. See Charles Taylor, 'The Politics of Recognition', in Amy Gutmann (ed.), *Multiculturalism and the 'Politics of Recognition'* (Princeton, NJ: Princeton University Press, 1992), 25–73.

[21] Young, *Justice and the Politics of Difference*, 168.

[22] Iris Marion Young, 'Asymmetrical Reciprocity: On Moral Respect, Wonder and Enlarged Thought', in Young, *Intersecting Voices* (Princeton, NJ: Princeton University Press, 1997), 46.

[23] Young, *Justice and the Politics of Difference*, 163.

[24] Young, *Justice and the Politics of Difference*, 173.

in a political community unless a claim to difference is presented as being, more fundamentally, a claim to *sameness*? In a decisive passage of a later work, Young notes that the claims to difference invoked by marginalized groups are 'claims for political equality, inclusion, and appeals to justice directed at a wider public which they claim that public *ought to accept*'.[25] The excluded demand that other members of the collective view such claims *as their own*. Notice how reversibility has already crept into a politics of difference. On the one hand, marginalized groups demand of the other members of the collective that they recognize themselves in those whom they have excluded, inasmuch as the normative point of joint action can and should accommodate the demands of the marginalized. On the other, the marginalized recognize themselves in those who have excluded them by demanding inclusion as members in full standing of the collective. Hence it is misguided to defend reciprocity by simply opposing difference to collective identity, arguing that 'groups do not have identity as such'.[26] The 'radical' democratic plurality which Young seeks to affirm by appealing to asymmetrical reciprocity is, from beginning to end, *plurality within the substantive unity of a collective*, a plurality of perspectives unified by a determinate normative point of joint action which is common to all participating individuals and groups, and which they seek to realize in and through their differences. Asymmetrical reciprocity is an oxymoron.

The basic idea which reappears in all of these permutations of reciprocity is the capacity of actors to take up each other's perspectives, in the face of conflict, with a view to rearticulating joint action in such a way that all affected parties can agree to it. Reaching a situation of mutual recognition, when a-legality calls legal (dis)order into question, involves resetting the boundaries of legal (dis)order in a way that elucidates the deeper agreement, the more fundamental unity, which *already* joins the parties in conflict. And that means reaching agreement about the three grounds that allow of qualifying behaviour as legal or illegal: (i) the collective to which an act ought to be imputed, such that all affected parties can say fully and without reservations, '*we* own this act' (our joint action); (ii) an interconnected distribution of ought-places, times, subjects, and act-contents in which joint action ought to play itself out (what*); and (iii) the normative point for the sake of which participant agents ought to engage in joint action (to be about?). Responding to a-legality by reciprocation entails creating a situation in which the boundaries that join and separate who ought to do what, where, and when are viewed by all participant agents as binding because they articulate their *prior* joint commitment to acting together for the sake of φ. A legal order that meets this criterion is 'well-ordered' in Rawls' parlance, that is, well grounded: a rational collective, in the full sense of the term. 'To recognize another as a person one must respond to him and act towards him in certain ways', notes Rawls.[27] The inverted proposition also follows from the principle

[25] Iris Marion Young, *Inclusion and Democracy* (Oxford: Oxford University Press, 2000), 86 (emphasis added).

[26] Young, *Inclusion and Democracy*, 82.

[27] Rawls, 'Justice as Reciprocity', 212–213.

of reciprocity: to respond to someone and act towards him in certain ways is to recognize another as a person. More pointedly, to respond to a-legality, in the spirit of reciprocity, is to include in the legal order what ought not to have been excluded therefrom—in light of the collective's *own* normative views. Accordingly, the principle of reciprocity entails collective self-reidentification as a rational process in which a group conserves itself as a self and as the same over time, while also integrating what *justifiably* questions how it draws the distinction between legality and illegality.

This is the core idea that, cutting across the divide between particularism and universalism, guides how a wide variety of normative theories of law and politics interpret the 'dialogical', 'deliberative', or 'discursive' nature of practical rationality in general, and legal rationality in particular. If the domain of politics includes the authoritative mediation and enforcement of joint action, then a reciprocity-driven politics of boundary-setting, whether premised on particularism or on universalism, advocates what I would like to call the *reducibility thesis*: reasonable political plurality is reducible to—and *ought* to be reduced to—the unity of a legal order. Hans-Georg Gadamer speaks for all devotees of a reciprocity-driven politics of boundary-setting when he asserts that 'social community, with all its tensions and disruptions, ever and ever again leads back to a common area of social understanding through which it exists'.[28]

7.3 THE NON-RECIPROCAL ORIGIN OF RECIPROCITY

The foregoing considerations show that, despite its insistence on the need to accommodate plurality, unity is the *alpha* and the *omega* of a reciprocity-driven politics of boundary-setting: it's *alpha*, in the form of a pre-given unity in the absence of which demands of recognition would not be intelligible as such; it's *omega*, in the form of a more inclusive unity that emerges, if things go well, from mutual recognition. Does this picture do justice to the nature of the closure—hence the inclusion and exclusion—that marks the emergence of a collective? More pointedly: does it do justice to the origin of reciprocity? The question seems legitimate because the genealogical analyses of chapter 4 suggest that legal reciprocity cannot itself *emerge* from a reciprocal act between 'all those affected'; on principle and not merely in fact, legal reciprocity has a non-reciprocal origin that establishes who are 'those affected'.

The concealment of this problem in communitarian thinking about the normativity of legal ordering is particularly clear in Walzer's reflections on distributive justice. 'The idea of distributive justice', he argues, 'presupposes a bounded world within which distributions take place: a group of people committed to dividing, exchanging, and sharing social goods, first among themselves. That

[28] Hans-Georg Gadamer, 'Rhetoric, Hermeneutics, and Ideology-Critique', in Walter Jost and Michael J. Hyde (eds.), *Rhetoric and Hermeneutics in Our Time: A Reader* (New Haven, CT: Yale University Press, 1997), 313–334, 332. Notice the proximity between what Gadamer calls 'a common area of social understanding' and what Rawls dubs an 'overlapping consensus'.

world . . . is the political community'.[29] If distributive justice requires a bounded political community, what is the nature of the closure which gives rise to it? Walzer's own interrogations seem to lead in this direction: 'We assume an established group and a fixed population and so we miss the first and most important distributive question: How is that group constituted?'[30] Having posed this query, one would have expected him to bring the primordial distributive act—the closure that includes a collective self and excludes other than self—within the compass of a theory of distributive justice. For, surely, everything that follows for a theory of distributive justice is contingent on the conditions governing this primordial closure. Remarkably, however, Walzer arrests his analysis just at this point. Having raised the question, 'How is that group constituted?', he immediately qualifies its scope: 'I do not mean, How was it constituted? I am concerned here not with the historical origins of the different groups, but with the decisions they make in the present about their present and future populations'.[31] Despite having insisted that the primary distributive act concerns membership, Walzer removes from a theory of distributive justice the very closure that, including a collective self and excluding other than self, gives rise to citizens and aliens in the first place. As we have seen, this closure comes about through an occupation, a unilateral seizure, that is never innocent. To a lesser or greater extent, the emergence of a legal collective is an act of conquest. If political and legal reciprocity emerge through a non-reciprocal act that partitions inside and outside, what could justify the assertion that 'no one on the outside has a right to be inside'?[32]

A similar problem confronts Rawls' rendition of reciprocity in the passage of his essay cited earlier:

> [T]he question of reciprocity arises when free persons, who have no moral authority over one another and who are engaging in or who find themselves participating in a joint activity, are among themselves settling upon or acknowledging the rules which define it and which determine their respective shares in its benefits and burdens.

The problem in this passage turns on the extension of reciprocity to the emergence of 'joint activity'. For, on closer consideration, Rawls does not—and arguably *cannot*—bring what renders reciprocity possible between members of a collective within the cincture of reciprocity. This is no mere oversight that Rawls can redress if he is to hold on to the veil of ignorance: reciprocity as deliberation between *citizens* presupposes a closure that by definition cannot itself be the outcome of reciprocal deliberation between citizens. Notice that the prior closure does not only concern who counts as a citizen. In effect, the initial boundaries

[29] Walzer, *Spheres of Justice*, 31. The normative implications of the non-reciprocal origins of reciprocity also remain beyond the pale of Miller's discussion of national identity and mutual recognition. See, in particular, Miller, *On Nationality*, 23 ff.

[30] Walzer, *Spheres of Justice*, 31.

[31] Walzer, *Spheres of Justice*, 31.

[32] Walzer, *Spheres of Justice*, 41.

that determine what counts, in Rawls' terms, as 'fair terms of cooperation' and 'reasonable conceptions of justice' are not and cannot themselves be the outcome of deliberation guided by the principle of reciprocity; to the contrary, a non-deliberative closure must already have taken place to get deliberation going.

Habermas encounters an analogous quandary: how does a practical discourse get started in the first place? The problem comes to the fore when Habermas attempts to defuse an objection that threatens to bring to naught his thesis about the equiprimordiality of democracy and the rule of law. Michelman has shown with respect to the enactment of a polity's first constitution that, in Habermas' own words, '[t]he constitutional assembly cannot itself vouch for the legitimacy of the rules according to which it was constituted. The chain never terminates, and the democratic process is caught in a circular self-constitution that leads to an infinite regress'.[33] Although Habermas acknowledges the gravity of the problem by referring to the foundation of a constitutional democracy as a 'groundless discursive self-constitution', he argues that it is possible to break out of this circularity provided one focuses on the 'future-oriented character, or openness, of the democratic constitution'.[34] The circularity thereby becomes a *hermeneutic* circle:

> whoever bases her judgment today on the normative expectation of complete inclusion and mutual recognition, as well as on the expectation of equal opportunities for utilizing equal rights, must assume that she can find these standards by reasonably appropriating the constitution and its history of interpretation.[35]

To secure its inclusion in a collective an individual or a minority group must appeal to—and aim to transform the meaning of—the values, interests, and purposes the individual or group *already* shares with other members of the collective. The individual or group must be able to present its identity as a particular manifestation of a general, more capacious collective identity. The emergence of mutual recognition, on this reading of a politics of inclusion, has the form of a dialectic of the general and the particular, such that an initial situation of non-reciprocity—where non-reciprocity denotes a yet-to-be-recognized claim to particularity within a whole—yields to a novel state of reciprocity and mutual recognition between equal—but different—individuals and groups. Legitimate struggles for differentiation are struggles for *internal* differentiation. Ultimately, a theory of constitutionalism that posits reciprocity as the rational principle governing a politics of boundaries can only view a-legal claims as *normative* claims to the extent that the latter can be viewed as claims to reciprocity, i.e. to particularity, cultural or otherwise, within political generality. Ineluctably, the motto of a reciprocity-driven politics of boundary-setting is this: *e pluribus unum*.

[33] Jürgen Habermas, 'Constitutional Democracy: A Paradoxical Union of Contradictory Principles?', *Political Theory* 29, no. 6 (2001), 774.

[34] Habermas, 'A Paradoxical Union of Contradictory Principles?', 774. It is for this reason that the Hegelian dialectic and its correlative notion of an ever provisional and transcendable limit is the preferred fall-back option for an interpretation of the postnational constellation which acknowledges that a practical discourse does not have a discursive origin. See n. 18 to this chapter.

[35] Habermas, 'A Paradoxical Union of Contradictory Principles?', 775.

But this surely begs the question: the problem is not merely how to achieve a greater inclusiveness to accommodate those who are subject to a form of untoward exclusion at the foundation of the polity to which they belong. A no less fundamental problem is that, more or less against their will, a variable range of individuals and groups may have been *included* in the first place; that, despite their opposition, they are deemed to *belong* to the polity. Why should they or those who later rally to their cause 'have the *task* of actualizing the still-untapped normative substance of the system of rights laid down in the original document of the constitution'?[36] Why should they have to view themselves as 'participants [who] must be able to recognize the project as *the same* throughout history and to judge it from *the same* perspective'?[37]

Here, then, is the fraught political dilemma confronting those individuals or groups who were included in the collective against their will. On the one hand, they can raise a constitutional claim that, if successful, allows them to obtain political and legal recognition for their group-related difference. But if they set foot down this path, they effectively identify themselves as participants in a project with which they do not want to be associated, hence as a minority group engaged in relations of reciprocity within a broader community. On the other, if they oppose their inclusion, refusing to appeal to the constitution's 'still-untapped' normative possibilities of inclusiveness, they expose themselves to the charge that their acts of contestation need not be accepted as such or even listened to because they are not, to borrow and emphasize Habermas' phrase, '*reasonably* appropriating the constitution and its history of interpretation'. So if they choose this second path, their acts of resistance are vulnerable to censure for being non-reciprocal acts, acts that fall prey to a performative contradiction—*the* cardinal sin of reason. More pointedly, if they refuse to participate in a practical discourse oriented to reaching agreement about the terms of their inclusion in the collective, they are no different to the sceptic who 'terminates his membership in the community of beings who argue—no less and no more'. That is to say, they have excluded *themselves* from the community of rational beings, and their demands need not be taken seriously; their refusal amounts to the 'suicide' of reason or to 'mental illness'.[38] The aforementioned dilemma surfaces time and again, during the later career of the collective, with respect to all those individuals and groups who view their inclusion in it as, well, the continuation of a prior annexation. The problem flagged in section 5.3 returns to haunt a reciprocity-driven politics of boundaries, namely, its normative blindness to situations in which inclusion is the *problem* signalled by a-legality, not its solution, that is, when recognition is not what is demanded but what is rejected as a form of domination. A genealogy of reciprocity does not show, as Habermas would have it, that legal orders find themselves somewhere 'between facticity *and* validity' (*Faktizität und Geltung*, as the German language title of Habermas' book puts it);

[36] Habermas, 'A Paradoxical Union of Contradictory Principles?', 774 (emphasis added).

[37] Habermas, 'A Paradoxical Union of Contradictory Principles?', 775.

[38] Jürgen Habermas, *Moral Consciousness and Communicative Action*, trans. Christian Lenhardt and Shierry Weber Nicholsen (Cambridge, MA: The MIT Press, 1990), 100.

it reveals a residual facticity *of* validity that is constitutive for every legal order, a facticity of validity which no collective can overcome and which is concealed—and on occasion actively suppressed—by a politics of boundary-setting for which instituting relations of reciprocity exhausts the normativity of legal ordering.

A lucid observation by Hannah Arendt casts a reciprocity-driven approach to legal ordering in a new light. 'We are not born equal', she notes; 'we become equal as members of a group on the strength of our decision to guarantee ourselves mutually equal rights'.[39] And, in an important article that echoes the passage cited hitherto, Arendt refers to the section of the *Nicomachean Ethics* in which 'Aristotle explains that a community is not made out of equals, but on the contrary of people who are different and unequal. The community comes into being through equalizing, *isasthènai*'.[40] That reciprocity is sparked by a non-reciprocal initiative means that a collective emerges by way of an initiative that *equalizes* the unequal by claiming that the legal order merely gives form to a prior equality between individuals who thereby become participant agents. This, concretely, is what lies behind the assertion that recognition allows participant agents to come to view themselves as what they are *de jure*, even if not yet necessarily *de facto*: free and equal citizens. Yet although Arendt correctly calls attention to the fact that justice can only arise through a process of equalization, she fails to discuss why this political achievement is irreducibly ambiguous. In a passage of the *Twilight of the Idols* that is both very close to and far removed from Arendt, Nietzsche exposes what she and all advocates of a reciprocity-driven politics of inclusion pass over in silence: '"Equality for equals, inequality for unequals"—that would be the true voice of justice: and, what follows from it, "Never make equal what is unequal"'.[41]

To conclude this section, the irresolvable difficulty confronting a reciprocity-driven politics of boundary-setting is a circularity that surfaces when it is asserted that a collective *ought* to include what has been *unjustifiably* excluded from legal (dis)order, or to exclude what has been *unjustifiably* included therein. For this circularity attests to a prior and unilateral closure which can never be fully justified vis-à-vis those who question it, other than by incurring in a *petitio principii*. But then with what right does a collective reject as irrelevant and unimportant those normative claims that definitively resist inclusion within the circle of reciprocity?

Note that this is not an argument against instituting relations of (putative) reciprocity in response to a-legality, nor against the role of reciprocity in making sense of the normativity of legal ordering. After all, as noted at the outset of this chapter, legal obligations and rights presuppose (putative) relations of reciprocity between participant agents in joint action under law. Rather than rejecting reciprocity out of hand, my aim is to expose its backside, which

[39] Arendt, *The Origin of Totalitarianism*, 301.

[40] Hannah Arendt, 'Philosophy and Politics', *Social Research* 57, no. 1 (1990), 83.

[41] Friedrich Nietzsche, *Twilight of the Idols and the Anti-Christ*, trans. Reginald John Hollingdale (London: Penguin, 1990), 113, cited in Bernhard Waldenfels, 'Inside and Outside the Order: Legal Orders in the Perspective of a Phenomenology of the Alien', *Ethical Perspectives* 12, no. 3 (2006), 362.

never abandons legal ordering as the process of instituting relations of reciprocity. Indeed, my reservations about an *exclusively* reciprocity-driven politics of boundary-setting boil down to this: every legal order claims to be binding, hence objective, by dint of having instituted or being capable of instituting relations of reciprocity between the members of the collective; but this claim has a blind spot that cannot be suspended by reciprocity. To the contrary: this blind spot is the condition of possibility of reciprocity.[42] And this means that acts of boundary-setting which institute relations of reciprocity are also always exposed to being a form of domination *because* they bring about and enforce relations of reciprocity.

Accordingly, instituting relations of reciprocity will not do away with a residual groundlessness of claims about what* our joint action *ought* to be about. The (authoritative) claim that there can be a threefold ground of joint action—a collective; a distribution of ought-places, times, subjects, and act-contents; a normative point—that allows of establishing conclusively whether behaviour is legal or illegal, rational or irrational, has a residual groundlessness which cannot be removed. This residual and irreducible groundlessness of joint action under law will not disappear as a *normative* problem if one attempts to write it off as the expression of 'defeatism', 'resignation', 'relativism', 'scepticism', or some such. To engage in this tactic is to collapse responsiveness into a politics of boundaries that neutralizes or assimilates normative claims that definitively resist inclusion in the legal order they question.

7.4 HUMAN RIGHTS AS THE RIGHTS OF STRANGERS

It remains to be seen what normative content is available to a politics of boundary-setting that is predicated on the finite questionability and finite responsiveness of collectives. I will call this *a politics of a-legality*. Before turning to outline its contours in the following section, it is first necessary to address head on a fundamental objection that a reciprocity-driven politics of boundary-setting could table against a politics of a-legality. The objection runs as follows: even if it is accepted that legal orders are exposed to more or less radical forms of political contestation, normative conflicts cannot be meaningfully settled unless the parties in conflict acknowledge that, prior to all conflict, and as the condition for its resolution, human rights are the manifestation of our common humanity. The bedrock normativity of legal orders is the reciprocity afforded by human rights. It would seem, therefore, that human rights confront a politics of a-legality with an intractable dilemma: it must either presuppose human rights, in which case it remains within the fold of a reciprocity-driven politics of inclusion; or it rejects the assumption that human rights speak to an all-inclusive form of reciprocity, in which case a politics of a-legality forfeits its normative content.

[42] Foucault obliquely refers to this blind spot of (normative) orders when, in the famous preface to *The Order of Things*, he asserts that 'there is order' (*il y a de l'ordre*) and speaks of the 'raw being of order' (*l'être brut de l'ordre*). See Michel Foucault, *The Order of Things* (London: Routledge, 2002), xxi, xxii (trans. altered).

With a view to parrying both horns of the dilemma I would like to begin by critically discussing two prominent philosophical defences of human rights as the foundational mode of reciprocity which lends legal orders their normative content. The first is Jürgen Habermas' defence of a universalistic reading of human rights in two articles, the first of which was published on the occasion of the bicentennial of Kant's famous essay, 'On Perpetual Peace'. In this article, Habermas offers the blueprint of a world polity in the form of 'cosmopolitan law' (*Weltbürgerrecht*). After making the case that Kant's 'federation of peoples' (*Völkerbund*) cannot safeguard the legal status and enforceability of the commitment by states to realizing world peace, Habermas champions the foundation of a polity along the lines of what Kant called a 'state of peoples' (*Völkerstaat*). This state sets aside the sovereignty of its Member States in view of creating a world community of equal and free citizens: 'The point of cosmopolitan law is, rather, that it bypasses the collective subjects of international law and directly establishes the legal status of the individual subjects by granting them unmediated membership in the association of free and equal world citizens'.[43] But the snag is that human rights, in the framework of Kant's federation of people, are unenforceable moral rights. Thus, to attain world peace through cosmopolitan law, Habermas rejects the distinction between human ('moral' rights) and fundamental rights (legal rights), audaciously proclaiming that '[h]uman rights are juridical *by their very nature*. What lends them the appearance of moral rights is... their mode of validity, which points beyond the legal orders of nation-states'.[44] The foundation of a world polity would secure their status as enforceable, subjective rights, and would assure all individuals of membership in a world polity as free and equal citizens.

In a later essay, Habermas backs off somewhat from his initial plea for what seems to be a world federal state, defending instead a more nuanced version of multi-level governance. In substance, he argues in favour of a 'world organization that can enforce peace and the implementation of human rights', leaving some issues—primarily economic and environmental—in the hands of regional polities such as the European Union, and other issues—cultural and the like—to individual states.[45] The picture that arises is, therefore, of a world polity set up in three 'layers' of legal orders: national, regional, and global. Whereas the material sphere of validity of the latter would be limited to enforcing human rights and securing world peace, its spatial, temporal, and subjective spheres of validity would be unlimited, as human rights are valid everywhere, everywhen, and for everyone. Human rights make possible a form of political inclusion without exclusion; or, more exactly, if there is exclusion from a global polity, it occurs only because those who breach human rights betray their own humanity, thereby excluding *themselves* from law and from political community.[46]

[43] Habermas, *The Inclusion of the Other*, 181.

[44] Habermas, *The Inclusion of the Other*, 190.

[45] Jürgen Habermas, *The Divided West*, trans. Ciaran Cronin (Cambridge: Polity Press, 2006), 136.

[46] It is in this sense that, according to Habermas, a world polity dedicated to realizing human rights would require a 'political closure', namely, the closure of rationality vis-à-vis irrationality. See Habermas, *The Postnational Constellation*, 90.

Moreover, inasmuch as the implementation and enforcement of human rights trumps all other legislation, the validity of the legal boundaries of national and regional polities is subordinated to the unlimited character of a universally valid global legal order. Accordingly, legal boundaries are the manifestation of national and regional particularism, which must give way, when human rights are at stake, to the unlimited dictates of universal reason. And to the extent that human rights articulate the *concept* of law as the set of rights whereby individuals coordinate their external freedom in relations of reciprocity, the limitlessness of a human rights order comes first—teleologically speaking, albeit not chronologically. So the reducibility thesis remains intact, provided the all-encompassing legal order is restricted to human rights with a moral content.

To assess this thesis, we would do well to reflect upon the most general conditions under which a multi-level world polity, as Habermas envisages it, could organize itself as a *legal* order. Patently, the three-step passage from nation-state to regional polity to world polity intends to mark the transition from substantive to formal political unity. 'If the international community limits itself to securing peace and protecting human rights, the requisite solidarity among world citizens need not reach the level of the implicit consensus on thick "ethical" valuations and practices that is necessary for supporting a common political culture and form of life among fellow-nationals'.[47] Habermas is persuaded that 'a coincidence in the moral wherewithal concerning massive human rights abuses and evident breaches of the prohibition of military attacks' would suffice.[48]

The first question that crops up, when pondering Habermas' proposal, is whether it takes us beyond the current *status quo* concerning Security Council resolutions—*quod non*. But this objection is too easy, and does not go to the heart of the matter. A more pointed question is, for example, whether agreement about what counts as *massive* human rights abuses does not already presuppose a local set of shared values. For example, can the European Union and its Member States be sure that African countries would not insist on viewing the EU's Common Agricultural Policy, given its devastating effects on agriculture in these countries, as continued, flagrant and massive human rights abuse? Can the industrialized Western nations and emergent nations, such as Brazil, China, and India, be sure that the environmental consequences of their economic activity would not count, in the eyes of those poor countries that are most threatened by such consequences, as massive human rights abuses that call for immediate and harsh intervention by the world polity? Even if this hurdle could be overcome, it remains the case that constitutions, when they positivize human rights, also establish the possibility, with only a few exceptions, of *limiting* the scope of those rights, to balance individual freedom and the common good. Could it be otherwise with a world polity? Would not the possibility of legislating limitations to the scope of human rights in a world polity already presuppose a more or less determinate global common good? Finally, *which* human rights are to belong to

[47] Habermas, *The Divided West*, 143 (trans. altered).

[48] Habermas, *The Divided West*, 143 (trans. altered).

the catalogue of rights to be safeguarded by the world polity? For example, in light of the enormous disparities in wealth and income between rich and poor countries, would it be possible to avoid including economic and social rights in the catalogue, if the world polity is to secure 'world peace'? Would this not require transferring the enactment and implementation of economic and environmental policies, which Habermas had assigned to regional polities such as the EU, to the world polity? But is there any hope of defining economic and environmental policies at the global level other than via a localized set of values deemed to be common to a world polity?

While it would be possible to continue elaborating on these examples, they suffice to call attention to the key problem confronting Habermas' move to secure world peace through the enactment and enforcement of human rights as legal rights. On the one hand, because their referent is the humanity of human beings, human rights betoken an order that is valid at all times, in all places, and for all individuals—an unlimited order. On the other hand, the moment human rights are positivized as fundamental rights, they are inevitably linked to a *limited* normative point of joint action under law. To positivize human rights in a global legal order requires a non-reciprocal act that seizes the initiative to *determine* the concept of humanity for legal purposes, to *limit* that which is germane from a legal perspective as constituting *our* 'common humanity'. And this non-reciprocal seizure entails a preferential differentiation concerning relevant and irrelevant practical possibilities, with a view to fixing what defines *us*, the members of a global polity, as human beings. This preferential differentiation calls forth the possibility of irreducible conflict about what constitutes the humanity of human beings.[49] In short, there can be no passage from human rights as moral rights to fundamental rights as legal rights, unless a manifold of individuals are deemed to take up the first-person plural perspective of a 'we'.[50] And this means taking up the perspective whence a collective determines—limits—who ought to do what, where, and when for the sake of φ. Accordingly, the institutionalization of human rights as fundamental rights would not evade the conditions that spawn political plurality—*radical* political plurality. Bluntly, legal determinations of humanity will not bring a-legality under normative control. Political plurality is irreducible because all legal orders, even those that would restrict themselves to legislating and enforcing human rights, must present themselves as limited (albeit putative) unities. No less than any other legal obligation, so also human rights as fundamental rights get entangled in the question a legal collective can respond to: what* ought *our* joint action to be about? The hiatus between the question posed by a-legality and the question to which a collective can respond has not been closed, but rather concealed, when it is taken for granted that what

[49] This became patent to Amnesty International, for example, when outraged social sectors excoriated it for betraying the human right to life when it finally jumped off the fence and took a stand on the issue of abortion.

[50] Van Roermund makes a related point when noting that human rights are constitutively 'selfish'. See his article, 'Migrants, Humans and Human Rights: The Right to Move as the Right to Stay', in *A Right to Inclusion and Exclusion?*, 161–182.

lends fundamental rights their binding character is their purely moral content, grounded as it is in the unlimited reciprocity of our common humanity.

I should note that the foregoing analysis is most emphatically *not* an argument against positing human rights as fundamental rights, any less than against human rights as such, of which I will offer an alternative defence in a moment. Nor am I suggesting that fundamental rights do not have an important role to play in helping to settle normative conflicts. And it certainly is not my intention to scoff at the model of global governance propounded by a thinker who has had the courage to make concrete institutional suggestions—something philosophers only do at their own peril—in an effort to find a way out of our contemporary predicament. My sole concern is to establish whether human rights, when positivized as fundamental rights, will do the job Habermas expects them to fulfil, namely, to include without excluding. The answer is 'no'. The closure required for a *Weltinnenpolitik* based on 'fundamental rights with a moral content' spawns, inevitably, a *Weltaußenpolitik*. A global regime of (enforceable) fundamental rights would be necessarily local, would have to emplace itself Enacting it would involve an irreducible element of occupation—of conquest. But, to belabour my caveat: I am concerned to ask how a collective could take responsibility, even if only indirectly, for the conditions governing its genesis, not to surrender to cynicism about human rights.

So much for Habermas' cosmopolitan project, which seeks to bring human rights within the circle of *legal* reciprocity. Without referring to Habermas by name, Seyla Benhabib perceptively argues that his approach makes of cosmopolitanism a reductive and totalizing project: reductive, because morality is reduced to law and politics; totalizing, because it takes for granted that an all-inclusive legal order can be enacted that allows of conclusively settling political conflict. To ward off these dangers, she advances an interpretation of legal orders that has these rest on human rights as the expression of *moral* reciprocity.

Her argument is couched in the framework of a vigorous defence of the rights of immigrants vis-à-vis state citizens. While she acknowledges that boundaries are constitutive for political communities, she argues that the political asymmetry between citizens and immigrants presupposes and rests on the symmetry of moral relations between human beings. Moral reciprocity, Benhabib argues, takes on the form of human rights claims. In contrast with the civic and territorial boundedness of political communities, human rights claims are boundless—hence universally valid—because they hold for everyone, everywhere, and everywhen. As such, human rights explain, amongst other things, why the interests of those who have been excluded without their consent ought to be taken into account by a democratic polity. To the extent that they institutionalize the insight that 'the rights of the citizens rest on the "rights of man" ',[51] modern constitutional democracies have the conceptual and normative wherewithal to mediate between political particularity and moral universalism. ' "We, the people" refers to a particular human community, circumscribed in space and time, sharing a particular culture, history, and legacy; yet this people establishes itself

[51] Benhabib, 'Another Cosmopolitanism', in *Another Cosmopolitanism*, 13–82, 32.

as a democratic body by acting in the name of the "universal" '.[52] Accordingly, universality, understood as the realization of the fundamental equality between individuals as human beings, is the principle that allows of settling the question concerning the just distribution of membership in democratic communities, even though this principle is never fully realized. Although her analysis focuses on immigrants and asylum seekers, the argument is extensive to all situations in which the 'rights of others' are at issue.

Closer consideration suggests that Benhabib's defence of the rights of others faces insurmountable difficulties. As she herself notes, the mediation between political particularity and moral universality confronts cosmopolitan right with a 'dilemma'. On the one hand, 'cosmopolitan right, if it is to deserve its name at all, must bind, that is, must guide as well as being enforceable on, the actions and the will of sovereign legal and political entities'.[53] This acknowledgment brings her perilously close to endorsing the positivization of human rights in a global regime of fundamental rights, like Habermas does. But, on the other hand, and fearing that this endorsement would transform cosmopolitanism into a project of reductions and totalizations, she adds that although 'cosmopolitan right trumps positive law', 'there is no higher sovereign that is authorized to enforce it'.[54]

The source of this dilemma is the attempt to reconcile two forms of reciprocity that are irreducible to each other. Moral norms, as defined by Benhabib, bespeak reciprocity between individuals as human beings, regardless of their political affiliation; by contrast, legally binding and enforceable norms ultimately presuppose the limited reciprocity of politics. I will return in a moment to consider whether human rights are adequately characterized in terms of reciprocal relations between human beings. For the moment, I will hold on to this assumption, showing how the dilemma comes to a head twice in the course of her discussion of human rights.

The first time occurs during her analysis of Arendt's famous reference to a 'right to have rights'. According to Benhabib, the word 'right' is used in two different ways in this phrase. The first usage 'evokes a *moral imperative*: "Treat all human beings as persons belonging to some human group and entitled to the protection of the same" '.[55] The second use of the term 'right' is *juridico-civil*, and implies membership in a political and legal community, such that 'I have a claim to do or not to do A, and you have an obligation not to hinder me from doing or not doing A'.[56] Crucially, Benhabib argues that the second usage 'is built upon [the] prior claim of membership' in the first.[57] But this alleged derivation will not work: to acknowledge that all human beings ought to be granted membership in some legal community by no means entails that this imperative would be violated 'if and when we were to refuse to enter into civil society with one another,

[52] Benhabib, 'Another Cosmopolitanism', 13–82, 32.
[53] Benhabib, 'Another Cosmopolitanism', 26.
[54] Benhabib, 'Another Cosmopolitanism', 26.
[55] Benhabib, *The Rights of Others*, 56–57.
[56] Benhabib, *The Rights of Others*, 56–57.
[57] Benhabib, *The Rights of Others*, 56–57.

that is, if we refuse to become legal consociates'.[58] The reason for the discontinuity between these two sorts of rights is straightforward: the fact that you, I, or anyone else can claim a right to membership in *some* community in no way implies that you and I have a joint interest that we are prepared to institutionalize by way of binding and enforceable rights in a community we call *our own*.

The point, then, is not so much that there is a difference in *concretion* between the first and second usages of 'right', such that a legal right is simply more determinate than a moral right. Rather, there is a difference in *kind* between the two: the latter betokens reciprocity between individual human beings, the former, reciprocity between political equals. To revisit an observation by Arendt cited earlier,

> equality, in contrast to all that is involved in mere existence, is not given us but is the result of human organization insofar as it is guided by the principle of justice. We are not born equal; we become equal as members of a group on the strength of our decision to guarantee ourselves mutually equal rights.

The incongruity between moral and legal rights appears a second time, when Benhabib attempts to posit a non-foundationalist human rights discourse as the touchstone of cosmopolitan right. The core of this discourse is what Benhabib calls 'egalitarian reciprocity', the idea that 'in the sphere of morality, generality means *universality*; universality refers to what would be valid for all human beings considered as beings equally entitled to respect and concern'.[59] 'Specific schedule[s] of rights', she argues, are derived from the egalitarian reciprocity that informs this universal 'principle of right'. Evidently, this differentiation reproduces the general distinction between, respectively, legal and moral rights. The perplexities that arise from attempting to derive the former from the latter become apparent in a passage in which Benhabib rehearses how egalitarian reciprocity would guide a dialogue in which a member and non-member of a polity exchange reasons about whether or not the latter should be admitted to membership:

> If you and I enter into a moral dialogue with one another, and I am a member of a state of which you are seeking membership and you are not, then I must be able to show you with good grounds, with grounds that would be acceptable to each of us equally, why you can never join our association and become one of us... Our reasons must be reciprocally acceptable; they must apply to each of us equally.[60]

But this is surely to beg the question: how can I enter into a *moral* dialogue with you about whether you may become a member of our polity, now or in the future? After all, the whole point of the dialogue is *political:* you request to join '*our* association', not *an* association in general. When providing you with reasons to this effect, I act as a member of the community, not as a human being. Accordingly, our dialogue is asymmetrical: when giving you reasons, I claim,

[58] Benhabib, *The Rights of Others*, 58–59.

[59] Benhabib, *The Rights of Others*, 133.

[60] Benhabib, *The Rights of Others*, 138.

explicitly or implicitly, that I and the other members of the community are entitled to determine *among ourselves* whether or not we will allow you to join our association, and on the basis of reasons that we regard as relevant from the point of view of *our* joint interest. To overcome this asymmetry, you must invoke a right to membership of some kind contained in or implied by the schedule of rights enacted by the political community to which I belong, not the fact that you and I are human beings.

As with Habermas, my concern is not to deny the urgency and seriousness of the normative issues raised by Benhabib's criticism of the politics of boundaries at work in contemporary immigration policy. To the contrary: I fully share her concern, first, that the closure which gives rise to a democratic community, separating inside from outside and members from non-members, cannot itself be democratically justified, and, second, that this calls into question the right to inclusion and exclusion collectives claim for themselves vis-à-vis outsiders. The events that took place at the Lampedusa CPTA reveal in the starkest possible manner when the collective claim to a right to inclusion and exclusion turns into the violence of a purely factual act of boundary-setting which mirrors, and carries forward, the occupation that gave rise to the collective. But the preferential differences between inside and outside, and member and non-member, cannot be mitigated or undone by appeals to human rights as the respect and equal treatment individuals owe each other as human beings. Rather than moralizing immigration and asylum policy, what is required is to *politicize* the questioning of boundaries, showing, in a concrete manner, under which circumstances immigrants and asylum seekers raise claims to inclusion that a collective *ought* to honour in light of its own normative views. A 'right to have rights' speaks to the emergence of political reciprocity—to proto-political reciprocity.[61] The same argument holds for other challenges to legal boundaries.

What, then, to make of human rights if they are not legal rights, i.e. fundamental rights? The question is important if one declines, as I do, the 'Kantian' invitation to view them as universal moral rights. For *rights* are correlative to directed or relational obligations, which bespeak the first-person plural perspective of a collective in joint action. But then what sense can one make of the 'humanity' of human rights, if these are to resist assimilation into the limited 'we' of a first-person plural perspective?

In a well-known essay Jeremy Waldron asserts that cosmopolitanism is characterized by its insistence that 'nothing human [is] alien'.[62] He alludes, of course, to the famous line in Terence's play, *The Self-Tormentor*: '*Homo sum, humani nihil a me alienum puto*', or 'I am a man, I consider nothing that is human alien to me'. Waldron's evocation of this line neatly encapsulates the cosmopolitan aim of realizing an all-inclusive collective grounded in the humanity of human rights.

[61] I develop these ideas more fully in my article, 'In Between: Immigration, Distributive Justice, and Political Dialogue', *Contemporary Political Theory* 8, no. 4 (2009), 415–434. Unfortunately, the journal truncated the article in its published version; a complete version thereof is available at <http://papers.ssrn.com/sol3/papers.cfm?abstract_id=1726285>.

[62] Jeremy Waldron, 'What is Cosmopolitan?', *Journal of Political Philosophy* 8, no. 2 (2000), 243.

It should come as no surprise that he views human rights as the hard core of *ius gentium*. But because strangeness is an enduring phenomenon of social life, whoever endorses this tenet inevitably ends up endorsing its inverted form: *what is strange or alien is inhuman*. The political consequence is predictable: why should a collective restrain itself when confronted with inhuman behaviour? Why not neutralize—and when push comes to shove obliterate—those who so ostensibly have placed *themselves* beyond the pale of 'our common humanity'?

An alternative begins to delineate itself when one acknowledges, against the claim that nothing human is strange, and against the assumption that what is strange is inhuman, that *the strange is human*. It is in this paradoxical way, I believe, that we need to understand the 'humanity' of human rights. The implication of this insight would be twofold. On the one hand, the humanity of human rights does not appeal to what a collective already includes or could include as its own practical possibilities, but rather, and primordially, to those practical possibilities which definitively surpass the scope of its joint action because they are normatively incompossible with the collective's own practical possibilities. Yet the invocation of humanity in human rights also postulates a *whole* from which a collective has definitively cut loose. It is a whole which precedes it, yet to which it has irrevocably lost access if it is to sustain itself as a collective: the legally unordered. Note that 'unordered' here does not mean what is simply unformed or inert but rather all those anonymous forms of sociality and socialization which precede the closure whereby a legal collective identifies itself as a limited whole and distinguishes itself from (what thereby becomes) the rest. Humanity is first and foremost this anonymous and pre-reflexive stratum of sociality and socialization, the background whence a legal collective wrests loose to emerge into the foreground. The primordial linguistic form of the human is the anonymity of 'one', or even 'anyone', rather than the distinctness of 'we', even though it is of course possible for someone to utter 'we humans' on behalf of a *limited* legal collective.[63] Even though there can be no return to this anonymous and pre-reflexive whole of humanity if the collective is to subsist as a self and as the same over time, the collective can never fully justify the closure which excludes a range of practical possibilities as incompossible with its own realm of practical possibilities. On the other hand, those normative claims that definitively resist inclusion in the legal order of a collective take on the form of a claim to a *right* against the collective, thereby exposing the residual facticity *of* legal validity which precludes that a collective can ever entirely justify why the limit between the collective self and other than self ought to be drawn as it has been and could be drawn. In this way, namely as the manifestation of an irredeemably *broken universality*, human rights retain a critical function with respect to legal orders without becoming a totalizing category, whether moral, political, or legal. Paradoxically, claims to human rights (in contrast to legal rights) articulate in the language of reciprocity what is definitively excluded from the circle of legal reciprocity available to a collective. They are not so much the archetypical 'rights of others', as rather the

[63] This would be the point at which, on another occasion, I would like to rejoin the critical analyses of Heidegger's characterization of *das Man* as inauthentic existence. See Heidegger, *Being and Time*, §27.

rights of strangers. *Claims to human rights indirectly evoke the normative blind spot of a collective's legal order.* Normatively speaking, human rights summon us, the collective, to political self-restraint because much of what is human is strange to us.

7.5 DIA-LOGOS

The upshot of the foregoing considerations is that an exclusively reciprocity-driven politics of boundary-setting cannot yield an adequate account of the normativity of legal orders and their boundaries, not even when human rights are postulated as the foundational mode of reciprocity. The problem turns on what I have called the strong dimension of a-legality. Is there a way of responding to this dimension of a-legality that does not collapse responsiveness into recognition, and that avoids rendering absolute the first-person plural perspective of a 'we'? If, moreover, reciprocity proves insufficient as a normative principle in the face of the strong dimension of a-legality, what understanding of normativity would such respons*a*bility enjoin? These are difficult questions; what follows is a tentative exploration that demands further development in a later study.

A-legality manifests itself, as noted earlier, in the form of a normative claim—an *ought*—that precedes what are deemed to be reciprocal expectations concerning what* our joint action ought to be about. At issue is not an asymmetrical reciprocity in the sense of Iris Marion Young, but rather an asymmetry that disrupts reciprocity. It is an ought that surges forth unilaterally, catching participant agents by surprise because it has already reached them in the form of an injunction that does not match the anticipation of what* one ought or ought not to do when 'we' are acting together, yet an injunction to which they must respond in one way or another.

What is the nature of this ought which disrupts reciprocity? The crux of the matter, as explained in chapter 5, is that a-legality is normatively complex: it raises a normative claim that, from the first-person plural perspective of the legal collective, concretely articulates orderable and unorderable practical possibilities. As orderable, a-legality raises a claim that can be accommodated in the legal order by transforming the boundaries that define the default-setting of (il)legality and therewith, albeit indirectly, shifting the limit between legal (dis)order and the unordered. As unorderable, a-legality raises a normative claim that exceeds the practical possibilities available to the collective: it reveals a normative fault line, an incompossibility between the range of possibilities accessible to a legal collective and what questions it. It is important to insist on the fact that normative claims that appear as purely orderable or as purely unorderable are extremes which can be approximated but never entirely reached in any given case of a-legality. A politics of a-legality is a politics of boundary-setting that responds to *both* dimensions of a-legality. Furthermore, which practical possibilities are our own, and which are beyond the pale of our joint action, is not something that is given in advance to a collective. As has been shown in chapters 5 and 6, part of what renders a-legality surprising is that it opens up some practical possibilities to which we had no prior access as possibilities which are our own, and others which are not.

How, then, ought 'we' to respond to a-legality? On an exclusively reciprocity-driven normative account of legal normativity, the collective ought to respond by (re)setting the boundaries of (il)legality in such a way that these boundaries institute relations of reciprocity and mutual recognition 'between those concerned'. But this principle only addresses the weak dimension of a-legality. When one jettisons the metaphysical thesis that boundary-setting is, at least in principle, the dialectical 'transition from the finite into the infinite' (Hegel *et aliud*), the *normative* problem confronting a politics of a-legality is not only to include what* has been unjustifiably excluded from a legal order, or to exclude what* has been unjustifiably included therein. It is also, and in particular, how a collective ought to deal with its normative blind spot. The question at the outset of this paragraph needs, accordingly, to be sharpened as follows: how ought a collective to respond to the strong dimension of a-legality?

To articulate this normative problem is to indicate how it should be dealt with. If, as I am arguing, every legal collective has a blind spot that is constitutive for the possibility of legal obligations, then the aim of a politics of a-legality cannot be to remove this blind spot or dissolve the zone of normative indifference which it calls forth. Instead, collectives *ought* to acknowledge that they have a normative blind spot which they can neither fully justify nor remove, and they *ought* to take this into account when responding to a-legality in the process of setting legal boundaries. What, concretely, is the normative content of this 'ought'? *Collective self-restraint*, I submit.

Collective self-restraint is something very different to relativism, if this means that 'anything goes' because there are no absolute truths or justifications concerning how legal boundaries ought to be set. The point of calling attention to possibilities that exceed the range of practical possibilities accessible to a collective is precisely that *not* everything goes for it; that the strong dimension of a-legality confronts a collective with normative fault lines which mark the end of its boundary-setting, both temporally and spatially. Not relativism but *relationalism* is entailed by the finite questionability and finite responsiveness of a legal collective, that is, the acknowledgment that who ought to do what, where, and when is relative to a collective: a *relational* obligation, giving a new twist to Gilbert's expression. But the acknowledgment of the relational character of legal obligations (and rights) is not sufficient to characterize the normative content of collective self-restraint; it also involves what can only be a *non-relational obligation*, that is, an obligation towards what resists integration into the circle of relations of reciprocity and mutual recognition made available by joint action under law. Most generally, this non-relational obligation involves introducing a certain forbearance or restraint into the process of setting the boundaries of (il)legality, such that the first-person plural perspective of the collective questioned by the strong dimension of a-legality is not rendered absolute.[64]

[64] Whereas legal obligations are relational, this non-relational obligation vis-à-vis the a-legal is, in my view, the properly *moral* core of boundary-setting by legal collectives. The morality of law would not reside in legal obligations being a particular instantiation of relations of reciprocity between humans as humans, but rather in the collective's disposition to restrain itself from neutralizing or destroying the bearers of normative claims which resist inclusion into the circle of legal reciprocity. On this reading,

The notion of restraint is certainly no newcomer to liberal theories of constitutionalism, which, in one reading, has been defined as 'the project of achieving government in accordance with the rule of law'.[65] This does not worry me; to the contrary: a politics of a-legality endorses constitutionalism thus defined—but only as far as it will take us in making sense of the normativity of boundary-setting. The caveat is crucial: every constitution, and every invocation of the rule of law, has its own normative blind spot which cannot be overcome. So although I am happy to support constitutionalism, I do so with the proviso that constitutionalism and collective self-restraint are not co-extensive terms: insomuch that normative fault lines are at stake, collective self-restraint demands abandoning constitutionalism in the sense noted above. Let us briefly look at how this interpretation of collective self-restraint meshes with traditional accounts of constitutionalism, to then consider why the normative content of collective self-restraint might also demand *violating and/or suspending* (constitutional) norms.

In its weakest sense, collective self-restraint is associated to majority rule in a constitutional democracy. As commentators never tire of noting, the majority can only claim to bind the minority by way of legal norms to the extent that institutional safeguards are put into place such that the minority of today can become, at least on principle, the majority of tomorrow.[66] The 'positive' or 'inclusive' function of fundamental rights has its place here. But this interpretation of the majority rule and of collective self-restraint presupposes and remains within the circle of legal reciprocity: at stake is holding open the tension between the practical possibilities that have been realized in the form of legal empowerments and those which could be realized as the collective's own possibilities. Here, collective self-restraint involves safeguarding the status of legal boundaries as a *limit* which can be shifted by including what had been excluded, and excluding what had been included. In a word, this reading of majority rule in a democracy interprets collective self-restraint in the process of boundary-setting as part and parcel of responsiveness oriented to instituting relations of reciprocity between the members of a legal collective. It bespeaks the weak dimension of a-legality.

A stronger form of collective self-restraint returns us to the distinction between legal (dis)order and the unordered. In effect, it is possible for a collective to restrain itself by *not* including what has been excluded from the domain of legal (dis)order, that is, by declaring off bounds a variable range of behaviour as the domain that *ought* to remain unordered from the first-person plural perspective of the legal collective. Collective self-restraint abandons behaviour

law's morality is all about preserving or sustaining the 'inter' of intersubjectivity as a *hiatus*, in the sense noted in section 6.5. But this topic requires more detailed consideration in a separate study.

[65] David Dyzenhaus, 'The Compulsion of Legality', in Victor V. Ramraj (ed.), *Emergencies and the Limits of Legality* (Cambridge: Cambridge University Press, 2008), 56. This is, admittedly, a narrow understanding of constitutionalism, but one which allows me to draw attention to a feature thereof I want to critically examine.

[66] A particularly perspicuous presentation of this idea is to be found in Hans Kelsen, *Vom Wesen und Wert der Demokratie*, 2nd edn. (Aalen: Scientia Verlag, 1981), 3–13.

to a law-free domain, to a domain which ought to be preserved *from* the scope of joint action under law. This, it seems to me, is the meaning of the 'negative' or 'exclusive' function of fundamental rights from the perspective of a politics of boundaries,[67] even though fundamental rights by no means exhaust this form of collective self-restraint.

There is yet a third form of collective self-restraint which is of particular interest for a politics of a-legality. Its normative significance becomes clearer if we revisit the notion of the *exception*. I introduced this concept in section 5.3 to make sense of the correlation between the strong dimension of a-legality and normative fault lines. Remember Carl Schmitt's characterization thereof: '[t]he exception is that which cannot be subsumed; it defies the general codification'. As such, the exception calls forth a response in the form of an *exceptional measure*. But what is an exceptional measure, and in what sense can it be a response, normatively speaking, to the strong dimension of a-legality?

The question is fraught. A wide range of contemporary political and legal theories peremptorily dismiss the notion of an 'exceptional measure', viewing such measures as the paradigm of arbitrariness and lawlessness. This wariness should not be taken lightly; the events that took place in Lampedusa are examples of the course which exceptional measures can take. But such situations do not exhaust the scope of the latter, which can also have a positive normative significance. Indeed, I want to argue that collective self-restraint can take on the form of an exceptional measure. On this reading, exceptional measures are the common root of boundary-setting undertaken either to neutralize and destroy, or to preserve and sustain, what radically questions the legal collective. Without denying the first manifestation of exceptional measures, I am interested here in exploring more fully the second manifestation thereof.

One way of launching this enquiry would be to argue that exceptional measures, in their positive normative significance, amount to prerogatives, as defined by Locke: 'the Power of doing publick good without a Rule'.[68] But the notion of the 'publick good' presupposes and is oriented to sustaining the collective as a *whole*. It makes of collective self-restraint a form of collective *self*-preservation, whereas what is of interest now is how such measures might preserve strangeness *as* strangeness, that is, as what falls beyond the pale of the 'publick good'. It is more instructive, in this respect, to look at Schmitt's uncompromising analysis of exceptional measures. In his view, the distinction between the enactment of general norms, including constitutional norms, and their application, via administrative acts, judicial decisions and the like, has no traction with respect to the exception. For, by definition, the exception is what cannot be subsumed under a general norm. Exceptions demand a response in the form of a 'measure' (*Maßnahme*). A measure is not merely

[67] It is in the spirit of this form of collective self-restraint that Teubner 'generalizes' the exclusive function of political constitutions and 'respecifies' it for a variety of societal systems, including science, education, health, etc. See Teubner, *Constitutional Fragments*.

[68] John Locke, *Two Treatises of Government*, Peter Laslet (ed.) (Cambridge: Cambridge University Press, 2009), 378.

an amendment of a norm, in particular a constitutional norm; rather, it is a violation, a 'breaking through' (*Durchbrechung*) of a legal norm in a specific sense of the term:

> a statutory violation of the constitution does not alter the constitutional norm. Rather, it constitutes an individual order that deviates from the norm in a single instance while preserving the general validity of the norm in other cases... Such statutory violations of the constitution are in essence measures, not norms. Hence, they are not laws in the Rechtsstaat sense of the word...[69]

If the exception, in the sense of the extra-ordinary, irrupts into a legal order, i.e. 'breaks through' the boundaries of (il)legality, so also an exceptional measure 'breaks through' a legal order by 'deviat[ing] from the norm in a single instance...' Schmitt also points to the possibility of suspending or setting aside 'general constitutional norms' in the face of an exception. In particular, he argues, constitutional limitations to state action, such as fundamental rights, can be suspended when the 'political form of existence' of the collective is endangered.

The thrust of Schmitt's thesis is to argue, against liberal constitutionalism, that measures derive 'their necessity... from the special condition of the individual case or from an unforeseen abnormal situation. When in the interest of the political existence of the whole such statutory violations and measures are used, the superiority of the existential element over the merely normative one reveals itself'.[70] In the same way that the decision by which a political unity gives itself a legal order and a legal constitution 'requires no justification via an ethical or juristic norm', so also 'a norm would not at all be in a position to justify anything' with respect to a *Maßnahme*. The problem with exceptional measures, he holds, is not that they cannot be legally justified; rather, it is the assumption that exceptional measures taken to defend the collective against what imperils its existence need to be justified. For 'the special type of political existence need not and cannot legitimate itself'.[71]

I would like to propose a normative reading of exceptional measures that is removed from both liberal constitutionalism and Schmitt. The defence of the rule of law by liberal constitutionalism is predicated on the assumption, *contra* Schmitt, that a collective *can and needs* to legitimate itself vis-à-vis what questions it by instituting relations of reciprocity which include what had been unjustifiably excluded from the legal order, or exclude what had been unjustifiably included therein. The a-legal can be brought into the fold of (il)legality by way of the dialectic of the general and the particular, a dialectic that is the rational warrant of what David Dyzenhaus has called the 'compulsion of legality': 'the compulsion to justify all acts of state as having a legal warrant, the authority of law'.[72] As should be clear from what I have stated earlier, it is by no means my aim to reject or to minimize the normative significance of the rule of law. But it should now be equally clear that constitutionalism does not warrant the 'authority of law'—or

[69] Schmitt, *Constitutional Theory*, 154.

[70] Schmitt, *Constitutional Theory*, 154.

[71] Schmitt, *Constitutional Theory*, 136.

[72] Dyzenhaus, 'The Compulsion of Legality', 39.

more precisely authoritative boundary-setting—with respect to the strong dimension of a-legality. For the concept of authority available to liberal constitutionalism amounts to the capacity to qualify behaviour in a way that views it as an instantiation (or breach) of general norms, that is, of a *limited* whole. If we are to speak of authoritative boundary-setting with respect to the strong dimension of a-legality, then it has to be indirectly, in the form of a *suspension or violation* of a (constitutional) norm, thereby acknowledging that there is something which definitively eludes the rule of law and its attendant forms of constitutional recognition. If a constitution affords a collective its master rule of legal rationality, by dint of establishing how relations of reciprocity and mutual recognition ought to be (re)instituted with a view to realizing the normative point of joint action under law, then the unconditional defence of the rule of law ends up concealing and suppressing the normative blind spot of a legal collective. Indeed, the price to be paid for the constitutional empowerment of a collective self is a radical disempowerment in the form of a range of practical possibilities which are rendered incompossible with the realm of practical possibilities opened up by a constitution. Constitutions empower *and* disempower. For this reason, whereas liberal constitutionalism equates 'lawlessness' with 'arbitrariness', I submit that lawlessness, in the form of an exceptional measure that responds to the strong dimension of a-legality, is a way of countering the irreducible residue of arbitrariness which dwells in the 'compulsion of legality'. More pointedly and perhaps paradoxically, lawlessness, when it takes on the form of collective self-restraint in the face of the strong dimension of a-legality, is an integral part of the *authority* of law, not its negation.

This interpretation of exceptional measures also takes issue with Schmitt's reductive account thereof. Schmit would have the suspension and violation of (constitutional) norms neutralize and destroy what poses a radical challenge to the collective. Here, in his view, is where sovereignty takes hold: the sovereign is he who decides on the exception. Measures have a purely existential rather than a normative significance because, revisiting his turn of phrase, a collective 'need not and cannot legitimate itself' as a unity. As concerns the radical normative challenge posed by the strong dimension of a-legality, Schmitt is right to aver, *contra* liberal constitutionalism, that a collective '*cannot* legitimate itself' vis-à-vis this challenge. The reason for which Schmitt is right on this is, however, different from that which he envisaged: ultimately a collective cannot legitimate itself with respect to what radically questions it, other than by falling prey to a *petitio principii*: a *self*-legitimation. If a collective cannot emerge absent a representational act that claims to act on behalf of a group without having been authorized to this effect, then, *contra* Schmitt, this founding representational claim, and those which follow it up, never cease to '*need* legitimation'. But the legitimation which could be provided by acts of boundary-setting that include what ought not to have been excluded, or exclude what ought not to have been included, is arrested, brought to a halt by normative fault lines. What remains for collective respons*a*bility, when legitimation comes to an end, is a suspension or violation of (constitutional) norms oriented to acknowledging that *legal boundaries need legitimation but cannot obtain it* vis-à-vis the a-legal, in the strong sense of the term. Collective self-restraint, in the form of the suspension or violation of (constitutional) norms, is the kind of respons*a*bility by which a legal collective can take respons*i*bility, albeit indirectly, for the conditions that govern its emergence. Here, then, is an 'existential' reading of exceptional measures that refuses to sever their link with normativity. In effect, collective self-restraint is the way in which a collective self *endures*, rather than overcomes, its finitude, a finitude which manifests itself obliquely by way of a normative blind spot it cannot dispense with, yet cannot justify. Here is a face of sovereignty that entirely escapes Schmitt's attention: *sovereign is he who decides on the exception by way of exceptional measures that seek to sustain rather than to destroy the strange as strange*. It is in this sense, or at any rate also in this sense, that sovereignty is a fault line concept, and not merely a boundary concept.

These considerations shed new light on the distinction between 'internal' and 'external' politics. When drawing on this distinction, I do not mean the distinction between domestic and foreign politics and policies. Both terms of the latter distinction are, of course, part and parcel of internal politics in the fundamental sense of a politics that seeks to respond to the question what* our joint action ought to be about. By the same token, this is the fundamental manifestation of a 'world internal politics'. For although the distinction between domestic and foreign spheres of political activity ceases to hold for global legal collectives, these necessarily engage in a *Weltinnenpolitik* oriented to setting the legal boundaries which establish who ought to do what, where, and when, and therewith indirectly posit the limit between what counts as legal (dis)order and the unordered. An internal politics, in this fundamental sense, is what attracts the attention of the members of a collective, inasmuch as it marks the range of what is orderable—practicable—in the course of boundary-setting. To revisit Husserl's comment, as cited in section 3.3, 'the practical interest is within (*Drinnen*)'. It stands in contrast to an 'irrelevant outside' that comprises what has been excluded from the range of practical possibilities accessible to joint action by a legal collective.

The question arises, on this reading of the internal/external distinction, whether it all makes sense to speak of an 'external' politics of boundary-setting. For if the outside is the domain to which a collective has no normative access if it is to pursue joint action under law, how can this domain be the object of a politics of boundary-setting at all? Is not a politics of a-legality necessarily restricted to an *internal* politics, even in those cases where limits are shifted in such a way that what had been excluded from legal (dis)order is included therein? Is a 'world external politics' anything other and anything more than *une façon de parler*?

The foregoing considerations suggest that exceptional measures, in the sense noted above, are a favoured vehicle of an external politics. A politics of a-legality can only respond to unorderable normative claims by acknowledging that they belong to an outside which it ought to safeguard *as* an outside. Collective self-restraint, in the form of exceptional measures aimed at preserving the normatively unorderable *as* normatively unorderable, is the core of a (world) external politics. Let me insist on the essential point. I don't want to play off against each other an internal and an external politics, such that setting the boundaries of legal orders engages in one or the other kind of politics. For, on a phenomenologically accurate description, a-legality reveals legal boundaries as being both limits and fault lines of normativity, where one or the other of these manifestations of legal boundedness may be predominant. Consequently, both dimensions of a-legality are involved in a normative account of the responsiveness available to a politics of a-legality. The act of positing the legal boundaries of a collective, in response to a-legality, has a complex structure: it can reach beyond extant legal boundaries, when shifting the limits of legal (dis)order, and it can suspend or violate extant legal boundaries to make room for and sustain an outside to which it has no normative access.

Philosophy reserves the term 'transcendence' for what is *beyond* the sphere of ownness. As such, transcendence is the favoured category by which to make sense of the 'inter' of intersubjectivity, whether individual or collective. In turn, the verb 'transcend', in the traditional philosophical readings thereof, is to 'reach beyond' oneself (or ourselves). A wide range of theories of law and legal obligation are theories of collective self-transcending, to the extent that they make normative sense of boundary-setting as realizing an ever greater inclusiveness. To reach out to other than self is to bring it into a legal relation with us by resetting the boundaries that establish who ought to do what, where, and when in order-to-φ. Not surprisingly, the philosophical articulation of such theories of collective self-transcending takes place in the form of a theory of practical rationality in general and of legal rationality in particular. To transcend ourselves means to 'include the other as one of us', and thereby to *overcome* transcendence by bringing about an ever more encompassing sphere of 'our own'. To transcend ourselves is, in this reading, to respond to what questions us by reciprocating, and this means, at bottom, a reaching out to bring in. As a result, the 'inter' of intersubjectivity becomes the mutuality of a legal relation within the encompassing unity of a collective: intersubjectivity within and as the expression of a single 'we'. Dialogue, as the favoured vehicle of transcending, gives way, if things go well, to a monologue.

The aim of this book is, most fundamentally, to oppose a reading of legal rationality that ends up collapsing transcendence into immanence—the compulsion of immanence, as one might put it, which is proper to the reducibility thesis. *Qua* rational endeavour, boundary-setting is not only a reaching out to bring in, but also *a holding back to hold out* (and in this sense to 'endure' collective finitude). The *also* is crucial: I reject the move to accept a normative reading of boundary-setting that would have it 'either' reach out to bring in 'or' hold back to hold out. In a word, a theory of boundary-setting as a theory of transcendence seeks to do justice to the 'inter' of intersubjectivity as the *hiatus*—a relation and a non-relation—between the own and the strange.

I welcome the hoary notion of 'dialogue' as constitutive of legal rationality and transcendence, but then in a reading that does not make of dialogue an attempt to reinstate and stabilize a monologue that has been interrupted. Legal responsiveness as dialogue is, quite precisely, a *dia-logos*, that is, a rationality of the in-between. On a normative reading of responsiveness, legal rationality has a complex structure: it is collective self-reidentification *and* collective self-restraint: a reaching out to bring in *and* a holding back to hold out. On the one hand, legal collectives cannot but redraw the distinction between legality and illegality in the face of what questions how they have drawn this distinction, and this means establishing anew what is to count as objective and subjective, rational and irrational behaviour. In turn, this implies that collectives cannot but respond to the question, what* is our joint action about? On the other hand, the authoritative act of collective self-reidentification which would realize the reference to the threefold ground of legal behaviour has a residual groundlessness—a normative blind spot—that cannot be overcome. Accordingly, legal rationality is not and cannot be exhausted by acts of collective self-reidentification oriented to reciprocation; legal rationality also demands self-restraint in the form of an indirect acknowledgment of the residual unjustifiability of what* is included in legal (dis)order and what* is excluded therefrom.

What, concretely, does this interpretation of a politics of a-legality look like? Consider, to begin with, the *Grogan* case, which has been discussed on several occasions in the course of this book. As the reader will remember, the European Court of Justice had been requested by the Irish High Court to establish whether Irish law prohibiting the distribution of information about abortion clinics situated in other Member States fell foul of European Community law. The case was explosive because it raised issues of public order for both legal collectives: for the Irish republic, in light of its constitutional protection of the rights of the unborn child; for the European Community, because the unfettered distribution of information about abortion clinics in other countries of the EC fell well within the scope of the fundamental freedoms to be served by the realization of an internal market. The way in which the European Court of Justice and the Irish Supreme Court dealt with this constitutional crisis is exemplary for the kind of exceptional measures I have in mind. The Irish Supreme Court could have quashed the High Court's referral of the case to the ECJ. And, indeed, it made no bones about its intention to protect the right of the unborn child under the Irish Constitution in a new act of collective self-reidentification, thereby responding to the practical question, what* is our joint action about? But by upholding the referral to a preliminary ruling procedure the Court *suspended* a constitutional norm. Paraphrasing Schmitt, its act, together with that of the High Court, '[suspended a] norm in a single instance while preserving the general validity of the norm in other cases...'. By holding back, the Supreme Court gave the ECJ the opportunity to deal with the case at hand in a way that could preserve the unity of the European legal order: holding out. The ECJ, for its part, declared abortion to be a service in an act of collective self-reidentification, thereby responding to the practical question, what* ought our joint action to be about? But it also held that the case at hand did not involve a restriction to the freedom to supply services, thereby abandoning the behaviour of Grogan and his colleagues to the aegis of Irish law. The reasoning underpinning its ruling left little room for doubt that the ECJ effectively breached its own established case law, in particular *GB-INNO-BM*. If the Irish High and Supreme Courts suspended a constitutional norm, the ECJ's preliminary ruling violated a constitutional norm, 'deviat[ing] from the norm in a single instance while preserving the general validity of the norm in other cases...'. The ECJ held back to hold out. Both the Irish and European courts engaged in acts of collective self-restraint by way of exceptional measures that released behaviour, even if only temporarily, from the circle of legal reciprocity. In this way, both courts engaged in a form of *external* politics, as much as in an internal politics centred on collective self-reidentification: they set the legal boundaries of (il)legality in a way that acknowledged, however obliquely, that there was a realm of practical possibilities concerning who ought to do what, where, and when to which they had no access, yet which required preservation, rather than neutralization or destruction.

Consider, secondly, the Quebec sessesion reference. The Canadian Supreme Court had been requested by the Canadian government to establish whether Quebec had a right to unilateral secession. The Court rejected such a right out of hand, arguing that it would amount to an oxymoron: whereas a right presupposes relations of legal reciprocity, unilateral secession is the denial thereof. Following the lead of the Canadian government, the Court's reasoning took for granted that the Quebecer secessionists were demanding a *right* to unilateral secession, hence that they implicitly recognized their status as members of the Canadian Confederation. This amounted to framing the secessionist challenge as a demand for a constitutional reform which, by implication, commits the secessionists to upholding the rule of law. But, as I have sought to show in chapter 5, the Court's reasoning fell prey to a *petitio principii*: the secessionists did not seek 'cultural' distinctiveness within the Canadian Confederation but rather *political* independence that could release them from the condition of unilateral annexation to which they were submitted at the time of Confederation—or so they held.

The Court responded to the secessionist challenge by resetting the boundaries of (il)legality, declaring that an act of unilateral secession would be unconstitutional. To this extent it engaged in a form of *internal* politics: collective self-reidentification. But the reference also included two important initiatives that can be seen as responsive to the strong dimension of secessionist a-legality. The first was the assertion that, in the course of negotiations pursuant to the secession, 'there would be no conclusions predetermined by law on any issue'.[73] Second, and congruent with the first initiative, 'to the extent issues addressed in the course of negotiation are political, the courts, appreciating their proper role in the constitutional scheme, would have no supervisory role'.[74] These initiatives bespeak forms of collective self-restraint: the Court *suspended* the constitution and legal reciprocity as concerns the content and the control of political negotiations about secession. To this extent, at least, it stoutly resisted the compulsion of legality, engaging in a form of external politics that held back to hold out.[75]

[73] *Reference re. Secession of Quebec*, §151. [74] *Reference re. Secession of Quebec*, §153.

[75] It is significant in this respect that any Member State of the EU is now permitted under Art. 49A of the Treaty of European Union 'to withdraw from the Union in accordance with its own constitutional requirements'. Neil Walker refers to this norm as laying down a 'hybrid' measure in that, 'while it provides a mechanism by which the Member States retain a unilateral right to withdraw, this is subject to a suspension of at least two years during which a negotiated settlement must be sought between the withdrawing party and the European Council'. See Neil Walker, 'The Migration of Constitutional Ideas and the Migration of the Constitutional Idea', in Sujit Choudry (ed.), *The Migration of Constitutional Ideas* (Cambridge: Cambridge University Press, 2006), 340.

Let us look, thirdly, at the U'wa challenge. The complexity of their normative claim is condensed into the cry, 'Who is the savage?', when they recoiled in horror from the oil drilling activities contiguous to their lands. As we have seen, the Colombian Constitutional Court responded by striking down the administrative act which granted oil drilling rights adjacent to their ancestral lands. The Court's ruling was an act of collective self-reidentification that reset the boundaries of (il) legality. By insisting on the need to harmonize conflicting interests it responded, in a new way, to the practical question, what* is our joint action about? By striking down the administrative act, the court's ruling remained within the orbit of an *internal* politics: it reaches out to bring in. This is not to minimize the significance of the Court's ruling; after all, the Council of State subsequently upheld the administrative acts which granted the oil drilling rights. Nor do I want to wax ecstatic about the ruling, as the Colombian collective could have gone much further in its response. For example, it could have introduced environmental measures in response to their anguished cry, thereby acknowledging that they are our *future*, rather than our past in the form of an allegedly 'primitive community'[76] or a 'pre-modern' and 'mythical way of understanding the world'.[77] But even such environmental policies, however sweeping and drastic they might be, would partake of an internal politics: they would remain within the range of practical possibilities—spatial, temporal, subjective, and material—accessible to *lex constructionis* as much as to the Colombian collective. However responsive, the Court ruling and such environmental policies would stay on this side of the normative fault line separating *lex constructionis* and Colombian law from U'wa law:

> The law of our people is different from that of the white man because the law of the riowa comes from men and is written on paper, whereas the law of our people was dictated by Sira, who inscribed it in the hearts of our wise men, the Weryahas. Respect for the living and the non-living, the known and the unknown, is part of our law: our mission in the world is to narrate, sing, and obey [this law] to sustain the equilibrium of the universe.[78]

Is an external politics imaginable in the face of this normative claim? As suggested earlier, this can only be an indirect or oblique respons*a*bility, one which suspends or violates (constitutional) norms to preserve a legal order's outside *as* its outside. One such unilateral initiative would be for the Colombian government *not* to initiate criminal proceedings against members of the U'wa for certain illegal acts they may have committed under Colombian law in the course of their resistance, such as the destruction of property, while also arranging for compensation by the Colombian collective to those who had suffered damage. The decision not to initiate criminal proceedings would be an exceptional

[76] Hart, *The Concept of Law*, 95.

[77] Habermas, *Theory of Communicative Action*, vol. 1, 43 ff. To call the U'wa 'pre-modern', because they 'lack' the modern consciousness of contingency, is to be blind to the *contingency of contingency*, to borrow a marvelous phrase from my colleague, David Janssens.

[78] 'Carta de los U'wa al hombre blanco'. One may ask to what extent the framing of their normative challenge has already begun in the translation of their extraordinary letter into Spanish.

measure, 'an individual order that deviates from the norm in a single instance while preserving the general validity of the norm in other cases...' (Schmitt). By suspending or violating the circle of legal reciprocity the decision would amount to a holding back that holds out. Other exceptional measures by which to respond to the strong dimension of U'wa a-legality are also conceivable. For example, the Colombian legal order can also hold back to hold out by abandoning a range of behaviour to the domain of the legally unordered, thereby making room for U'wa law.

And, to conclude, there is Breivik: 'I concede the deeds, but deny that I am guilty'. What took place in Oslo and the island of Utøya intimates the point at which the strong dimension of a-legality calls forth the unconditional reaffirmation of legal order. By declaring Breivik guilty, the Oslo District Court set anew the boundaries of (il)legality which lay down who ought to do what, where, and when. The court's ruling is an act of collective self-reidentification oriented to upholding the Norwegian collective as the same and as a self over time. To this extent, the court engaged in a form of *internal* politics that responded to the practical question, what* is our joint action about?

Is there any room here for something like an external politics that seeks to preserve, rather than destroy, the normative claim raised by Breivik's acts?

The first forensic report, which declared Breivik to be criminally irresponsible because he acted in a condition of insanity, would have deprived his act of any normative character whatsoever. The farmhouse and the island of Utøya would cease to be strange *ought*-places, even from Breivik's point of view, or so the initial report effectively held. Legally speaking, the declaration of insanity would have created a pure disjunction between fact and norm; what took place, however grievous, would cease to raise a question concerning what is relevant and important to the collective. His act would have interfered with legal empowerments made available to the Norwegian legal order, but would not reveal a *practical* incompossibility. It would have been no different to a 'natural' catastrophe, which, in a sense, is what paranoid schizophrenia is. Breivik himself was acutely aware of this and fought hard during the trial hearings to discredit the first forensic report. He argued that his was an 'act of political violence' and that the report might have been influenced by the government's attempt to 'keep his ideology from getting out'.[79] By the same token, if the court had accepted the first report, it would no longer have been necessary to take seriously Breivik's claim that he spoke and speaks on behalf of a group. His act would have been the act of a lone individual. But this reading, which was finally rejected by the court, neutralizes the seriousness of the challenge posed by his deed. While the killing may have been perpetrated by Breivik on his own, there is ample evidence, not least on the internet, that he by no means stood alone when asserting that liberal collectives are informed by an 'ideology of hatred and multiculturalism'.[80] Breivik and his

[79] Richard Galpin, 'Anders Behring Breivik says that insanity report is lies', *BBC News*, 25 April 2012, <http://www.bbc.co.uk/news/world-europe-17836180> (accessed on 13 February 2013).

[80] See, e.g. <http://www.gatesofvienna.blogspot.com> (accessed on 1 February 2012). The name of the site alludes, of course, to the siege of Vienna by the Muslim Ottoman Turks in 1683.

brethren raised and continue to raise a *normative* challenge. The judicial declaration of Breivik's insanity would not have changed that.

By condemning Breivik to preventive detention, the Oslo District Court's ruling was both an act of collective self-reidentification and an act of collective self-restraint. In particular, by dismissing the diagnosis of paranoid schizophrenia and embracing the view that he was criminally responsible, the court obliquely acknowledged that his was a normative challenge that ought to be *heard* in the course of the trial, even if what he had to say and how he behaved during the trial was 'almost unbearable' for those who listened.[81] By declaring Breivik criminally responsible and allowing him to have his say during the trial, the court resisted collapsing transcendence into immanence, holding back to hold out. The ruling, on the interpretation I am defending, engaged in internal and external politics, the two faces of a politics of a-legality.

Let me note, to conclude, that the aim of this section is not to unveil a novel form of legal ordering, one which would set the ongoing process of boundary-setting on an entirely new and sure normative footing. What I have tried to do is to provide a better normative account and interpretation of the rational significance of the practices in which the legal boundaries of collectives are or can be set: a politics of a-legality. The normative core of such a politics is, I argue, a *dia-logos*. On this reading, the normative dimension of legal responsiveness and rationality consists in resetting the preferential distinction between the legal* and the illegal* in a way that institutes (putative) relations of reciprocity, while also acknowledging that the institution of such relations is always exposed to being a form of domination *because* relations of reciprocity are instituted. Only indirectly, in the mode of collective self-restraint, can legal rationality respond to normative claims which surpass its own practical possibilities. If acts of collective self-reidentification that determine what* our joint action ought to be about are the heart of an internal politics, even when it takes on the form of a *Weltinnenpolitik*, collective self-restraint is, by contrast, the normative core of an external politics, and a fortiori of a *Weltaußenpolitik*.

Harking back to section 7.1, the further question is how to interpret equality, justice, freedom, and security if it can no longer be taken for granted that these concepts draw their normative meaning only from the criteria governing the practical question, what* ought our joint action to be about? What would be required is a reconceptualization of these concepts in terms of a politics of a-legality, in the twofold sense of an internal and an external politics of boundaries. This endeavour will have to wait for a later occasion.

[81] Traufetter, 'Ein fast uneträglicher Auftritt'.

Conclusion

This book has argued that boundaries, limits, and fault lines are not merely ancillary features that could be dispensed with when accounting for how law is structured and how it emerges; they are central features that require systematic consideration in a general theory of legal order and legal ordering. A 'general' theory, I say, because we are witness to the emergence of new legal orders that do not fit into the paradigm of state/international law, and to the renewed visibility of legal orders that have been around for a very long time, many of them far older than states (in the modern sense of the term) or international law. I will have nothing more to say here about the concepts of legal order and legal ordering advanced heretofore. Instead, the concluding question I would now like to briefly examine is how this concept might contribute to casting light on the process that, according to many, marks an epochal rupture in our understanding of law by dint of exposing borders as contingent features of law: *globalization*.

Any interpretation of globalization takes its point of departure, explicitly or implicitly, in one or other interpretation of the spatial significance of this process. Indeed, globalization means, in its most elemental formulation, 'growth to a global or worldwide scale'.[1] The notion of 'scales' of law has presented itself as a convenient way of conceptualizing this transformation. On one influential reading, whereas legal theory has focused during the last centuries on the 'scale of the state', the pluralization of legal orders requires introducing a multiscalar analysis, in which 'local law is a large-scale legality, nation-state law, a medium-scale legality and global law, a small-scale legality'.[2] Sassen questions this too simple scalar analysis of normative orders. While conceding that it is appropriate to refer to a properly global scale in the case of global institutions and processes, she argues that subnational localities also operate as sites for globalization. Revindicating the importance of place and emplacement in this second form of globalization, she proposes to 'disaggregat[e] the global into particular, cross-border circuits connecting specific localities, thereby partially bringing the vague notion of the global to the more concrete notion of networks of places'.[3] These networks of places mark the emergence of normative orders that are both sub-national and global in reach. In short, the local can be global in scale, even though the global need not be local in scale.

The entire thrust of my argument demands that Sassen's insight be radicalized. As concerns law, there are not two kinds of globalization processes—global globalization and local globalization—but one: legal globalization can only come

[1] 'Globalization' entry in the *Webster's Online Dictionary*, <http://www.websters-online-dictionary.org/definitions/globalisation> (accessed on 28 October 2012)

[2] De Sousa Santos, *Toward a New Legal Common Sense*, 426 (emphases omitted).

[3] Sassen, *A Sociology of Globalization*, 13.

about in the form of the *localization* or emplacement of law. In the same way that cross-border 'mergers and acquisitions', cross-border 'transactions among immigrant communities and communities of origin', cross-border 'networks of activists', and cross-border 'criminal networks', which comprise what she calls 'non-cosmopolitan globalities', are nascent networks of places, so also the cosmopolitan globalities of organizations such as the WTO and the International War Crimes Tribunals emerge and consolidate themselves as interconnected distributions of places by emplacing themselves as *spatial unities*.[4] Notice that this is something other than the misleading neologism of the 'glocal', in which the global and the local would be wedded; rather, the global is no more and no less a form of the local than all other forms of 'local' law. In short, the notion of local law is pleonastic. What is profoundly misleading about all analyses of legal orders that take their cue from the notion of a scale, cartographic or otherwise, is that they are blind to the fact that while we can certainly use maps when thinking about the space of law, we are and remain *in* the space of law when using maps. The 'in-ness' of 'in' refers to being in a *space of action*, which is organized in terms of the contrast between inside and outside. As a result, the encounter between global law and other kinds of legal orders is always *lateral*.

And here again we need to clear up a misconception about globalization as it pertains to law. The misconception begins, at a purely linguistic level, with the convention that the nouns 'globe' and 'world', and their corresponding adjectives, are synonyms, such as when one refers interchangeably to global law and to world law. This is not unusual; it follows common usage of these terms, which is reflected in the *Webster's* definition of globalization as 'growth to a global or worldwide scale'. While there is nothing wrong with this linguistic convention, the conceptual and normative problems begin when the convention is taken to mean that a global or world legal order is no longer organized as an inside in contrast to an outside. Although the domestic/foreign distinction is a contingent feature of law, not so the distinction between the own and the strange, which is a necessary feature of the structure of legal orders as such. And this is because legal orders, including global legal orders, partake of the structure of what phenomenology calls a 'world', or more exactly, a 'home-world'—a *Heimwelt,* even if only partial.

Indeed, the phenomenologically versed reader will have quickly spotted, early on in chapter 1, that I am trying to justify my claim that legal orders are necessarily organized as an inside over and against an outside by reference to the phenomenological notion of a world. This is not the place to engage in a full-blown discussion of this vast topic. A couple of indications will suffice with regard to the point I want to make. For phenomenology, a world is not simply the sum total of things, such that, in seizing this aggregate (assuming one could), the world would have been understood *as* world. Moreover, the world is not given as a *thing* among other things. More pointedly, the planet, although a very large thing, is not a world, phenomenologically speaking. The 'globe' of 'global justice' or the 'world' of 'world constitutionalism' (to name only a couple of the

[4] Sassen, *A Sociology of Globalization*, 29, 6.

cognate expressions that have proliferated over the last decennia) is not the world in its fundamental sense; both expressions refer to a thing among other things, even if a thing too large for anyone or even for the whole of humanity to take in at one glance. For the same reason, space law, which Wikipedia defines as 'an area of the law that encompasses national and international law governing activities in outer space',[5] is not law that is 'outside' of the world, simply because it is in 'outer space'. On the contrary, the very distinction between an 'inner space'—i.e. planetary law—and an 'outer space'—i.e. extra-planetary law—is itself only possible within a *single* legal world.

From this fundamental perspective, to treat the globe and the world as synonymous terms is to incur a category mistake. A world is a *nexus or whole of meaning-relations*, which is *co*-given and *pre*-given with the things, events, and acts that populate it. Things, events, and acts are present, i.e. appear *as* something (a contract of sale, a court, abortion), against the backdrop of this unity of relations, which, itself, appears indirectly in and through these things, events, and acts. In the absence of this co- and pre-given world we could not even begin to make sense of a novel apparition as more or less unintelligible; that something cannot be completely understood presupposes a nexus of meaning-relations with respect to which it appears as 'meaningless'. A further point on which phenomenology has insisted is that a world is *subject-relative*. When describing the structures of the world, one describes its mode of *givenness*, that is, how it appears to *us*. In contrast to science, which seeks to factor out subject-relative aspects of knowledge in its quest for objectivity, phenomenology has pointed out that the scientific endeavour presupposes and takes place on the ground of an experience of the world that is subject-relative. Crucially, insomuch that a world is subject-relative it not only 'appears' (to someone), but appears as a *limited* nexus of meaning-relations: as 'horizonal'.

Moreover, although a world is always co-given as a limited unity of meaning-relations, its limited character usually remains more or less invisible and unthematic for us. Husserl refers to this as the 'natural' attitude or orientation towards the world. The normality of living within and towards the co-given nexus of meaning-relations, and the goals, interests and themes it makes available, can, however, be broken—*interrupted*—such that the world becomes visible *as* a world. Like Husserl, Heidegger insists that the 'worldliness' of the world only manifests itself as such when our orientation in and within the world is interrupted. But in discussion with Husserl, Heidegger shows that such interruptions are not something that is the object of a methodological 'decision' to bracket the world, but rather an event that unexpectedly takes place in the course of our day-to-day practical activities, such that these activities become visible as literally 'mundane', that is, as taking place within a pre-given whole (*Ganzheit*) of meaning-relations.[6]

[5] See the apposite Wikipedia entry at: <http://en.wikipedia.org/wiki/Space_law> (accessed on 12 February 2013). It would be possible to show how space law, if it is to be law, would have to be organized as a space of action, hence that it would have to be populated by ought-places and not only by positions, in Heidegger's sense of the term 'position', and that the three-way distinction between legality, illegality, and a-legality would be effectual therein.

[6] Heidegger, *Being and Time*, §§15 and 16.

My own enquiry into legality, illegality, and a-legality follows an analogous trajectory, tracing the passage from the articulation of the legal / illegal distinction in the ordinary course of joint action under law to its interruption by a-legality. The interruptions wrought by a-legality reveal boundaries to be the limit between a familiar inside and a strange outside, between what Husserl calls a home-world (*Heimwelt*) and an empty outside that suddenly is 'filled', however partially, in the form of a strange world (*Fremdwelt*).[7] The thesis that globalization reveals spatial closure to be a merely contingent feature of legal orders, as assumed by systems theory, legal positivism, and normative theories of law, not only involves a reification of the world into a thing among things, but also a certain 'forgetfulness' about the worldliness of a legal world. More precisely perhaps, it involves 'forgetfulness' about the orderliness of legal orders: about their structure as subject-relative and limited, albeit transformable, unities of spatial, temporal, subjective, and material relations. The more one insists on globality as divesting legal orders of spatial closure, the more the worldliness of legal worlds becomes concealed.[8]

If this approach helps us to clarify the structure of legal order and legal ordering, so also, I now want to claim, it goes some way to understanding what is at stake, conceptually and normatively, in globalization. Conceptually, the emergence of global legal orders as a form of local law bespeaks the primordial experience of pluralization, the *dis-location* whereby a place which had pointed beyond itself to the other places which make up the spatial unity of a state, gives way to and is overlain by a place that points to another unity of places whence it draws its normative meaning as an ought-place. It is this process of dis-location which Sassen describes when referring to the emergence of global networks of places which are both sub-national and transnational. More generally, the account of emergent legal orders developed in this book is in line with the process of *globalization as unification and pluralization* which is unfolding before our eyes. Indeed, what we see happening is that normative orders with a global reach emerge by breaking out from state law and, in some cases, consolidate themselves as legal orders by way of more or less robust structures of authority that mediate and uphold joint action by participant agents.

Certainly, dis-location does not on its own suffice to characterize globalization as a spatial phenomenon. The concrete spatial experience which gets papered over in references to the 'small scale' of global law is far more accurately conveyed in terms of the remarkable 'compression' of space (and time) wrought by globalization. This phenomenon is also understandable against the background of a phenomenological account of practical orientation in and towards a world. Sassen notes that new technologies allow individuals and organizations to orient themselves towards other individuals and organizations 'located far away, thereby destabilizing the notion of context, which is often associated with that of the local

[7] Husserl, *Zur Phänomenologie der Intersubjectivität*, 214 ff.

[8] As happens, for example, when Waldron refers to 'world or universal law'. See Waldron, '*Partly Laws Common to All Mankind*', 203.

and with the notion that physical proximity is one of the attributes of the local'.[9] In fact, the dis-location wrought by the emergence of global legal orders entails what is physically distant becoming practically proximate, and what is physically proximate receding into a practical distance. While global legal orders would not be possible without the technologies that allow of rendering practically proximate what is physically distant, these technologies are themselves vehicles of the form of spacing which Heidegger calls *Entfernung* or 'approximation': a bringing close of what is far by dint of including it in a world of practical involvement with others and with things.[10] The technological approximation of the physically distant in global legal orders presupposes and is one of the modalities of the approximation whereby a collective gathers together and brings near the places which are relevant and important for the sake of φ, while pushing into the distance of an empty outside what is irrelevant and unimportant from the point of view of joint action under law, however close, physically speaking. It is in this way, again, that legal globalization, as the 'compression' or 'shrinkage' of space, is only possible through the emplacement or localization of law. Legal globalization is part and parcel of the 'enworlding' (*Verweltlichung*), however partial, which takes place through the emergence of joint action under law—*globalization as enworlding*—even though not all legal enworlding is a globalization.

Finally, defending the thesis that legal enworlding requires a closure leads to normative perspectives about globalization that in important ways are at odds with both particularism and universalism. It seems to me that, in different ways and with different accents, both universalistic and particularistic readings of legal ordering end up rendering absolute the sphere of ownness which lends legal orders the structure of a home- or familiar world. This is most obviously the case in particularism, at least in its communitarian forms, in which the task of legal ordering is to reappropriate a directly accessible sphere of ownness which constitutes the origin of a political community. The polity's boundaries operate a neat partition between the own and the strange, such that they include the home-world and exclude strange worlds. Particularism vigorously defends pluralism against the monism of globalization. But it is a pluralism premised on the assumption that the contrast between the own and the strange falls together with the contrast between, respectively, the domestic and the foreign. This is but *monism multiplied*, whereby each political community is a unity in the form of a home-world.[11]

Universalism vigorously opposes the particularistic reading of legal boundaries, pointing to their twofold function, which is to separate and join. On the one hand, boundaries separate, thereby accommodating a plurality of home-worlds. On the other, boundaries could not separate unless, more fundamentally, they join together within the framework of a unity. So universalism can claim to

[9] Sassen, *A Sociology of Globalization*, 21. See also David Harvey, *The Condition of Postmodernity* (Oxford: Blackwell, 1989), 260 ff, on the 'compression of time and space'.

[10] 'Approximating [*Entfernen*] amounts to making the farness vanish—that is, making the remoteness of something disappear, bringing it close'. Heidegger, *Being and Time*, §23 (trans. altered).

[11] This assumption also underpins Schmitt's thesis that '[t]he political world is a pluriverse, not a universe'. See Schmitt, *The Concept of the Political*, 53.

respect plurality, while also championing a unity in which each of this plurality of perspectives can recognize itself as being part of a whole. Such, in its view, is the promise, if not yet the reality, of *globalization as universalization*. At the end of the day, universalism is beholden to monism: plurality within the unity of one world. But there is a decisive detail that universalism tends to pass over in silence: globalization has to begin *somewhere*. This means that globalization would take on the form of a progressive inclusion of the other 'as one of us'. In pressing for 'one' world, universalism effectively advocates the emergence of an all-encompassing *home-world*. Although there is no openness without a prior closure, the closure of a (collective) self is in principle provisional and called on to be overcome through a dialectic of collective self-mediation, mirrored in a self-mediation by other collectives: a 'fusion of horizons' as the fusion of worlds. When understood as a universalizing process, globalization unfolds as a *dialectic of the limit*, the vehicle that allows us to become, albeit in a future that must be indefinitely postponed, what we already are *in posse*, if not *in esse*: one humanity under one law. For universalism, globalization is the historical process of 'making the strange our own'.[12]

Both monistic interpretations of globalization—particularism and universalism—operate, I believe, with a reductive conceptualization of the strange and of strange worlds. By taking for granted that the boundaries of political communities include the home-world and exclude strange worlds, particularism turns a blind eye to the fact that the foreign need not be strange and that the strange need not be foreign. In particular, as I have insisted time and again, the strange can irrupt from within the heart of what is deemed to be the collective's own legal order. By assuming that the boundaries of collectives are defeasible in a way that allows for the progressive reduction of a-legality to (il)legality, universalism collapses the fault lines of globalization into the limits of ever-expanding legal orders, such that the 'fusion of horizons' is the progressive integration of the others into our home-world, which ought to welcome all others—provided their claims are 'reasonable'.

The strength of universalism resides in arguing that legal boundaries *include what they exclude*. For only to the extent that legal orders in some way include what they have excluded can legal collectives *respond* at all to a-legality by shifting their limits. Legal boundaries would not be 'porous' or 'permeable', hence amenable to transformation, unless what a legal order has excluded is, in some normative sense, included therein. This, it seems to me, is the defensible insight of universalism, an insight that should be staunchly defended against the particularistic assumption that boundaries simply include the collective self and exclude other than self. Yet legal responsiveness never merely integrates a-legal behaviour into the collective; responsiveness also always *neutralizes* a-legality, levelling down the extraordinary to a variation of the ordinary. To lose sight of the finite responsiveness of legal collectives is to strip a-legality of its normative complexity, reducing

[12] Gadamer, 'Rhetoric, Hermeneutics, and Ideology-Critique', 314 (translation altered). In this sense, the controversy between Gadamer and Habermas is very much a storm in a glass of water. See Karl-Otto Apel et al. (eds.), *Hermeneutik und Ideologiekritik* (Frankfurt: Suhrkamp, 1971).

the threat posed by the subversion of a legal order into a mere opportunity for and celebration of legal change. Notice how universalism inverts the particularist position: whereas the latter defends political plurality by letting legal boundaries separate, the former advocates human unity by letting legal boundaries join. By contrast, a strong form of political plurality, one that eschews the simple monism of universalism and the multiplication of monism propounded by particularism, emerges when we acknowledge that legal boundaries not only include by excluding but also always exclude by including This, you will recall, is the upshot of the finite responsiveness and finite questionability of legal orders. A-legality retains its irreducibly ambiguous status when it is acknowledged that, although the limits of legal orders can be shifted by resetting the boundaries of (il)legality, political pluralism is irreducible to an all-encompassing legal unity, that is, when it is recognized that globalization gives rise to fault lines. Insofar as legal ordering excludes by including, legal boundaries are not only provisional; they are also *definitive* in the form of those aspects of a-legal behaviour that resist inclusion in a given legal order and its variable but finite possibilities. To deny, with universalism, that globalization gives rise to fault lines is to endorse, however unwittingly, *globalization as imperialism*.

This interpretation of how legal boundaries do their work of including and excluding suggests a view of *globalization as emergent intertwinement*, namely, the intertwinement of home- and strange worlds manifest in the experience of familiarity *and* irreducible strangeness; of legal orderability *and* unorderability; of possibilities which appear as our own joint possibilities *and* others which do not. It should be clear that what I have in mind is not a 'multipolar' world, whether or not it is carved up into regional blocks. This amounts to assuming that each of the 'poles' demarcates a self-contained domain of ownness that stands over and against other such spheres. To characterize globalization as the emergent intertwinement of home- and strange worlds is to reiterate one of the central claims of this book: if a foreign place need not be strange, so also a strange place need not be foreign. Crucially, when I say that legal orders intertwine, I mean that there is no common core shared by all of these orders, no common normative standard for universal reciprocity in an all-inclusive legal order. True, it would not be possible to distinguish between a home-world and a strange world unless these appear against the background of the *one world*. But the one world intimated by a-legal behaviour is the whole of anonymous and pre-reflexive forms of sociality and socialization from which a legal collective has cut loose and to which there can be no return if it is to sustain itself as a self and as the same over time. In any case, the metaphor of an intertwinement of home-world and strange worlds also evinces why a theory of legal ordering can defend irreducible political plurality without simply having to endorse massive incommensurability. Intertwinement speaks to both interference and interconnection without an all-encompassing normative framework. It is this, precisely, what it means that boundaries are *in-between*, and that globalization demands a *dia-logos*: a politics of a-legality.

Bibliography

Agamben, Giorgio. *State of Exception,* trans. Kevin Attel (Chicago, IL: Chicago University Press, 2005).

Amazon Watch. 'Colombia: Resistencia Uwa contra petroleras y megaproyectos, 2009-10-08': <http://www.amazonwatch.org/newsroom/view_news.php?id=1943> (accessed on 13 September 2010).

Amnesty International, 'Italy. Temporary Stay—Permanent Rights: The treatment of foreign nationals detained in "temporary stay and assistance centres" (CPTAs)', 20 June 2005: <http://www.unhcr.org/refworld/country,,AMNESTY,,ITA,,43b14cd04,0.html> (accessed on 12 February 2013).

Amselek, Paul. *Méthode phénoménologique et théorie du droit* (Paris: Pichon, 1964).

Apel, Karl-Otto, Claus von Bormann, Rüdiger Bubner, Hans-Georg Gadamer, Hans Joachim Giegel, and Jürgen Habermas. *Hermeneutik und Ideologiekritik* (Frankfurt: Suhrkamp, 1971).

Arendt, Hannah. *The Origins of Totalitarianism* (New York: Harcourt Brace, 1951).

——. *The Human Condition* (Chicago, IL: Chicago University Press, 1985).

——. 'Philosophy and Politics', *Social Research* 57, no. 1 (1990), 73–103.

Augenstein, Daniel and David Kinley. 'Beyond the 100 Acre Woods: Navigating the Jurisdictional Jungle of Extraterritoriality, Multinational Corporations and Human Rights Violations', in D. Bilchitz and S. Deva (eds.), *Human Rights Obligations of Business: Beyond the Corporate Responsibility to Respect?* (Cambridge: Cambridge University Press, 2013).

Balibar, Étienne. *Politics and the Other Scene,* trans. Christine Jones, James Swenson, and Chris Turner (London: Verso, 2012).

Barlow, John Perry. 'A Declaration of the Independence of Cyberspace': <https://projects.eff.org/~barlow/Declaration-Final.html> (accessed on 13 February 2013).

BBC News, 'Somali charged over attack on Danish cartoonist', 2 January 2010: <http://news.bbc.co.uk/2/hi/europe/8437652.stm> (accessed on 13 February 2010).

Beck, Ulrich. *What is Globalization?,* trans. Patrick Camiller (Cambridge: Polity Press, 2000).

Beitz, Charles. *Political Theory and International Relations,* rev. edn. (Princeton, NJ: Princeton University Press, 1999).

Benhabib, Seyla. *Situating the Self* (London: Routledge, 1992).

——. *The Rights of Others* (Cambridge: Cambridge University Press, 2004).

——. 'Another Cosmopolitanism', in Robert Post (ed.), *Another Cosmopolitanism* 13–80 (Oxford: Oxford University Press, 2006).

Benveniste, Émile. 'Le langage et l'expérience humaine', in Émile Benveniste, Noam Chomsky, Roman Jakobson et al. (eds.), *Problèmes de langage*, 3–13 (Paris: Gallimard, 1966).

Bilaterals. 'Colombian U'wa indigenous leaders to visit US, urging investors and US Congress to respect human rights': <http://www.bilaterals.org/spip.php?article13824> (accessed on 13 February 2013).

Blumenberg, Hans. 'Kontigenz', in Kurt Galling (ed.), *Die Religion in Geschichte und Gegenwart. Handwörterbuch für Theologie und Religionswissenschaft*, vol. III, 3rd edn, 1794–1795 (Tübingen: J.C.B. Mohr, 1959).

——. *The Legitimacy of the Modern Age*, trans. Robert Wallace (Cambridge, MA: The MIT Press, 1985).

Bourdieu, Pierre. *Esquisse d'une théorie de la pratique*, repr. (Paris: Seuil, 2000).

Brague, Rémi. *Aristote et la question du monde* (Paris: Presses Universitaires de France, 1988).

Bratman, Michael. *Faces of Intention: Selected Essays on Intention and Agency* (Cambridge: Cambridge University Press, 1999).

Broekman, Jan M. *A Philosophy of European Union Law* (Louvain: Peeters, 1999).

Bundesverfassungsgericht. 'Maastricht-Urteil', BVerfG 89, 155 of 12 October 1993, Az: 2 BvR 2134, 2159/92.

——. 'Lissabon-Urteil', BVerfG, 2 BvE 2/08 of 30 June 2009.

Canadian Supreme Court, *Reference re Secession of Quebec* [1998] 2 S.C.R. 217–297.

Caramel, Laurence. 'Forum de Florence: offensive de la gauche radical', *Le Monde*, 16 November 2002. Cited in Henri Maler, 'Le Monde en quête de "phénomène de société"', on the website of Observatoire des Médias ACRIMED: <http://www.acrimed.org/article811.html> (accessed on 12 May 2013).

Casey, Edward. *Getting Back Into Place: For a Renewed Understanding of the Place World* (Indianapolis, IN: Indiana University Press, 1993).

Cassirer, Ernst. *Philosophy of Symbolic Forms*, vol. 2, trans. Ralph Mannheim (New Haven, CT: Yale University Press, 1955).

——. *Symbol, Technik, Sprache* (Hamburg: Felix Meiner Verlag, 1985).

Castoriadis, Cornelius. *The Imaginary Institution of Society: Creativity and Autonomy in the Social-Historical World*, trans. Kathleen Blamey (Boston, MA: The MIT Press, 1998).

Christodoulidis, Emilios. 'End of History Jurisprudence: Dworkin in South Africa', in F. Du Bois (ed.), *The Practice of Integrity: Reflections on Ronald Dworkin and South African Law*, 64–85 (Cape Town: Juta, 2004).

——. 'The Objection that Cannot be Heard: Communication and Legitimacy in the Courtroom', in Antony Duff, Lindsay Farmer, Sandra Marshall, and Victor Tadros (eds.), *The Trial on Trial, Vol. 1: Truth and Due Process*, 179–202 (Oxford: Hart, 2004).

——. 'Against Substitution: The Constitutional Thinking of Dissensus', in Martin Loughlin and Neil Walker (eds.), *The Paradox of Constitutionalism: Constituent Power and Constitutional Form*, 189–208 (Oxford: Oxford University Press, 2007).

——. 'Strategies of Rupture', *Law and Critique* 20, no. 1 (2009), 3–36.

Clarkson, Carrol. 'Who are "We"? Don't Make Me Laugh', *Law and Critique* 18, no. 3 (2007), 361–374.

Coleman, Jules. *The Practice of Principle: In Defence of a Pragmatist Approach to Legal Theory* (Oxford: Oxford University Press, 2001).

Constitutional Court of Colombia. *Derechos Fundamentales de Comunidad Indígena* (Case SU-039/07): <http://www.corteconstitucional.gov.co/relatoria/1997/SU039-97.htm> (accessed on 13 February 2013).

Craig, Paul and Gráinne de Búrca. *EU Law: Text, Cases, and Materials,* 4th edn. (Oxford: Oxford University Press, 2008).

da Cunha, Euclydes. *Rebellion in the Backlands,* trans. Samuel Putnam (Chicago, IL: University of Chicago Press, 1944).

Deleuze, Gilles and Felix Guattari. *A Thousand Plateaus: Capitalism and Schizophrenia,* trans. Brian Massumi (London: Continuum, 1987).

Derrida, Jacques. *L'écriture et la différence* (Paris: Seuil, 1967).

——. 'Declarations of Independence', *New Political Science* 15 (1986), 7–15.

De Sousa Santos, Boaventura. *Toward a New Legal Common Sense,* 2nd edn. (London: Butterworths, 2002).

Dworkin, Ronald. 'Is Law a System of Rules?', repr. in Ronald Dworkin (ed.), *The Philosophy of Law,* 38–65 (Oxford: Oxford University Press, 1977), 38–65.

——. *Taking Rights Seriously* (Cambridge, MA: Harvard University Press, 1978).

——. *Law's Empire* (Cambridge, MA: Belknap Press, 1986).

——. *A Matter of Principle,* repr. (Oxford: Clarendon Press, 2001).

Dyzenhaus, David. 'The Compulsion of Legality', in Victor V. Ramraj (ed.), *Emergencies and the Limits of Legality,* 31–59 (Cambridge: Cambridge University Press, 2008).

Edmonton, James. 'Norway awaits Anders Breivik trial with mixture of revulsion and fascination', *The Guardian,* 13 April 2012: <http://www.guardian.co.uk/world/2012/apr/13/anders-breivik-trial-norway> (accessed on 13 February 2013).

European Commission. Communication 459/98, 'Towards an area of freedom, security and justice', in *Bulletin of the European Union* 7/8, 152–157 (1998).

——. 'Community Acquis', *Glossary*: <http://europa.eu/legislation_summaries/glossary/community_acquis_en.htm> (accessed on 13 February 2013).

European Court of Human Rights. *A, B and C* v. *Ireland* [2010], Application No. 25579/05: <http://hudoc.echr.coe.int/sites/eng/Pages/search.aspx#{"fulltext":["A","B and C v. Ireland"],"documentcollectionid2":["GRANDCHAMBER","CHAMBER"],"itemid":["001-102332"]}> (accessed on 9 May 2013).

European Court of Justice. *Van Gend & Loos* (Case 26/62) [1963] ECR 3–16.

——. *Costa* v. *ENEL* (Case 6/64) [1964] ECR 585–600.

——. *Regina* v. *Pierre Bouchereau* (Case 30/77) [1977] ECR 1999–2015.

——. *GB-INNO-BM* (Case C-362/88) [1990] ECR I-667–679.

——. *Grogan* (Case C-159/90) [1991] ECR I-4733–4742.

Fischer-Lescano, Andreas and Gunther Teubner. 'Regime-Collisions: The Vain Search for Legal Unity in the Fragmentation of Global Law', *Michigan Journal of International Law* 25, no. 4 (2004), 999–1046.
Fitzpatrick, Peter. *Modernism and the Grounds of Law* (Cambridge: Cambridge University Press, 2001).
Forst, Rainer. *Contexts of Justice*, trans. John M.M. Farrell (Berkeley, CA: University of California Press, 1994).
Foucault, Michel. *The Order of Things* (London: Routledge, 2002).
Fox, Lorna. *Conceptualising Home: Theories, Laws and Policies* (Oxford: Hart, 2007).
Friends of the MST: <http://www.mstbrazil.org/whatismst> (accessed on 10 October 2010).
Gadamer, Hans-Georg. 'Text and Interpretation', in Diane P. Michelfelder and Richard E. Palmer (eds.), *Dialogue and Deconstruction: The Gadamer-Derrida Encounter*, 21–50 (Stony Brook, NY: SUNY Press, 1989).
——. 'Rhetoric, Hermeneutics, and Ideology-Critique', in Walter Jost and Michael J. Hyde (eds.), *Rhetoric and Hermeneutics in Our Time: A Reader*, 313–334 (New Haven, CT: Yale University Press, 1997).
——. *Truth and Method,* 2nd edn., trans. Joel Weinsheimer and Donald G. Marshall (London: Continuum Books, 2005).
Galpin, Richard. 'Anders Behring Breivik says that insanity report is lies', *BBC News*, 25 April 2012: <http://www.bbc.co.uk/news/world-europe-17836180> (accessed on 13 February 2012).
Gernet, Louis. 'Le temps dans les formes archaïques du droit', *Journal de psychologie normale et pathologique* 53 (1956), 183–206.
Gilbert, Margaret. *On Social Facts,* repr. (Princeton, NJ: Princeton University Press, 1992).
——. *A Theory of Political Obligation* (Oxford: Oxford University Press, 2008).
Glenn, H. Patrick. *Legal Traditions of the World,* 2nd edn. (Oxford: Oxford University Press, 2004).
'Globalization', *Webster's Online Dictionary*: <http://www.websters-online-dictionary.org/definitions/globalisation> (accessed on 28 October 2012).
Goyard-Fabre, Simone. *Essai de critique phénoménologique du droit* (Paris: Klincksieck, 1972).
Gray, Kevin. 'Property in a Queue', in Gregory S. Alexander and Eduardo M. Peñalver (eds.), *Property and Community*, 165–195 (New York: Oxford University Press, 2009).
Grupo Antimilitarista Tortuga. 'Carta de los U'wa al hombre blanco': <http://www.nodo50.org/tortuga/Carta-de-los-U-WA-al-hombre-blanco> (accessed on 13 February 2013).
Gusdorf, Georges. *Mythe et métaphysique* (Paris: Flammarion, 1953).
Gutmann, Amy and Dennis Thompson. *Democracy and Disagreement* (Cambridge, MA: The Belknap Press, 1996).
Habermas, Jürgen. *Communication and the Evolution of Society,* trans. Thomas McCarthy (London: Heinemann Educational, 1979).

——. *The Theory of Communicative Action*, vol. 1, trans. Thomas McCarthy (Boston, MA: Beacon Press, 1981).
——. *Moral Consciousness and Communicative Action,* trans. Christian Lenhardt and Shierry Weber Nicholsen (Cambridge, MA: The MIT Press, 1990).
——. 'Reconciliation through the Public Use of Reason: Remarks on John Rawls' Political Liberalism', *Journal of Philosophy* 92, no. 3 (1995), 109–131.
——. *The Postnational Constellation,* trans. Max Pensky (Cambridge: Polity Press, 2001).
——. 'Constitutional Democracy: A Paradoxical Union of Contradictory Principles?', *Political Theory* 29, no. 6 (2001), 766–781.
——. *The Inclusion of the Other: Studies in Political Theory,* trans. Ciaran Cronin and Pablo de Greiff (Cambridge: Polity Press, 2005).
——. *The Divided West,* trans. Ciaran Cronin (Cambridge: Polity Press, 2006).
——. 'Legitimation through Human Rights', in Pablo de Greiff and Ciaran Cronin (eds.), *Global Justice and Transnational Politics*, 197–213 (Cambridge, MA: The MIT Press, 2002).
Hall, Thomas D. 'Borders, Borderlands, and Frontiers, Global', in Maryanne Klein Horowitz (ed.), *New Dictionary of the History of Ideas,* vol. 1, 238–242 (New York: Charles Scribners and Sons, 1994).
Hart, H.L.A. *The Concept of Law,* 2nd edn. (Oxford: Clarendon Press, 1997).
Harvey, David. *The Condition of Postmodernity* (Oxford: Blackwell, 1989).
Hegel, Georg Friedrich Wilhelm. *Science of Logic,* trans. John Niemeyer Findlay (London: Allen & Unwin, 1969).
Heidegger, Martin. *Being and Time,* repr., trans. John Macquarrie and Edward Robinson (Oxford: Blackwell, 1995).
Held, Klaus. 'Heimwelt, Fremdwelt, die eine Welt', *Phänomenologische Forschungen* 24 (1991), 305–337.
Honig, Bonnie. 'Between Decision and Deliberation: Political Paradox in Democratic Theory', *American Political Science Review* 101, no. 1 (2007), 1–17.
Houtzager, Peter P. 'The Movement of the Landless (MST), Juridical Field, and Legal Change in Brazil', in Boaventura de Sousa Santos and César A. Rodríguez-Garavito (eds.), *Law and Globalization from Below: Towards a Cosmopolitan Legality,* 218–240 (Cambridge: Cambridge University Press, 2005).
Husserl, Edmund. *Logical Investigations,* vol. 2, trans. J.N. Findlay (London: Routledge & Kegan Paul, 1970).
——. *The Crisis of European Sciences and Transcedental Phenomenology*, trans. David Carr (Evanston, IL: Northwestern University Press, 1970).
——. *Zur Phänomenologie der Intersubjektivität,* Iso Kern (ed.) (The Hague: Martinus Nijhhoff, 1973).
——. *Experience and Judgment: Investigations in a Genealogy of Logic,* Ludwig Landgrebe (ed.), trans. James S. Churchill and Karl Ameriks (London: Routledge & Kegan Paul, 1973).
——. *Ideas Pertaining to a Pure Phenomenology and to a Phenomenological Philosophy,* vol. II, trans. Richard Rojcewicz and André Schuwer (Dordrecht: Kluwer Academic Publishers, 1989).
Husserl, Gerhart. *Recht und Zeit* (Frankfurt: Klostermann, 1955).

——. *Recht und Welt* (Frankfurt: Klostermann, 1964).

International Federation of Consulting Engineers. 'Conditions of Contract for Construction for Building and Engineering Works Designed by the Employer': <http://fidic.org/books/construction-contract-1st-ed-1999-red-book> (accessed on 9 May 2013).

Johnson, David R. and David Post. 'Law and Borders—The Rise of Law in Cyberspace', *Stanford Law Review* 48 (1995), 1367–1402.

Journal d'un avocat. 'Autoréduction, ou extorsion?': <http://www.maitre-eolas.fr/post/2009/01/05/1263-autoreduction-ou-extorsion> (accessed on 13 February 2013).

Kelsen, Hans. *Pure Theory of Law*, 2nd edn. of the *Reine Rechtslehre*, trans. Max Knight (Berkeley, CA: University of California Press, 1967).

——. *Das Problem der Souveränität und die Theorie des Völkenrechts: Beitrag zu einer reinen Rechtslehre*, 2nd edn. (Aalen: Scientia Verlag, 1981).

——. *Vom Wesen und Wert der Demokratie*, 2nd edn. (Aalen: Scientia Verlag, 1981).

——. *Allgemeine Staatslehre*, repr. (Vienna: Österreichische Staatsdruckerei, 1993).

——. *Introduction to the Problems of Legal Theory. 1st edn. of the Reine Rechtslehre*, trans. Bonnie Litchewski Paulson and Stanley L. Paulson (Oxford: Clarendon Press, 2002).

——. *General Theory of Law and State*, repr. (New Brunswick, NJ: Transaction Publishers, 2007).

Kerckove, Michel and François Ost. *Le système juridique entre ordre et désordre* (Paris: Presses Universitaires de France, 1988).

Koskenniemi, Martti. *The Gentle Civilizer of Nations: The Rise and Fall of International Law 1870–1960* (Cambridge: Cambridge University Press, 2002).

Kurdzialek, Marina. 'Chaos', in Joachim Ritter, Karlfried Gründer, and Gottfried Gabriel (eds.), *Historisches Wörterbuch der Philosophie*, vol. 1, 980–984 (Darmstadt: Wissenschaftliche Buchgesellschaft, 1971).

Laclau, Ernesto. *Emancipation(s)*, repr. (London: Verso, 2007).

Laclau, Ernesto and Chantal Mouffe, *Hegemony and Socialist Strategy: Towards a Radical Democratic Politics*, 2nd edn. (London: Verso, 2001).

Lessig, Lawrence. 'The Zones of Cyberspace', *Stanford Law Review* 48 (1996), 1403–1411.

——. *Code: Version 2.0* (New York: Perseus Books Group, 2006).

Lindahl, Hans. 'Acquiring a Community: The *Acquis* and the Institution of European Legal Order', *European Law Journal* 9, no. 4 (2003), 433–450.

——. 'Inside and Outside the EU's Area of Freedom, Security and Justice: Reflexive Identity and the Unity of Legal Space', *Archiv für Rechts- und Sozialphilosophie* 90, no. 4 (2004), 478–497.

——. 'Finding a Place for Freedom, Security and Justice: The European Union's Claim to Territorial Unity', *European Law Review* 29, no. 4 (2004), 461–484.

——. 'Give and Take: Arendt and the *Nomos* of Political Community', *Philosophy and Social Criticism* 32, no. 6 (2006), 785–805.

——. 'Constituent Power and Reflexive Identity: Towards an Ontology of Collective Selfhood', in Martin Loughlin and Neil Walker (eds.), *The Paradox of Constituent Power: Constituent Power and Constitutional Form*, 9–24 (Oxford: Oxford University Press, 2007).

——. 'The Paradox of Constituent Power: The Ambiguous Self-Constitution of the European Union', *Ratio Juris* 20, no. 4 (2007), 485–505.

——. 'Collective Self-Legislation as an *Actus Impurus*: A Response to Heidegger's Critique of European Nihilism', *Continental Philosophy Review* 41, no. 3 (2008), 323–342.

——. 'Discretion and Public Policy: Timing the Unity and Divergence of Legal Orders', in Sacha Prechal and Bert van Roermund (eds.), *The Coherence of EU Law: The Search for Unity in Divergent Concepts*, 291–313 (Oxford: Oxford University Press, 2008).

——. 'The *anomos* of the earth: political indexicality, immigration and distributive justice', *Ethics and Global Politics* 1, no. 4 (2008), 193–212.

——. 'Border Crossings By Immigrants: Legality, Illegality, and Alegality', *Res Publica* 14 (2008), 117–135.

——. 'In Between: Immigration, Distributive Justice, and Political Dialogue', *Contemporary Political Theory* 8, no. 4 (2009), 415–434. A non-truncated version is available at: <http://papers.ssrn.com/sol3/papers.cfm?abstract_id=1726285> (accessed on 21 June 2013).

——. 'A-Legality: Postnationalism and the Question of Legal Boundaries', *Modern Law Review* 73, no. 1 (2010), 30–56.

——. 'Recognition as Domination: Constitutionalism, Reciprocity and the Problem of Singularity', in Neil Walker, Jo Shaw, and Steven Thierney (eds.), *Europe's Constitutional Mosaic*, 205–230 (Oxford: Hart, 2011).

——. 'We and Cyberlaw: Constitutionalism and the Inclusion/Exclusion Difference', *Indiana Journal of Global Legal Studies* 20, no. 2 (2013), (forthcoming).

Locke, John. *Two Treatises of Government,* repr., Peter Laslet (ed.) (Cambridge: Cambridge University Press, 2009).

Loidolt, Sophie. *Einführung in die Rechtsphänomenologie* (Tübingen: Mohr Siebeck, 2010).

Loughlin, Martin. 'In Defence of Staatslehre', *Der Staat* 48, no. 1 (2009), 1–28.

——. 'What is Constitutionalism?', in Petra Dobner and Martin Loughlin (eds.), *The Twilight of Constitutionalism?*, 47–71 (Oxford: Oxford University Press, 2010).

Luhmann, Niklas. *A Sociological Theory of Law,* trans. Elizabth King-Utz and Martin Albrow (London: Routledge & Kegan Paul, 1985).

——. *Social Systems*, trans. John Bednarz Jr. with Dirk Baecker (Stanford, CA: Stanford University Press, 1995).

MacIntyre, Alasdair. *After Virtue,* 3rd edn. (London: Duckworth, 2007).

Merleau-Ponty, Maurice. *Phenomenology of Perception,* trans. Colin Smith (London: Routledge, 1989).

——. *Prose of the World,* trans. John O'Neill (Evanston, IL: Northwestern University Press, 1973).

Michaels, Ralf. 'The True *Lex Mercatoria*: Law Beyond the State', *Indiana Journal of Global Legal Studies* 14, no. 2 (2007), 447–468.
Miller, David. *On Nationality* (Oxford: Oxford University Press, 1995).
Mommsen, Theodor and Paul Krueger (eds.), *The Digest of Justinian,* trans. Alan Watson (Philadelphia, PA: University of Pennsylvania Press, 1985).
Mouffe, Chantal. *The Democratic Paradox* (London: Verso, 2000).
Mueller, Milton. *Ruling the Root: Internet Governance and the Taming of Cyberspace* (Cambridge, MA: The MIT Press, 2002).
Myers, Fred R. *Pintupi Country, Pintupi Self: Sentiment, Place and Politics among Western Desert Aborigines* (Washington, DC: Smithsonian Institution Press, 1986).
Nagel, Thomas. *Equality and Partiality* (New York: Oxford University Press, 1991).
Näsström, Sofia. 'The Legitimacy of the People', *Political Theory* 35, no. 5 (2007), 624–655.
Negri, Antonio and Michael Hardt. *Empire* (Cambridge, MA: Harvard University Press, 2000).
Nietzsche, Friedrich. *Twilight of the Idols and the Anti-Christ,* trans. Reginald John Hollingdale (London: Penguin, 1990).
Nonet, Philippe and Philip Selznick. *Law and Society in Transition: Toward Responsive Law* (New Brunswick, NJ: Transaction Publishers, 2001).
#Occupy Wall Street. 'Declaration of the Occupation of New York City': <http://www.nycga.net/resources/documents/declaration/> (accessed on 13 February 2013).
Osborn, Ann. *The Four Seasons of the U'wa: A Chibcha Ritual Ecology in the Colombian Andes* (Wantage: Sean Kingston Publishing, 2009).
Oudejans, Nanda. *Asylum: A Philosophical Inquiry into the International Protection of Refugees* (Oisterwijk, Netherlands: BOXPress BV, 2011).
Peñalver, Eduardo M. and Sonia K. Katyal. 'Property Outlaws', *University of Pennsylvania Law Review* 155 (2007), 1095–1186.
Perez, Oren. 'Using Private-Public Linkages to Regulate Environmental Conflicts: The Case of International Construction Contracts', *Journal of Law and Society* 29, no. 1 (2002), 77–110.
Pettit, Philip. *A Theory of Freedom: From the Psychology to the Politics of Agency* (Cambridge: Polity, 2001).
——. *Republicanism: A Theory of Freedom and Government,* repr. (Oxford: Oxford University Press, 2002).
Plessner, Helmut. *Laughing and Crying: A Study of the Limits of Human Behavior,* trans. James Spencer Churchill and Marjorie Grene (Evanston, IL: Northwestern University Press, 1970).
Pogge, Thomas. *Realizing Rawls* (Ithaca, NY: Cornell University Press, 1989).
Radbruch, Gustav. *Rechtsfilosofie*, 2nd edn. (Heidelberg: C.F. Müller, 1999).
Rawls, John. *A Theory of Justice* (Cambridge, MA: The Belknap Press, 1971).
——. 'The Justification of Civil Disobedience', in Samuel Freeman (ed.), *Collected Papers*, 176–189 (Cambridge, MA: Harvard University Press, 1999).
——. 'Justice as Reciprocity', in Samuel Freeman (ed.), *Collected Papers*, 190–224 (Cambridge, MA: Harvard University Press, 1999).

——. *Political Liberalism*, exp. edn. (New York: Columbia University Press, 2005).
Raz, Joseph. *The Concept of a Legal System: An Introduction to the Theory of Legal System* (Oxford: Clarendon Press, 1970).
——. *The Authority of Law*, repr. (Oxford: Clarendon Press, 2002).
——. *Between Authority and Interpretation* (Oxford: Oxford University Press, 2009).
Reidenberg, Joel R. 'Lex Informatica: The Formulation of Information Policy Rules through Technology', *Texas Law Review* 76, no. 3 (1998), 553–593.
——. 'Technology and Internet Jurisdiction', *Pennsylvania Law Review* 153 (2005), 1951–1974.
Reinach, Adolf. *Zur Phänomenologie des Rechts: Die apriorischen Grundlagen des bürgerlichen Rechts* (Munich: Kösel Verlag, 1953).
Réseau Agir contre le Chômage et la précarité. 'Rennes: autoréduction des chômeurs galeries Lafayette': <http://www.ac.eu.org/spip.php?article1947> (accessed on 13 February 2013).
Réseau Agir contre le Chômage et la précarité: <http://www.ac.eu.org/> (accessed on 13 February).
Ricœur, Paul. *Time and Narrative*, vol. 3, trans. Kathleen Blamey and David Pellauer (Chicago, IL: Chicago University Press, 1990).
——. *Oneself as Another*, trans. Kathleen Blamely (Chicago, IL: Chicago University Press, 1992).
——. *The Course of Recognition*, trans. David Pellauer (Cambridge, MA: Harvard University Press, 2005).
Rinoceros: International Information Portal for Global Justice and Solidarity. 'First People of the Kalahari': <http://www.rinoceros.org/article9826.html> (accessed on 13 February 2013).
Rodríguez-Garavito, César A. and Luis Carlos Arenas. 'Indigenous Rights, Transnational Activism, and Legal Mobilization: The Struggle of the U'wa People in Colombia', in Boaventura de Sousa Santos and César A. Rodríguez-Garavito (eds.), *Law and Globalization from Below: Towards a Cosmopolitan Legality*, 241–265 (Cambridge: Cambridge University Press, 2005).
Robé, Jean-Philippe. 'Multinational Enterprises: The Constitution of a Pluralistic Legal Order', in Gunther Teubner (ed.), *Global Law Without a State*, 45–77 (Aldershot: Dartmouth, 1997).
Sassen, Saskia. *Territory · Authority · Rights: From Medieval to Global Assemblages* (Princeton, NJ: Princeton University Press, 2006).
——. 'Places and Spaces of the Global: An Expanded Analytic Terrain', in David Held and Anthony McGrew (eds.), *Globalization Theory: Approaches and Controversies*, 79–105 (Cambridge: Polity, 2007).
——. *A Sociology of Globalization* (New York: W.W. Norton, 2007).
Scattola, Merio. 'Die Grenze der Neuzeit: ihr Begriff in der juristischen und politischen Literatur der Antike und Frühmoderne', in *Die Grenze: Begriff und Inszenierung*, Markus Bauer and Thomas Rahn (eds.), 37–69 (Berlin: Akademie Verlag, 1997).
Schmitt, Carl. *Verfassungsrechtliche Aufsätze aus den Jahren 1924–1954*, 4th edn. (Berlin: Duncker & Humblot, 1958).

——. *Political Theology: Four Chapters on the Concept of Sovereignty,* trans. George Schwab (Cambridge, MA: The MIT Press, 1985).
——. *Über die drei Arten des rechtswissenschaftlichen Denkens,* 2nd edn. (Berlin: Duncker & Humblot, 1993).
——. *Staat, Großraum, Nomos: Arbeiten aus den Jahren 1916–1969* (Berlin: Dunker & Humblot, 1995).
——. *The Nomos of the Earth in the International Law of the Jus Publicum Europaeum,* trans. G.L. Ulmen (New York: Telos Press, 2003).
——. *The Concept of the Political,* exp. edn., trans. George Schwab (Chicago, IL: University of Chicago Press, 2007).
——. *Constitutional Theory,* trans. Jeffrey Seitzer (Durham, NC: Duke University Press, 2008).
Schütz, Alfred. *On Phenomenology and Social Relations* (Chicago, IL: Chicago University Press, 1970).
——. *The Phenomenology of the Social World,* repr., trans. George Walsh and Frederick Lehnert (London: Heinemann Educational Books, 1976).
Schütz, Alfred and Thomas Luckmann. *The Structures of the Life-World,* vol. I, trans. Richard M. Zaner and J. Tristam Engelhardt Jr. (Evanston, IL: Northwestern University Press, 1973).
Schütz, Alfred and Thomas Luckmann, *The Structures of the Life-World,* vol. II, trans. Richard M. Zaner and David J. Parent (Evanston, IL: Northwestern University Press, 1989).
Schwartz, Mattathias. 'Pre-Occupied: The Origins and Future of Occupy Wall Street', *The New Yorker,* 28 November 2011: <http://www.newyorker.com/reporting/2011/11/28/111128fa_fact_schwartz> (accessed on 13 February 2013).
Scott, S.P. (trans. and ed.), *The Digest or Pandects of Justinian, The Civil Law* (Cincinnati, OH: The Central Trust Company, 1932).
Shapiro, Scott. *Legality* (Cambridge, MA: Harvard University Press, 2010).
Silberbauer, George. *Hunter and Habitat in the Central Kalahari Desert* (Cambridge: Cambridge University Press, 1981).
——. 'A Sense of Place', in Ernest S. Burch, Jr. and Linda J. Ellanna (eds.), *Key Issues in Hunter-Gatherer Research,* 119–143 (Oxford: Berg, 1994).
Situationist International Online. 'Address to All Workers, Enragés-Situationist International Committee, Council for Maintaining the Occupations', trans. Ken Knabb: <http://www.cddc.vt.edu/sionline/si/address.html> (accessed on 13 February 2013).
Spiegel Online. 'Norwegischer Attentäter: Richter unterbrechen wirre Breivik-Tirade', 14 November 2011: <http://www.spiegel.de/panorama/justiz/norwegischer-attentaeter-richter-unterbrechen-wirre-breivik-tirade-a-797587.html> (accessed on 13 February 2013).
Stein, Ursula. *Lex Mercatoria: Realität und Theorie* (Frankfurt: Vittorio Klostermann, 1995).
Stone Sweet, Alec. 'The New *Lex Mercatoria* and Transnational Governance', *Journal of European Public Policy* 13, no. 5 (2006), 627–646.

Strawson, Peter F. *Individuals*, repr. (London: Methuen, 1984).

Ströker, Elisabeth. *Investigations in Philosophy of Space*, trans. Algis Mickunas (Athens, OH: Ohio University Press, 1987).

Tamanaha, Brian. *A General Jurisprudence of Law and Society* (Oxford: Oxford University Press, 2001).

Taylor, Charles. *Philosophy and the Human Sciences. Philosophical Papers 2* (Cambridge: Cambridge University Press, 1985).

——. 'The Politics of Recognition', in Amy Gutmann (ed.), *Multiculturalism and the 'Politics of Recognition'*, 25–73 (Princeton, NJ: Princeton University Press, 1992).

Teubner, Gunther. 'Global Bukowina: Legal Pluralism in the World Society', in Gunther Teubner (ed.), *Global Law Without a State*, 3–28 (Aldershot: Dartmouth, 1997).

——. *Constitutional Fragments: Societal Constitutionalism and Globalization* (Oxford: Oxford University Press, 2011).

Theunissen, Michael. *The Other: Studies in the Social Ontology of Husserl, Heidegger, Sartre and Buber*, trans. C. McCann (Cambridge, MA: The MIT Press, 1984).

The Voluntary Human Extinction Movement. 'U'wa tribe's suicide pact': <http://www.vhemt.org/uwa.htm> (accessed on 13 February 2013).

Traufetter, Gerald. 'Ein fast unerträglicher Auftritt', *Spiegel Online*, 14 November 2011: <http://www.spiegel.de/panorama/justiz/attentaeter-breivik-vor-gericht-ein-fast-unertraeglicher-auftritt-a-797671.html> (accessed on 12 February 2013).

Tribunal de Grande Instance de Paris. 'Ligue contre le racisme et l'antisémitisme et Union des étudiants juifs de France c. Yahoo! Inc. et Société Yahoo! France' <http://www.lapres.net/yahfr.html> (accessed on 13 February 2013).

Tully, James. *Strange Multiplicity: Constitutionalism in an Age of Diversity* (Cambridge: Cambridge University Press, 1995).

——. *Public Philosophy in a New Key*, vol. 1 (Cambridge: Cambridge University Press, 2008).

Twining, William. *General Jurisprudence: Understanding Law from a Global Perspective* (Cambridge: Cambridge University Press, 2009).

Twomey, Patrick. 'Constructing a Secure Space: The Area of Freedom, Security and Justice', in David O'Keeffe and Patrick Twomey (eds.), *Legal Issues of the Amsterdam Treaty*, 351–373 (Oxford: Hart, 1999).

Van Roermund, Bert. *Law, Narrative and Reality: An Essay in Intercepting Politics* (Dordrecht: Kluwer Academic Publishers, 1997).

——. 'Constituerende macht, soevereiniteit en representatie', *Tijdschrift voor Filosofie* 64, no. 3 (2002), 509–532.

——. 'First-Person Plural Legislature: Political Reflexivity and Representation', *Philosophical Explorations* 6, no. 3 (2006), 235–252.

——. 'Migrants, Humans and Human Rights', in Hans Lindahl (ed.), *A Right to Inclusion and Exclusion? Normative Fault Lines of the EU's Area of Freedom, Security and Justice*, 161–182 (Oxford: Hart, 2009).

——. 'Kelsen under the Low Skies. Recognition Theory Revisited and Revised', in Robert Walter, Clemens Jabloner, and Klaus Zeleny (eds.), *Hans Kelsen anderswo. Hans Kelsen Abroad*, 259–279 (Vienna: Manz Verlag, 2010).

——. 'Objectifying Legal Norm Claims: Validity and Self-Reference.' In *The Pure Theory of Law Revisited: The Jurisprudence of Hans Kelsen*, John Gardner, Leslie Green, and Luis Duarte de Almeida (eds.), 11–41 (Oxford: Oxford University Press, 2013).

——. *Legal Thought and Philosophy: What Legal Scholarship is About* (Cheltenham, UK: Edward Elgar, 2013).

Van der Walt, André. *Property in the Margins* (Oxford: Hart, 2009).

Vargas Llosa, Mario. *The War of the End of the World*, trans. Helene Fane (New York: Faber and Faber, 2004).

Vidal-Folch, Xavier. 'Los límites del club Europa: La futura ampliación hasta 28 países abre el debate hasta dónde llega Europa y dónde debe terminar la UE', *El País*, 14 December 1999: <http://elpais.com/diario/1999/12/14/internacional/945126012_850215.html> (accessed on 12 May 2013).

Viénet, René. *Enragés and Situationists in the Occupations Movement*, trans. Loren Goldner and Paul Sieveking (New York: Autonomedia, 1992): <http://www.cddc.vt.edu/sionline/si/enrages.html> (accessed on 13 February 2013).

Waldenfels, Bernhard. *Spielraum des Verhaltens* (Frankfurt: Suhrkamp, 1980).

——. 'Experience of the Alien in Husserl's Phenomenology', *Research in Phenomenology* 20 (1990), 19–33.

——. *Antwortregister* (Frankfurt: Suhrkamp, 1994).

——. 'The Other and the Strange', *Philosophy and Social Criticism* 21 (1995), 111–124.

——. *Order in the Twilight*, trans. David J. Parent (Athens, OH: Ohio University Press, 1996).

——. *Vielstimmigkeit der Rede: Studien zur Phänomenologie des Fremden 4* (Frankfurt: Suhrkamp, 1999).

——. *Bruchlinien der Erfahrung* (Frankfurt: Suhrkamp, 2002).

——. *Verfremdung der Moderne: Phänomenologische Grenzgänge* (Essen: Wallstein Verlag, 2001).

——. 'Inside and Outside the Order: Legal Orders in the Perspective of a Phenomenology of the Alien', *Ethical Perspectives* 12, no. 3 (2006), 359–381.

——. *Hyperphänomene: Modi hyperbolischer Erfahrung* (Frankfurt: Suhrkamp, 2012).

Waldron, Jeremy. 'What is Cosmopolitan?', *Journal of Political Philosophy* 8, no. 2 (2000), 227–243.

——. *'Partly Laws Common to All Mankind': Foreign Law in American Courts* (New Haven, CT: Yale University Press, 2012).

Walker, Neil. 'The Idea of Constitutional Pluralism', *Modern Law Review* 65, no. 3 (2003), 317–359.

——. 'The Migration of Constitutional Ideas and the Migration of the Constitutional Idea', in Sujit Choudry (ed.), *The Migration of Constitutional Ideas*, 316–344 (Cambridge: Cambridge University Press, 2006).

——. 'Taking Constitutionalism Beyond the State', *Political Studies* 56 (2008), 519–543.

——. 'Beyond Boundary Disputes and Basic Grids: Mapping the Global Disorder of Normative Orders', *International Journal of Constitutional Law* 6, no. 3–4 (2008), 373–396.

__________, Stephen Tierney, and Jo Shaw (eds.), *Europe's Constitutional Mosaic* (Oxford: Hart, 2011).

Walzer, Michael. *Spheres of Justice: A Defense of Pluralism and Equality* (New York: Basic Books, 1983).

Weiler, Joseph. 'The Fischer Debate—The Dark Side', in Christian Joerges, Yves Mény, and Joseph Weiler (eds.), *What Kind of Constitution for What Kind of Polity? Responses to Joschka Fischer*, 235–247 (Florence: European University Institute, 2000).

Wikipedia. 'Brent Spar': <http://en.wikipedia.org/wiki/Brent_Spar_oil_rig> (accessed on 13 February 2013).

——. 'Space Law': <http://en.wikipedia.org/wiki/Space_law> (accessed on 13 February 2013).

——. '*Jyllands-Posten* Muhammad cartoon controversy': <http://en.wikipedia.org/wiki/Jyllands-Posten_Muhammad_cartoons_controversy#cite_note-4> (accessed on 13 February 2013).

Weyrauch, Walter and Maureen A. Bell. 'Autonomous Lawmaking: The Case of the Gypsies', *Yale Law Journal* 103, no. 2 (1993), 323–399.

Weyrauch, Walter et al. (eds.). 'Symposium on Gypsy Law (Romaniya)', *American Journal of Comparative Law* 45 (1997), 225–289.

Young, Iris Marion. *Justice and the Politics of Difference* (Princeton, NJ: Princeton University Press, 1990).

——. *Intersecting Voices* (Princeton, NJ: Princeton University Press, 1997).

——. *Inclusion and Democracy* (Oxford: Oxford University Press, 2000).

Zahavi, Dan. 'Husserl's Intersubjective Transformation of Transcendental Philosophy', repr. in Rudolf Bernet, Donn Welton, and Gina Zavota (eds.), *Edmund Husserl: Critical Assessments of Leading Philosophers,* vol. 4, 359–377 (London: Routledge, 2005).

Index

Arendt, Hannah 84n, 194n, 62, 238, 244–5
A-legality
a politics of 222, 239, 248–60
and enmity 179–80
and strangeness 37–8, 156–7, 159–61
concept of 3–4, 13, 30–1, 36–38, 158–61
limits and fault lines 3–4, 164–78
weak and strong dimensions 164–74
Alterity
and selfhood 83–4, 91–4, 95n, 96, 106, 113
and strangeness 157, 179
Authority
and joint action 87–88, 90, 96–8, 100, 102, 105–107, 112, 117, 137, 144–6, 159n, 164, 169, 172, 177–80, 193, 197, 207, 218–221, 229
its normative content 252–253

Benhabib, Seyla 214n, 231n, 243–6
Boundaries
as fault lines 3, 6, 8, 175–182, 187, 207, 209, 215, 225, 249, 250, 253–4, 258, 266–7
as limits 40–43, 52–3, 55, 57–8, 63, 69, 76, 79, 90–5, 100, 141, 153–4, 158, 158n, 162–3, 174, 176–7, 181, 194, 197, 203, 212, 227, 231, 236n, 242, 247, 250, 263–4
spatial, temporal, subjective, and material 3, 14, 17, 18–24, 28, 39–40
their functions 3, 12, 26, 32, 40–1, 50, 52, 99, 157, 233, 265–7
Boundary-setting
and collective self-identification 187–8, 202–14
constitution and enforcement 202–5
deferral of collective identity 214

Chaos
and magma 186
meanings of 184–186
Christodoulidis, Emilios 183, 215–216
Civil Disobedience
and a-legality 182–4
and reciprocity 184
Collective (or joint)
action 4, 5, 6, 8, 17n, 35n, 29–30, 84, 86–88, 90–6, 99–100, 117–8, 126–7, 126n, 131–2, 134, 135–6, 138–142
genesis or emergence of 144–155, 215–218
ontology of 8, 85, 178, 209
Communitarianism
and boundaries 5, 228, 234
and reciprocity 228–9, 232, 234, 265
Constitution
as a first-person plural concept 99–101
as a master rule for inclusion/exclusion 137, 144, 253
the 'first' 146–8
Constitutionalism
and the rule of law 250, 252
Schmitt's critique of liberal constitutionalism 251–2
Cosmopolitanism
and boundaries 5, 214n, 240–7
and human rights 242–6
and reciprocity 230–2
Cyberlaw
Declaration of Independence for Cyberspace 67–68
Jyllands-Posten controversy 68–69
the *Yahoo*! Case 68

Deleuze, Gilles 45–49
Derrida, Jacques 146n, 163n, 214n,
De Sousa Santos, Boaventura 58n, 70n, 72, 79n, 190n, 261n
Dialectic
and revolution 169–70
and the reducibility thesis 241, 255
and transformation 213
Hegelian 175, 214n, 231n, 236n
Dialogue
and rationality 133, 177, 208, 245, 255
as *dia-logos* 155–157
audi alteram partem 208
monologue 255
Dworkin, Ronald 16, 35, 121n, 127n, 208n, 216n, 250–252
Dyzenhaus, David 250

Exception
and collective self-restraint 249, 250–4
and exceptional measures 176, 179–80, 221, 251–3

Fault Lines
concept of 3–4, 175–8
of globalization 7, 266

Fault Lines (*Cont.*)
normative ruptures 158–161, 209, 211, 213, 215–6, 216n, 218
(world) internal politics/(world) external politics 184, 243, 254, 257–60
First-person (Plural) Perspective
and joint action 4, 6, 8, 26, 29–30, 44, 52, 55–6, 76, 77, 81, 83, 85, 87, 90–1, 94–6, 99–100, 102, 120, 125–8, 138, 174–5, 178, 196, 207, 223, 242, 246, 248, 250
comes second 154, 162, 175, 218
enlarged 106–113
Frontiers 52–5, 56, 63, 95, 174, 194

Gadamer, Hans-Georg 120, 211, 234, 266n
Gilbert, Margaret 5, 86–7, 126–7, 136, 144–6, 150, 226, 249
Globalization
as emergent entwinement of home-worlds and strange worlds 267
as enworlding 265
as localization 55, 58n, 74, 106, 115, 261–2
as unification and pluralization 264
as universalization/imperialism 266–7
globe and world 262–3
'scales' of law 190, 261

Habermas, Jürgen 134n, 157n, 183–4, 228, 230–2, 236, 237, 240–3, 258n, 266n,
Hart, H.L.A. 15–6, 79–80, 81n, 258n
Hegel, G.F.W. 175–9, 214n, 231n, 236n, 249,
Heidegger, Martin 23, 97n, 119, 120n, 121n, 123–4, 125n, 126n, 127n, 185n, 211, 247n, 263, 265
Hiatus
between question and response 180, 205, 205n, 208–9, 242
the in-between 255, 267
the morality of law 249–50n
Human Rights
as legal rights 240–3
as the rights of others 244–6
as the rights of strangers 247–8
Husserl, Edmund 93–4, 119, 123, 125, 126n, 129, 130n, 131, 133, 157, 160–1, 166, 168, 189n, 191n, 195–6, 217, 254, 263–4

Identity
and individuation 78–81, 95, 99, 107, 113, 187, 196
as sameness (*idem*) 12, 77, 82–3, 86, 89, 90, 91, 108, 112, 187, 198
as self hood (*ipse*) 12, 77, 82–3, 86, 89, 90, 91–92, 108, 112, 198
de-identification 218–221
misidentification 197
re-identification 197–201
Inclusion/exclusion
as a normative problem 225–7
in relation to equality, justice, freedom, and security 223–5
preferential differentiation 28–9, 38, 44, 46, 48, 74, 76, 94, 104, 104n, 115, 193, 203, 206, 222, 227, 242, 246, 260
Self-inclusion/other-inclusion 12, 92, 153, 180–1, 197, 224
Self-exclusion/other-exclusion 153, 180, 181, 197, 224
Indexicality
and the first-person perspective 4, 83, 91, 102
political uses of 200, 216
Intentionality
and ordering 128
legal 118–9
normative difference 153, 204
significative difference 119, 123, 153, 185
Interpretation
and intentionality 119–22, 127, 129–32, 142
hermeneutics 109–10
Ius gentium
and the U'wa 64
Waldron 64, 64n, 246–7

Kelsen, Hans 13–15, 16–8, 19n, 29, 51n, 67, 71, 79, 80, 82n, 87, 88n, 99, 118–120, 122–4, 125, 129, 132n, 156–148, 150, 152, 169, 250n

Lex mercatoria
global law 2, 44, 58–9, 63, 77, 97, 194, 217–8
lex constructionis 58–60, 63–4, 93, 128, 181, 258
U'wa people 60–64
Limits
concept of 3, 40–1, 95
contingency 96, 97n, 174–175, 225, 258
inclusion and exclusion 90–94, 174, 193–4, 197, 222–4
Luhmann, Niklas 29, 30n, 153

Merleau-Ponty, Maurice 56, 201, 210n, 214n
Movimento dos trabalhadores rurais sem terra (Brazil) 53, 166–8, 177
Multinationals 2, 8, 13, 56–8, 77, 97, 133, 196

Nomos
nomadism 44–9
Schmitt on taking, distributing, and exploiting 194–195, 200n
smooth/striated space 45, 48

Occupation and Conquest
and Identification 194–196
Besetzung (Husserl) 161, 166, 195–6
Occupy Wall Street 195–196, 200n, 203–4, 217, 218
Order/Ordering
breach of 1, 26–8, 29, 53, 58, 63, 69, 87, 90, 102, 108, 132, 140, 145, 157, 166, 228, 240, 253
concrete 1, 3, 11, 18, 24–5, 27, 29–30, 32, 38–39, 40–1, 65, 70, 80–82, 85, 94, 100, 117, 121, 133, 138, 141, 155, 157, 191n, 220, 264

contingency and loss of order 96–97, 175, 225, 225n, 258n
ordo ordinatus/ordo ordinans 6, 115
the unordered 2, 4, 5–6, 11–2, 94–95, 153, 157–63, 165, 167, 172, 185–6, 193, 197, 203, 212, 220, 223, 229, 247, 250, 254
the orderable 6, 164–5, 167, 175, 187, 248, 254
the unorderable 4, 6, 165, 175–6, 187, 207, 208, 248, 254
transgression of 1, 3, 13, 33–6, 52, 54, 58, 63, 69, 143, 155, 202, 210–1, 217, 228
Overlapping Legal Orders
structure explained 70–3
the EU and its Member States 73–4

Paradox
of authority 253
of boundaries 152
of constituent power 209, 211, 216
of identification 199–200, 209, 219
of origins 147–8, 201, 214, 226
of representation 148–151, 154, 199, 201, 213, 216
Pettit, Philip 82–4, 87, 88n, 102, 110, 134n, 183–4, 208, 218, 223
Plurality
estrangement 6, 38, 141, 160
legal pluralism 70, 70n, 79, 79n, 91, 101–2, 105, 142, 190
pluralization 6, 101–2, 105, 141–2, 155, 181, 218, 261, 264
Possibility
as practical possibility 3–4, 6, 8, 132, 132n, 147, 154, 156–8, 160–5, 169, 173, 174–177, 179, 185, 203, 207, 209, 213–4, 217, 242, 247–9, 250, 253, 254, 257, 258, 260
capacity 131–2
compossibility and incompossibility 156, 165, 165n, 175, 176, 248, 259
legal empowerments 99–100, 132, 132n, 147, 150, 157, 161, 164–5, 167, 174, 176, 197, 212, 214, 217, 250, 263

Question/Questionability
finite 8, 85, 209, 239, 249, 267
precedence of 18, 39, 162–163, 163n, 164, 180, 203–4, 205, 205n, 207, 208
primordial and derivative 203
What* ought our joint action to be about? 8, 142, 150, 164, 172, 197–7, 201–3, 206–7, 209, 225–7, 242, 256, 260

Rationality
and understanding 134–156
and interpretation 122, 134, 142–3
dia-logos 255–6, 260
grounding 27, 97n, 133–4, 136–7, 139, 142, 143–4, 147, 149, 177, 224, 225, 230, 233, 236, 239, 243, 245, 246, 256
objectivity and subjectivity 133, 135–6, 139, 141, 144–8, 152, 154, 212, 222, 263
petitio principii 7, 177, 183, 211, 222, 238, 253, 257
reason-giving and justification 133–4, 136, 137, 139, 143, 177, 211, 229
responsive 222
Rawls, John 83n, 134n, 182–34, 207n, 228, 229–231, 232–4, 235–6
Raz, Joseph 16, 79–81, 121n, 122n
Reciprocity
and civil disobedience, 183–4, 208
and dialogue 208
and (human) rights 170, 244–245
and joint action 8, 153–4, 167, 184, 206–7, 207n
and particularism 7, 228–230
and universalism 7, 230–32
asymmetrical 63, 232–233
normativity and normative blind spots 7, 171, 209, 222, 227–34, 239, 239n, 258, 249, 253–4, 256
Representation
and authorization 145, 147, 150
and militancy 216
originalism 148, 151, 213, 215, 229
presence and absence 126n, 146, 149, 151, 200
Response/responsiveness
as indirect action 203
finite 8, 85, 209, 239, 249, 266–7
primordial and derivative 203
responsability 208, 208n, 248, 253–4, 258
retroactivity of 18, 39, 147–8, 150, 153, 163, 163n, 164, 177, 203–5, 205n, 208, 210, 212–4, 216, 221
Revolution
emergence of legal orders 148, 149, 169–70, 215–216
May 1968 168–70, 181, 217, 218
Ricœur, Paul 12, 82–6, 89, 91–2, 96, 157n, 181, 189n, 191, 193, 198, 213–4
Roman Law
and property law 50, 63–64, 140, 166–7, 258
Frontiers 49, 52–53
public and private boundaries 50–51

Sassen, Saskia 50n, 57–8, 72, 101, 104–5, 190n, 261, 264, 265n
Scattola, Merio 49–55
Schmitt, Carl 38n, 155, 176–80, 186, 194–6, 199, 213–4, 251–4, 256, 259, 265n
Schütz, Alfred 86, 126n, 152n, 162
Secession
and a-legality 173, 177, 181
Quebec secession reference 170–2, 177, 178, 181, 196, 217, 218, 257
Space law
and the world 263
Strawson, Peter 82n, 188–94, 197–8, 200

Strange(ness)
and a-legality 3, 4, 6, 13, 37–38, 41, 42–3, 55, 57, 63, 69, 74–5, 76, 94n, 154, 156–63, 171, 173, 209, 247–8
and collective self-restraint 251, 254, 255
and enmity 179–80
in contrast to familiarity/ownness 181, 197
phenomenological characterization 156–160
Ströker, Elisabeth 37n, 189n

Taylor, Charles 28, 29n, 136n, 232n
Territory
as necessarily exclusive 47–8, 72, 105
of states 2–3, 5, 14, 24, 40, 41–2, 45, 52, 56, 58, 59, 61, 65, 71–2, 75, 220, 243
Teubner, Gunther 56n, 58n, 59, 63, 98, 251n
Twining, William 30, 70, 75, 78, 80–1, 127, 142, 173, 190, 196n

Unity
and political plurality 9, 180, 181, 234, 242, 267
legal 16–7, 25, 154, 180, 181, 267
reducibility thesis 234, 241, 255
Understanding
and intentionality 122, 125, 127, 130, 132, 134, 142–3
and possibility 132–3, 164
pre- and post reflexive joint action under law 25–6, 28, 127, 136–7, 138, 150, 201, 247, 267
hermeneutics 119, 120
Universalism
all-inclusiveness 5, 6, 7, 43, 182, 214n, 222, 230–2, 234
and reciprocity 240–6
as imperialism 265–6
broken 247

Van der Walt, André 35n, 53–54, 167
Van Roermund, Bert 4, 82n, 107, 146n, 195n, 216n, 242n

Waldenfels, Bernhard 28, 29n, 94n, 109, 120n, 123, 146, 153, 157n, 162n, 163n, 179n, 185, 201n, 222, 238n
Waldron, Jeremy 64, 231n, 246, 264n
Walker, Neil 101n, 106–7, 110, 170n, 257n
World
difference with planet and globe 263
Home-world (*Heimwelt*) 7, 93–4, 160, 262, 264–7
phenomenological sense of 262–4
Strange world (*Fremdwelt*) 7, 69, 173, 264–267

Young, Iris Marion 232–33, 248

The manufacturer's authorised representative in the EU for product safety is Oxford University Press España S.A. of El Parque Empresarial San Fernando de Henares, Avenida de Castilla, 2 - 28830 Madrid (www.oup.es/en or product.safety@oup.com). OUP España S.A. also acts as importer into Spain of products made by the manufacturer.

Printed and bound by CPI Group (UK) Ltd, Croydon, CR0 4YY

12/09/2026

02215930-0004